MAN OUT

MAN OUT

MEN ON THE SIDELINES
OF AMERICAN LIFE

ANDREW L. YARROW

BROOKINGS INSTITUTION PRESS
Washington, D.C.

Copyright © *2018*
THE BROOKINGS INSTITUTION
1775 Massachusetts Avenue, N.W., Washington, D.C. 20036
www.brookings.edu

Library of Congress Cataloging-in-Publication data are available.
ISBN 978-0-8157-3274-7 (cloth : alk. paper)
ISBN 978-0-8157- 3275-4 (ebook)

9 8 7 6 5 4 3 2 1

Typeset in Electra

Composition by Elliott Beard

To my son,
Richard Yarrow,

to the memory of my parents,
Marian Radke Yarrow and Leon Yarrow,

and to my partner,
Jennifer Pettyjohn

Contents

Acknowledgments

Many people have contributed their time and insights to make this book possible, and I have numerous people to thank. My editor, Bill Finan, at the Brookings Institution Press, has carefully and thoughtfully nurtured this project to completion. Valentina Kalk, the former director of the press, was enthusiastic about the project from the beginning. I probably would not have been inspired to write about these issues if not for several people I have worked for and with over the years—notably Isabel Sawhill and Ron Haskins at Brookings and David Blankenhorn, who leads the Better Angels initiative. The idea for the book germinated during casual discussions with my cousin Rebecca Miller. I owe the title to my friend Steve Powell. Susan Schulman, my agent, has been supportive since the first draft of the book proposal. I am grateful to the Annie E. Casey Foundation for providing support for this project, particularly to Mike Laracy at the foundation. Lois Kazakoff, editorial page editor of the *San Francisco Chronicle*, has been especially supportive, publishing many of my articles on different facets of this topic. Laura Winter built the compelling, interactive website www.manout.us. Lauren Swaim helped with research on young men. Janet Walker, Carrie Engel, Marjorie Pannell, Steven Roman, Yelba Quinn, Elliott Beard, Christian Purdy, and others at the Brookings Institution Press, as well as copyeditor Jill R. Hughes, provided all manner of assistance.

This work would not have been possible without the assistance of many scholars, social service providers, organizations, and countless men and women.

The roster of scholars, practitioners, and advocates who have helped and guided me include—in addition to Sawhill, Haskins, and Blankenhorn—David Autor, Brad Wilcox, Steven Hipple, Rose Woods, Steven Haugen, Larry Mead, David and Amber Lapp, Eugene Steuerle, Kathryn Edin, Naomi Cahn, June Carbone, Jacob Hacker, Cynthia Osborne, Sylvia Allegretto, Jean Twenge, Ronald Day, Vernon Wallace, Gary Barker, Peter Fenn, Melissa Boteach, Katherine Gallagher Robbins, Warren Farrell, Joseph Cordell, Olivia Golden, Rob Okun, Mitch Pearlstein, Donald Gordon, J. Steven Svoboda, Harry Crouch, Naomi Goldberg, Julie Vogtman, Helen Fisher, Chuck Derry, David Cooper, Frederick Marx, Tyvon Hewitt, Dan Singley, Pierre Azzam, Sonia Molloy, Mark Kisselica, Kimberly Young, Helen Fisher, Irene Caniano, Lindsey Monte, Gail Melson, Richard Reeves, and many officials, therapists, members of the legal and law enforcement communities, and others who wish to remain anonymous.

I was privileged to get to know the men of the New York–based Fortune Society, which assists former prisoners; the Baltimore Center for Urban Families, which assists lower-income fathers; Washington, D.C.'s Latin American Youth Center; and men in job-search support groups like 40-Plus in Washington, D.C., and Neighbors Helping Neighbors in New Jersey.

I am also thankful to a number of recruiters, commanders, and others in the U.S. Army, including Nelson Ballew, Andrea Zucker, Fonda Bock, Captain Peter Ahching, Colonel Patrick Michaelis, Sergeant First Class Tifani Hightower, Command Sergeant Major Michael Gragg, and Master Sergeant Jeffrey Klimek.

The men and women of Horicon, Wisconsin, and Frackville, Pennsylvania, were generous with their time and insights. Lorraine Stanton provided especially valuable assistance in connecting me with other Frackville residents.

Others who have provided valuable input and access to some of those who I have interviewed, as well as editorial suggestions, include Richard Yarrow, Laurie Kaye Schwartz, Jennifer Pettyjohn, Kevin Purcell, Ned Rosenau, John Fugazzie, Charla Payne, and Morris Waxler.

I especially owe thanks to about two hundred men and women from nearly thirty states who spoke with or wrote to me. The stories and thoughts they told me are what humanized this book and brought different threads together in ways that data cannot. I wish I could name them, but for understandable reasons they requested the anonymity provided by pseudonyms and somewhat disguised descriptions of their lives.

Preface

During the last few years, we have started to hear about "failing" or "missing" American men. Much of this discussion has focused on two topics: men who aren't working and fathers who have little or no attachment to their children. The 2016 election led many political scientists and commentators to write about "angry white men" as a voting bloc.

Man Out is not another hyperbolic argument about the "decline of men," the changing nature of masculinity, or the white working class. Much has been written about the "end of men," the "boy problem," and the dwindling share of men in higher education, from snarky chick lit to socioeconomic analyses.[1] Some have argued that 40,000 years of male supremacy may be coming to an end as women and girls not only do better in schools and colleges but also may have skills that are more in demand in a twenty-first-century economy in which brawn and brute strength no longer count for much. These trends and arguments are important and relevant, but they are largely tangential to this story.

Instead, this book looks at the large and expanding subcultures of men who have been shoved to the sidelines or have chosen to disengage from many of the traditional responsibilities of American manhood. Sometimes it will seem that I am harshly criticizing these men; at others, vigorously defending them. Sometimes I may sound quite conservative; at others, a left-wing radical. In the end, my goals are to bring awareness to a constellation of issues and to help improve the lives of millions of men (and women and children).

Shoehorning oneself into one or another ideological straitjacket doesn't help.

Although some earlier research, as well as analysis and commentary, has been quite good, it has had two particularly glaring flaws stemming from a narrowly focused myopia: (1) it has been siloed—for example, treating fatherhood, work, or family issues as largely, not entirely, distinct from other issues such as masculinity, men's health, technology, civic engagement, and incarceration—and (2) it has ignored other tragic, shameful matters affecting millions of American men or viewed them as essentially unrelated phenomena.

First, America's "man problem" (which is not uniquely American) is much more far-reaching in terms of "symptoms" or "problems," as well as scope, than nearly all prior writing has discussed. The men affected also have tended to be corralled into a couple of sociological buckets: men of color and heterosexual, middle-age, white working-class men from the Rust Belt or "Greater Appalachia."[2] In fact, the demographic terrain for men who are on the sidelines of American life goes well beyond these buckets to include middle- and upper-middle-class men and young men of every race, ethnicity, and sexual orientation from every part of the United States. A number of scholars, ethnographers, journalists, commentators, and practitioners in various walks of life understand the relatedness of the issues explored in this book, but these issues have sat like disconnected puzzle pieces waiting to be put together.

The second flaw follows from the first: while the still sparse sociological and journalistic portrayals of "real men" have included some excellent works, they have missed swaths of sidelined men—in well-heeled suburbs, coming out of prison, on dating apps like Tinder, on dark and off-the-grid corners of the internet ranting about women, among young men with some college education or degrees from nonelite schools, in troubled and failed marriages and cohabitation, among missing fathers and isolated single men, among men struggling with their masculinity, and among addicts of computer games, alcohol, opioids, and other drugs. These men are more likely to be less educated and lower income, but the comfortable stereotype that they are only lower-middle-class white men dislocated by technology and globalization is wrong.

America's "men out" are disconnected from work, family and children, civic and community life, and relationships. They are often angry with government, employers, women, and "the system," or they may have given up and given the finger to social norms. Some have done time in prison, and some have done too much time in front of screens. Their wives, partners, and other women frequently don't want them; their children are estranged from them;

their neighbors and onetime friends are embarrassed by them. Indeed, male-female animosity, especially among younger men, is considerably greater than we would like to think. Some men have turned from relationships to a hookup culture facilitated by apps, and others have migrated from the labor force to a fantasy world of starting their own businesses or writing the Great American Novel. Many adult men economically and psychologically survive by living with older parents. Many depend on the nation's relatively weak safety net—mainly food stamps, Medicaid, and disability insurance. Some gay, bisexual, and transgender men exhibit these traits, but this is largely the story of heterosexual men.

Man Out draws together these seemingly disparate threads and probes what's behind them. Some men have been pushed out of the mainstream; some have chosen to be on the outskirts of twenty-first-century America. When this issue is posed as this simplistic dichotomy, this is where arguments get heated. For most of these men, differing degrees of both situations are at play. This continuum is key to the construct of "man out."

The phrase, a play on the often lobbed call for implicitly "unmasculine" men to "man up," is intended to avoid blanket value judgments, stereotypes, and ideologically tinged assertions that these men either have irresponsibly "dropped out" and are no-good shirkers or have been "pushed out" by a callous capitalism or allegedly nefarious women. Avoiding the terms "pushed out" or "dropped out" leads to the book's other widely used locution—that these men are "on the sidelines" or "have been sidelined" from American life. In short, I believe it is wrong to solely (or largely) blame these men by implying that their circumstances are primarily a result of their choices, or alternatively, to see them mainly as victims of larger "social forces"—though this is also not to say that these men are not victims or not to blame for their circumstances, to varying degrees.

Among this diverse population, it is not clear how so many got there, particularly from a somewhat (but not entirely) romanticized narrative about mid-twentieth-century life. In those days at least most white men were doing pretty well, and many black men were at least beginning to see the end of the Jim Crow world of legalized racism.

The question of why so many men seem to be sidelined is also politically and morally fraught, which is another reason why most who have danced around it have used a narrow lens that is often tinted to their ideological predilections. Most simply stated, the implicit debate about elusive causation comes down to economics or culture.

Very crudely, those on the political left have largely ascribed many of these problems to a harsh economy and policies favoring the rich that have destroyed or failed to create decent jobs with decent pay and benefits and have made social mobility ever more difficult in an increasingly unequal society. This view is shared by many men who supported Donald Trump and would hardly call themselves left wing. Extensive, incisive research by economists like David Autor, Alan Krueger, and others provide good fodder for this argument.

Similarly, those on the political right, such as Senator Ben Sasse (R-Nebr.) or scholar Charles Murray, have generally argued or suggested that the causes are primarily cultural or moral: Growing numbers of men are lazy, have little in the way of a work ethic, are immature and want to be taken care of—whether by the state, parents, or partners. They are narcissistic and irresponsible as fathers or husbands or even reliable mates—a complaint echoed by many women who would hardly call themselves right wing. Changing values and norms, as well as an overly generous welfare state, they argue, have enabled this behavior and broader state of affairs.[3]

As suggested, another way that this economics-versus-culture debate has been posed is this: Are they victims, or culprits, or something in between? Has society failed them or have they failed? How much of this is a story of economic injustice, of dwindling well-paying jobs—blame Wall Street, China, government policies that fail the middle class and the poor, you name it? Or is this a story of a culture gone to hell, one in which, as Nietzsche said, "Everything is permissible" or about which Daniel Patrick Moynihan, the late, great senator from New York, said that "deviancy" is "defined down"?

Many thoughtful scholars and commentators recognize that causal factors include some of both. It isn't a black-or-white choice, with strident Marxist determinists on one side and vulgar culture warriors on the other. But the devil, as always, is in the details.

Man Out explores interactions between economics and culture—some more demonstrable, some more hypothetical. Some show up in data, while others come from inferences from the real experiences and attitudes of men and those around them.

Let's be clear about three things at the outset:

First, many men are on "the outs," struggling, suffering, or screwing up to varying degrees. However, women, on average, still tend to get the shorter end of the stick. Women are more likely to be paid less, ghettoized into low-wage, low-status traditionally female occupations such as health aides, and in child care, housekeeping and cleaning, and food service. Although men, particularly highly educated ones, are more involved in parenting and doing household tasks than a generation or two ago, women still do the lion's share of this vital, unpaid work. Despite vast strides by women since the 1960s, men largely preside at the pinnacle of economic and political power. The vast majority of serious intergender violence is committed by men, and even in the wake of the Harvey Weinstein and other #MeToo revelations, most real incidents of rape and sexual assault of women are still not reported (however, false claims by women of sexual assault probably occur more than many people may want to admit). As tensions between the sexes appear to be growing significantly, a vocal minority of men are unabashed misogynists, spewing vile comments and behaving horrifically. Proclaiming the "ascendance of women" or the "death of men" or of "male hegemony" is quite premature.

Second, this is not the story of most men. There are about 120 million adult males in the United States in 2018, roughly 100 million of whom are of "working age," largely between their early 20s and late 60s.[1] Most have decent (even good) jobs, are good fathers and husbands, and strive to succeed for themselves, their families, and even the nation. Many more who lack good jobs and are "episodic fathers" are doing the best they can, to paraphrase Princeton sociologist Kathryn Edin.[5] They keep trying against the odds.

Third, many women also live on the periphery of U.S. life. I'm not only talking about poor single moms, many women of color, and the most tragic victims of male violence and discrimination—although they hardly live the American Dream. Rather, there are millions of women who also have been shut out of good jobs, have dropped out of the labor force, aren't doing well by their children, have squandered their money, are isolated and uninvolved in public life, and are drug, alcohol, or sex addicts. However, their stories tend to be different in kind and degree, and their outcomes are often colored by the still powerful effects of sexism.

Nonetheless, men out, or men on the sidelines, is the deeply troubling and vitally important story—or set of intertwined stories—of somewhere between one in five and one in four, or several tens of millions of, American men.[6] And the numbers show no signs of decreasing.

Chapter 1 presents the broad case that a lot of American men are not doing well *as men*. *People* struggle and are left on the sidelines for many reasons—because of their health, their economic circumstances, their character or psychology, their race or gender, their genes, where they live, bad luck, and so forth. Usually multiple factors are at work. This book argues that a large minority of adult males in the United States are struggling, on the sidelines, to a significant degree because they are men. Basic questions are posed: Who are these men? What does it mean to be "sidelined"? What are some of the possible reasons, including cultural, socioeconomic, historical, and personal factors? Why have they largely remained invisible?

Chapter 2 looks at the 20 million or more working-age men who are not employed. It explores such questions as, Why aren't they working? Who are they? What are they doing instead? How does this fit in with broader economic changes? What does this mean economically for these men, their families, the government, and the U.S. economy?

Chapter 3 explores how "masculinity," a cultural construct that has been undergoing rapid change during the last fifty years, negatively impacts millions of American men. It may be "traditional" masculinity, or new ideals of manhood, or the tensions between these that may be harming men—and, all too often, the women and children in their lives and society at large. What does it mean to be "masculine," and if that meaning isn't clear, what does that ambiguity mean for men? What do feminism as a political philosophy and women's individual or group beliefs about men mean for American males? How does this play out in a dramatically changing world of dating and male-female relations more generally? Why do so many heterosexual men seem so hostile toward women? Do men face "reverse discrimination" and need to fight back? Alternatively, do men need to fight old and damaging norms and stereotypes of masculinity?

Chapter 4 focuses on younger men, so-called millennials in their 20s and early to mid-30s. In many ways, it is in this age group—not that of the 55-year-old former factory worker—that American men are most likely to be struggling or sidelined. Why are they doing so poorly economically, living at home, anxious or angry, and seemingly unable to launch and assume adult responsibilities?

Chapter 5 examines how the internet may be harming many men and how many sidelined men may be using "new technologies" in unhealthy or unsavory ways.

Chapter 6 looks at men and marriage. To what extent are the class-based decline in marriage and the sidelining of American men related? Why are so many heterosexual men not marrying and starting families, and why do increasing numbers of women see husbands as irresponsible and—perhaps, worse—unnecessary?

Chapter 7 examines "fathers without children," reversing the more familiar trope of fatherless children to see why millions of American men are not a part of their minor children's lives and what that means to the fathers. In addition, how are the many problems of men out affecting their children?

Chapter 8 looks at middle-age men, those we so often hear about as having lost jobs and bringing their anger into politics—except that this chapter is about why growing numbers of men are in poor physical and psychological health.

Chapter 9 asks to what extent mass incarceration has contributed to the sidelining of so many American men and explores the struggles of millions of formerly incarcerated men.

Chapter 10 takes the man out phenomenon into the public square. It asks, Why are many men no longer "joiners" (while more women are)? Why are men less likely to serve their country in the armed forces or their communities as volunteers? How is the political gender gap that has emerged in the last generation related to the sidelining of American men?

Finally, chapter 11 asks what can be done to bring millions of men from the sidelines into lives and a society in which they are productive, happy, responsible, economically secure, healthy, and engaged with their families, friends, communities, and country. In addition, how do we navigate out of the current fog of gender roles in ways other than browbeating guys with politically correct nostrums or falling back into sexist and misogynistic patterns? Possible answers lie in public policy (and not just economic policies) and in cultural change.

A Personal Note

Research for this book entailed in-person, telephone, and online interviews with hundreds of men, as well as women and parents of young men, from the majority of the fifty states. They ranged in age from 18 to 96; were black, white, Latino, and Asian American; and occupied virtually every rung of the socio-economic ladder—from the very poor, to the middle class, to those making incomes well into six figures. As noted, they were primarily heterosexual. They included men from several working-class and middle-class communities as well as from several more affluent areas, groups of formerly incarcerated men, missing fathers, and significant numbers of millennial men under about age 35. An interactive website developed for this book, www.manout.us, elicited comments from many more men (and some women) in nearly twenty-five states. Understandably concerned about their privacy, virtually all of those whose stories and quotes appear in this book have been given pseudonyms and somewhat vague but accurate descriptors.

In addition, I spoke with scholars, advocates, and practitioners ranging from economists, sociologists, psychologists, and social workers to army re-cruiters, therapists, physicians, civic leaders, business leaders, and human re-source managers; federal, state, and local government experts and officials; men's rights advocates; female and male gender-equity proponents; members of service and volunteer organizations; those serving and studying fathers and children; criminal justice and domestic violence experts; political commen-tators; gay rights leaders; feminists; divorce lawyers; and more. Their politics often didn't fit a simple left-right characterization, although some were more clearly from one side of the spectrum or the other. Quantitative data were drawn from U.S. government (and some international agency) sources, academic research, and personal communication with experts. As both a journalist and a historian, I have also drawn on media reports and historical works.

These people, excluding those who understandably wanted their anonymity preserved, are noted in the acknowledgments.

To state the obvious, I am a man. I am white. I have had the privilege of a very good (perhaps too extensive) education, very good parents, good and interesting jobs, a brilliant and wonderful son (if I may kvell for a moment), and economic security. I have also had personal reversals, but I have not had anything like the difficulties of most of the men I've talked with and write about.

That said, it is not just as a historian, journalist, social analyst, or commentator that I have seen what has been happening to too many American men. Aside from having many friends and acquaintances who have experienced pieces of the man out story, one especially powerful part of my research took me to see what has become of the worlds of my long-deceased parents.

My father grew up in the gritty working-class coal country of central Pennsylvania, but my childhood memories are of a town where people generally worked hard, provided for their families, worshiped in mostly Catholic churches and synagogues, and thought about the good of the community and nation. My mother grew up in the rural dairy country of Wisconsin, in a small town rimmed by cornfields and cows, where a farm machinery factory employed unionized workers, the yards were tidy, men went boating and hunting, a light progressivism hung in the air, and the main street was lined with mostly Protestant churches, shops, and more than a few taverns.

These worlds have radically changed. In my father's hometown, there's no work in the mines, two prisons have become the major employers, the streets and railroad-flat homes like my grandmother's are shabbier or in rubble, and the nearby yeshiva my father attended is no more. Drug overdoses are frequent news, and anger has replaced the kind of patriotism portrayed in *The Deer Hunter*, the 1978 film set a little farther west in Pennsylvania. My mother's hometown still is surrounded by farms and its factory is humming, but wage levels, in real terms, and the number of local workers are less than when I visited as a child for family Christmases. Solid, wood-frame houses like my aunt and uncle's have been supplemented by trailer homes, and anger and opioids also have established a big beachhead.

In both, the main streets are filled with empty storefronts, residents talk of a decline of neighborliness, and there are men from their 20s to their 60s who can't seem to make it. My father's hometown was a stronghold of FDR Democrats, and my mother's was a town of moderate Republicans. Unions were strong in both places, as were Elks and Kiwanis clubs and other traditionally men's organizations. While there are still Democrats in these microcosms of states won by Donald Trump in 2016, both are dominated by conservative Republicans, and the unions and once strong men's groups are a shadow of what they once were.

MAN OUT

CHAPTER 1

American Men on the Sidelines

The mass of men lead lives of quiet desperation. What is called resignation
is confirmed desperation.

—*Henry David Thoreau, "Economy"*

No one knows my struggle, they only see the trouble.

—*Tupac Shakur, "Thugz Mansion"*

Twenty to twenty-five million men—the population of Florida or Texas—are
on the sidelines of American life.[1] They have the same Y chromosomes as the
men you see at work, the men who play with their children, go out with their
wives or partners, are involved in their communities, and earn a living to save
for their children's education and their families' retirement. But these "men
out" are doing few if any of these things.

They are still counted by the U.S. Census, but for all practical purposes
they are absent from much of mainstream life. What they do doesn't register
in either the gross domestic product (GDP) or in the glimmer of a child's eye.
They aren't engaged in their communities or country.

Viscerally, we know these sidelined men are out there. But they don't fit
old stereotypes of failure. We haven't been able to name them or come to
grips with who they are. We haven't identified the problem or its dimensions.
Why is this happening? What can we do? We see separate problems like white
men who aren't working, who are angry, whose education ended long before

a bachelor's degree. We see black men whose lives don't seem to matter. We see adult boys living in their parents' basements. We see drug and technology addicts, absent fathers, misogynists. We see men struggling with masculinity. We see men struggling with relationships and marriage and ones with physical and mental health problems. But we don't see a single, larger story.

This is a cultural, economic, and political phenomenon that many have caught glimpses of but no one has defined. It is corroding American life in myriad ways. This problem without a name is fed by and affects the economy and politics, changing norms and technologies, and it bleeds into individual and social psychology and public health, as well as dating, marriage, and fatherhood. As Bob Dylan said, "Something is happening here, but you don't know what it is."

This raises several basic questions: Who are these men, what are their lives like, and what makes them different from the majority of American men, who still navigate life pretty well? What are some of the qualities, barriers, pathologies, and other challenges these men face, and what are the common threads that tie together these various manifestations of dysfunction?

Many men try hard to do the right thing and succeed. Many see the problem in terms of being casualties of economic and cultural change. These men are at least partially correct. Rather than receiving a dishonorable discharge, they have been deported from mainstream America.

In this chapter we begin to explore the following: Who are America's sidelined men? Why is this happening? (And why do often politicized explanations that lean too heavily on cultural factors, on the one hand, or economic factors, on the other, present an unsatisfactory, one-dimensional view?) What does being on the sidelines mean for these and other men, for women and children, for civic life, economic well-being, and everyday life? And is this the future for ever more American men?

WHO ARE THEY?

Sidelined men are a disparate population. Not all men out exhibit all of the characteristics mentioned above and discussed in the following pages. And the extent and the severity of their challenges differ. However, like the overlapping sections of a Venn diagram, all of them exhibit at least some of these qualities.

These men—different in many ways but kindred in ways we generally don't want to admit—cut across demographic categories. The Trump-era stereotype of the laid-off white worker—that is, the former Stakhanovite in bedroom slippers—is but a slice of a bigger, more complex story. Central casting may put them in pickup trucks in Appalachia and the Rust Belt. But the cast is far larger.

Some groups—less educated white men, poorer African American men, young men, single men, and many middle-age men who are still far from the birthdays that will open the doors to Social Security and Medicare—are disproportionately represented. But there are men who at least once were middle and upper middle class, gay men, married men, and Latino men. Some are just trying to begin adulthood; others are well into middle age. Some are ex-offenders, but most have never committed a crime. They are Democrats, Republicans, and independents and are often detached from, disgusted with, and isolated from politics and public life. They can be found in all corners of the nation—from big cities and suburbs to rural areas and small towns. While many do live in Appalachia, the rural South, and formerly industrial areas, a surprising number live in exurbs, suburbs, and cities from Silicon Valley to New England. Not off-the-grid hermits holed up in mountain bunkers, they live next door or in our own homes.

It is impossible to pinpoint their numbers except to say that one-fifth to one quarter of the 100 million or so American males who are between their early 20s and mid- to late 60s exhibit many of the key characteristics.[2]

Many don't work and either can't find jobs or aren't looking. These out-of-work, often alone men have disembarked from the labor force and other social institutions or have been thrown overboard. Their skills may be out of date and their former salaries too high for a profit-maximizing economy that sometimes gets airbrushed with exciting-sounding words like "competitive," "global," and "digital" but leaves them in the dust. The aging of the population has coincided with age discrimination against ever younger "older workers." And there's an increasing brokenness to their bodies and psyches.

Few are buying homes, and many are more likely to have—*or be*—liabilities than assets. Nor are they paying much in the way of taxes, although they are more than likely drawing on government benefits like food stamps and Medicaid and driving up government spending.[3]

They generally aren't active in public life. Some younger men lack maturity. Others have become loners or suffer from poor health. They may be angry, or they may just be blank. Many are less than responsible, reliable, and loving fathers, husbands, partners, or workers, even when they do have jobs. A significant number feel they've been mistreated by women, unfair laws, and an unjust economy. Many drift in and out of relationships, having children with multiple women, prowling the virgin yet hardly virginal terrain of hookups and Tinder. Others who are married are neither good providers nor taking care of the kids and home, letting their wives support them—an embarrassment at best, a costly ball and chain and divorce material at worst. Other sidelined men turn to parents; millions of adult men in their 20s and 30s are back in their childhood bedrooms or basements. Spending all too much time online in a world of video games, social media, porn, and dyspeptic Reddit threads and quasi-fascist corners of the internet, they have largely gone offline from the real world of other, in-the-flesh human beings. They are beyond "bowling alone"; it's more likely that they can't find the bowling alley, and if they do, they don't know what to do with the ball.[4] Many feel disparaged, rightly or wrongly, which erodes their self-esteem and makes their lives even worse.

Midlife—one's 40s to early 60s—once was the time when men were at the pinnacle of their careers. They had put in their time, climbed the corporate or organizational ladder, and attained what was likely to be the highest income of their lifetimes. They could support their families and look forward to a secure retirement. If they weren't genuinely happy or content, at least they had checked all the boxes of middle-class success in the mid-twentieth century. Most still do, and many 25-year-olds are getting good jobs, marrying, and leading good lives, while more than a few 70- to 75-year-olds are hard at work in jobs they love.

The growing population of men out has become a drain on their families and the economy. Whether one sees these men as victims or as responsible for their own circumstances, they not only represent hundreds of billions of dollars in lost potential GDP, as well as tax revenues and increased government expenditures that together help drive up deficits, but they also are a cost to family and friends, who often pay to sustain them.

Are these men victims or are they culprits? The question is fiercely and inconclusively debated, yielding much more heat than light. Neither the left nor the right has a monopoly on this story. For now, let's sidestep the question and say that most men out are some of both. Regardless, their lives are rimmed with losses, defeats, and sadness.

They aren't all ne'er-do-wells, but they *aren't* doing well for themselves, their families, their communities, or their country. They are disappointments to their children, wives (and girlfriends, if they have any), and employers or former employers. They, too, are disappointed, but more than likely they are hurting—economically, psychologically, and physically. Many are in poverty or in pain, are depressed and isolated, feel shame or anger, and are lost. They comprise millions of personal tragedies, and their collective condition has negative repercussions for the nation. And their numbers seem to be increasing.

Lorne, a middle-age white man in the Midwest who was last employed eight years ago, is angry. Very angry. He hasn't "dropped out" of the workforce, he said emphatically when I spoke with him. "I've been kicked out." Citing, at once proudly and cynically, his two science and math degrees and his career in information technology (IT), he said that he and men like him "are overeducated, overtrained, and overskilled."

Lorne is angry at not only recruiters, women, journalists, and scholars who write about men like him but also society in general. He focuses his ire on what he calls "the deliberate and strategic discrimination in human resources departments, against middle-age white men." The "recruiting industry," a phrase used with scorn, is "female-dominated," filled with "young, single women" and biased against men "to compensate for years of so-called misogyny."

Society is brimming with "hatred" toward people like him who aren't working, he said. They think that such people are mooching off the government. Lorne was quick to note, "The government hasn't given me a dime. I've paid for everything with my own hard-earned savings."

He recounted his efforts to find jobs, telling the story of one potential employer who took him to court for harassment because he sent an indeterminate number of follow-up emails after an interview. "My job-hunting efforts have been criminalized, in the true, literal sense," Lorne said. "You wonder why I gave up looking for work?"

When the subject of available low-wage jobs came up, Lorne said he's not "culturally suited" to working in a pizza parlor or other places where "high school dropouts" and college students taking summer jobs toil. As a former IT worker, he said, his "expectations" are higher.

Lorne is not alone in his bitterness. A lot has gone badly wrong in his work life. Naturally, he has looked for explanations and has come up with a long list of culprits. But having others to blame—rightly or wrongly—doesn't ease his pain. He made a point of saying that he understands why suicide rates among men are up, concluding grimly, "I fully embrace the fact that I will die of starvation when my savings are gone. Bring it on!" Yet men like Lorne are largely out of sight.

WHY ARE THEY INVISIBLE?

Even more than the poor, or people of color, or underpaid workers, or the LGBTQ community, or women, men out are largely invisible. They are unorganized and lack advocates. They have no lobbyists on K Street or grassroots activists to support them. There are no charities for failing men, and very few scholars of gender studies focus on them. While these men out face a host of problems, as do other marginalized groups, most social scientists and the commentariat have put their problems into discrete silos: it's a labor force problem, or a fatherhood and family problem, or an opioid or public health problem, or a political problem.

But there is another significant reason for their invisibility: gender-role norms and shame. Men are supposed to be strong, stoic fighters. If they're not at the top of their game or vigorously competing, they're not in the game. At the same time, our postfeminist culture tells us that women are still largely oppressed, the victims of a patriarchal, sexist society in which men cling to their privilege and too many are likely to be guilty of sexual harassment, if not assault. It follows that if men remain the unjust winners, it's ludicrous or tin-eared to think of them as losers. In general, this story is correct, just like it's true that America is generally a rich country. Yet the United States has many poor and economically struggling people, just as a still male-dominated society has many sidelined, struggling men.

Shame is compounded by another concept that few want to discuss: masculinity. For those on the left, feminists, and many women, the very term connotes retrograde norms and attitudes that are one step out of the cave. For those on the right, many men, and some women, the vague idea of masculinity suggests a positive, tough, in-charge persona. None of these groups has much of a place for struggling men. For a lot of sidelined men, establishing and maintaining a "masculine" identity is just one more cross to bear. Definitions of masculinity are in flux, leaving them confused or angry about how they should play their gender role. The acting coaches have left the theater. This is another key, similarly siloed dimension of the man out problem.

Different dimensions of many American men's problems have been creeping into the headlines and public awareness. However, several key things have been missing from these discussions.

First and foremost, the array of problems has been spliced apart and widely treated as separate issues; connections among them have not been carefully explored. This set of man out issues has yet to be identified as what is in many ways a single, broader problem. Unfortunately, most economists, social scientists, and advocates who have ventured into this world fail to see the politically inconvenient connections among many subpopulations of men and among different social problems.

The list of those who have entered into parts of this discussion is long: (1) the "men's rights" types, (2) those on the right denouncing a lost work ethic, (3) worker activists on the left pointing to forty-five years of declining inflation-adjusted median male wages, (4) women decrying irresponsible or misogynistic men, (5) Donald Trump and the Tea Party fanning the flames of hypernationalist discontent, (6) deincarceration supporters, (7) public health leaders seeing disturbing trends in men's health, (8) those promoting civic engagement and greater comity in public discourse, (9) feminists and progressive men's groups that want to reduce "toxic masculinity," (10) family and fatherhood activists, (11) education and workforce development proponents who want to expand opportunities and access for both, and (12) economists and others in public policy who see the costs to the U.S. economy and want to figure out what to do. However, few of these seem to realize that they are often talking about the same men.

Second, economics and politics are key, but despite much populist rhetoric, few people, other than labor organizers and advocates, are truly standing up for men who have been pushed to the precarious margins of the U.S. economy. Which political leaders have taken a stand on, which research organizations have focused on, and which foundations or nonprofits have taken up men's issues?[5] Similarly, absent fathers and ex-offenders don't elicit much sympathy, but many of these men are not being given a fair shake. Politically correct scholars and advocates are generally loath to touch the subject of a "man problem." As Simone de Beauvoir wrote in the 1940s, who would ever get "the notion of writing a book on the peculiar situation of the American male?"[6]

Third, for those whose focus is on economics, the at least equally influential role of culture and historical changes in norms, values, and mores is rarely spoken in the same breath. The ticklish questions of men's choices and what choices we as a society tolerate—or have forced or nudged so many people into—have been avoided.

TEN STATISTICS

Ten statistics about ten seemingly unrelated phenomena, when brought together, are intriguingly suggestive of this interlocking story:

- Fewer than seven out of ten American men age 20 and older work; in the
  1950s, nine out of ten worked. Just over eight in ten working-age (25–64
  years old) men work, compared to nineteen out of twenty in the mid-
  twentieth century.[7]

- Inflation-adjusted ("real") wages for the bottom 60 percent of men fell between 1973 and 2016, with the most dramatic declines occurring among
  the bottom 40 percent, and despite growth during the final Obama years,
  real median wages for all men were slightly lower in 2016 than at their
  peak in 1973.[8]

- By the mid-2010s, just half of men were husbands; in 1960 three-fourths
  of men were married.[9]

- Today, and in the years before Donald Trump became president, only two
  out of three children had both parents living with them; when John Kennedy was elected president, nine out of ten children did.[10]

- In 2015, 35 percent of 18- to 34-year-old American men lived with their
  parents (compared to 29 percent of millennial women); in 1975 about 28
  percent did.[11]

- There were projected to be 37 percent more women in college than men
  in 2017–2018, whereas in 1970 there were about 35 percent more men
  than women in college.[12]

- In 2013 mortality rates among less educated, middle-age white men and
  women were about 20 percent higher than they were in 1998, life expectancy among American men had fallen in the mid-2010s, and life expectancy for white men in rural West Virginia was more than eight years less
  than it was in the affluent suburbs of Washington, D.C., 100 miles away.[13]

- Men are about 50 percent less likely than women to trust government.[14]

- In the 2016 election there was a 24 percentage point voting gap between
  genders, with white men being much more likely not only to vote for
  Republicans but also to express disillusionment and anger toward gov-

ernment; until about 1980, men and women voted roughly evenly for Democrats and Republicans.[15]

- Male membership in civic groups—including service organizations like the Masons, Rotary, Elks, and Kiwanis—has fallen by between one-half and two-thirds since the 1960s.[16]

The pattern is striking. On a number of these metrics, there has been a similar rate of decline, in some cases more than a 20 percentage point falloff.

Although there are many ways to slice and argue about statistics, and categories often overlap, in 2017 there were more than 20 million nonworking adult American men; 4.7 million men 25 and older working part-time, including 1.4 million men not by choice; 13–14 million young adult men living with parents; about 10 million fathers of minor children who did not live full-time or at all with their kids, including several million never-married fathers; 2 million incarcerated men, 4 million more on parole or probation, and at least 17 million male ex-felons; 15 million hard-core male video gamers; about 12 million men living alone and more than 10 million men who said they didn't have anyone to turn to in a time of crisis; nearly 13 million men who were substance abusers; at least a million men in drug and alcohol abuse treatment centers; 33,000 men who committed suicide; and countless men ranging from the virulently misogynistic to those who felt confused and threatened about their masculinity.[17] These men are all around us.

While it is more socially acceptable for women—particularly mothers—not to work, comparable numbers for women on other metrics paint a very different picture: in 2017 there were about 2 million mothers who did not live with their children; 200,000 incarcerated women; 9,000 women who killed themselves; 6 million women who abused drugs or alcohol; and 10 million millennial women living at home.

Each of these statistics is not necessarily either a damnation or a marker of a man out. Many nonworking men are looking hard for work, and thousands of fathers who don't live full-time with their kids are still good dads. Online gaming can be an engrossing pastime, pharmaceutical companies bear much of the blame for America's opioid crisis, and gender norms must be pretty up in the air when *Time* magazine releases a cover story called "Beyond 'He' or "She.'"[18]

This is where we once again need to stand back from pat judgments. By themselves, these numbers don't necessarily mean that American capitalism is ruthlessly amoral or that men are good-for-nothing louts.

What these numbers mean—at least at this point in this book—is that too many men are on the sidelines of American life, not living the kinds of good lives that should be possible in a prosperous, tolerant, fair, friendly, and happy society.

In short, the man out problem has a number of intertwined dimensions in which causal lines run in various directions. The siloed "labor force problem" stems from and stokes degraded values, the growth in economic inequality, mass incarceration, government policies that have hurt working Americans, and internet addiction, among many other factors. So too is the "masculinity crisis" a function of, and contributor to, declining labor force participation, misogyny, and virulent expressions of male anger. America's "marriage and fatherhood crises" also swirl back into inequality, dwindling values of responsibility, gender-role confusion, and mass incarceration. Growing physical health, mental health, and substance abuse problems among men reflect problems in the labor force and economy, in marriages and male-female relations, and in knowing what it means to be a man.

The problem is multifactorial, some would drily say. It involves a little bit of everything (which at some point becomes a heuristic cop-out). Anyone who argues that men's declining labor force participation can be reversed largely by increasing economic growth or reducing inequality (as if either is easy), that father absence can be significantly reduced by marriage promotion, or that misogyny can be dealt with largely by teaching males a more egalitarian version of masculinity misses the larger issue. None of these, or other problems of men out, can be truly addressed without confronting these multiple factors together.

If an observer from Mars were looking at the Earth in the 1950s or 1960s and asked who was at the top of the global heap in power and opportunity, the answer would have been clear: American men, white men in particular. It is important not to idealize the mid-twentieth century as a time when everything was smooth sailing for men and to gloss over how much worse life was for most women and for African Americans and other people of color, as historian Stephanie Coontz points out in her 1992 book, *The Way We Never Were*. Nonetheless, if that same Martian returned today, it would see a much different picture.[19]

Certainly it is true that many women, especially women of color, are still more likely to fare poorly in the United States, despite significant strides

during the last half century. They are grossly underrepresented in government and executive suites. They are shunted into traditional "women's work"
and paid, on average, 20 percent less than men; the differential is less for
those in the same jobs, but it still exists, even though well-educated urban
younger women are starting to earn more than their male counterparts.[20] In
many other countries, women have it much worse. In some, mostly northern
European countries, women are doing better than those in America.

Variants on men out also have started to appear in western Europe and
other developed countries, although adult male employment rates are higher
in almost every other rich country than in the United States. Britain has
record numbers of "kippers" (kids in parents' pockets, eroding retirement savings). As in the United States and France, about one-third of Britons under 35
live at home. The figure climbs to more than 40 percent of young Germans
and a staggering 65 percent of young Italians. These male *bamboccioni* or
mammone are not so flatteringly called "big babies." In Japan the so-called
soushoku danshi, or "herbivore men," appear to have little interest in marriage, sex, dating, and even careers.[21]

MORE THAN A FEW GOOD MEN

It is important to emphasize that although an awful lot of American men may
be down for the count, most men are still very much in the ring. Men still
dominate the penthouses of American society and the commanding heights
of power. Most work hard to support themselves and their families. They are
ambitious and goal-oriented and are good husbands and fathers. The majority are still engaged in civic life, have embraced mature adulthood, and have
more than a passing acquaintance with the notion of responsibility and other
"good" values. They aren't in trouble with the law. They don't fritter away
their time playing computer games or streaming endless movies.

Millions of them toil ten- and twelve-hour days at virtually every type of
job. They work because they need to earn a living, sometimes working more
than one job, sometimes because they are committed to their employer's
mission. They can be found picking up their kids at school and playing in
adult softball leagues. When they go on a date, they are looking for a serious relationship, not a one-night stand. They keep themselves fit and well-
groomed and are at ease when carrying on a conversation. They may have
dreams of better tomorrows, but their dreams are ones that they put effort
into achieving.

At home—meaning independent domiciles, not group houses, man caves, or parents' spare bedrooms—more and more men help with child care, cooking, and housework. A growing minority has gone further, becoming egalitarian partners and very involved fathers.

Most men are neither damned losers nor neolithic misogynists. They have their faults and problems, but theirs are everyday ones that they manage. And they soldier on.

In fact, most Americans who are doing extremely well are men. Although women outnumber men as entrants into a great number of prestigious professions and one quarter of wives earn more than their husbands, more than 95 percent of Fortune 500 CEOs are men; 88 percent of financial services executives are men; 82 percent of the directors, producers, and writers of the 250 top-grossing films in 2017 and 80 percent of the members of the 115th Congress are also men.[22] Eighty-eight of the one hundred wealthiest Americans are men. And 71 percent of federal and state elected officials are male (and all but 6 percent of the 71 percent are white). At the same time, three-fourths of the workers in the nation's ten lowest-paid occupations are women. And median weekly earnings for full-time male workers were $944 at the end of 2017, which is $173 more than those of women.[23]

What makes thriving men different?

Some of the difference is a matter of social structure and class. Smart boys who grow up in upper-middle-class households exposed to greater intellectual stimulation are much more likely to make it into elite colleges and universities, get high-powered professional jobs, and become good husbands and fathers.[24] On the other hand, males from poorer families all too often face a brick wall, as "sticky" social mobility has made rags to rags a more common intergenerational story than rags to riches. Men with modest skills and education are more likely to face the slings and arrows of labor market misfortune. Yet there are many exceptions to this story line, and many bad boys grow up to be good men (and many good boys don't sparkle later in life).

Beyond class and social structure, much of the success formula has to do with what values, skills, and attitudes, as well as knowledge, boys and young men learn from parents, school, media, and their communities. Boys who learn to obey rules and assume responsibilities and are neither too coddled nor neglected are likelier to carry these lessons into manhood. Boys who receive more reinforcement for doing well and aren't allowed to get away with so much bad behavior and mediocre performance also have a better chance of being successful men. Although ambition and drive may not be rewarded as much as we'd like, those who are ambitious and instilled with a strong work ethic early on do have a better chance at doing well in many realms of life. Likewise, boys and young men who get a bigger dose of good manners, leavened with a more flexible conception of gender roles, probably will do better with girlfriends, wives, partners, children, and employers.

Commitment to values and open-mindedness are key, whether they are achievement-driven, hipsters, entrepreneurs, diligent employees, rock-solid family men, patriots, or activists. Their beliefs matter, yet they are tolerant of the beliefs of others. They are generally strong and confident yet flexible and self-questioning. They are very much engaged with the present, but they don't simply "live for today"; they also have an eye on the future. Their perspectives, goals, time horizons, and social circles are broad, and their lives are about more than themselves.

That most men are doing well, that the subordinate status of women and the legacy of eons of sexism have faded to a good degree, and that the same is occurring in other countries do not make America's man out problem go away.

FORCED EXILE OR CHOSEN RETREAT?

Bill's story is one illustration of how so many American men are falling onto the sidelines. He has lived for about fifteen years in an upper-middle-class suburb of one of the East Coast's big cities. He is well-spoken and knowledgeable about current affairs. He is white and has two master's degrees. He had worked for several companies by his mid-40s, when he started taking too many days off and quit his job. Wanting to start a new career as a teacher, he got a third master's degree in education and was hired as a middle school chemistry teacher, only to be fired before his first school year was over.

At age 47, he stopped looking for work, and despite many offers of help from his wife and extended family, he rarely left home, became increasingly angry, and refused to take his children to appointments and school sporting events. His wife, also a professional with two master's degrees, worked full-time at modest pay, supporting him and their two children. Bill was repeatedly urged to look for a job, first by his wife, then by his children. Hearing such a basic, reasonable request, he would be resentful and stomp off. Instead he has spent a decade and a half of what some still call "the prime" of his life watching movies and reading.

Bill is now in his early 60s. Since his late 40s, he has been jobless by choice. After his wife filed for divorce, he moved into a rental room in a

nearby house. With no earnings, no wife to support him, his children and extended family alienated from him, and still no motivation to work, his present
is barren and his future is bleak. Yet, generally, he sees nothing wrong with
his decisions or where they have left him. His son, now out of college, sadly
said, "I always wished that Daddy could have gotten a job and be someone I
could look up to."

At first, economic arguments seem most compelling. A brutal economy
may appear to explain why great numbers of men, particularly those with
little education and few skills, can no longer find jobs. Deindustrialization
and automation, which have taken a particularly heavy toll in male occupations since the 1970s, eviscerated a once strong male working class. Despite a
generally buoyant stock market, significant productivity growth, and officially
low unemployment, Americans' economic fortunes started to diverge in the
late 1970s and 1980s, only to diverge more severely after strong economic
growth in the late 1990s. Former president Obama called rising inequality
"the defining issue of our time," as the top one-fifth of earners—especially
those in the storied "1 percent"—largely flourished while the bottom four-
fifths saw their incomes after inflation stagnate or fall and the middle class
"hollowed out."

Is the divide between the men in command and the men on the sidelines
yet another manifestation of growing inequality in America? Are we seeing
a new version of *Upstairs, Downstairs*—with a shrinking majority of diligent
workers, partners, fathers, and citizens and a growing minority who have
more or less abdicated or been exiled from these essential adult roles?

However, only those who follow a strong reductionist approach would say
that an economy failing the middle and working classes is the sole or major
cause of men not participating in civic or political organizations, not committing to relationships or marriage, not working, not being good fathers, dying
younger, and hiding out in basements, transfixed by video games and popping
open another beer.

Economic factors certainly have seared the lives of many men and women
in contemporary America. Ruthless corporations and financial institutions
and laws rigged in favor of the wealthy and powerful have fleeced millions
of hardworking American women and men. An economic democracy the
United States is not.

Moreover, many sidelined men emphatically say they don't want to be
seen as failures and dropouts. They say they want to work, marry, own a house,
and achieve the American Dream. They have tried hard, and they rightfully

bristle at the suggestion that they are irresponsible or lazy. They simply feel beaten down. With wages of $12 per hour, part-time or contract jobs, and no pensions or retirement security, they are paupers compared to CEOs and others taking home millions per year. They also stand in stark contrast to the great mid-twentieth-century American middle class, which generally had ever rising wage and benefit packages during the quarter century after World War II.

Yet economic circumstances have been bad before and are worse today in other parts of the world. In times past—including much more economically challenging times—and in many countries that are not as rich as America, men have persevered and fought back. They have taken less than ideal jobs (which American women are more likely to do than men), spent long hours working, kept searching for work, and even demonstrated in the streets. Overall, they did not tune out. But despite a boiling anger across the land, a defining trait of so many sidelined men is their passivity and resignation.

Those who focus on growing gender disparities in educational achievement believe that some boys and young men have learned that it's "not cool for them to perform or be smart," as the principal of the Bronx Leadership Academy said.[25] On average, they don't perform as well as girls and young women from kindergarten to graduate school.

There are also ominous signs of declining health, particularly among less educated males: rising alcohol and opioid abuse and poisonings, suicide, increasing reports of physical and psychological pain, growing disability rolls, and even declining testosterone levels. Death rates for middle-age whites with a high school education or less have been on the rise since at least 1999. Suicide has increased dramatically among men. So too has impotence, particularly among younger men. Thanks to the magic of spam, reminders of "erectile dysfunction" fill many an inbox. Meanwhile, military leaders point to a sharp decline in the numbers of men who are physically or psychologically fit for service.[26]

The distinctly worse and intertwined problems of racism, crime, and unemployment facing black men have become much more salient in the wake of police killings in Ferguson, Missouri, and elsewhere. The long shadow of four hundred years of U.S. slavery and racism has contributed to a dyad of oppression and dysfunction for too many young African American men. The deincarceration and Black Lives Matter movements are responses to the doors of opportunity being slammed shut on so many black men.

Feminism has done much for women, but it has had a more nuanced effect on men. On the positive side, it has pushed men toward accepting women as equals and adopting more equal gender roles. Actors Alan Alda and Robin Williams in the late twentieth century helped make sensitivity and engaged fatherhood de rigueur in many quarters. The ranks of stay-at-home married dads has increased—to 209,000 in 2016—still a fraction of 1 percent of the nation's approximately 36 million fathers of minor children.[27]

However, feminism has confused, upset, and, in some people's eyes, emasculated a number of men—not only Arnold Schwarzenegger's "girly men" but those who realize that they can't compete with women in the classroom, the conference room, or the bedroom. It has also created many unsettling ambiguities; many men who have internalized traditional masculine norms but rejected them in theory don't really know what playbook to use. If men and women are equal, why do men pick up the tab, and why are fathers second-class parents at home and in the eyes of employers and courts?

The erosion of patriarchy is not to be bemoaned. Still, there is a palpable and bittersweet nostalgia for the debonair and successful Cary Grant, Gary Cooper, Don Draper, or the "working-class hero"—the masculine mystique of mid-twentieth-century America. Somewhere between the poles of James Bond and the Man in the Gray Flannel Suit were men who were bold yet dependable. There was no irony about being male.

Some female and male pundits and website warriors fight the gender wars. Some women use the seductive but vague notion of "masculinity" to demand that males "man up." But for those who think that the adjective to modify masculinity is "toxic," the message seems to be to "man down." Across the gender divide, from the far reaches of the men's rights'/separatists' "manosphere" to many more mainstream men, salvos against feminism often devolve into derision toward women. In men's defense, survey data show that nearly as many women as men are drawn to "traditional" conceptions of masculinity.[28]

Gender dynamics are a complicated dance of lingering prejudices and beliefs and changing expectations about men's and women's roles. Feminism, new laws, mixed messages from popular culture, the uncloseting of gay men, changing norms about sexuality, and women's own ambivalence (or, if one takes a harsher view, double standard) all have contributed to muddling the minds of Joe Sixpack or even B. A. Bob about what it means to be a man. Barack Obama got nailed for his 2008 remark about unemployed Rust Belt workers "clinging to guns or religion," but many men may have tried to shore up their masculinity with an overly zealous interest in guns, cars, and violent games and sports.

Politics might appear to be another culprit, or refuge, for men on the side-lines. George Wallace in 1968, Kevin Phillips's *Emerging Republican Major-ity* (1969), Archie Bunker, Ronald Reagan, Newt Gingrich and the Contract with America, the Tea Party, and Donald Trump seem to chart a half-century trajectory for the political potency of embattled white men. Although Trump could not have made it to the White House without the support of various other constituencies, pundits endlessly hailed the rise of the white American male *sansculottes*.

However, digging deeper, the capture of politics and policymaking by the rich has left some men and women to rightly question whether their voices matter. This is quite different from much of American history—at least for white men until the 1970s—when most white people at least felt represented by their government. This phenomenon comes on top of a decades-long as-sault on government whose unspoken subtext is that one would be a fool to try to effect positive changes through the core institutions of American democ-racy. This post-Nixon, Reagan to-Trump-driven assault on the public sphere has particularly captivated working- and middle-class white men. But men's retreat from public life goes far beyond such politics and antigovernment polemics.

Political scientists such as Robert D. Putnam have highlighted the exodus from civic organizations as young and middle-age men are hardly beating down the doors of Rotary Clubs or churches.[29] Nor are men joining much else. As shout-outs to veterans at stadiums and on airplanes grow louder, few men choose to serve their country in the armed forces or AmeriCorps.[30]

The sizable gender gap in voting and the Trump-era trope of angry white men are much discussed. The gendered nature of the erosion of public life, public service, and public trust in government, however, has largely gone unrecognized, as men are increasingly loners and rebels and women have become more likely to be active and "joiners."

IS THIS A CHOICE?

Men out are neither purely victims of social and economic ills nor irredeem-ably irresponsible. Too many of these arguments for one or the other are made through blinkered "progressive" or "conservative" lenses.

Socioeconomic injustices are certainly worthy of attack, but to what degree are millions of men making a *choice*, or a series of choices, to give up on aspirations, institutions, and norms, and not engage with a changing world—a world that is leaving many men behind? Of course, "choices" are made in contexts and in response to circumstances. Whether we believe in an all-powerful God, fate, or ineluctable "economic forces," much of the time we are determinists; we tend to think that larger forces are at work, and we discount the role that choice plays in life.

No one happily chooses to be poor, laid off, lonely, powerless, or sick. However, one makes better or worse choices, and one does choose how to respond to difficult circumstances. One can choose to fight back or to strive individually or collectively to make life better. Or not.

But who is to say what's a "better" choice? One could argue that hanging out in the basement or garage, primed to come up with the "next big thing," may seem more rewarding than taking an unsatisfying job. Surveys seem to show that nonworking millennials are somewhat happier than their peers with jobs. Or one could argue that dating and not assuming the economic costs of a family offer more options and safety than "settling down" and becoming a long-term partner and father. Similarly, taking OxyContin or heroin or that fifth shot of vodka may feel better than living with physical and psychological pain. And in the libertarian spirit of "live free or die," it may seem like a wise, principled choice in a broken polity to tend one's own garden rather than commit to the furtherance of liberty and justice for all through a "government of the people, by the people, and for the people."

CULTURE AND HISTORY

Since the mid-twentieth century, when male employment rates were at their highest and slowly starting to decline, there have been two narratives about middle-age men who didn't work: either they wanted to "escape the rat race" or they were having "midlife crises."

In 1965 psychologist Elliott Jacques coined the term "midlife crisis" to describe mostly male, angst-ridden patients seeing their mortality over the horizon and their youthful dreams fade. Enter the red sports car and the young blonde. The idea caught fire as Hollywood played off the glamour and dangers of midlife crises in movies like *American Beauty*. Research has disproved the inevitability of "midlife crises," but the notion lives on.[31]

At about the same time that Jacques came along, the idea of escaping the rat race of stressful, unfulfilling jobs became a popular, if unacted-upon, goal. This was seen as liberation from the stultifying life of being the "company man," the "lifer," who punched his time clock for forty years in exchange for the proverbial gold watch. Echoing Henry David Thoreau's *Walden,* in which the author said that "most men live lives of quiet desperation," John Updike's *Rabbit* novels vividly recast that idea for the late twentieth century in his antihero Harry Angstrom. Trapped in suburbia and marriage, the Angstrom character was aptly called by the *New York Times* "an older and less articulate Holden Caulfield." This was given added oomph by a 1960s counterculture that derided nine-to-five work.[32]

This route to "freedom" undoubtedly was also a rationalization for abandoning once sacrosanct responsibilities of the Protestant work ethic. Despite the allure of getting off the treadmill and "firing your boss," as one book put it, few men actually did so, except for well-to-do aging hippies who gave up the corporate life to open a B&B, start a winery, or write a novel in a mountain cabin. One of many critics of this metaphor for mind-numbing conformity, the Reverend William Sloane Coffin, said, "Even if you win the rat race, you're still a rat."[33] Ideas about midlife crises and the rat race reflect that a lot of jobs can be bad for the soul, but nonwork can also scorch the soul.

In many ways the perfectly reasonable idea of greater freedom and choice got hijacked. Somewhere between Ivan Karamazov declaring that "if God does not exist, everything is permitted" and the 1960s ethos of "do your own thing" or "whatever turns you on," fewer and fewer behaviors became cultural requisites. Instead they became lifestyle choices. No one really said that it's okay to not work, or not work hard, or not be a good spouse or parent, or not be a good neighbor or citizen. But other values began to take precedence. Reinforced by an unholy alliance of advertising-driven consumerism, a pseudo-liberationist psychology, and a bastardized Buddhism, Americans (and others) more and more got the message that self-fulfillment and living for the moment were paramount life goals. The operative phrase from Jefferson's Declaration of Independence for a bookshelf's worth of post-1960s self-help books became "the pursuit of happiness."

Two influential books from the late 1970s—Daniel Bell's *The Cultural Contradictions of Capitalism* and Christopher Lasch's *The Culture of Narcissism*—made parallel, but different, arguments that capitalism creates needs for self-gratification that undermine both the work ethic and civic engagement.[34] Narcissism and solipsism result, which weaken responsibility to others and belief in collective action, whether by government, civic clubs, unions, or neighborhood associations. Self-centeredness is a stingingly logical consequence of the post-1960s embrace of psychologist Abraham Maslow's idea that once an individual's needs for food and shelter are met, higher-level needs, such as self-esteem and, ultimately, "self-actualization," become most important. It's also a very convenient philosophy for marketers to adopt in a rampantly consumerist society.

When Daniel Patrick Moynihan, building on the work of the pioneering French sociologist Émile Durkheim, spoke of "defining deviancy down," he argued that a society can tolerate only so much "bad" behavior before it lowers its standards; what was once considered deviant increasingly enters the normative realm of tolerable behavior.[35]

In a sense, that is what has happened. Cultural change and changes in attitudes are natural in any dynamic, open society, and the last fifty years of changes in beliefs and norms about gender roles and identity have ushered in a freer and less sexist and homophobic society. But the legions of American men who are on the fringes of American life reflect something else.

At about the same time that Moynihan wrote, during America's cultural revolution of the late 1960s and 1970s, the leftist philosopher Robert Paul Wolff suggested that liberal "tolerance" may come at the expense of the common good. His contemporary Herbert Marcuse called such tolerance a "non-partisan tolerance" that "refrains from taking sides." The consequence: almost anything is okay.[36]

As more and more has become permissible, ever more adult males (and people in general) have been given license to behave in ways that were once out of bounds, not part of the standard operating procedure for American men. Seemingly dissimilar, but strangely consonant, voices provided sanction—from Timothy Leary, Hugh Hefner, and Ronald Reagan to welfare proponents, permissive parents, and ardent libertarians: Turn on and tune out. Love the one you're with. Government is not the solution to our problems; government is the problem. Protect the needy. Give children freedom. Live as you choose, so long as you don't hurt others.

But as Kris Kristofferson and Janis Joplin said, "Freedom's just another word for nothing left to lose."

So we return to Moynihan's implicit question: Do we accept behaviors that are emblematic of these sidelined men?

Many women, children, parents, teachers, employers, economists, social scientists, and policymakers would say a resounding no. This large-scale exodus represents a huge economic loss, the difference in potential output between millions of men working and not working. A smaller workforce leads to a smaller economy. It also increases government costs, supporting these men on disability, Medicaid, and other means-tested programs.

Aside from the huge economic losses, there are arguably even greater emotional losses for wives watching their husbands become freeloaders, for unmarried women viewing many single men as hapless losers, for parents disappointed by seeing their adult sons (and some daughters) in pajamas half the day, and for children and dads not having each other in their lives. As we have seen, there are also losses for America's public life as men show less and less interest in constructive politics and organized groups.

But let's not forget the inner lives of these men on the sidelines. Most of them are hurting. Most don't want to be where they are. We need to put "choice" in quotation marks. Few men consciously "choose" to adopt "bad" behaviors, even if social sanctions against doing so have lessened.

We will come back to the economic circumstances that have done so much to sideline and even discard so many men and women, but that does not absolve us from recognizing that psychology—anger and resignation becoming volition—and culture are major parts of the story. Maybe phrases like "*coerced choice*" or "*negative nudges*" are more apt. While some conservatives rightly highlight perverse incentives for "bad" behavior, many others tar these men, like "welfare mothers" before them, as lazy leeches and bemoan—with considerable justification—a culture gone to hell.

If the culture is forcing or enabling so many men to "choose" to be on the sidelines as workers, fathers, citizens—a notion sure to elicit yowls from those on the left—then we must ask, What values and norms changed? How did these choices become acceptable, and who, if anyone, benefited from these changes? There have been clear winners and losers from these changes, and sidelined men are decidedly among the losers. However, those on the left, fearful of "blaming the victim" or being politically incorrect, generally have been as complicit as those on the right in denying the economics-culture nexus.

Mitt Romney may have lost the 2012 presidential election thanks in part to his horribly insensitive, incorrect, and politically inept comment that 47 percent of Americans could not be convinced to "take personal responsibility and care for their lives." Yet Romney touched on a theme that has swirled for years around our cultural landscape.

"Responsibility," a fraught term, particularly for liberals, is one oft-cited value that allegedly has gone to the winds. Hard to clearly define, it is not so hard to recognize in its absence. One can see a decline of responsibility in all too many corners of America—from the hyper-rich hiding their trillions in the Cayman Islands and companies offshoring profits in tax havens to the supposedly liberal counterculture that put "self-actualization" first and said to hell with work, marriage, commitment, parenthood, and society.

Other values often said to have gone missing include self-reliance, drive, the work ethic, ambition, self-respect, courtesy, patriotism, civic engagement, altruism, and toughness. All of these were nearly universally seen as positive and have been variously referred to as "traditional," "American," and "masculine."

For all the talk of a degradation of values, rarely have the distinctly male elements of this issue been considered. To the extent that cultural values have deteriorated—or, to be more neutral, changed—there has been little attention to how and why they have changed differently for men, or some men, than for women.

As suggested, many factors have been fingered for the decline in values—an economy of exclusion, the imperative to maximize earnings, demagogic attacks on government, the withering of organized religion, and the hippie-inspired "let it all hang out" philosophy gone mainstream. As one army brigade commander told me, "I have a three in ten problem. Three in ten [recruits] have the moral, mental, and physical qualities" to succeed.[37]

The "traditional" role of the man as provider may have been sexist, keeping women in what Betty Friedan more than fifty years ago called the "comfortable concentration camp" of housewifery, but it did bespeak responsibility. Men worked; fought, through unions, for decent wages and benefits; went about supporting their families; and stood tall in their communities and country. A man who wasn't working and married and at least a half-decent father was either a "bum" or a "beatnik," straying onto the "path less traveled" or so devastated by mental illness or trauma to be generally pilloried or pitied. In the world of *Father Knows Best* and *The Dick Van Dyke Show*, these men didn't exist. If they did, they were often portrayed as comedic figures, defying social norms.

The "anything goes" culture spawned by the revolution in norms and mores of the 1960s and 1970s also has given some men a cultural pass to live what was once quaintly called "alternative lifestyles." The sexual revolution, too, has given men another pass to hook up or become serial daters and not step up to the plate as husbands, fathers, or reliable partners. And technology—the internet, social media, smart phones, gaming, even earbuds—has done more than oceans of LSD to make it easy to tune out from a world of in-the-flesh human interaction.

Today some men have supports that they didn't have in the past—working wives, longer-living parents, and a modest government safety net. However, factors such as these only go so far to explain why such values have withered away for too many American men. In general, it's not because they are "lazy" or "cheats" but because a changed culture has made it at least somewhat okay to retreat from productive, caring, and civic-spirited lives. This brings us to an even more charged set of "explanations": just as an overly simple economic history might blame the increasing power of capital relative to labor, financialization, automation, or globalization, a simplistic cultural history could lay the blame for these negative cultural changes on hippies, Hollywood, and pop psychology.

Answers to why up to one quarter of America's men are sidelined are badly needed. This first requires understanding the problem in its many dimensions.

Returning to Bob Dylan: "There must be some kinda way out of here." But until problems are seen for what they are, and the reality of American men on the sidelines is seen as a composite problem, how can we even begin to look for remedies? In the following pages, we will explore both the economic and cultural dimensions of this problem, recognizing that solutions will require changes in both.

Once again, it is worth turning to Moynihan, who pithily provided powerful frameworks for analysis and bringing about change: "The central conservative truth is that it is culture, not politics, that defines the success of a society. The central liberal truth is that politics can change a culture and save it from itself."[38]

CHAPTER 2

The Male Nonworking Class

Early in the morning, factory whistle blows,
Man rises from bed and puts on his clothes,
Man takes his lunch, walks out in the morning light,
It's the working, the working, just the working life.

—*Bruce Springsteen, "Factory," 1978*

Work. It was what men did (and most still do). During the halcyon decades of America's booming post–World War II economy; throughout all of American history, except when periods of economic depression threw millions into unemployment or bread lines. Indeed, for centuries and millennia, men worked. They needed to work to survive, but it was also a cultural given. Even if work consisted of long hours of arduous, brutal toil and could be exploitative, men did it, day in and day out. It was socially unacceptable for able-bodied men not to work; if they didn't, they were "bums."[1] Work has also given meaning, structure, and identity to people's lives. Studs Terkel, the oral historian who published the book *Working* in 1974, at a then unforeseen turning point in U.S. history, portrayed barbers and cops, stockbrokers and welders and others as hardworking, responsible, and finding at least a modicum of fulfillment in their jobs.[2]

Flash back to the "greatest generation," the Americans who defeated fascism and came home to build the most prosperous country in human history. During the Eisenhower administration, when *I Love Lucy* made its debut and

Joe McCarthy was censured by the Senate, 95 percent of men between the ages of 25 and 54 worked. They worked in factories and offices in an era of plentiful jobs, unions that defended their jobs (at a time when 35–40 percent of male wage and salary workers were union members),[3] and a swiftly rising standard of living. Men could support their families—even the large ones of the baby boom era—with what was known as the "family wage."[4] Women were still subservient, and African American men still lived with the legacy of slavery and Jim Crow that had shamefully clouded American life and ideals since the seventeenth century. Yet, as John Kennedy famously said, in the midst of a purring economy, a "rising tide lifts all boats." And men were at the helm.

Flash forward. While most men today work, the proportion of adult men who do not is higher than at any time since statistics started to be collected sixty years ago. There are many caveats to these numbers, but between one in four and one in five men between their early 20s and mid- to late 60s—about 20 million—aren't working, three to four times the proportion during the 1950s, with an even larger number not working full-time.

Some are like Hank, a white man now in his late 50s. He grew up on a farm in the old Cotton Belt in the Southeast but made his way to college, where he was always on the dean's list. He developed a specialized agricultural software program in the 1980s that catapulted him into the upper middle class. He married young, but his business success led him to conventions where he would meet other women. Divorced and remarried many times, he always seemed to have a chip on his shoulder. He was abusive to his children, telling one son he was "worthless." When a dog bit him, he pulled out his shotgun and killed it.

Hank's ex-wives say he paid very little in child support. Since he posts pictures of his fancy cars on his Facebook page, they assume he's hiding his money. But a friend claims he's broke: "He doesn't have a pot to pee in." Going off the grid, Hank eventually moved in with his elderly father somewhere in rural Appalachia.

Other nonworking men are like Yates, a white man who had been a partner at a law firm and had gone to one of the country's top law schools. When the firm's billings started to decline, he was told that either he had to drum up more business or he would be laid off. In his early 40s, Yates decided to leave, taking a modest severance package.

He and his wife and young child moved from their house into a rental apartment, and his wife got a job. The couple fell far behind on their taxes, initiating a long history of troubles with the IRS. Then his check to their daughter's private school bounced.

By day Yates was the ideal stay-at-home dad. By night he was drinking, self-medicating with prescription drugs, and staying up late looking at porn on the internet. His wife later found out that he was also active in chat rooms with other women and had contacted a prostitute. They tried couples therapy and Yates did a stint at a rehab center.

Yates's wife finally gave up and divorced him. He still is very involved with his child, but he remains out of work and moved in with a woman who is supporting him.

We will meet many men like Hank and Yates, some with similar stories, others whose tales are quite different. They are not one "type" of man—a point I will run the risk of emphasizing too much—although those without a college degree are disproportionately represented. Not working is but one of many characteristics of America's men out, and some sidelined men do work but exhibit other characteristics of being "out." However, the absence of work in their lives is one key characteristic, one that has attracted increasing attention and alarm among economists, commentators, policymakers, and the public.

This chapter offers a tour d'horizon and analyzes the decline in male employment, how nonworking men live, how a changing economy and policies that have abetted many of the changes have contributed to the rise of a male nonworking class, how cultural factors have also contributed, and what the economic costs are to individuals and the nation. Let's start with the numbers.

Bear with me for the next few paragraphs on the statistics, because there is much misunderstanding, and many different stats are put forth about who is counted as working and not working. At the very lowest end, there is the *unemployment rate*, hovering near historic recent lows of about 4 percent. With roughly 100 million men of "working age," a contested concept that also needs explanation, that's about four million unemployed men. These are only men who are out of work and have actively looked for a job in the last four weeks. "Marginally attached" workers, meaning those who say they want a job but haven't looked for one in the last four weeks, and those who work part-time not by choice, add a few million more men. The numbers of men collecting unemployment insurance are lower than either of these two metrics—called U-3 and U-6 by the U.S. Bureau of Labor Statistics (BLS)—because many people don't qualify or bother to apply.[5]

Then there is the *labor force participation rate*. This includes civilian, noninstitutionalized working and unemployed men. For all males 20 and older, 28 percent (or about 32.6 million guys) were not in the labor force in March 2018. This, of course, is a rather unhelpful statistic, since millions of younger males are in school and millions of older men are retired. So the BLS zeroes in on "prime working age" men, people between 25 and 54 years old. This number, about 11 percent of whom are not "participating" in the labor force (about seven million men), is also a deceptively foolish metric. It may have been meaningful eighty years ago, when life expectancy was 65 instead of about 80, but today most Americans expect to work at least until retirement age (whether 65, 66, or 70 for full Social Security benefits or 62 for early benefits), many men under 25 are in the labor force, and many men who are in their early 30s have yet to "launch." Those 60 and older are the one age group in which work is increasing. The "prime age" descriptor that was more or less accurate in 1965 has become a misnomer. In 2017 about 16 percent of 25- to 64-year-old men (or about 13.5 million) weren't in the labor force, a rate slightly higher than even during the depths of the global recession in 2010. In the very prime years between 45 and 54, 14 percent of men were not in the workforce. However you look at it, of all the wealthy country members of the Organization for Economic Cooperation and Development (OECD), the United States—which has favorably compared its supposedly dynamic free-market economy and labor market to the allegedly sclerotic European and Japanese economies—has the lowest proportion of its adult male population working or seeking work. The only exception is Italy, although participation rates have also declined, albeit by lesser amounts, in countries ranging from Australia and Finland to Korea and France. The United States would come out even lower if both the numbers of men in prison and those in informal work were included, since men in the United States are much more likely to be locked up than men virtually anywhere else, and because Europeans are somewhat more likely than Americans to be involved in the black-market economy.[6]

Although increasing school enrollment and retirement in an aging population make the definitions and stats somewhat fuzzy at either end of the "working age" range, we have not yet exhausted our ways of counting the number of nonworking men. Somewhat under half of the nation's six million "disconnected youth"—people between 16 and 24 who are neither in school nor working—are men (disproportionately black youth), although a small portion may be in internships, so we should add at least another 1.5–2 million not-working young guys, or, looking at the 16- to 29-year old age group, more than four million. Then, with five million men over age 65 working, we can infer that some additional older men want to, need to, or expect to work but aren't; this total could be anywhere from one to several million. Nowhere in the above stats are counted the two million men behind bars, five times the number back in the 1970s.[7]

Counting those who are unemployed, not in the labor force, incarcerated, NEETs, and 65 and older men who would be happy to hold a job, we are now at more than 20 million nonworking American men. Since this is a point-in-time number, some of these men will go back to work. This number requires several caveats. "Unemployed" men looking for work are part of the labor force and many will find jobs. It is also hard to say how many young students go in and out of school and work, how many incarcerated men would work if not behind bars, and how many near-elderly men may alternate between saying they're retired or out of work. As one 60-ish New York white man, who had been earning upward of $150,000 a year, said, "I retired after failing to find a suitable opportunity." This number more or less jibes with another workforce construct—the "employment-to-population (e:p) ratio"—which tells us that 21 percent of 20- to 64-year-old American men are not employed and 33.5 percent of males over 16 were not working in early 2018. If incarcerated men were included as part of "the population," these numbers would increase by about 2 percentage points. Similarly, if students were excluded, the number would fall. Still, the percentage of men not working is about three times what it was when Harry Truman was president.[8]

A final set of wrinkles to this statistical story involves part-time and "contingent," or contract, work. Many men are missed by nonwork statistics because they say they're retired or do part-time or consulting work. About one-sixth of the 80.2 million men age 20 and over with jobs in February 2018—including those outside the 25–64 year age bracket—worked less than 35 hours a week at generally lower hourly pay. Most say they do so by choice, but about one quarter report that they do so involuntarily. Because the "part-time workers for economic reasons" cannot find full-time jobs, they are counted in the BLS's U-6, the unofficial unemployment rate.[9]

Perhaps even more important, and even more difficult to get a handle on, are the blurry worlds of the "self-employed" and the "gig" or "1099" economy, in which millions of men work on short-term contracts, without job security, and on demand. Some may be highly successful consultants, inventors, or best-selling authors, while others are gardeners, janitors, handymen, or those who occasionally are hired for freelance work.[10] Still other men make some money at home, using the internet to buy and sell goods on platforms like e-Bay or Fulfillment by Amazon. Harvard economist Lawrence Katz and Princeton economist Alan Krueger estimated that 14 percent of the U.S. labor force were employed either by contract firms or temporary agencies or were independent contractors in 2015, although labor activists have good reason to believe that some employers have misclassified workers to avoid paying benefits and complying with labor laws. McKinsey estimated in 2016 that 13 percent of the working-age population were engaged full-time in gig economy work, with another 14 percent being "supplemental independent contractors." If we add some of these to the total number of nonworking men—which is both statistically and conceptually difficult since data vary, some may also have full-time jobs, gig workers are often part-time workers, and definitions and self-definitions of "gig" workers vary—we might arrive at the startling figure that one-third of, or as many as 30 million, genuinely working-age American males are not in full-time jobs. Some economists believe that the United States undercounts those who are not full-time workers. On the other hand, the numbers would go down a bit if those in the armed services and the underground economy were counted. (But is a drug dealer really considered a working man?)[11]

The proportions of men working vary by their level of education, marital status, age, race, and ethnicity, whether they grew up in a single-parent household, and other factors—which we will return to later—but the numbers who are not working have shown a long-term, across-the-board increase.

The ranks of women, including mothers, in the labor force increased dramatically between the 1960s and about 2000, when their numbers also started to fall. This decline is perhaps attributable to college-educated women who have delayed childbearing and are staying out of work much longer than earlier cohorts of working women. Again, the United States is fairly unusual among OECD countries in having falling female labor force participation rates.[12]

For men, the historical association between masculinity and work adds important cultural and psychological dimensions to this story. Behind the numbers are 20 to 30 million individual stories—often sad tales of lives derailed and complicated economic, sociological, and historical narratives. But a number of obvious questions leap out at us:

- Who are these men?

- What are they doing and thinking?

- How do they survive?

- Why is this happening?

- What are the costs, in terms of economic insecurity, public benefits paid, and poor health, as well as opportunity costs, or what potential gains in individual and national income are given up by so many men not working?

THE NEW NONWORKING CLASS

The data give only a two-dimensional portrait of America's vast male nonworking class. Who are they, what are their lives like, and what do they feel and think?

Some, like James, in the San Francisco Bay Area, or Rick, in New Jersey, worked for decades in good jobs before being laid off in their 50s and, despite their best efforts, have been unable for years to find work. Michael, on the Carolina coast, essentially stopped doing the odd jobs he had pieced together into a living when his wife left him. Young men in their late 20s and early 30s, like Jeremy, from a fading industrial town near the Great Lakes, and Chuck, who had a master's degree and a good job in Southern California, fell ever deeper into the abyss of opioids and heroin, don't work, get money from their parents, and collect disability benefits. Then there are men like Ed, who, after losing his job with a publishing company, could only find "grunt" jobs, and his wife of more than thirty years divorced him. Or there's Tyrone, imprisoned for years in a maximum-security facility in upstate New York, who can barely get an interview from employers who fear ex-convicts.[13]

Attempts to explain the decline in male workers tend to focus on structural factors such as technology and trade, which have reduced the demand for workers with low to moderate skill levels. Because having less than a college education has become a proxy for people with fewer skills, they have had a tougher time than well-educated, more likely to be employed, higher-income Americans. This theory of so-called skill-biased technological change has a lot of merit, suggesting that if the nation only educated and trained its people better, the problem would be at least partially solved.[14] This, in turn, suggests that there is a mismatch between labor supply and demand. The difficulty with this idea is that low-skill service jobs have proliferated and generally require much less training than many of the routinized "middle-skill" jobs that have disappeared and that many economists and policymakers focus on. It is true that demand for workers with very high skill levels has increased and that getting a bachelor's degree is generally still worth hundreds of thousands of dollars of additional income over a lifetime.[15] The dirty little secret, though, is that employers aren't exactly beating down the doors of graduates from non-elite (i.e., most) colleges—grads who are lampooned as not being able to write a coherent paragraph, do simple calculations without their smart phones, and think critically. In addition, while manufacturing and other traditionally male jobs that required brawn have been vanishing, and boys and men are doing less well than girls and women in terms of education, these factors by no means fully explain the sharp drop-off in men working.

The aging of the population plays a role, as baby boomers have moved into age brackets in which participation normally dips. Yet the one age group in which men are working more than they were thirty years ago is those 60 and older, as the average retirement age for men increased between 1985 and 2015 by nearly three years, to about 65. Some of the overall decline comes from a precipitous falloff among very young adults, whose college attendance rates have increased (though much less so for young men). There's also a relation-ship between poor health and not working, although this is a chicken-or-egg question that we will wrestle with later. The American Time Use Survey (ATUS), conducted by the U.S. Census Bureau and the BLS, has found that about one in eight 25- to 54-year-olds say they are in school, and one in five are disabled. About four-fifths of the nearly four million disabled men in this age bracket are not working. In addition, there's much debate about cause, effect, and correlation between the decline of marriage, unstable lives, and work.[16]

Many men have been laid off, haven't been able to find jobs, and have stopped trying to find full-time employment, slipping into "retirement," "con-sulting," or receiving support from their wives or the government. Many have tried very hard, sending out hundreds of résumés, getting increasingly frus-trated, as their anger toward employers morphs into a more generalized anger. Young and not-so-young men have stayed in, or gone back to, school, returned to the parental nest, or gone on disability. Others either see available jobs as "beneath them," fit for only immigrants or women, or too low-paying when their wives, parents, or the government can support them—even though many nonworking men's partners don't work either and government benefits are generally not enough to live on. Although their numbers have grown slightly, how many male preschool teachers or home health aides do you know? Even higher-paid "women's work" such as nursing attracts few men.[17] Hundreds of thousands of men who might once have worked—disproportionately men of color—are locked up in America's sprawling prison system.

We will hear a lot more about these and other men and the many variations on men out, but the point to reemphasize is that these men come from every type of background. Many are less educated and lower middle class and live in blighted rural and urban areas of America.[18] Yet the demographic pool of unemployed men is deeper. By the late 2010s, it began to include more and more educated men, too—five, ten, or even fifteen years out of school, well into midlife, and from middle- and upper-middle-class communities across the country. In the aggregate, however, there are demographic differences: college-educated men, married men, early middle-age men, Asian American men, and men from affluent zip codes are more likely to work.

Young men, those born since the early 1980s, are particularly likely to be not working, and the falloff in employment rates for men under 35, especially the less educated, has been steep. In 2014 just 71 percent of 18- to 34-year-old men were employed, compared to 84 percent in 1960. Some of this, but far from all, can be explained by increased college matriculation.[19]

For example, the biggest falloff in the proportion of men working since the late 1960s has been among those with a high school diploma or less. Similarly, 83 percent of unmarried men between 25 and 54 were employed in 2015, compared to just over 90 percent of married men. African American men are less likely to be working than whites, who are slightly less likely to work than Latino and Asian American men. The high numbers of incarcerated and formerly incarcerated black men plays a role, but employers are also more likely to hire immigrants or women than black men for low-skill jobs. The racist stereotype that Latinos, Asian Americans, and other immigrants work harder than black men persists. However, these racial and ethnic differences all but disappear if one looks at married 25- to 54-year-old men of all four major racial and ethnic groups.[20]

In some parts of Appalachia, northern Michigan, the Deep South, and the Southwest, more than 40 percent of men aren't working. In a few sparsely populated counties in northeastern Kentucky and on some Indian reservations, a majority of men don't work. On the other hand, in census tracts on the well-heeled Upper East Side of Manhattan, and in places like Silicon Valley and Bethesda, Maryland, just 3 percent of men are not working.[21]

THE EIGHT-HOUR DAY AND BEYOND

If full-time work is a daily eight- or ten-hour commitment, including commuting, what do men who don't work do with all those hours? This subject is complex, rife with controversy and vitriolic assertions, and varies among men, although there are few reliable quantitative data. In one poll, among nonworking men between the ages of 45 and 54, 60 percent claimed to be disabled. According to Rose Woods, senior economist for ATUS, nonemployed men spend more than seven hours of each day engaged in "leisure" activities, about four hours and twenty minutes watching TV, nearly an hour and fifty minutes on "household activities," and three quarters of an hour on the phone. Other analyses have found nonworking men spending long hours playing video games but only about ten minutes per day on volunteer work. One study found that less educated men—those more likely not to be working—spend less time looking for work than better-educated males. In yet another sign of the spread of nonwork among less educated men, men without a high school diploma added eight more "leisure" hours per week between 1985 and 2005, while college-educated men saw a decline of six hours. Not to wade too deeply into these very charged subjects quite yet, nonworking men spend only minutes more per day than those with full-time jobs caring for children, cooking, and cleaning up—numbers that have barely changed from the 1960s to the presumably more egalitarian twenty-first century.[22]

These categories are very broad and have little to say about differences among single men, educated men, middle-age men, and other different demographic "types" of men.

Here is where we need to turn largely to qualitative data—in other words, people's stories. Talking to men, the women in their lives, therapists, and others, we can piece together the varied textures of the lives of men who aren't working. If one is a subscriber to what Max Weber called "the Protestant work ethic" and thinks of those earnest Puritans who saw toil as the road to salvation, the picture isn't pretty.

The internet—games, surfing, Facebook, porn, and all manner of time-gobbling electronic enticements. TV . . . and more TV. Puttering around. Booze, pot, and pills. Reading, occasionally. The IPO (initial public offering) fantasy, usually fantastical, occasionally productive: they talk about starting a wildly successful business with nary a business plan, or about developing a product or service that no one has ever thought of before. Among those who fancy themselves as creative, they think about writing the novel that will make them the next John Grisham or the screenplay that Steven Spielberg will immediately put into production. They sleep. They hang out with the guys in neo-frat-house basements. More likely, they spend their time just being alone.

Of course, many nonemployed men look for work—very hard. They spend hours scouring job listings, sending out résumés, reaching out to their networks, having coffee with contacts, going on interviews. Some support groups, such as Neighbors-helping-Neighbors (NhN) in two largely white New Jersey communities, have sprung up. At one NhN meeting, a man said he was there because his wife expected him to find a job. Another guy broke into tears, telling how his lack of work had led him to "lose the love of my life." A regular attendee recalled a man who stopped coming to the group meetings and is living in the basement of his aging mother's home. A great number of the men were angry—at employers, capitalism more broadly, politicians, how society and their families have treated them. But the facilitator kept bringing them back to the job at hand: focusing on how to get a job.

This isn't Appalachia, the Midwestern Rust Belt, or poor, urban America. Both of these New Jersey towns are reasonably well-to-do bedroom communities, with median incomes about half again as high as the typical American income. Connected by New Jersey Transit to Manhattan, Westwood is in affluent Bergen County and has a smattering of big, nineteenth-century homes, free outdoor concerts, and is almost evenly divided between Democrats and Republicans. Cranford, to the south in Union County, is also more than 90 percent white, has a similar median household income of close to $80,000 a year, and, like Westwood, voted narrowly for Hillary Clinton in 2016.

IF WORK EQUALS INCOME, WHAT DOES NONWORK EQUAL?

Work may be essential to psychological fulfillment, as Freud suggested, and the availability and terms of paid work may be dictated and controlled by the market. Yet, more prosaically, for most people work is about earning a living. Henry David Thoreau and the producers of *Lifestyles of the Rich and Famous* can debate what constitutes a good material standard of living. Economists and policymakers, from those who set poverty thresholds to philosophical titans like Amartya Sen, have devoted lifetimes to this question.[23]

In very practical terms, life in the United States today is expensive. Without riffing on another round of stats, and acknowledging that the cost of living is much higher in San Francisco than in Kansas, changes in median prices of some of the most important goods and services are far greater than economy-wide average price increases, which the widely cited Consumer Price Index (CPI) reports. The three *Hs*—housing, health care, and higher education—are often beyond the reach of the typical American.

So how do nonworking men make do?

Like the "what do they do" question, the "how do they make do" ques tion is also laden with sketchy statistics and highly politicized hypothesizing. As the number of married women who are primary breadwinners has risen, wives are one big answer. One survey found that 22 percent of nonworking men are supported by their wives, although the vast majority of nonworking men do not have a spouse who works. Some girlfriends and unmarried mothers may support their nonworking male partners, but the convergence of low labor force participation rates and wages and the fragility of relationships and cohabitation suggests that the numbers are small. Many young men are supported by their parents. Some do odd jobs in the black-market cash economy. Some men are trust-fund children, and others may have squirreled away a good nest egg from a more successful phase of their lives, but these numbers are also relatively small, since men out tend to skew toward the lower end of the socioeconomic spectrum.[24]

Beyond this, we're left with the kindness of strangers—that is, government or charity. Some recently unemployed workers briefly can claim unemployment insurance (UI). According to American Enterprise Institute political economist Nicholas Eberstadt, in 2013, 48 percent of households headed by nonworking 25- to 54-year-old men were on Medicaid and 52 percent were collecting Social Security Disability Insurance (SSDI) and other disability benefits, with about 41 percent on food stamps. These numbers are somewhat misleading, since many nonworking men are not heads of households; only about 3.5–4 million men in this age range were disabled in 2016, and roughly three quarters of a million were working; and another three million men between 55 and 64 reported a disability, yet nearly one-fourth were working. All told, the percentage of 25- to 54-year-old American men who are on SSDI has risen from about 1 percent in the late 1960s to 3 percent in the mid-2010s. Yet, if this rate had not increased, just 1.2 million of the nation's 62 million men in this age bracket in 2017 would not be on disability—hardly 52 percent of even the seven million "prime age" nonworking men.[25]

For most men, this is not about being parasites or "takers." It is a fall from grace. They may be poorer men, but they include guys like Matt, a white former financial services editor with a wife and two children in elementary school, who lost his job of more than twenty years. While he's fortunate that his wife is working, because her pay and benefits are relatively poor, they went on Medicaid. And that has hardly been a piece of cake. "They don't call back or fax, so I had to drive more than an hour to drop off paperwork to prove who I was, with pictures of my passport," Matt recalled. "I haven't had to use it yet, but I hold back on going to the doctor because of high co-pays."

Needless to say, this is also quite costly for the public purse, although author Justin Gest makes the trenchant point that many, if not most, of these men don't consider UI, Medicaid, disability, or even food stamps as "welfare." That's for people "below them," often seen as the "undeserving poor."[26]

Income—or the lack of it—is only one of several related economic strikes against nonworking men. With a decent paycheck, people are able to save—whether for a rainy day, their children's college tuition, a home, a vacation or new car, or retirement. It hardly bears saying that no income means no savings; no savings means no new car, nothing for the rainy day, and little retirement security.

Health insurance and pensions are the other two big economic benefits associated with full-time work since the mid-twentieth century. Without work, one receives no pension. As for health insurance, the options are receiving coverage from a spouse's employer, Obamacare if one can afford it, Medicaid if one is poor enough, or none.

Although white men in general have more in savings than women or men of color, the overall savings picture in America is pretty bleak. Nearly 44 percent of all households are "liquid asset poor," a term used by the nonprofit organization Prosperity Now to mean they have less than three months of savings to cover expenses if they lose a job or are hit by an emergency. National saving rates dipped to 2.5 percent at the end of 2017.[27] Nonworking men—especially single and less educated men of all races—are especially likely to be asset poor as their lifetime earnings, marital status, and psychological and physical well-being tend to lag behind those of full-time workers.[28]

As with savings, it's impossible to have an employer-sponsored pension or to amass much in Social Security earnings or in a personal IRA if one isn't working. Again, the aggregate numbers for the United States aren't good, although men generally remain in better shape than women. Only half of *workers* have any retirement savings plan, and most of these are in defined-contribution (DC) plans such as 401(k)s, with little money accumulated and the burden of risk on the worker, rather than on employers, as in "traditional" defined-benefit (DB) plans, in which employers pay a regular annuity upon retirement. The proportion of workers in the more secure DB plans has declined precipitously since 1974 due to changes in the law. One consequence, which can be read as either disturbing or hopeful, is that those with DC plans work about two years longer than workers with DB plans.[29] Nonworking men may have 401(k)s from former jobs, and some pay a penalty to withdraw funds before retirement. But the larger fact is that if nonworking men face economic difficulties now, and pose economic and social problems for the country today, their lack of savings and pensions poses huge problems for when they reach their late 60s and on into old age.

MANY MEN ARE STILL PRETTY SUCCESSFUL

Although between 20 percent and 25 percent of working-age men are not working full-time, more than three-fourths are. Pay and social class divisions have widened considerably since the days of Ozzie Nelson, Fred Flintstone, and the organization man, but 71 million men 20 and older were employed in 2017. The majority had health, pension, and vacation benefits—although the first two of these are far less generous than they once were. Men on average still make more than women, although the gender pay gap shrinks when looking at comparable jobs and for younger workers; in some "knowledge economy" places such as Manhattan, it has been reported that working women younger than 30 have median incomes that are 17 percent higher than men's.[30]

One in six men earns more than $100,000 a year, more than twice the proportion among women. Among the highly educated urban elites, both men and women are brimming with ambition, working longer hours than ever. Most low-wage occupations are dominated by women, and unmarried men have about twice the wealth that single women do, although the dollar figures for those without a college education are so low that the difference amounts to the cost of a kitchen appliance or two.[31]

SOMETHING IS HAPPENING, BUT WE DON'T KNOW WHAT IT IS

We come back to the question, Why are so many American men not working?

Labor market economists would argue that the biggest reason why men are not working has to do with fundamental changes in the economy and the labor market itself. Traditionally male, middle-skill jobs started to disappear in the 1970s, falling from 58 percent of employment in 1981 to 41 percent in 2017. Service jobs began to replace manufacturing jobs as what came to be known as automation (or "technology") and "globalization" were said to take no prisoners in working-class male America. If the proportion of these heavily male, middle-skill jobs had held up in the decades after 1979, the United States would have about 15 million more jobs.[32]

"It is widely assumed that the traditional male domination of postsecondary education, highly paid occupations, and elite professions is a virtually immutable fact of the U.S. economic landscape," say MIT scholars David Autor and Melanie Wasserman. "But in reality, this landscape is undergoing a tectonic shift. Although a significant minority of males continue to reach the highest echelons of achievement in education and labor markets, the median male is moving in the opposite direction. Over the last three decades, the labor market trajectory of males in the U.S. has turned downward along four dimensions: skills acquisition; employment rates; occupational stature; and real wage levels."[33]

However, as we've noted, the vanishing male worker has become not just a phenomenon of the lunchbox-and-hard-hat population. Industrial employment has declined sharply, but despite what some would like us to believe, the drop in manufacturing jobs accounts for only a small proportion of the nonworking class.[34]

According to Sylvia Allegretto, an economist at the University of California, Berkeley, "While there are a lot of different stories one can tell, with differences between rural, formerly industrialized, and urban areas, it all comes back to an economy that isn't working for a lot of people."[35]

Among those "stories" are that the proportion of over-25 men in school increased by seven-tenths of a percentage point and the share citing "home responsibilities" inched up by three-tenths of a percentage point between 2004 and 2014. Some studies have found that an increasing proportion of young men simply don't want to work. Population aging also plays a role but is confounded by the reality that older men are working more, whether by choice or out of economic need, while men under 55 or 60 are working less. The decline in male work has paralleled the decline in marriage—not to mention rising mortality rates and a host of other characteristics of men out—with greater declines in both among less educated men.[36]

Again, we fall into the chasm of causality. Were these choices (hence, causes) or rationalizations (hence, effects) related to not working? The nature and direction of any purported causality are hotly debated.[37]

Visit Pittsfield, Massachusetts, where enormous former General Electric (GE) factories and overgrown onetime GE parking lots stand silent behind razor wire facing ramshackle wood houses and old brick apartment buildings. Family Dollar and Goodwill stores have moved in; many buildings are boarded up with "no trespassing" signs; and a billboard visible when one drives into town advertises Naloxone, a principal treatment drug for opioid addiction. Behind the Walmart are more empty factories, the remains of a mid-twentieth-century boom when GE employed 13,000 people in this western Massachusetts city.

Look, too, at the coal country of Appalachia, the Steel Belt of the Midwest, or the old textile towns of the Southeast, and you'd be tempted to believe that mass layoffs and the notion of "they're closing the factory down" have decimated the male workforce. Yet very little of the national decline in labor force participation among men has been due to large-scale industrial layoffs. Two of the three biggest mass layoffs in recent decades occurred in 1993 at IBM and Sears, and the global recession of 2008–09 led financial firms like Citigroup, which dismissed 50,000 workers in late 2008, to shed workers.[38]

It's certainly not men's *fault* that a changing economy and labor market have shafted millions of them. Lifetime jobs with paternalistic employers that offer regular raises, good benefits, and steady hours have become a vanishing species. Risks have increased. Yet even in this economy—broken in many ways but still the wealthiest in the world—why are so many men not looking for work? Or not taking jobs that do exist? Or not retooling to acquire skills that would help them find a job?

It might seem easy to infer that the American male work ethic seems to have gone the way of the Victrola and the rumble seat. From Middle American employers to U.S. Army recruiters, many say that too many men fail drug tests and lack basic skills, such as being able to do simple math or write a coherent sentence. Multiple time use studies have shown that "the average day of a male nonworker looks very much like the average day of a worker—"on his day off," as economist Alan Krueger cleverly put it.[39] As a strange de facto coalition of conservatives, women who are disenchanted with men, human resource directors, and some cultural observers would say, a lot of these guys are lazy bums.

Many women from well-to-do suburbs, fading rural and industrial areas, and big cities alike repeated variations on this theme. Linda is a middle-age, white California woman whose brother left his wife and kids and now "lives either on the street or in an SRO [single room occupancy]." She told me that too many men have "buckled under the weight." They have a "lack of self-worth, no drive, and too many 'fun' distractions." Many of these women, liberal Democrats, see no dissonance in expressing views very similar to those of conservative Republicans and their think tank brethren.

There are several facts, supported by cultural and historical observations, that might buttress this argument. In other economic hard times, such as the Great Depression, men tramped the streets looking for work or migrated with or without their families in rail cars and beat-up Model Ts in search of jobs elsewhere in the country. Instead of resigning themselves to unemployment, in such times of economic collapse, they gave it their all and even rose up in protest. Demonstrations brought tens of thousands protesting against unemployment to the streets of New York, Pittsburgh, Washington, D.C., and elsewhere between 1930 and 1932. These men, steeped in the long-standing American ethos of self-sufficiency, didn't want to be on the dole; they wanted jobs. In part because of their activism, President Franklin Roosevelt created the famous "alphabet soup" of public works programs like the CCC (Civilian Conservation Corps), WPA (Works Progress Administration), and PWA (Public Works Administration).

In the late 2010s, almost no out-of-the-workforce men protest the lack of jobs. Instead of taking to the streets to demand work, they keep their bitterness largely behind closed doors and fill their lives with what the ATUS quaintly calls "leisure"—that is, games, drugs, hanging with buddies, or becoming recluses in homes that are not so much theirs as those of their parents, wives, or girlfriends. Others pretend—or pridefully claim—that they are "working for themselves."

Human resource and management consulting professionals argue that women tend to be better than men at soft skills, such as communications, interpersonal relationships, compassion, and emotional self-awareness, which are said to be more in demand in the twenty-first-century workplace.[40] That may be true, but men tend to have greater physical strength, to be somewhat better at math, and may benefit in some occupations from continuing sexism.

Some commentators have hailed the rise of a bold new "freelance nation," a "create your own economy" with great new horizons, the "sharing economy," and the aforementioned gig economy as a welcome antidote to gray-flannel-suited organization men. Unfortunately, most of these quasi-workers for the likes of Uber and TaskRabbit are not blazing a trail to a glorious new economy. Rather, they are often the detritus of an economic system that has thrown millions of people out of familiar work and blocked millions more from decent jobs and offered instead a career ladder with poverty-level earnings and volatile incomes. Most are victims of what economist Jared Bernstein has called the "you're on your own," or "YOYO," economy. At best, they are underemployed or part of the black- or gray-market economy. Tamer versions of Walter White in Breaking Bad may not be so uncommon.[41]

Age discrimination is another reason sometimes put forth to help explain why some men aren't working. Employers want younger workers who will accept less pay and who have fresher skills, more fire in their bellies, and present a more attractive public face for their firms. Majorities of men and women between the ages of 45 and 74 believe that people their age face such bias at work. This discrimination manifests itself most often in inability to get hired or finding it takes much longer to get a job, according to an AARP survey. Other respondents said they were either not promoted, or reassigned to unappealing tasks, or laid off or fired because of their age. Women are somewhat more likely to be victims of bias or discrimination, and research has shown that physical appearance matters more for women's employment status. As one financial industry hiring manager candidly said, "There's some suspicion of middle-aged white guys when they're out of work." Only half of employed men said that job security was good, and three in seven said it's "not easy at all" to find a new job in 2016. While age discrimination is a real part of the story of nonworking men, the fact is that employment rates have fallen the most among men 35 and under.[42]

James, a San Francisco Bay Area white man in his late 50s, attributes his plight at least in part to age bias. He had worked in IT project management his entire career, finding good, new jobs every five to seven years. Then the good, new job didn't show up.

"While I have some software development experience and I've recently retrained, I have not found work yet," he said. "So I'm taking on whatever side jobs I can get short of Uber." Although some employment options pay low wages, James says he's lucky to get occasional part-time work in his field and turn his hobby of metal fabrication into a paying proposition. "But we're running negative every month, even with my wife's salary," he said. Even though his wife has a job with decent pay, he said that she's "terrified." It doesn't help that they live in one of America's most expensive metropolitan areas or that his daughter and her boyfriend, both around 30 and earning little money, live with them.

While James's family is hanging together, another family member who was a help desk manager "hit the wall hard." Unable to find a job, he stopped trying, spending more and more time on Facebook, playing video games, and drinking. When his wife told him he must "do something or else she'd be out of there," he, too, started driving for Uber, the drive-for-hire company that has become a refuge for many men.

James derides "traditional, conservative" bromides like "just hang in there and it'll be OK." Having seen many other highly skilled men his age "beat up" by automation, outsourcing, bad bosses, and companies with little loy-alty, he said, "It's not working for us anymore. Opportunities are going to the younger, stronger, and cheaper." He is especially bitter about how tech industries discard older workers. Without the latest training, he said, "we are scorned as being out of touch with a technological future we invented and are, in fact, very good at." He said he's lowered his consulting rates to compete with foreign workers on H1B visas (in specialty occupations), workers whom he once hired.

James is thankful that he owns his house and expects income from Social Security—if the program stays afloat. "We can cover the mortgage and pay for some basic bills," he said. "I don't see us on the streets, but it's hard to imagine retiring. If we want to do anything else, we're going to have to work."

Middle-age, middle-class men who lost jobs, can't find good ones, and have become discouraged and angry are all around, but few people want to acknowledge them, James told me. They're an embarrassment. They don't fit most economists' or politicians' picture of struggling working-class men who lost industrial jobs. Nor do they fit the cheery low-unemployment data that lead equally cheery and out-of-touch Wall Street commentators to talk about "tight labor markets." "All around are guys my age who were on a corporate-ish track, and those jobs went away. The social contract was broken. Corpora-tions threw out an entire generation or two of workers. And we're all trying to find out what to do next."

James walked around his neighborhood and pointed to solidly middle-class houses, many concealing stories of men who have been sidelined. Behind one door lives "an IT guy who was laid off a couple of times." He found a job even-tually, but "it was a step down in money and prestige." Another neighbor is nervous, working for a well-known tech company that's been laying off work-ers doing tasks so specialized that, according to James, "there are only three companies in the world that have that job."

James continued his tour, identifying the home of a man who lost his professional job and finally got work in sales, commuting hours every day for a fraction of his former pay. "Then there's the guy in back," he added with a sneer. He recruits low-cost IT talent from eastern Europe.

At the very worst, a half million married men and three million children that they fathered have virtually zero income, including from government as-sistance, according to social scientists Kathryn Edin and Luke Shaefer. The vast majority of America's half million or more homeless people are single men, which may be because nonworking, desperately poor men, including veterans, are less likely than women to seek mental health treatment because of culturally instilled ideas about masculinity.[43]

Or they have chosen to take a more or less permanent detour from the world of work. Many nonemployed men have looked long and hard for jobs and given up or taken a break. For others the search is perfunctory; they quickly and shamelessly wave the flag of surrender. In either case, some wind up in de facto "man caves," where the internet, the beer fridge, endless movies (usually puerile, violent, or sexist), sports memorabilia, near-empty bags of marijuana, loneliness, and lassitude define their lives. In a strange permutation of Virginia Woolf, the basement has become a room of their own.

BACK TO THE FUTURE

If Marty McFly in Robert Zemeckis's 1985 film had been a cultural anthropologist instead of a teenage boy with a souped-up time-traveling car, he would have seen a very different male labor force, economy, and norms about working in mid-twentieth-century America.

The Eisenhower years occurred in the midst of the most spectacular thirty-year economic boom in U.S. history. (As other rich countries saw rapid growth and nearly nonexistent unemployment between the end of World War II and the early 1970s, the Germans called these years the *Wirtschaftwunder*, and the French, *les trentes glorieuses*.) Just a few facts about this oft-repeated story of America's "glory days" bear repeating. The economy (then called "gross national product," before the days of gross domestic product, or GDP) was growing at 5 percent a year in the early 1960s. The real, or inflation-adjusted, hourly compensation of the typical, or median, worker increased by about 100 percent in the quarter century beginning in 1948, almost exactly tracking productivity growth, and home ownership rose from 44 to 62 percent between 1940 and 1960. As government and Madison Avenue somewhat hyperbolically told Americans, and as U.S. propaganda agencies tweaked the Soviets, there was "abundance for all in a classless society."[44]

Businesses profited, building their grand modernist headquarters in midtown Manhattan, many piggybacking on dazzling technological inventions coming out of World War II, such as the jet airplane, plastics and other synthetics, and computers. Some companies, including Bell Labs and IBM, dedicated huge and productive sums to research and development. A voracious consumer society developed, with rapidly rising disposable income and relatively low prices. New homes were cheap and easily financed, Ford Fairlanes and Chevy Bel Airs had $2,000 sticker prices, vacation travel became common, TV swept the nation, and Walt Disney's Magic Kingdom created a revolution in entertainment and travel cross-marketing.[45]

Labor unions were at the zenith of their power, counting two in five wage-earning men as members. They negotiated contracts with yearly pay increases, health insurance, generous company-paid defined-benefit pension plans, and paid time off, based on the model of the 1950 agreement between the United Auto Workers and General Motors that *Fortune* magazine called the "Treaty of Detroit."[46]

Government also played an enormous role in stoking economic growth. Federal, state, and local governments poured money into building the interstate highway system, the St. Lawrence Seaway, airports, schools, and universities. The U.S. Defense Department—including its famed Defense Advanced Research Projects Agency, credited with developing the internet, and the new National Institutes of Health—invented products and processes that saved and transformed lives. The demand-driven economic theories of John Maynard Keynes were in vogue for Democrats and Republicans alike; alternative voices from Chicago (or Vienna) got little hearing.

Equally remarkable was the fact that the lower classes were growing richer slightly faster than the upper classes, and America became a fairly egalitarian middle-class nation. Despite the glaring poverty that Michael Harrington exposed in *The Other America* (1962),[47] continuing racial injustice, and sexist norms that imprisoned women in the informal economy of housewifery, the "rising tide" slogan that JFK borrowed from a New England chamber of commerce was spot on—at least for white men.

On television, fictional besuited characters like Ozzie Nelson on *Ozzie and Harriet* and Jim Anderson on *Father Knows Best* were proof that the "family wage" meant men could work and support their wives and children on one paycheck. Even in the fantasy caveman days of *The Flintstones*, a working-class crane operator like Fred provided Wilma and Pebbles a comfortable life.

Yes, there was the conformity described in Sloan Wilson's *Man in the Gray Flannel Suit* (1955) and William H. Whyte's *The Organization Man* (1956), the quiet desperation of John Cheever's men on Metro-North, and drudgery on those humming auto-assembly lines, but men worked. Cultural expectations that men would work were successfully reinforced by rising wages and expectations.

THE POST-1973 TRANSFORMATION

Another familiar story exists about how, since about 1973, with a few exceptions, U.S. economic growth has been sluggish, the typical male worker's wages have stagnated, benefits have been cut, and economic inequality has grown.[48] Median male income in inflation-adjusted dollars in 2016 was below not only its 1973 peak but also what it was in 2007, 2002, and 1986. Less educated men have experienced real declines in wages, while only men with graduate degrees have seen their pay rise. Former treasury secretary Larry Summers famously revived a term coined by Alvin Hansen, another Harvard economist, from the 1930s, to describe the state of the twenty-first-century U.S. economy: "secular stagnation."[49] The midcentury middle-class, male breadwinner model—never entirely true, as one-third of women were in the workforce in the 1950s—became untenable for most families by the late twentieth century.

Women went to work in droves; the percentage of females 16 and older in the labor force increased rapidly between 1965 and 2000, from 37 percent to 60 percent. Fully half of the growth in the workforce in the last forty years of the twentieth century has been reversed by the free fall in the ranks of working men. Between 2015 and 2017, women accounted for virtually the entire growth in U.S. labor force participation. Some of this influx was driven by changing, more egalitarian norms championed by the women's movement. Some was due to the fact that a single male income simply could no longer support a family.[50]

Despite rafts of research and endless blather by politicians and those with publishing platforms from the *New York Times* to Facebook, explanations including the growth in the female workforce, the rise of global trade and competition, increased automation and productivity, outsourcing, the decline of unions, and immigration are important but do not fully account for what has happened to men. Widespread automation and other technological developments have eliminated many middle-skill (and some higher-skill) jobs, such as cashiers, factory workers, and lab technicians, in the United States and other developed countries; they have also reduced job security and put downward pressure on wages. Much industrial production has moved to China, Mexico, and other countries with lower-cost labor. Other factors, including a slack labor market that's not producing enough good jobs, a mismatch between jobs and skills, less willingness to move for jobs, and a less work-oriented culture, also have played a role in the decline of work.

But another part of the story is distributional: Who gets the goodies? This is where corporate and financial industry greed, government policies favoring big businesses and the well-to-do, and less generous government safety net policies come into play.

Since Republicans, Democrats, and people of other political stripes have railed about the savaging of the middle class, it is worth saying a bit about the significant growth in economic inequality in America since the 1970s.

The U.S. economy, while less peppy and more volatile than during its golden mid-twentieth-century years, has still grown in recent decades, but most of the gains have gone to the wealthy and the upper middle class. Between 1993 and 2015, more than half of the nation's overall income gains went to the 1 percent of people with the highest incomes, with their real incomes soaring by 94 percent. At the same time, the bottom 99 percent saw a cumulative gain of just 14 percent. The typical worker's wage increased by just 6 percent between 1979 and 2013, although the increase in this median is almost entirely accounted for by rising pay for women, with wages for those at the bottom declining. Factoring in tax law changes, which have enormously benefited the wealthy and somewhat benefited lower-income Americans, real after-tax and transfer income grew by 192 percent between 1979 and 2007 for the top 1 percent compared to only 41 to 46 percent for the bottom 80 percent.[51] Compare that to the broad-based 100 percent pretax wage gain in the quarter century between 1948 and 1973.

Growing inequality "is the defining issue of our time," former president Barack Obama said. Economists Paul Krugman, the Nobel Prize–winning columnist for the *New York Times*, and David Autor at MIT have called it "the great divergence" and "job polarization," in which increased demand for better-educated workers has led to less demand for middle-skill workers.[52]

The top 10 percent of American wage earners rake in more than half of the nation's income, compared to about one-third during the more equal post–World War II years. There are other ways to look at income inequality (leaving aside the even thornier subject of wealth inequality). For one, in 2015 compensation of CEOs at the nation's largest companies was three hundred to seven hundred times that of the typical worker, compared with about twenty times in 1965 and thirty times as late as 1978. Labor's share of national income has fallen markedly in the twenty-first century, from 66 percent during the Kennedy years, to about 64 percent at the dawn of the millennium, to 58 percent in 2016.[53]

Moreover, social mobility in the United States has fallen behind that of most of western Europe. It has become "stickier" as those on the bottom rungs of the ladder have less of a chance to move up than they did in the past, inevitably dampening motivation for some to work harder. What former labor secretary Robert Reich called "the secession of the successful" is perpetuated by class divisions in educational attainment and other opportunities; whereas six in ten children of the top 20 percent of the income distribution get a college degree, only one in ten from the bottom 40 percent do. But many other economic and economic policy factors also explain why only half of children born in the 1980s earn more than their parents, compared to 90 percent of those born in the 1940s.[54]

The Occupy Wall Street movement, the Bernie Sanders presidential campaign, and other leftist activities have focused on the "1 percent." The superwealthy top 0.1 percent have seen astronomical gains. And the well-educated upper-middle-class professionals and managers—one-sixth to one-fifth of the population—in their suburban mega-mansions, gentrified urban townhouses, and pricey apartments, also have done quite well. Their real after-tax income grew by 70 percent from the beginning of Ronald Reagan's presidency to the end of George W. Bush's. For them, as one 2017 *Wall Street Journal* headline screamed, "Everything Is Awesome!"[55]

But economic changes don't happen in a vacuum. This is where culture and politics start to creep into a seemingly economic story.

As CEOs turned to maximizing shareholder returns, cost cutting became all the rage. Of course, the biggest cost for most businesses is labor. So end the raises and start cutting pay. End lifetime job security and put more workers on shorter-term contracts. "The new employment relationship" became, in the clever words of economist Peter Capelli, "like a lifetime of divorces and remarriages." ProPublica journalist Peter Gosselin has called ours a "no promise" society.[56]

Remember all those hot-shot investment bankers in the 1980s, the downsizing consultants in the 1990s, and hedge fund managers in the 2000s? And let's not forget the fancy-sounding new financial instruments and all the loose lending, when it seemed like even the mangiest squirrel could get a loan and the undercapitalized peddlers of credit default swaps could make a killing.

Thanks to this "financialization" of the economy, the U.S. financial sector, which expanded its share of America's GDP by at least 50 percent between 1980 and 2010 to 8–9 percent, played a leading role in bringing us the global recession, continued high debt, unstable markets, greater inequality, and some even say lower GDP.[57]

While we're traversing the relatively recent stretches of memory lane, let's take the bypass marked "Culture." In what has come to be known as "winner-take-all" markets, where quarterbacks like Tom Brady and Peyton Manning make nearly $40 million a year and singer Taylor Swift earned more than four times that amount in 2016, the super-rich became objects of adulation. TV shows like *Lifestyles of the Rich and Famous*, which debuted as Reagan was proclaiming "morning in America," and the *Real Housewives* reality series about upper-class women, which made its debut at the height of the early 2000s housing bubble, celebrated wealth. In its press release announcing the latter, the Bravo network said the women lead "glamorous lives" with "diamond parties" amid CEOs and professional athletes, and "viewers have been riveted by the fictionalized versions of such lifestyles."[58] Never mind that such lifestyles were out of reach for all but a fraction of the top 1 percent. The American credo, which had morphed from "the pursuit of happiness" to a still reasonable "abundance for all" in the mid-twentieth century, was transmogrified into an equation of opulence with success.[59]

In inner suburbs, bulldozers razed middle-class ranch houses, to be replaced by cavernous, if often cheaply constructed, mansions with marble kitchen counters and appliances by high-end, high-status manufacturers that could never be mistaken for Sears or GE. Even if it became hard for some of the upper middle class to pay for the two BMWs, the private schools and college tuition, the exotic vacations, the designer clothing, the nannies, and the mediocre triple-digit meals, the top quintile wasn't doing badly in the post-1980 (or post-2009) economy.

If 1960s hippies, consumer culture theorists, and even John Kenneth Galbraith questioned America's postwar materialistic binge, it was a lot tamer and more democratic than the contemporary veneration of bling. As the Gordon Gekko character in *Wall Street* (1987), near the beginning of this normative change, famously said, "Greed is good."

Popular culture, which has a major role in shaping norms and values, of course, doesn't exist independently of economics and politics. During recent decades, as billions of dollars in contributions and lobbying have doused America's political system, it's no surprise that studies show that those with more money—and who want even more—get their way in Washington far more often than those who are middle class, working class, or poor. To make a very long side story short, in many ways our political system has been captured, with the wealthy, big business, and big finance essentially buying policies that are in their interests.[60]

So what did they get for their money—aside from more money?

When Ronald Reagan declared that "government is not the solution, it's the problem," big parts of the post–World War II social contract that had created a rising tide with ever more jobs paying ever higher wages started to unravel. Taxes, particularly on the wealthy, were cut and cut again under presidents Reagan, George W. Bush, and Donald Trump,[61] thanks to the magical thinking of "supply-side economics" that doing so would increase economic growth and, hence, tax revenues. W's father, George H. W. Bush, called this "voodoo economics" in 1980, and he was right, as federal deficits have soared above $1 trillion per year, and spending on public investment and social welfare has fallen in many areas.

The second whammy was deregulation. Using the supposedly sound notion that free markets are uniformly good, sold to the world as "the Washington Consensus," laws that aimed to promote fair business practices in sectors ranging from airlines, energy, and utilities to telecommunications and finance were weakened or shelved. Antitrust enforcement similarly declined. Aside from the failure of many promised benefits for consumers to materialize— think of airlines' wonderful service, bargain prices for cell phones, and those low bank and credit card fees—workers took a hit. Deregulation went hand in hand with shifting production to lower-wage areas and heeding business schools' mantra of "just in time" production, leading to mass layoffs.

The final government blow was the attack on unions and weakening of labor laws. As noted, by the early 1950s, unions were an accepted part of an economy in which business, government, and labor could work together. While corruption and long strikes diminished popular opinion of unions long before Reagan was elected president, the Reagan administration—together with business-led state "right to work" campaigns—made it more difficult for unions to organize and operate. If union density had remained even at 1979 levels, weekly wages for the typical male worker would have been $2,700 higher in 2013, according to the left-leaning Economic Policy Institute. At the same time, the federal minimum wage wasn't raised during the Reagan years and hasn't been since 2009. At $7.25 an hour from 2009 to 2018, the minimum wage would have been about $3 higher if it had just kept pace with inflation since its high point in 1968, and would have reached around $19 an hour if it had kept up with productivity growth. In addition to their injustice, low wages are not exactly the bells and whistles to entice more people to work. By comparison with western Europe, low-skill jobs in the United States pay less and provide fewer (i.e., usually no) benefits.[62]

As you may notice, most of these arguments about how a changing U.S. economy hurt millions of workers and their families come from, or bear out, a left-of-center interpretation.

However, there are other facts and interpretations that lend credence to other arguments. And this is where the nuances of language become important. Have many men been "pushed out" of the labor force, as the above-mentioned economic changes suggest, or have they "dropped out"? The answer is not a simple either/or. It is some of both. But how much can be attributed to one or the other? The devil is in both the details and the interpretation.

Charles Murray, an economist at the center-right American Enterprise Institute (AEI), writes, "A substantial number of prime-age [30–49] white working-age men dropped out of the labor force for no obvious reason." Such men, particularly unmarried ones, are "less industrious" than a generation or two ago, and there has been a striking "increase in the number of people seeking to get [disability] benefits who aren't really unable to work." Murray calculated that the percentage of men and women *qualifying* for disability benefits because they're unable to work rose from 0.7 percent of the labor force in 1960 to 5.2 percent a half century later. The increase in disability, which some see as a cover for laziness, is said by conservatives like Scott Winship of the congressional Joint Economic Committee to be a major factor in men not working, although President Obama's Council of Economic Advisers found this increase to have had only a very small effect.[63]

Murray and Winship are hardly alone. Many conservative politicians, human resource professionals, and other Americans speak of a lost or waning work ethic.

Kellyanne Conway, one of President Trump's top advisers, said, "If you're able-bodied and you would like to go and find employment and have employer-sponsored benefits, then you should be able to do that."[64]

Steve, a manager at a New Jersey firm who had his own hard times out of work, told me that millennials (born between 1981 and 1995 or 1997) in particular "don't have the same level of commitment. I'll work all hours, but they come in at nine and leave at five or whenever they want."

Jonathan, a white Ohio man who works the second shift in the same factory where his father worked, called his two adult sons "lazy." "They lived with my wife and me well into their twenties until we had to kick them out so that we could move on with our lives," he said.

Nicholas Eberstadt describes nonworking men as "dropouts" who are "doing little to improve themselves." What's happening, he says, is "a moral crisis," adding that "the growing incapability of grown men to function as breadwinners cannot help but undermine the American family." Eberstadt, who has trotted out data on Medicaid, disability, and other public benefit use among these men, also published *A Nation of Takers*, a phrase that helped Mitt Romney lose the 2012 presidential election.[65]

Ben Carson, President Trump's secretary of housing and urban development, resurrected the old conservative line that "welfare" programs like SSDI and Supplemental Security Income (SSI) create "dependency" and reduce the incentive to work (read: make people lazy).[66]

While there are glimmers of truth to such ideas, they egregiously fail to explain why a greater proportion of men are in the labor force virtually everywhere else in the developed world. The much more extensive social welfare policies of a Germany or Sweden result in more—not less—work. People do make decisions to work by comparing the benefits of work with the costs of not working, but the lack of "benefits" from work—low wages and lousy jobs—may compare unfavorably to leisure subsidized by wives, parents, or government. Why this is happening gets back to both progressive arguments about socioeconomic injustice and conservative arguments about moral or cultural decline.

This conservative trope drives men like Sam, a 55-year-old white man who once worked in Silicon Valley, crazy. He bristles at the idea that "every educated American male who is out of work for an extended period of time is a lazy, irresponsible lout." Sam quit his IT job a few years ago. He'd been working for twenty-six years but wanted to "take a year off." Since that year has passed, he has started looking for jobs that "look to be a good match." He assiduously applies for job after job in his field. Nothing has come up.

Nonetheless, a case can be made for what some may call a "moral crisis" and others less judgmentally call a radical change in norms and values. As we have seen, many men out are divorced or have never married, but whether nonemployment or the breakdown of the traditional nuclear family in many corners of America is a cause, effect, or something else is a tricky, fraught subject. There is a relationship, and big pieces of the story do constitute a crisis that goes beyond work to the family, the psyche, civic life, public health, how men view money, and the values relating to money. To these cultural issues, we will return.

A 2014 poll of nonemployed men by the Kaiser Family Foundation, CBS, and the *New York Times* found that 44 percent would not take available jobs that they believed were "beneath them." Some economists would say that these men's "reservation wage," the lowest wage they would work for, is too high. Not a few employers say that "Now Hiring" signs attract few men, who say this "isn't the kind of work I'm interested in."[67] Self-esteem is understandable, as an out-of-work programmer or college professor probably would not leap for joy to be on his feet all day selling housewares at Walmart or driving for Lyft in the middle of the night.

As expressed by Lorne, the laid-off midwestern IT worker we met in chapter 1, "I'm not culturally suited to working in a pizza parlor." He had no compunction about saying that he is "better" than that and that his "expectations are higher." Rising expectations, stoked at least as much by popular culture as by generations of increasing living standards, may have turned what were once considered decent jobs into "boring" ones. Anecdotes abound of men who once might have dutifully obeyed their boss now getting into arguments and getting fired or quitting. Where once lived pride in work, disdain and shame seem to have moved in.

Yet many other men do take lower-paid, lower-status jobs. Joe, a white California man nearing 60, had worked for decades as a librarian. During the four years after he lost his job, he said, "I was working two minimum-wage jobs to survive after being on unemployment for two years. I got divorced and lost my house to foreclosure." Even after getting a full-time job and remarrying, he says, "I make $50,000 less now than before I was laid off. I live paycheck to paycheck to support everyone—my wife and myself, my ex-wife, and my two children."

Hardly on the outskirts of the U.S. economy, a striking number of middle-age men I spoke with talked about being pushed into lower-paid jobs. Andy had long worked in the movie business, living in an expensive West L.A. home. He lost his job in his early 50s and is now making do as a salesman. Braden, another 50-something guy in the Northeast, whose income had been well into six figures, found a well-paying job, although his earnings now are one-third of what he once made and he continues to pay alimony to his ex-wife based on his once much higher income. Both are white. Neither is suffering. But both have been on a downward trajectory.

None of these men are part of the nonworking class, and Andy and Braden are still financially comfortable. Yet they have taken blows to their self-esteem. Work, of course, is not just about money. It can be a marker of status, a source of pride, something that brings happiness or fulfillment, a place for sociability, and a sign of masculinity to many men.

We will turn to issues of masculinity and psychological well-being, but for now it suffices to say that growing numbers of men are emotionally hurting. This has led not only to increased depression, alcohol abuse, and suicide but also to physical pain and the consumption of opioids and other drugs intended to ease that pain.

Clearly, the costs of 20 million men not working are manifold and enormous. Many of these men descend into poverty or, at the very least, their financial circumstances become precarious. The personal economic costs ramify across their lifetimes in terms of lost savings, foreclosures, much less opportunity to lead good lives, poor prospects of paying for additional education that might improve their lot, and little economic security in retirement.

Indeed, the very concept of retirement turns into a cruel joke for many of these middle-age men. If they're not working now, at least in part thinking that available jobs don't fit their self-image, they could well find themselves working part-time or more than full-time at age 70 or 75 in low-wage jobs they never imagined they would be in.[68] Nonemployment at 50 or 55 may mean working the sales floors of Home Depot or Walmart ten or fifteen years down the road—that is, if retail jobs are even available in the 2020s and beyond.

The economic costs to the United States are huge. Although the average GDP per worker was about $112,000 in 2016, according to the World Bank, if one believes that most nonemployed men would be in the lowest-paid one-fourth of male wage and salary workers, output per worker is notably less. Since the upper bound for men's income in the bottom quartile is about $32,000 and the upper bound for those in the bottom decile is about $20,000, and the ratio of wages to GDP is about 44 percent, that would suggest GDP per low-income worker may approach $60,000.[69] Although some nonemployed men have much higher potential earnings, the absence of 20 million male workers could crudely translate into more than $1 trillion in lost GDP. Since no economy will ever put to work every adult—because there will always be a significant number of ill and disabled people, adults getting education or staying home to take care of children or aging parents, and people between jobs—we are still looking at perhaps three quarters of a trillion dollars in lost annual income. Moreover, expected continuing declines in labor force participation will lead to even slower economic growth, up to 0.5 percentage points per year, between 2017 and 2027, several studies have projected. Precise numbers may be impossible to come by, but, as economist Alan Krueger has said, "We're not fully utilizing the human resources we have, and that means the economy is not performing as well as it could be. That means our overall standard of living is lower because overall output is lower."[70]

Add to that the costs of Medicaid, SSDI, and other public assistance, not to mention the huge health care costs at least indirectly associated with millions of men not working, and we're talking about upward of a trillion dollars lost each year in the United States. Moreover, in a country with federal deficits of $1 trillion in 2019,[71] and state governments without sufficient money to pay for public higher and K–12 education, among other bills, this forgone income translates into hundreds of billions of dollars in lost tax revenues. Over a generation, the economic costs are trillions upon trillions of dollars.

And these are just the economic costs. As economist David Autor told me, "They go beyond lost earnings and tax revenues. They affect career potential, marriageability, role models, involvement in crime, and a lot of costly social ills." Beyond quantifiable earnings, productivity, and output, creativity is lost. When people are not working, whether with colleagues or alone, ideas are not generated and shared, which sometimes means they are not transformed into products or services that improve the lives and happiness of millions—from a more efficient car or a useful app to better care for the elderly or a new piece of music.

As we will see, the growth of the male nonworking class also has myriad ill effects on health and psychology. It affects—and is affected by—marriage, fatherhood, relationships, and attitudes toward women. There are costs to America's civic life and politics. For most of these men (as well as many nonworking women), *time* itself—which means a portion of life—is lost.

FRACKVILLE, PENNSYLVANIA
PORTRAIT OF A TOWN

Frackville is the kind of place that fits Donald Trump's rhetoric about the decline of America's coal industry. About sixty miles northeast of Harrisburg, Pennsylvania's capital, Frackville lies in the heart of one of the Western Hemisphere's largest deposits of anthracite coal.

Just north of town, along the Gold Star Highway, stretch miles of deep black fields and hillsides of strip-mined coal on land owned by Gilbertson Coal Company. There were forty-one collieries northeast of Frackville, with company-built "patch towns" for workers, during mining's heyday in the first half of the twentieth century. Today almost all of the mines have been abandoned, the patch towns have burned down, and there are largely only the ghosts preserved in photos and miners' gear in the Frackville Museum.

Instead of coal dust, today very different dark shadows hang over Frackville The town is home to two prisons built between 1987 and 1993, which house almost as many inmates as Frackville's entire population. The maximum-security prison has 1,200 inmates, and 2,400 more are incarcerated in the medium-security prison; together, the two prisons employ more than 1,000 people.[1]

A number of townspeople live in "half a double" houses, narrow two-story 1920s vintage attached homes, often with pitched roofs, although larger split-levels and other detached houses are dotted about the southwest side of town. Many of the former, with foreclosure signs out front, can be bought for as little as $25,000. The gold-domed Holy Ascension Orthodox Church, serving descendants of the Poles, Lithuanians, and Ukrainians who settled in

Frackville, and the once stately Peoples Bank, with its Doric columns, stand in stark contrast to a main street with too many abandoned lots and cracked shop windows. One store window, with a large "Trump for President" sign, advertises that it is "buying entire contents of homes—cleanouts available." In another, only debris can be seen through the window.

On the window of one store is taped a "Stomp Out Suicide" sign. It announces an all-day "awareness event" to benefit Schuylkill County's task force on suicide prevention that rather improbably included "raffles, DJ, children's activities," and a sheriff's department "drug take-back."

I often heard downtown Frackville compared to Beirut, a city still widely associated with devastation.

It is obvious that "the town has deteriorated like other small towns," commented Lorraine Stanton, who created and has run the Frackville Museum above Borough Hall for nearly forty-five years.

"It's a whole cauldron of things," said Gavin, a 26-year-old Frackville native who moved to San Francisco to become a freelance fashion writer. "A dearth of jobs is a big part. Social pillars like the church, the Knights of Columbus, and Rotary have been dwindling. There's been a brain drain."

"Doomsday . . . day of reckoning," "escape plan," and "Thessalonians 4" read handmade bumper stickers on an old red Plymouth parked by a row of half a doubles. The sidewalk, lined with aboveground power lines, is cracked, as are the tiny concrete porches.

Although other residents are less pessimistic and glimmers of a town spirit can be seen, Gavin added, "People feel bitter and cheated and a lack of hope."

The prisons have changed the town's population as many family members of inmates have moved in. With 3,700 residents, 98 percent of whom are white, Frackville has less than half the number of people it had in 1940. The well-paying but dangerous mining jobs that once supported thousands of working-class families and made the town and area thrive have given way to poverty and near-poverty. The median household income, at about $39,500, is about two-thirds of the U.S. median.[2]

"The jobs don't pay as well, and the husband and wife both have to work, and they still have to budget themselves," said Lorraine, who was 91 when I visited in 2017.

The shopping mall, which just opened in the 1970s, is shuttered, and the ATI Specialty Metals plant laid off forty people when it shut down at the end of 2016. However, Walmart and Wegmans Food Markets have built sprawling distribution centers to the south, near I-81. Along with the prisons, these are

Frackville's principal employers. Full-time warehouse jobs pay about $12–$13 an hour plus benefits, and a Wegmans job description characterizes part-time "product selector" jobs as requiring lifting "35–65 pounds repeatedly," "bending, twisting, reaching" with warehouse temperatures that vary by more than 50 degrees.[3] National retailers, including Dollar General and Saks Fifth Avenue, also have opened fulfillment centers in the area.

Aside from the younger people who have left—like Lorraine's son, a professor at Ohio State University—Frackville also once had a sizable number of Jews, many of whom operated several dozen stores along Lehigh Avenue. My grandmother and aunt were among them, running a shoe store downstairs from their four-room railroad flat. Their store and home were demolished twenty years ago, and the lot remains empty, as are others in the town. The synagogue, chartered in 1884, and the shul are gone, as is a small Jewish museum in nearby Pottsville. A few kosher stores still exist in the even more depressed city of Shenandoah, where my father grew up, a ten-minute drive north of Frackville, and they are now joined by halal and Hispanic markets there. Hidden in the hills farther north is a small, gated Hebrew cemetery, maintained by Jews in Harrisburg and across the winding highway from much larger Christian cemeteries.[4]

Family life in Frackville has also seen better days. The last public schools in Frackville closed, so the few young families have to send their children to towns ten to fifteen miles away.

"Families are breaking up because of divorce, and babies are being born out of wedlock," said Patti Domalakes, whose ancestors came to the area from Poland before the First World War. "The fathers aren't present and they're not passing on to their sons how to lead a family."

Joe Jordan, a Frackville native who achieved fame with his brother in the 1960s for Top 40 hits like "Gimme Some Lovin'," said that his daughter had adopted a six-year-old girl who had been abandoned by her parents. "The kids are promiscuous, couples aren't as devoted, and they run off and leave it to the state," he said.

While stories of nonmarital births are rife, Patti, like others, blames the men. "They buy into this handout culture. Women are strong and fill the void." She said men "gave up" on leading the local Boy Scout troop, so women stepped in.

Paul Domalakes, Patti's husband and a defense attorney and part-time public defender, told me, "There's a whole underclass of people living with different people and having children with different people." Many are convicted on drug charges. They are quickly fired from temp jobs and are in-eligible for subsidized housing in nearby towns because of their convictions. "They wind up in cheap housing and it's a downward spiral."

Paul's brother, John, is a judge who has seen an "explosion" on his docket of domestic abuse, child abuse, and divorce cases, as well as so many drug cases that "we need another round of jury selection." Both men and women are abusing opioids, heroin, and fentanyl, he said. "But most deaths are young men under 30. Many come from difficult home situations. They didn't do well in high school. They found it difficult to get a job. Most have girlfriends in and out of their lives. The newspaper has a section listing births, and half are not from married couples. Many get welfare, food stamps, and disability."

"I've done this for twenty years," he added. "I've seen parents in court, and now I'm seeing their children."

Gavin said this is especially true among his peers who stayed in Frackville. "More guys are not committing to being fathers," he said. Two young women he knows from high school got pregnant with men who later left them, and one of the women has had a baby with a second man. Neither woman is married.

He also said that a dozen or more of his high school classmates have died from drug overdoses, and others suffer from depression. "A lot of them don't have a sense of purpose, so they get high, finding solace in drug dependency," he said. "I think they feel like they had no future."

The number of fatal overdoses in the county more than doubled, from twenty-five in 2015 to fifty-nine in 2016.[5] Frackville has a buprenorphine treatment center for opioid addiction, and many drug and alcohol rehab or detox facilities are in nearby towns. The Holiday Inn Express on the interstate has held public meetings about access to Narcan, a drug that can save those who have overdosed.

Just as opioid deaths are much more common in the Frackville area than nationally, so too are suicides. Twenty-six men and seven women killed them-selves in Schuylkill County in 2016, twelve of them under age 40 and sixteen in their 40s and 50s.[6]

While the national pattern of rising suicide among middle-age men holds true in Frackville and its environs, all too many men in their mid- to late 20s are not doing well and seem to not know what to do. "There's a circuit of bush parties in the woods, where guys drink bad beer, hanging out, doing the kinds of things they were doing in high school," Gavin said. "Some aren't doing anything, and some work at minimum-wage jobs and live with their parents."

What German social theorist Jürgen Habermas called "the public sphere" and Robert Putnam called "social capital" has dwindled in Frackville, as elsewhere in America. The Rotarians have few members. All of the town's ten Little League teams have disappeared. The three Catholic churches have combined into one. The former Episcopal church was converted into a private residence. The little synagogue closed around 2007. And the Catholic school that Gavin attended is no more.

Paul Pilconis, a Vietnam veteran and retired steelworker in his mid-60s, recalled the bar that his grandparents owned, "where everyone used to meet." When he was a young man, he remembers, there were "thirty-some places to go to drink. It was like *Cheers*, where everyone knew your name. Now there are no bars like that, no meeting places for older people, and none of the picnics like you used to have."

Patti and others attribute this retreat in part to the internet and declining morals. The judge said that "they don't teach morals in families, the churches, or the schools." It is also of a piece with the drug problem, the rise in nonmarital births, the lack of good parenting, and what some view as the "handout" culture.

Lorraine, too, is angry about a new generation of men "who don't have a work ethic because they never worked" and turn to public benefits. "Our family was too proud for welfare," she said. She went on to say she gets very angry at "these men and women who have gold bracelets and smoke," have children with a succession of partners, and don't work. "Our taxes are paying for that." The anger is diffuse, deep, and widespread. "There are a lot of welfare people here," she said. "If I put my children through college, why can't you? I had to pay $675 for my glasses, and those on welfare don't have to pay."

In nearby Shenandoah, a group of young men beat to death one of the many Mexican men who have come to the area to pick the orchards. When two from the group were eventually convicted, other young white men were outraged, blamed the incident on immigrants, and said there wouldn't have been such an uproar if a white man had been killed. The sheriff and another officer were convicted of trying to cover up the crime.[7]

It's a familiar story of struggling Americans who blame those below them on the social ladder. So too is the story of seething anger toward the government.

"The government has become our parents," Patti said. "There are too many government programs to solve problems that they can't. They give out handouts without a message, without faith."

Joe has a different take. "Back then you honored the president. Now you throw mud at him."

Despite everything, many townspeople haven't given up. Patti started the Frackville Beautification Group in the 1990s, is active on a downtown revitalization team, and presses state and federal officials to improve the roads. Lorraine is involved with Frackville Seniors, which supports the fire companies, the library, and Christmas light displays. But men, who once led thriving civic organizations—especially younger men—are hard to find in such efforts.

In Lorraine's well-tended museum, several rooms are filled with photos of miners going to work and the old coal breakers near Frackville, high school football team banners, "Elk of the Year" award plaques, mannequins in early twentieth-century garb, and Jordan Brothers music memorabilia.

A deep sense of nostalgia hangs in the air over Frackville. Even 26-year-old Gavin said that "people are pining for memories of when they grew up. It was very sweet, but it's heightened because they've been sliding into a future that is much more uncertain and disappointing."

CHAPTER 3

Masculinity, Mating, and Misogyny

> The three most destructive words that every man receives when he's a boy
> is when he's told to "be a man."
>
> —Joe Ehrmann, former NFL defensive lineman

No concept is as charged and confusing for men today as "masculinity" or "manhood." What does it mean to be male? Ideas differ around the world and have changed throughout history, but what norms and expectations are associated with "being a man" in the contemporary United States? How do they differ by race and ethnicity, class, age, sexual orientation, and marital or relationship status? How do they influence men's behavior in the heterosexual dating and mating market and their views about women? And how does the cultural ambiguity and ambivalence about being male lead many men to be on the sidelines, intersecting with other issues and trends discussed in this book?

This chapter follows an especially winding road, examining a number of topics that aren't typically brought together. However, they all have to do with how men, women, and society normatively view what a man should be and do. These issues—largely unaddressed in economic and sociological writings about "missing men," "absent fathers," "working-class white men," "poor African American men," and so forth—are key to the man out problem.

Thus, we will venture into traditional ideas of masculinity and newer, postfeminist ideas of the "new man" and tensions between them. We will explore how these norms and values play out in dating and male-female relations. We will look at cultural tropes about the "decline of men," women not needing men, and men portrayed by Hollywood as losers or villains. Then we will turn to the anger and misogyny that too many men express, in part as a way to define their own masculinity. Finally, we will look at two faces of men's activists—what might be loosely called the men's rights movement and the progressive, pro–gender equity men's movement.

A strictly biological definition of a man is pretty straightforward, all gender-bending aside. Since gender is a cultural construct, what do little boys, and girls, and adult men and women learn about masculinity? The answer, never simple, is more complex than ever in the early twenty-first century.

Attributes such as toughness, strength, power, dominance, self-reliance, sexual virility, aggressiveness, self-control, courage, homophobia, risk-taking, honor, and stoicism come to mind. Roles like provider, protector, warrior, athlete, and leader were long accepted as decidedly masculine. Just as these have been cultural requisites, or "dos," there have been many long-standing "don'ts": real men don't cry, don't talk about their feelings, don't give up, don't avoid a fight if provoked, aren't "sissies," aren't passive, aren't vulnerable, and expect women to take care of the kids and the home.

Traditional masculinity's most extreme consequence has always been how male "aggressiveness" easily morphs into violence. From the schoolyard to the streets to the home, males are violent. This is not new. How much this stems from biology and how much from acculturation is debatable, but four out of five of the nation's five million violent crimes in 2015 were committed by men, although the U.S. Justice Department reports no statistically significant gender difference in victimization rates for all violent crimes together. Perpetrators of mass shootings in recent years have been nearly all male.[1]

A great number of men and women, particularly social scientists, believe that adherence to, and promotion of, such roles, behaviors, and character traits constitute a "toxic masculinity." A British group cleverly calls this cluster of "stereotypes aimed at making you a manly man, proper bloke, or top lad" "propamanda." Many of these norms disempower and degrade women, as feminists have used terms like "machismo" and the more politicized phrase "hegemonic masculinity." But living up to the norms of traditional masculinity has also put an enormous emotional burden on boys and men. If they even half accept these norms and fail to live up to them, they feel like failures. On the other hand, traditional "male" values, such as providing for one's family, courage, honor, self-reliance, and leadership, in most circumstances are positive, should be gender-neutral, and, if anything, are in too short supply in modern America.[2]

In addition, masculinity has long been defined in opposition to femininity. Despite poets', philosophers', and psychologists' longtime recognition of overlap, in the popular mind the two were largely antonyms until the very late twentieth century. This polarity is captured in comments by guys like Ike, a young African American man in Washington, D.C.: "Society tells us not to express ourselves. We're not allowed to cry, because that's what girls do."

We have a rich vocabulary of words and phrases denoting (often crudely) normative masculinity: "dude," "bros," "alpha males," "stud," "babe magnet," "sissy," "wimp," "faggot," "crybaby," "wuss," "mama's boy," "grow some balls," "act like a man," "man up."

Another black man from the Washington, D.C., area said, "I feel it's manly to have many partners and have a crude and degrading attitude toward females, even if I don't feel that way." According to a 2017 poll, 60 percent of millennial men said they get the message that "a real man should have as many sexual partners as he can."[3] And for these men the old double standard persists. A young white Rhode Island man recalled his high school days, when boys "celebrated the guys who were very sexually active and slut-shamed the girls who were sexually active."

For all the talk of sex, however, declining male libido—the very ability to have sex—is rarely talked about (at least by men) beyond doctors' offices. Online pornography and depression are seen as major reasons for this problem. "It doesn't surprise me that there's more masturbation and that the capacity for healthy sexual relations is compromised," said one Maryland therapist who works with young men. A further knock on men's virility comes from findings that sperm counts have declined by more than 50 percent since 1973.[4]

Other male virtues cited by a young Latino man in Washington, D.C., were "You always have to be strong and you always have to provide."

Christopher, a 30-year-old white Virginian who described himself as "liberal," nonetheless said,

> I despise men who, I irrationally think, are acting too much like women. Cologne, slim-fitting suits, fancy hairstyles, skinny jeans—I would never be caught dead wearing these things. And men do not

wear pink pants! I am reactionary in this regard. I don't care. I also confess to being homophobic. I once joked to myself about starting a Facebook group: Homophobes for Marriage Equality. I'm glad they have equal rights, but I don't want to be around them when they're availing themselves of these rights.

As we've seen, work and "providing" have been central to male identity. The working man was not only the family provider but also the brawny backbone of the industrial economy and the stoic, salary man of Sloan Wilson's or John Cheever's America. In colonial and revolutionary America, "manhood rested on the establishment of a household, the securing of a career, and the self-control over one's masculine comportment," writes historian Thomas Foster.[5] Some men have seen a big paycheck as a sign of masculinity—a big problem when pay has been declining for most men. It is also a bit ironic for a progressive, high-earning elite to tell "working-class men to abandon the breadwinner masculinity [that] privileged men still enjoy," as University of California law professor Joan C. Williams has written.[6] We also know that a 50-year-old man not working is seen as more problematic than a woman that age not working, given the cultural constructs that guide most people's thinking. And a lot of men are uneasy about having a woman as their boss.

Many traditionally masculine qualities have a long lineage in American history. Teddy Roosevelt extolled "the strenuous life." Authors and artists like Jack London, Owen Wister, and Frederic Remington glorified the swashbuckling frontiersman and that most archetypal of American males, the cowboy. In the mid-twentieth century, Humphrey Bogart, Gary Cooper, Marlon Brando, and Gregory Peck captured the ideal of the lone male hero in films like *Casablanca* (1942), *High Noon* (1952), *On the Waterfront* (1954), and *To Kill a Mockingbird* (1962). Then there were Dirty Harry and Rambo, Shaft and Rocky. And 007, the epitome of tough, always-in-control virility. NFL sportscasters have portrayed men as "machines," tough and unfeeling. The male as the cool sexual conquistador came to the fore in the mid-twentieth century with role models like Hugh Hefner, Mick Jagger, Wilt Chamberlain, and Warren Beatty. By the 2010s, after Arnold Schwarzenegger's moment in the male sun, the American über-man was Dwayne Johnson (aka "the Rock"), named "Man of the Century" by *Muscle and Fitness* magazine in 2016 not only for his exploits in the wrestling ring and on screen but also in the winner-take-all economy, where he led the Hollywood pack with $64.5 million in income that year.[7]

Boys have learned how to be "real men" for generations—from parents, school, popular culture, and observing the world around them. Some of these lessons definitely have begun to change. For example, a 2016 YouGov poll found that about 30 percent of men between 18 and 44 called themselves "completely masculine," compared to 65 percent of those age 65 and older. Nonetheless, studies have found that significant majorities of young men in 2017 still said they had gotten the message that men must follow these traditional behavioral norms. For example, 75 percent of them felt social pressure to "act strong even if they feel scared or nervous inside."[8]

"Masculinity" carries an added charge among men of color. Most Latino men have been acculturated to the norms of machismo, a term appropriated derisively by feminists as a form of hypermasculinity. Despite the prominent roles of mothers and grandmothers in Latino families, as Alejandro, a Latino man in Washington, D.C., told me, it's about "treating women as objects of lust, where you can have them, possess them, but in return, they can't possess you. You can charm and be a heartbreaker, but you're not charmed by any one girl." A Salvadoran immigrant said, "In my country, most believe a woman is less than a man, and is only good for this or that."

The circumstances of African American men lend particular credence to the concept of "intersectionality." Race, gender, and class intersect with a vengeance for poorer black men. The objects of hundreds of years of American racism, disadvantaged in the job market, stalked by police, unlikely to be married, and incarcerated at frightening rates, poor black men can't prove their manhood with a big paycheck or societal power. Thus, toughness, violence, and sexuality are what's left on the "man card." As Tyvon Hewitt, an African American trainer of minority youth, said, "If toxic masculinity is a cold for white men, it's the flu for Latinos and African Americans." Being a father is also a sign of being a man for many African American men, despite statistics seeming to show that many of them aren't around their children.[9]

FEMINISM, GAY MEN, "NEW" MANHOOD, AND BEYOND

While these masculine ideals certainly have survived, beginning in the mid-twentieth century, "second-wave" feminists like Simone de Beauvoir and Betty Friedan began to chip away at the masculine mystique and the seemingly eternal and natural preeminence of men.[10] Feminism gained particular strength by the 1970s, playing a major role—along with the demise of the "family-wage" economy—in bringing tens of millions of women into the U.S. workforce.

Although men today still hold most of the reins of power and control most economic resources, late twentieth-century feminism helped women achieve tremendous gains in a number of arenas and fostered a sea change in attitudes. Few men (or women) believe—and even fewer would openly say—that women are inferior, that their place is in the home, and that there shouldn't be some vague notion of equality between the sexes.[11]

As a result, some traditional norms and attributes of masculinity began to fall into disrepute. A lot of male behaviors long taken for granted at home, in workplaces, in relationships, and throughout society became politically incorrect, if not downright piggish.

So enter the new, sensitive man.

Alan Alda, the paragon of this new persona, collaborated with actress Marlo Thomas on the Ms. Foundation's 1972 children's album, *Free to Be . . . You and Me*, which essentially told toddlers that gender roles could be fluid. Alda's activism on behalf of the failed Equal Rights Amendment led the *Boston Globe* to call him "the quintessential Honorary Woman: a feminist icon," while defenders of traditional masculinity derided him "as a synonym for wussiness," as *New York Magazine* put it.[12]

Like Alda, other "new men" such as Fred Rogers on *Mr. Rogers' Neighborhood* or Woody Allen in films like *Annie Hall* (1977) talked about feelings, were gentle and intellectual, and wore sweaters. Old-style masculinity took frontal assaults in gender-bending movies like *Tootsie* (1982) and *Mrs. Doubtfire* (1993). A raft of TV talk-show hosts—from Dick Cavett and Merv Griffin to Phil Donahue and David Letterman—also were poster boys for the new man. Enter the style-conscious "metrosexual" man in the 1990s. By the twenty-first century, upscale urban men had become especially concerned about grooming and their appearance, working out at health clubs to have buff bodies and buying products and getting treatments to make them look appropriately cool. HSBC, the global bank and financial services company, even gushed over "the rise of the YUMMY," the young urban male with his "vanity and penchant for trend-chasing."[13]

Meanwhile, from *The Mary Tyler Moore Show* to *Homeland* and *Veep*, women were taking the glamorous or powerful roles once assigned just to men—reporter, CIA operative, president of the United States. Almost like real life.[14]

The gay rights movement, with prominent men coming out, and the decline of homophobia also have had a huge impact on ideas about what it means to be male. For many straight men, the stereotype of "effeminacy" remains and the use of derogatory terms hardly has disappeared from the schoolyard to online chatter. As one young gay black man in an eastern city said, "In communities of color, being gay is unacceptable." However, positive images also have influenced what's desirable for many heterosexual men. Supposedly gay male attributes such as being stylish, physically fit, well-to-do, and sociable are widely appealing. Yet gay male stereotypes can be as stifling as heterosexual masculine norms, leaving some gay men to feel that they aren't living up to these "ideals." They also aren't entirely true, because gay men and couples have higher poverty rates than heterosexual men, and nearly half of Washington, D.C.'s homeless youth are LGBTQ.[15]

Just to make things a little more confusing, a lot of gay men hold firmly to traditional masculine ideals. Athletic prowess, leather-jacketed toughness, and controlled emotions are among the qualities associated with "butch" men. An online "butch board" for so-called straight-acting men was filled with posts about sports, "studs," and the military. As one of these men wrote, "I don't think there's anything feminine about being a gay man. . . . Many, many, many gay men are extremely masculine" without having to put on an act.[16]

The coming out and empowerment of the LGBTQ population has been liberating for many lesbian, gay, bisexual, and transgender Americans, but it has also muddied the waters of masculinity in other ways. "Queer," once a term of masculine derision for homosexual men, has been embraced as an umbrella descriptor by nonheterosexual men and women. Surveys have found that young men are more likely to identify themselves as "mostly straight" rather than "bisexual."[17] Reports on intersexuality—biologically ambiguous or androgynous people—have added to the sense that maleness and femaleness are not as clear-cut as "male" and "female" electrical connectors. Further confounding old libidinous ideas of masculinity, new concepts of asexuality and involuntary celibacy have come out of the closet.

In short, for a lot of gay as well as straight men, masculinity is a conundrum. Countervailing ideas compete for cultural airtime.

Given the new script, many Generation X and millennial men adopted—or were socially coerced into adopting—traits like sexual egalitarianism, thoughtfulness, and expressiveness. For a lot of children brought up after about 1990, no more blue or pink bedrooms or, after Title IX, sports that were only for boys. Being gay or transgender became cool in some circles. On most college campuses, where gender studies (read: women's studies) have proliferated, any guy who doesn't accept and profess such views is the odd man out at best, an antediluvian male supremacist at worst.

One iconoclastic white college student in California—who opposes toxic masculinity, lauds feminism's goals of equality, and agrees with women who say there aren't enough good men—told me about taking a gender studies class and doing the unthinkable: he wrote a paper about how gender inequality manifests itself as men being disadvantaged.

Here's the rub: although feminism has enabled women to make huge advances, and also has done many good things for men—whom Friedan called "fellow victims"—its effects on men have been much more ambiguous. A "cultural lag between the genders" has opened up, with women developing a new, more defined set of beliefs and greater ambition, and men unable to figure out how to respond to these changes and how to act.[18]

Some men feel that women have taken "their" jobs and that they are victims of reverse discrimination. Men watch glumly as women have surpassed them in most educational metrics. They listen equally glumly when traditionally feminine attributes—such as good communications and interpersonal abilities—are said to be today's in-demand skills of the twenty-first century. To many, women's gains are a zero-sum game. "Obviously, the more traditional jobs that women take, the fewer opportunities for men," a 60-year-old white Maryland man said. "Simple math."

Antifeminism has been simplistically associated with loony right-wing politics and less educated working-class men. Televangelist Pat Robertson notoriously once said that the women's movement encouraged women "to leave their husbands, kill their children, practice witchcraft, destroy capitalism and become lesbians."[19] Most men's feelings about the ascent of women are much more psychologically complex.

As male identity has become more fluid, which mask should they wear? Should they act like Marlon Brando in The Godfather (1972), Robin Williams in Good Will Hunting (1997), or some hybrid like Tony Soprano, the tough mobster who spills his innermost feelings on his psychiatrist's couch, or Phillip Jennings, the occasionally brutal, always pensive, and often tender KGB agent in The Americans? Indeed, behavioral norms have become rife with contradictions and minefields: Who picks up the tab on a date? Is it too dangerous to be alone in the same room with a woman, fearing innuendos at best, sexual assault allegations at worst? Women say they want men to be equal parents and caregivers, yet women and society signal that mothers remain the most important parent. The macho man may be out of style in theory, but women looking for a male partner appear to value many aspects of traditional masculinity.[20]

Especially disturbing are the palpable anger and misogyny among great numbers of men. Whether perplexed and frustrated by the normative limbo for men or just plain angry at a society that has left them on the sidelines seeking a scapegoat, the degree of animus and vitriol is striking.

Few subjects elicited as much passion as feminism and the state of male-female relations among the several hundred men interviewed or surveyed for this book. Many honestly, or dutifully, said that feminism and women's equality have been good for all. A significant number qualified this by saying that women have taken men's jobs or that "women's separatism" or "extreme leftist feminism is a pox and a disgrace" for men and women alike, in the words of a 30-year-old white, married Wisconsin man. Among twenty-six men in thirteen states directly asked whether feminism has been good or bad, half said its impact has been good, while the other half either said it was bad or expressed mixed feelings. Only about one-third rated the state of male-female relations as very good.

A striking number of men believe that women receive "preferential treatment in legal decisions, employment decisions, and divorce decisions," in the words of a nonworking Virginia man in his mid-30s.

A white millennial man in Kansas was even more blunt: "Feminism is reverse sexism. Men shouldn't have to pay for everything and give up their rights." An employed Minnesota man, also white, who said he has "always treated men and women equally," nonetheless added that "feminism is often taken to an extreme by a select group that doesn't desire equality but rather women's superiority."

Although a large number of men said that they and their employers derived big benefits from the talents of women, there was also the feeling that "workplaces can be plagued by oversensitivity," as a young white California man in his first job said.

Luis, a millennial Latino man from Southern California who grew up in a macho culture, suggested that "changing the name 'feminism' might help, since it may turn off a lot of hypermasculine men."

Tensions were particularly pronounced when it came to dating and male-female relationships. As a divorced white Texas man in his early 40s said, "Sheryl Sandberg's advice to young women to date 'bad boys' means that the eventual hubby feels like he's a consolation prize."

THE "DECLINE OF MEN" TROPE

Adding fuel to the fire is the real and perceived idea of the "decline of men" and the concomitant rise of women, who often seem or profess to "no longer need" men. Declinism, always a popular subject, has periodically dogged men throughout American history. Michael S. Kimmel, in his book *Manhood in America: A Cultural History* (2012), points to Benjamin Rush's 1788 meditations on threats to republican manhood from effeminate aristocrats and lazy laborers. Widespread worries around the turn of the twentieth century led to muscular Christianity, the Boy Scouts, and the YMCA's vision of Jesus as an exemplar of "magnificent manliness." Fears about boys and men being "sissies," "wimps," or other less than masculine creatures have been recurrent themes in U.S. history. Even in that virile era of astronauts, three-martini lunches at the 21 Club, and the Kennedy brothers playing football, historian and JFK speechwriter Arthur Schlesinger Jr. wrote, "There are multiplying signs, indeed, that something has gone badly wrong with the American Male's conception of himself." Thus Kennedy created the President's Council on Physical Fitness, basically a federal push to get boys to be more athletic (read: masculine).[21]

The "decline of males" theme surfaced again with anthropologist Lionel Tiger's 1999 book of that name. Using the language of evolutionary biology, he argued that contraception has given women the power to control the future of the species, that work no longer rewards "strength and endurance," and that nasty feminists have redefined "how words may be used or forbidden to be used." More sensational were Guy Garcia's *The Decline of Men* (2008) and Hannah Rosin's *The End of Men and the Rise of Women* (2012).[22]

In some ways, the alleged decline of males starts in school. Look at an Ivy League class photo from the 1950s and you'll see a sea of clean-cut white male faces. After World War II, 70 percent of college students were men. In 1979 women had caught up in college enrollment, and by 2016 they accounted for 57 percent of undergrads and graduate students. Professors now see classrooms full of women, as females outnumbered men on campuses by almost 3.5 million in 2016—13.3 million versus 9.9 million. Often, female students are the chipper faces in the front rows, raising their hands, while young men slouch in the back, dozing or doing a poor job hiding their smart phones on their laps. By 2015 three in eight women had a bachelor's or higher degree compared to about three in ten men. Of course, there are many academically stellar male students, and this gender gap is also class-based, with little difference between the sexes in the highest-income quartile. It is also race-based, as the difference in college graduation rates among African American men and women is greater than it is for whites.[23]

Rolling back to elementary and secondary school, girls leave boys in the dust on eight major standardized tests. Girls have long outperformed boys in reading, with the average gap in eighth and twelfth grades essentially equivalent to girls being one grade level ahead. Boys also get poorer grades, act out and have more behavior problems, and are less likely to graduate from high school, although some of this may come down to two factors: teacher bias favoring girls and evidence that boys growing up in troubled households are less resilient than girls. Perhaps the masculinity trap plays a role, with learning consciously or unconsciously seen as "uncool" or effeminate; twice as many boys as girls say that school is "a waste of time." As J. D. Vance wrote of his West Virginia town in *Hillbilly Elegy,* "Boys who got good grades were 'sissies' or 'faggots.'"[24]

American "anti-intellectualism" is a long-running story too, as historian Richard Hofstadter argued in the 1950s, but in recent years it has become decidedly more gendered. Girls and women were largely discouraged or shut out of learning until the mid-twentieth century, but now knowledge has become a primarily female virtue. Two-thirds of adults who say they never read a book are men, and book clubs might as well be called "women's night out," although men remain somewhat more likely to read newspapers and online news sites.[25]

At the same time that girls have been outperforming guys in school, younger women have become the majority in high-status professions like the law and are more prominent in positions of power. There are also reports, seized on by some aggrieved men, that childless millennial women in some fields and some cities are being paid more than single men. Women also have become the primary joiners: after courts struck down the legality of almost all males-only clubs in the 1980s, a good number of these organizations could not have survived without large numbers of women joining.[26]

All of this has contributed to an image problem for men. On the one hand, we still have the Rock, Bond, and other Hollywood and sports figures who are as hypermasculine as ever. On the other hand, we have sensitive guys like Jerry Seinfeld or Bono telling Congress about the dangers of toxic masculinity.[27] However, a third, less flattering view of men has also become au courant in popular culture since the 1990s.

Perhaps it all began with Kramer, the prototypical nonworking man-boy on the *Seinfeld* show, which debuted in 1989. Then came slacker movies like *Wayne's World* (1992) and TV series like *Beavis and Butthead* and *Jackass*, in which overage frat-boy types hung out in the basement, played heavy metal music, got high, and obsessed about "babes." The Coen brothers' *The Big Lebowski* (1998) follows an unemployed "dude" on his ventures through L.A. looking for roach clips. The lazy stoner became the stock-in-trade of actor Seth Rogen. In *Knocked Up* (2007) he played a guy who survived on disability payments and whose only claim to a vocation was running a porn site. The epitome of such men is Homer Simpson—lazy, vulgar, ignorant, and angry, in contrast to his sensible wife and whiz-kid daughter. As comedies, these movies and TV shows are not intended to elicit sympathy but to get laughs at the expense of nonworking, directionless, mindless loser men.

More subtle has been the change in big-screen heroism. While there are still a lot of male heroes, and while female heroes are still in a minority, even action films like *The Last Jedi* have a surfeit of men who are more likely to be whimpering, impulsive, or villainous (Luke Skywalker aside, of course!).

Portrayed as a troglodyte, a wimp, or a loser, told in one ear to "man up" and in the other to shed his toxic masculinity, what is a man to do? Women want "manly" guys. No, they want smart, thoughtful guys. These mixed messages and the confusion they engender (pun intended) have done a number on many American men's sense of their identity as a man. They also have gone a dangerously long way toward poisoning male-female relations. The notion of a battle between the sexes is as old as the hills (at least from the 1914 D. W. Griffith film to the 1973 Billie Jean King–Bobby Riggs tennis match), but the ante has been upped.

DATING, MASCULINITY, AND MALE-FEMALE RELATIONS

The dating world is ground zero for men's (and women's) uncertainties—and the fear and loathing they spawn—about what a "man" should be. At a time when marriage rates are plummeting among the less educated, marriage is being postponed by the educated until what used to be considered midlife, and dating apps like Tinder and websites like Match.com have millions of users, it's worth asking Freud's famous question, "What do women want?," and juxtaposing it with its parallel, "What do men want?"

It is abundantly clear that when it comes to men, some women increasingly aren't getting what they want. Most women still seek a responsible, working, ready-for-parenthood man. Many are clear that unemployed or underemployed men need not apply. A Pew survey found that 78 percent of never-married women say it's "very important" that a potential spouse have a steady job; by comparison, 46 percent of never-married men agree. And the proportion of women who want a good marriage has been going up, while the percentage of young men who want matrimonial bliss has fallen since the late 1990s.[28]

"There just aren't enough good men," or so say millions of single women; at least there aren't enough "regular good men" who aren't movie-star handsome or wealthy and don't have a wall full of prestigious degrees. Somewhere between urban legend and demographic determinism are tales of 40-year-old single "women being more likely to be killed by a terrorist than to get married." Yes, *Newsweek* actually reported this in 1986, only to have its sensational statistic quickly debunked. But the idea lives on and has more than a whiff of truth to it. In Washington, D.C., for example, there are about 1.4 college-educated single women for every college-educated man between 18 and 30.[29]

The horror stories of disappointed single women searching far and wide for a "good man" are legion (not that men don't have horror stories of their own). Well-educated urban women in the dating market complain that the only good men are gay or married. They are especially likely to recite a litany of cads and failed dates: men who have little to talk about except themselves or sports, men who are ill-mannered and slovenly, men who just want to "score," men who are overly needy, men who turn into stalkers, men who are commitment-phobic, men who have conveniently misplaced their wedding rings, men who can't find their wallets when the restaurant check arrives, and men who—when asked what they do—speak vaguely of "working for themselves." Women who have been married and supported husbands or ex-husbands who do little or no paying work and little in the way of taking care of kids or households also have choice words to describe their men.

The internet is afire with women's complaints about the modern man. One New York woman's diatribe that garnered 1.7 million Facebook "likes" described a city of "misfit men" where they make brunch reservations but can't make eggs, buy bottles of wine instead of flowers, and don't "chase you" but instead "chase you away." On websites like gurl.com and straightwhiteboystexting.org, women write of discarding "a decomposing trash heap of a boyfriend" and "send[ing] the SWB to hell."[30] Many women routinely say that men aren't worth a damn, rattling off perceptions as if they were rigorously proven facts: They're untrustworthy. They have affairs. They play video games. They drink.

The miasma of changing but poorly defined gender roles has not been easy for men. Some of them feel whipsawed by conflicting if not hypocritical expectations from women and do not really know what role to play: women want a man who is a feminist but still pays for everything; one who is suave and a well-toned hunk, a high-earner who is good in bed but who appreciates women for "who they are," not just their "looks"; one who listens, is sensitive and smart, but is also a knight in shining armor to protect them. Gender differences in communication styles, which linguist Deborah Tannen wrote about in the 1990s, can create misunderstandings at best, disasters at worst. An especially disturbing offshoot is how traditional masculinity teaches men to hear no as a problem to be solved, not a simple "That's it—no."[31]

Women and girls also get mixed messages in this long era of changing gender roles and norms, although the practical, behavioral, and psychological consequences tend to differ. Like most men, most women try their best to navigate these treacherous waters as best they can.

But there are significant gender differences. Eighty-three percent of college-age women want a traditional romantic relationship, compared to 63 percent of men their age, with a similar spread in the percentage of women (65 percent) versus men (45 percent) who want a hookup to lead to a committed relationship.[32] Women are also much more likely than men to seek a partner with an income and earning potential, whereas many men appear to want, in Donald Trump's caught-on-tape words, "pussy." Male accomplishment and power are still an aphrodisiac for women, while high-powered women either scare or turn off some men. As an e-Harmony advice column for women put it, "It's about the attraction, not your success."[33]

While the "terrorist" line is nonsense, what is new is the change in supply and demand. In 1960 there were 139 unmarried working men for every 100 unmarried women between the ages of 25 and 34; in 2014 there were 84 unmarried working men for every 100 women in that prime dating and mating age bracket. In Memphis that ratio falls to 59 to 100. It gets much worse for highly educated employed young women: there are only 67 working men between 25 and 34 with postgraduate degrees for every 100 unmarried women of the same ages and educational attainment. As women and men tend to date and marry those from their own social class, what was once a buyer's market for women has flipped to become a buyer's—or, perhaps more accurately, a renter's— market for men. As a Princeton University alumna wrote to female students in 2013, "Here's what nobody is telling you: Find a husband on campus before you graduate. You will never again be surrounded by this concentration of men who are worthy of you."[34]

This asymmetric marriage market is far worse among African Americans. The long-standing dearth of available and marriageable black men has left black women twice as likely to be single as white women (although the gap closes later in life). Nearly half of 25- to 34-year-old black men either do not have a high school degree, are formally unemployed, or are in prison. The short-lived VH1 TV show *Flavor of Love*, starring Flavor Flav of the rap group Public Enemy, captured what a lot of black women think: black men are non-working deadbeats and drug addicts.[35]

Between differing expectations and dismal statistics, what is a woman to do? Because many men steer clear of women who are too smart or successful, some women talk of dumbing themselves down or "trading down" to find a man. Others turn to the magic of plastic surgery and the short skirt and low-neckline blouse. Perhaps more than in the past, many women use sex as a bait, hoping they will catch and keep the prize fish.

Still others have gone off the dating grid, asking, like *New York Times* columnist Maureen Dowd, "Are men necessary?"[36] Growing numbers of women don't want to marry and, among divorcees, a significant number say they don't want to remarry, while men are much more interested in going back to the trough. So the $64,000 question is this: Are more women losing interest, or are more men losers (or both)?

Neither the travails of dating nor premarital sex are new, but six things are new in the twenty-first century: (1) the changing demographic ratio of employed, educated men to women; (2) a grossly unequal economy producing bad jobs that couples can't survive on in the lower tiers of the socioeconomic scale; (3) the decline of work among men; (4) heightened ambiguity about gender roles; (5) online dating; and (6) hookups.

DO ONLINE DATING AND THE HOOKUP CULTURE
SHAPE MEN'S ATTITUDES?

Online dating, which began around the turn of this century, has thrown into contact—and into bars and beds—millions upon millions of men and women who otherwise never would have met. Match.com reports that nearly half of America's 87 million singles use online dating sites. Tinder, which started in 2012 as an app to basically facilitate no-strings sex, produced 26 million matches per day in 2017. These have led to successful relationships and mar-riage, but they've also spawned many a nightmare.[37]

"People have so many options to hook up, so they try to keep their options open and keep looking for the perfect person," said a white New York woman with two advanced degrees who uses an online service. "But it also creates distance, as people can string things out with messages and never pick up the phone. It's so impersonal, it makes it very easy to blow someone off." If an actual date follows, it's often a prelude to either an immediate expectation of sex or "ghosting," disappearing without so much as a good-bye or "I'm sorry, this doesn't seem right."

Despite its anodyne claims that it "helps expand your social group," Tinder has taken online dating a step further, becoming the ideal app for this age of parlous male-female relations. Swipe right and nearby potential matches, often looking for quick, convenient sex, appear. Said to be used equally by women and men, Tinder is viewed by some as a way to boost male egos and, with its emphasis on appearance, the quintessence of objectifying the opposite sex.[38]

With even more anonymity than Match, and with Tinder's emphasis on sex, a number of women say that the app has become a hotbed of male vul-garity and misogyny. As one woman recounted, "He only waited twenty-two words to mention his erection." Another woman told *Vanity Fair* that the app makes women feel like "an option" for men who have "pussy affluenza." To many women, men on Tinder are "fuckboys," while men's sobriquet for women is "Tinderellas."[39]

Tinder is very much consonant with the broader advent of the hookup culture, one embraced by both women and men but also often seen as an affirmation of traditional masculine notions of sexual prowess. Eschewing romantic relationships, or even the counterculture's political gloss of "free love" or the studied, flirtatious game culminating in the one-night stand of late twentieth-century singles culture, hookups are more transactional—and dangerous.

Hookups, whether one-on-one, at a party, or in another group situation, are essentially agreements, sometimes explicit, often tacit, to have sex. Al-though many women and some men see a hookup as a prelude to a rela-tionship, hookup norms generally make emotional attachment a taboo and prescribe "meaningless" (as opposed to "meaningful") sex, according to Lisa Wade, author of *American Hookup*.[40]

A Kinsey Institute researcher estimated that 60–80 percent of college students have had at least one hookup, likely an exaggerated number given that other surveys show that two in five students are virgins or have had only one relationship by the time of graduation. Nonetheless, in colleges, high schools, and the adult world, casual hookups or app-assisted ones like those enabled by Tinder, Grindr (for gay men), or Bumble (geared to women) are common.[41]

Some say that hookups are actually beneficial to women since they enable them to focus on academics and finding a job without getting bogged down in relationships.[42] However, many women, men, and social scientists believe that hookups favor men, reinforcing toxic masculine aspirations to chalk up sexual conquests. Hookups can leave women devalued and traumatized, and they face greater risks—sexual violence, pregnancy, and sexually transmitted diseases. Often lubricated with abundant alcohol and drugs, hookups frequently go bad, veering from consensual sex to sexual assault and rape, with as many as half of college women reporting incidents of unwanted sex, typically during a hookup. By contrast, men still generally decide whether a woman is relationship material or just the hot body du jour, and men are much more likely than women to demand and get oral and anal sex. As writer Amber Lapp says, "Hookup culture, strongly masculinized, demands carelessness, rewards callousness, and punishes kindness."[43]

"It's possible for a man to brag about a hookup, perhaps as a 'conquest,'" one male college student observed. "It isn't possible for a woman to do that. If she discusses it with others, it's something to be kept mostly quiet. If she's seen walking late at night with her hair disheveled, it's a 'walk of shame.'"

The hookup and Tinder cultures are at one end of a continuum in today's dating world, with casual, serial relationships more the norm for most in their 20s, 30s, and older. Marriage is a more distant goal for many better-educated men and women and elusive for many less educated Americans.

This new dating and mating environment parallels changing attitudes about the opposite sex and new and dangerous tensions between men and women. It is clear that a lot of women see the pool of males as filled with too many losers, and many men are less than enthusiastic about the state of male-female relations. This has coincided with a striking rise in misogyny among some men, especially younger ones.

MEN AREN'T NEEDED, OR SO THEY SAY

Before we go into the dark world of misogyny, it should be noted that this is a two-way street: women, too, play a part in these tensions, and their role should not be overlooked. We often hear about the lack of "good men" or that "women don't need men." The quote, often wrongly attributed to Gloria Steinem, that "a woman needs a man like a fish needs a bicycle" is all too frequently recounted, dripping with what writer Cathy Young has called "ironic misandry." Tales of abusive, cheating, good-for-nothing men have been a staple of country music from Nancy Sinatra's "These Boots Are Made for Walking" (1966) to the Dixie Chicks' "Goodbye Earl" (2000), but a host of contemporary angry songs portray men as liars (Beyoncé's "Resentment," 2006), violent (Queen Latifah's "U.N.I.T.Y," 1993), rapists (Angel Haze's "Cleaning Out My Closet," 2012), and as the eponymous subject of Kate Nash's "Dickhead" (2007). The theme that men are unnecessary at best is popular in the "angry woman" genre, with songs like "Independent Woman" (2001) from Destiny's Child and "I Don't Need a Man" (2006) by the Pussycat Dolls. As the latter sing:

> I don't need a man to make me feel good
> I get off doing my thing
> I don't need a ring around my finger
> To make me feel complete
> So let me break it down
> I can get off when you ain't around, oh!

With support from both radical feminists and a number of Homer Simpson–like characters in contemporary popular culture, trashing men, or at least making fun of them, has become a reliable punch line, accepted by many women who would rightly find similar putdowns of women sexist and anything but cool. Words putting down male behavior, such as "mansplaining" or "manterrupting," have entered the popular argot. Social media sites overflow with women's horror stories about men they've dated or married, not to mention news stories like one in the "science" section of the Broadly website, "Men Are Creepy, New Study Confirms." [44]

MISOGYNY

Women and men have always joked about or put down the opposite sex, but the hostility on both sides has become more shrill, much as in politics and other spheres of contemporary American life. The internet and social media play a big role in disseminating and reinforcing these less than savory views, but the medium isn't entirely the message. Modern misogyny has other roots.

Although there may be roots in sexism or some men's perception of "reverse sexism," misogyny goes far beyond holding traditional views of masculinity or arguing that feminism has had some negative effects on men. The Southern Poverty Law Center, known for its monitoring of racism and other prejudice, has designated misogynists a "hate group."[45]

What does misogyny in the late 2010s look like? And why is it on the rise?

When Fox news presenter Megyn Kelly called Donald Trump to account for calling women "fat pigs, dogs, slobs, and disgusting animals," he tweeted that she was a "bimbo" and later said she had blood "coming out of her wherever." The 2016 election brought out Trump supporters wearing T-shirts and buttons with slogans like "Hillary sucks, but not like Monica" and "Life's a Bitch: Don't Vote for One."[46]

Trump may have made misogyny more acceptable, but he hardly accounts for the extent or depth of so many men's apparent loathing of women. Female journalists, politicians, ex-girlfriends, and ex-wives are frequent targets of anonymous online abuse. Scorned and angry men post nude photos of their exes as "revenge porn," and high school he-men "sext" photos of girls they've slept with. Words like "bitch" and "slut" are prominent in the misogynist vocabulary. Grisly fantasies of rape, murder, and other violence are described in detail. In March 2013, T-shirts emblazoned with "Keep Calm and Rape a Lot," "Keep Calm and Hit Her," and other offensive phrases were for sale on Amazon for several hours until the company became aware of them. Rap music frequently glorifies rape, from early Dr. Dre songs like "B*tches Ain't Sh*t" (1992) to Eminem's "Love Game" (2013), which plays out a particularly violent rape-murder. Lest anyone think that such thoughts or language are restricted to doltish or provocative men, clearly many powerful, well-educated, seemingly liberal men from Bill Cosby and Harvey Weinstein to Anthony Weiner and Charlie Rose (hardly "men out") are only somewhat more discreetly guilty. A study of male economics Ph.D. students found that the most used words to anonymously describe women in an online jobs forum included "slut," "tits," "vagina," "hot," and "feminazi."[47]

One internet warrior raging against "misandrists" wrote, "They should all be jailed for minimum two years in re-education camps, with special favors, and much shorter sentences for the females who learn to suck cock." Another wrote about women with "flabby, bitchy, asses who want to castrate men." And the bile goes on.

Some misogynists have acted on their hatred. John Russell Houser shot and killed two women and injured eight others in Lafayette, Louisiana, in 2015 after going on talk radio to denounce "the growing power of women." The year before, in Isla Vista, California, Elliot Rodger, an "involuntary celibate," or "incel," killed six and wounded seven others after the 22-year-old complained on YouTube that women wouldn't pay attention to him and said that he wanted to "slaughter every single spoiled, stuck-up blond slut I see."[48]

It's not surprising that sexual violence is widespread, although data are notoriously unreliable in light of what many women and police say is underreporting and what some men say is overreporting. Justice Department statistics show a decline in rape since the 1970s, although headlines often proclaim that rape and domestic violence are "soaring," and some data show a sharp rise in reports of sexual assault on college campuses. Stories of parties where men drug and rape women are all too common. A woman at a Minnesota college recounted how all of her friends who went to a party during the first week of classes had been drugged, raped, and woke up in a field far from the campus.[49]

Yet some men emphasize an alternative view of the problem of sexual assault. Even before the #MeToo movement, they were saying they were afraid to go on dates, be alone with women, or even give a pat on the shoulder, out of fear they would be accused of sexual assault or harassment. Some of the problem swings back to issues with masculinity. Moreover, sexual assault in which men are victims has been an all but taboo subject, even though the Centers for Disease Control and Prevention (CDC) report that men are nearly as likely as women to experience coerced sex other than rape.[50]

"Definitions have been expanded over the last few decades to include ridiculous things," said Harry Crouch, president of the National Coalition for Men (NCFM). "One military man was kicked out because he touched a woman's button while dancing." The fight against what one Maryland group, SAVE Services, calls "rape hoaxes" was given considerable ammunition by the infamous, and discredited, *Rolling Stone* article about an alleged fraternity gang rape at the University of Virginia. One web blog, *Community of the Wrongly Accused*, collects stories of purportedly made-up rapes. President Trump's education secretary, Betsy DeVos, gave succor to these men in 2017, saying, "Their stories are not often shared," and the department issued guidance to colleges to raise evidentiary standards to protect the accused. The department's acting head of the Office for Civil Rights, Candice Jackson, went further. "Ninety percent" of accusations "fall into the category of 'we were both drunk,' 'we broke up, and six months later I found myself under a Title IX investigation because she just decided that our last sleeping together was not quite right,'" she said. Jackson later apologized for the comment.[51]

MEN'S RIGHTS AND THE MANOSPHERE

The false sexual assault argument, along with arguments about female-favored divorce laws and perhaps reverse discrimination, is the somewhat legitimate tip of the iceberg of a significant male subculture called the "manosphere" and the loosely related men's rights movement.

Groups like the National Coalition for Men started to spring up in the 1970s, in part in reaction to feminism, in part as an offshoot of the consciousness-raising groups of that era, and in part to draw attention to long-ignored men's problems. Joseph Pleck, in *The Myth of Masculinity* (1981), offered an early critique of traditional masculinity and the harm that it did to men. More influential was Robert Bly's *Iron John* (1990), which drew on Jungian psychology and myth to argue that "the warriors inside American men have become weak" and to exalt an archetypal "Wild Man" whose "job is to teach the young man how abundant, various, and many-sided his manhood is."[52]

In response to the growing crisis of absent fathers, as well as divorce and custody laws that favored mothers, a fatherhood movement gained steam in the 1990s. David Blankenhorn drew attention to what he called "our most urgent social problem" in his book *Fatherless America* (1995). Together with social scientists Wade Horn and Mitch Pearlstein, Blankenhorn issued the movement's "call to action" in 1999. With more fervor, Nation of Islam leader Louis Farrakhan organized the Million Man March in Washington, D.C., in 1995, with the intention of raising awareness about the dire social and economic conditions of great numbers of African American men and combating negative stereotypes about black males. Promise Keepers, an evangelical group founded in 1990, urged men "to drop the normal posturing and humble ourselves in Jesus Christ," and make seven promises, emphasizing strong male relationships and marriages based on biblical values; the group also staged a massive rally in Washington in 1997.[53]

Warren Farrell, author of *The Liberated Man* (1974) and *The Myth of Male Power* (2001), initially tried to ally the nascent men's movement with feminism, arguing that gender equality required a joint male-female effort to support equal economic, political, and family rights. When leaders of the National Organization for Women opposed the presumption of joint custody, saying it was a ruse by men to not pay child support, Farrell became an ardent advocate for fathers and something of a pariah among feminists. "The parallel to equality in the workplace for women is for men to have equal opportunity as fathers," Farrell told me.[54]

The broad idea of promoting more engaged fatherhood has drawn together strange bedfellows, from conservative Republicans and the Christian right to a host of social scientists, fathers, men's rights advocates, feminists, and leading figures on the left, such as former president Obama. Yet it remains an uphill struggle.[55]

More radical are men's groups like the California-based NCFM, which denounces the many ways in which "men have been systematically discriminated against." These include not only parenting rights and sexual violence laws that neglect male victims but also government benefits and the dearth of research on men and men's health. NCFM president Harry Crouch acknowledges that "feminism did some good things" but argues that half of sexual assault allegations are untrue, that 50–70 percent of domestic violence is perpetrated by women, and that 70–90 percent of courts' divorce orders give sole or primary physical custody to mothers.[56]

While one prominent fathers' rights advocate called much of the men's rights movement "nuts," there are more extreme tributaries. The "manosphere" is a mostly online assemblage of websites like MenAreBetterThanWomen.com, Reddit feeds, and largely millennial followers that simultaneously denounce women and proffer advice on how to pick up women. A guru for "pickup artists" (PUAs), Roosh V has written sex travel guides like "Bang Brazil" and talks of "hate fucks." Brimming with misogyny and men's tales of being dumped or spurned by women (usually called by more derogatory terms), one "manifesto" proclaims, "The Manosphere is the Big Bang of chaotic masculine disruption that will eventually bring into existence a new personal world of freedom for those who choose to be free."[57]

The bible of the manosphere is a 2016 film and concept called "the Red Pill."[58] Drawing on the Keanu Reeves character in the 1999 film *The Matrix*, who takes a red pill to exit a pseudo-reality for a genuine one, Red Pillers' reality is that men are the oppressed gender. As in other corners of the manosphere, the Red Pill seems deeply contradictory in that women are described in graphically vile terms yet are to be seduced as much as possible. It's tempting to see this as a to-the-barricades call for revolution by rape.

Another manosphere manifestation is known as Men Going Their Own Way (MGTOW). MGTOWs seek to avoid relationships with women, whom they see as manipulative, and focus on taking care of themselves. The MGTOW Facebook page shows a fork in the road, with one path leading to a stormy world labeled "Misandry" and the other leading to a sunny paradise labeled "Freedom." As a Maryland therapist said, "It's their way of creating an island of sanity in what seems like a turbulent world of relationships. It's a sanctuary of sorts. They feel they can't navigate these constantly changing relationship environments."[59] Self-proclaimed MGTOWs may be relatively rare, although a striking number of heterosexual young men do not want to date or become involved with women.

THE PROGRESSIVE MEN'S MOVEMENT

Far from the manosphere and the MGTOWs is another men's movement that highlights and promotes men's departure from toxic masculinity and embraces more egalitarian ideas and roles. Rob Okun, a member of the steering committees for the North America MenEngage Network and the Center for Men and Masculinities, has been publishing a quarterly magazine, *Voice Male: The Untold Story of the Profeminist Men's Movement*, in Amherst, Massachusetts, since 1983. It aims to show "a way for men to live that is centered not on their masculinity, but on their humanity."[60]

Michael S. Kimmel and Michael A. Mess have edited a textbook of essays on the "pro-feminist men's movement." *Manhood 2.0*, developed by the nonprofits Promundo and Child Trends, is one of a growing number of curricula to teach young men that masculinity doesn't have to be toxic. The American Psychological Association also launched a division for psychologists studying men and masculinity.[61]

Many men have comfortably adapted to—or grown up with—more egalitarian gender norms that don't require being male to mean being hypermasculine. As Marcos, a Latino man in his early 30s in Washington, D.C., said, "Equality is beneficial to men because it makes our society more productive. More folks, men and women, are working, providing for families, contributing to the economy, and innovating." A white Minnesota man in his 50s was also positive about changing gender roles. "It's allowed men to have more authentic relationships with women," he said. And Julie Vogtman, senior counsel for the Family Economic Security Program at the National Women's Law Center, whose husband "does more than I do," said that "many men are taking on more child care and work in the home than they used to do."[62]

Although this book will have more to say about marriage and fatherhood, it's clear that some men are doing well with less traditional masculine prescriptions and proscriptions, while others are having a very hard time. Some of these men out believe that women have taken the field, leaving more and more males on the sidelines. Feeling put down, scorned, and rejected by women seeking higher-quality male companionship, their own feelings of oppression and inferiority too often translate into rage.

CHAPTER 4

The New Lost Boys

Millennials at Home and at Sea

When I'm lyin' in my bed at night
I don't wanna grow up
Nothing ever seems to turn out right
I don't wanna grow up.
　　　　　　　—*Tom Waits, "I Don't Wanna Grow Up," 1992*

In Milton Bradley's Game of Life, the popular, not so subtly normative, mid-twentieth-century board game, players quickly proceeded to college or on a vocational track and soon after got jobs, married, bought a house, and added the little pink or blue plastic pegs that represented babies

Once upon a time, in those increasingly misty days in the 1960s and early 1970s, the typical man married at 23 and the typical woman at 21—six and half years younger than today for both.[1] That man took a job, usually for life, climbed the career ladder, bought a house, had a houseful of kids, and was a responsible adult at an age that is now in the inner suburbs of adolescence. Constricted as this picture may seem, those who didn't follow that path were either gay, rebels without much of a cause, enthralled by *Playboy* magazine's curious notions of "bachelorhood," or just plain losers. But their numbers were small.

That picture has changed radically, as 13 million young adult males in their 20s and early 30s now live at "home," having moved back or never left.

They live with middle-age and aging parents. Millions more are living with other relatives, friends, or roommates, and at least three quarters of a million are behind bars. Similarly, about 13 million are not working. For those who are, median wages have fallen and their jobs are less secure than a few decades ago. To top it off, childless women in their 20s earn more on average than childless men. Most of the 38 million men who are so-called millennials haven't married, and most births to under-30 couples are outside of marriage. It's as if 25 or 28 is the new 15.[2]

These men are more likely than men of other generations or women of their generation to not be religious, not vote, not be patriotic, and not be willing to sacrifice. Depression has become more common with these men as "deaths of despair," in the words of Princeton economists Angus Deaton and Anne Case—from opioid, heroin, and alcohol overdoses and suicide—have spiked upward. And they are less likely to work.[3]

Even though the data speak for themselves, millennials need a good publicist. They've gotten a particularly bad rap as lazy, entitled, irresponsible slackers. They've been variously called the "go-nowhere generation," "the new unemployables," and "man-boys."[4] This stereotype immediately brings to mind young men, although there has been surprisingly little discussion of millennial gender differences and how the state of young men differs from that of young women beyond the fact that young women outnumber young men in higher education.

Life is not a bed of roses for many young people in other developed countries, although phenomena such as high rates of nonmarital childbearing and opioid addiction are uniquely American, and the social policy context in some OECD nations provides more supports. However, in Japan, asexual "grass-eating men" frustrate women, and millions toil in dead-end jobs, as depicted in Tomoyuki Hoshino's novel We (2017). Close to half of 20-something Spaniards are out of work. And up to half of young men in southern and eastern European countries live with their parents.[5]

Named generations are slippery, artificial constructs, and there isn't even a lot of consensus about who millennials are. There has been some hubbub that the number of millennials, 71 million strong in 2016, is surpassing the number of baby boomers. Although the U.S. Census has included all those born between 1982 and 2000 as millennials, the most common definition of members of this benighted generation is that they were born between 1981 and about 1996.[6] Nor is it so clear that borderline members of the supposedly distinct Generation Z or iGen, born between about 1997 and 2012, will be terribly different from millennials in terms of their life trajectories and beliefs.[7]

This chapter examines why so many under-35 men are on the sidelines. Is it because they are immature, have been raised to be dependent, and have "failed to launch"? Have the economic problems discussed in chapter 2 also been responsible for huge numbers of young men returning to live in their parents' homes or with roommates, not marrying or "starting life," and all too often being angry, anxious, and addicted?

MEN OUT ARE ESPECIALLY LIKELY TO BE YOUNG

A sizable proportion of America's men out consists of these young men in their 20s and early to mid-30s. Indeed, there are far more of them than the middle-age white factory workers who have lost their jobs. While there are striking class divides between successful millennials and those who have been left behind, these young men out come from all races and ethnicities, all parts of the country, and from every imaginable background. However, compared to the overall U.S. population, they are disproportionately Latino, African American, and Asian American.

Jeremy, 26 and white, went to Catholic school as a kid in a once-thriving factory town near the Great Lakes. His parents were both teachers, education was a priority, and he had aspired to be valedictorian and go to a top state university ever since middle school.

However, larger economic problems intervened. His town's steady loss of jobs led the school and church to close, so Jeremy transferred in tenth grade to another Catholic school in a town about fifteen miles away. New to the school, he sought to be accepted and fell in with a group of guys who smoked pot and vied for sexual conquests. His once straight-arrow academic pursuits fell by the wayside, and when it was time to apply for college, he was rejected by the school he had always hoped to attend.

Instead, he got into a lower-tier college known for students' widespread drug use. Jeremy got a job waiting tables at a national chain restaurant but spent his money on Percocet. When the dealers weren't on campus, he would drive to the city a few hours away to buy what he needed. Nonetheless, after two years of getting at least somewhat back into his academic groove, Jeremy was able to transfer to the university of his childhood dreams.

Then things took another turn for the worse. Jeremy got into heroin and would be strung out in bed for days in the apartment he shared with a hometown friend, only to make his way back to classes for a few days. There were not only shady characters drifting in and out but also robberies, and friends described Jeremy's behavior as increasingly bizarre. Fortunately, his roommate told his parents, who called Jeremy's parents. Although they were in the midst of a nasty divorce, they drove together to the campus and brought him home.

He got drug treatment and eventually made it back to the first college he had attended, from which he recently graduated. The last that he was heard from, he had a girlfriend but was living at home and not working.

Then there are guys like Connor, a young white man who aspired to be a doctor yet dropped out of college twice and is making $10.50 an hour at a big-box store in central Arkansas.

Since his parents were intent on his becoming a minister, he started college, studying religion and foreign languages. After initially getting good grades, the pressure of taking multiple language classes started to turn him off from his studies. He switched majors several times, but he stopped caring about assignments. Neither the major his parents had chosen for him nor his new majors appealed to him. His grades suffered because he didn't really know what he wanted to do, and he seemed to be rebelling against his parents' wishes.

The warnings from his college counselor fell on deaf ears until the counselor called Connor's parents. His parents told him that if he wasn't going to take college seriously, then he shouldn't be wasting their money paying for it. So he dropped out again.

A few months later he decided to try school once more, transferring to a college closer to his parents so that he could live with them. When the new school told him that none of his earlier credits would transfer because his GPA had been so low, he decided he'd rather quit college than retake all those classes.

Connor needed money, so he took odd jobs as a restaurant host, a laborer, and filing papers in a lawyer's office. When a friend with a degree in management information systems told Connor how much he was making, Connor got defensive, saying he could make just as much money without a degree.

But his dreams of becoming a doctor seem far away, even though his parents still have some savings in case he makes a third attempt at college.

There always have been men who have failed, faltered, or fumbled, but stories like Jeremy's and Connor's were the exception, at least for young white men, during the decades after World War II. By their early to mid-20s, most of these men had achieved, or were on their way to achieving, five milestones of adulthood: (1) working in a full-time, permanent job, (2) finding a woman to marry, (3) moving into their own home, (4) having children, and (5) saving money. By the 2010s, for many young men the first, third, and fifth of these milestones were simply out of reach, while the second and fourth were no longer priorities.[8]

"EMERGING ADULTHOOD" OR "FAILURE TO LAUNCH"?

Trying to account for these changes from the standpoint of developmental psychology, Clark University psychologist Jeffrey Jensen Arnett coined the term "emerging adulthood" in 2004. Putting a somewhat rosy spin on things, Arnett spoke of this life stage—from about 18 to 30—as both a time of instability and "feeling in between" and one of "identity exploration and possibilities." By contrast, the mid-twentieth-century psychologist Erik Erikson wrote of the teens and 20s as a time when an individual ideally develops an ego identity and finds intimacy.[9]

"Arnett's thinking—that it's a great thing that they can do volunteer work in Africa—is very upper middle class," said Jean Twenge, author of *Generation Me* and *iGen* and a psychology professor at San Diego State University. "Working-class kids can't do that. If you're not working or working at a junky job, that's not 'exploring your options.' It's going nowhere at all."[10]

Unlike Dustin Hoffman's character in *The Graduate* (1968), who was adrift for a single summer after college graduation, a huge proportion of millennial males (and a good number of millennial women) remain "in between," mired in "role confusion" (what Erikson negatively juxtaposed with ego identity), and men out throughout their 20s and beyond. *Failure to Launch*, the title of a 2006 romantic comedy, became a popular phrase among many social scientists and journalists, just as "adulting" has become popular among young people, who "adult less than 50 percent of the time," according to the Urban Dictionary.[11]

Mid-twentieth-century norms of maturity have given way to what looks an awful lot like immaturity. These norms go seamlessly hand in hand with traditional norms of masculinity. Author Gary Cross writes, "The culture of the boy-men today is less a life stage than a lifestyle."[12] Once again, lousy economic conditions are important, but lifestyles are not forced on people; they also choose whether or not to live in accord with certain norms and mores.

Which brings us to Peter Pan. Are these young men who have climbed off the once normative developmental ladder a twenty-first-century version of Pan's "lost boys"?

It's long been known that boys mature later than girls, even though in recent years we have seen the contrary trends of earlier puberty and prolonged adolescence for both sexes. Nonetheless, the definition of "boy" and "girl" long meant someone under the age of 18. In this era of political correctness, calling someone who is at least 18 a "boy" or "girl" instead of "young man" or "young woman" is widely seen as demeaning. Yet for many of them, this moniker of maturity may not fit.

Looking back, for much of the twentieth century, at 18 you either went to work or to college, and in Eisenhower- and Kennedy-era America, you were typically a real, adult "man" or "woman" by your early 20s, self-supporting, married, and ready to start a family. During World War II, millions of 18-year-old men idealistically and courageously volunteered to fight to defeat fascism. Go further back in history, and teenage boys worked in the family business or on the family farm.

Such creatures today are virtually extinct. For all too many early twenty-first-century young men, the biblical precept no longer holds: "When I was a child, I used to speak like a child, think like a child, reason like a child; when I became a man, I put childish things behind me."[13]

Boyhood, or at least a crude caricature of adolescence, has crept ever further into more men's life cycles as the "prime of life" has become like an eroding tropical island, squeezed into fewer years of an ever longer life span. In popular culture the battle cry of *Wayne's World* (1992) was "Party on, Wayne," while in *Step-Brothers* (2008) Will Ferrell and John C. Reilly played 40-year-old adolescents with thinning hair and sagging paunches getting their jollies from pissing matches and karate competitions in the basement.

How did this happen?

Once again, cultural and economic factors vie for attention.

HELICOPTER PARENTS AND THE TROPHY GENERATION?

Often cited among the cultural changes is a widespread change in parenting and expectations for children. Enter the so-called helicopter parents and their offspring, the "trophy generation." Much-maligned baby boomer parents hovered over their children from infancy to college, planning their lives to the nth degree for the sake of their kids' intellectual and social stimulation and safety, as well as to demonstrate to one and all that they have been good, involved parents. From the first pretoddler play group to the digital tether of constant texts and emails at college, these are busy, low-flying helicopters.

They coddled, choreographed, and chaperoned their children from music lesson, to soccer practice, to play dates, to Cub Scouts or Brownies, volunteering in their children's classrooms, and—often relearning geometry or rereading *Lord of the Flies*—doing their homework for them. Wendy Mogel, a clinical psychologist and author of *The Blessing of a B-Minus* claims that children of helicopter parents often have been unable to become adults because of their parents' overprotectiveness and failure to let them struggle.[14]

"Free-range" childhood, in which children fended for themselves after school, gave way by the turn of the twenty-first century to empty streets as kids either were shuttled to programmed activities or became glued to their screens. "When I was growing up, we'd go out from morning to evening," recalled a 66-year-old white Vietnam veteran in Pennsylvania. "I'd take my bike and a baseball bat and I'd meet other kids, and we'd have a pickup game and bike on and meet other kids and have another game. There were no leagues or uniforms or organizing by parents."

Like millennials, these largely baby boomer helicopter parents are popular media targets and widely seen as doing more harm than good. *Time* magazine managed to knock both with a 2014 cover story titled "Millennials Are Selfish and Entitled: Blame Helicopter Parents." The *National Review* damned both in "Blame Parents for Millennials' Laughable Fragility."[15]

Schools and sports teams, undoubtedly pressured by these parents, have brought us grade inflation and awards for all, with the fictive notion that everyone is a winner. Having taught at a university for a number of years, I can't count the numerous times when students doing mediocre work complained that they didn't get As and students who did poor work griped about not getting Bs.

In addition, some parents deem all manner of things dangerous—from playground equipment and peanut butter to the perceived need to institute "trigger warnings" about domestic violence in F. Scott Fitzgerald's *The Great Gatsby* and "microaggressions," such as expecting a black student to have the most informed views on racism. Some students say this description is a caricature, true of only a few of their more radical peers. Comedians like Jerry Seinfeld and Chris Rock are wary of performing at colleges, saying that students can't take a joke. The needs to succeed and be safe—regardless of whether effort is put into achieving these—have led to increased anxiety and depression on campuses, college counselors report.[16]

Sergeant First Class Tifani Hightower, an army company commander in Brunswick, Georgia, told me, "Parents don't push kids to try things, and they

give them an out—they can quit softball if they don't like it. . . . In this trophy
generation, everyone's a winner. Parents give kids the message to be afraid of
failure."[17]

Many millennials agree. "American men my age are severely lacking in
confidence," said Manuel, a Washingtonian in his early 30s. "We've been told
we're entitled to things, yet we've never been pushed to work to earn those
things."

Christopher, the 30-year-old Virginia man, agreed:

Too few upper-middle-class millennials like myself were given the opportunity to fail on our own merits. It was great that our parents gave
us books and had computers in their houses early on and were willing
to drive us to extracurricular activities. I'm also eternally grateful that
my parents could afford speech therapy and the medication I needed.
But when I got my driver's license and started driving to high school,
my parents paid for car insurance and gas. When I was too lazy to fill
out college application forms, my mom did them for me. And when I
made the mistake of going to graduate school, thinking it would be an
automatic ticket to a good job, my parents made the mistake of lending
me the money to pay for it.

For those not getting trophies—at least in the white, upper half of the
income distribution—the *Diagnostic and Statistical Manual of Mental
Disorders*, 5th edition (*DSM-5*), and the therapeutic professions are here
to help. "Everything that deviates becomes a psychological diagnosis," a
Baltimore-area therapist who works with adolescents told me. One in seven
5- to 17-year-old boys is diagnosed with attention deficit hyperactivity disorder
(ADHD), compared to one in sixteen girls, according to the CDC. Male children of white, better-educated parents are more likely to receive this diagnosis
than African Americans, Latinos, or kids whose parents didn't graduate from
high school. Boys are also twice as likely to be diagnosed with behavioral or
conduct disorders, clinical diagnoses that were added to the *DSM-5* in 2013,
and three to four times as likely to be diagnosed with autism.[18]

"Once you start labeling and diagnosing, it becomes a self-fulfilling
prophecy," the therapist added. "It works against young men feeling capable,
competent, self-assured. They're so cowed and intimidated by how they're
diagnosed and labeled and scrutinized. It leaves precious little initiative."

Of course, the helicopters mostly fly in middle- and upper-middle-class neighborhoods. Not all parents fit this mold, and huge numbers of American children face the opposite problem to overprotective coddling—that is, absent parents, disengaged parents, and abusive parents. Poor and working-class boys often don't have fathers to guide them, and boys tend to be more adversely affected by single-parent families than girls.[19] Although Jason, a millennial from a well-to-do family, said he "secretly envies guys further down the economic ladder because they had to struggle and discipline themselves more than I did," in reality, most of those who started on the bottom rungs are still there, and those rungs have become more precarious over the last few decades.

SOME ECONOMIC INDICATORS MAY BE SUNNY, BUT IT'S STORMY FOR MILLENNIAL GUYS

Men of all ages have suffered and been sidelined in the world of work, but economic metrics paint a portrait of a generation of young men who are especially likely to be on the outs.

Whereas 25 percent of 25- to 34-year-old men had incomes of less than $30,000 a year in 1975 (in 2015 dollars), in 2016, 41 percent did. Poverty rates have risen considerably since 1980. In 2014 one in five young adults lived below the official poverty line, up from one in seven when Ronald Reagan was elected president; for an individual, this means they had incomes below about $12,000. One-third had incomes below 150 percent of the federal poverty guidelines. Median income for young men has declined since 1975, with a steeper falloff for 25- to 34-year-old men—from about $46,000 to $40,000— and the sharpest rate of decline occurring since 2000. Even college graduates earned less in 2013 than in the late 1990s, although fortunes improved a bit in the mid-2010s. Stanford economist Raj Chetty, a leading expert on social mobility, found that fewer than half of all millennials born in the 1980s grew up to outearn their parents, compared to 92 percent of those born during World War II. Equally ominous is the Federal Reserve statistic that median net worth for those under 35 has fallen by more than one-third in the last decade to a paltry $10,400.[20]

Economic factors discussed in chapter 2 apply to millennial men with a vengeance. "No demographic group has been as adversely affected by the recession as young adult men under 30," an American Academy of Political and Social Science report proclaimed.[21]

Work has become progressively less common. Only 71 percent of 18- to 34-year-old men were employed in 2014, compared to 84 percent in 1960.

By 2015, 22 percent of men in their 20s without bachelor's degrees had not worked at all in the past year, a proportion that had more than doubled since 2000. Teenage work has also sharply declined, from 76 percent in the late 1970s to 55 percent in the mid-2010s among high school seniors, perhaps setting the stage for the decline in young adult work. Again, the class divide is severe: the employment rate for all millennials with at least a bachelor's degree was a staggering 35 percentage points higher than it was for those their age who failed to finish high school (87 percent versus 52 percent), and the rate for men without a college degree fell by a full 10 percentage points during the first fifteen years of this century. While rising college attendance since the 1960s and 1970s accounts for some of the overall decline in young male employment, male graduation rates have essentially flatlined in the 2010s.[22]

A particularly troubling subset of these young men is the population that some alternatively have called "disconnected youth" or "NEETS," meaning not in education, employment, or training. Young women are more likely than men to be in this population, and they are disproportionately people of color. About 4.3 million males between 16 and 29 fell into this category in 2015. Among 16- to 24-year-olds, 26 percent of black men were "disconnected," compared to 20 percent of Latinos and 17 percent of whites.[23]

In contrast to many millennial men, Randy, 31, knows he has had a privileged life. He grew up in a wealthy enclave near Los Angeles, is white, was an Eagle Scout, participated in several extracurricular activities in high school, and graduated from the University of California. He spent his mid-20s in East Asia, teaching English, traveling, and working with friends on a startup in China after he learned Mandarin. He also has a trust fund.

Smart, articulate, and generally upbeat, he came back to the United States when he was 27 but has never been able to find anything better than temporary or contract work. "My idea was to build a career straddling America and Asia," he said. "It's been four years and it's been a rough go of it. There aren't too many opportunities for people with my background." Randy compares his generation to that of his baby boomer parents. As he tells it, they were interested in particular careers and "just walked into" them.

He says his generation's priorities are different: "We don't need a big house and fancy car, just a reasonable house and car. We want jobs we believe in, not just a paycheck."

Nonetheless, Randy feels unsettled and wants to be "established." And despite his family's money, he said, "I know that if I had more discretionary income, I'd be in better shape. Right now I pinch pennies." He also knows that if he could get a full-time job with health insurance, he could get the medication he needs.

While some of his peers have found good careers and married, a lot of them came out of the once free California state university system with $70,000 in college debt. He tells of a good friend who had a panic attack on the job, leading him to resign, after which the friend and his wife moved in with the friend's parents. Another man he knows suffers from depression and lived with his parents until he was 30.

As far as work, he said, "I don't want to work the crappy, entry-level job and grind through that for ten years, maybe making $35,000. I have a high opinion of my abilities, but maybe I'm fooling myself. So should I take a crappy job?"

Randy was a Bernie Sanders supporter because of what "the country has gone through under this neoliberal capitalist society," he said. Yet he's anything but enthusiastic about the Democratic Party and less than hopeful about American politics. "The left says they'll give us gay marriage and abortion, but otherwise they're pretty much the same as the conservatives."

The inequality seen in America at large is especially glaring among America's 38 million millennial men—not a happy portent for those hoping for a more egalitarian society. Whereas the tale of two cities for the entire nation may be one of a gated community and a big city, for young adult males it is one of an exclusive resort and a sprawling metropolis. Even though the number of low-income young men has risen since 1975 as the ranks of middle-income young men have fallen, approximately 1.5 million young men are flourishing: to be precise, 7.6 percent of 25- to 34-year-olds earned more than $100,000 in 2016. By and large, these are men from upper-middle-class homes with two parents who made it into the more-competitive-than-ever elite universities; had a bevy of job offers; work in elite technology, financial, or consulting firms; travel and eat out in fancy restaurants; and have gotten married themselves. Cordoned off from most of their generation, they are like Ray, a 27-year-old working in Chicago for a large internet company. As he said, "All the people I'm friends with are doing well." It is worth noting that some prospering millennials provide financial assistance to their parents.[24]

Among those fortunate enough to have gone to college, but not among the one in fourteen with six-figure salaries, two-thirds had student loan debt, with one-third reporting debt of more than $30,000. Although there are many college dropouts with debt, those with college debt were better off than the 66 percent of young men (compared to 60 percent of women) who did not have a bachelor's degree in 2016. High levels of debt have become one factor leading millennials to put off marrying or buying a house. Student loan debt hit $1.4 trillion in 2017, with the average class of 2016 grad having more than $37,000 to pay back. "My husband and I are positioning ourselves to buy a house," said Juan, a 30-year-old college-educated gay Latino man in Washington, D.C. "But because we graduated with so much debt, we talk about moving back in with my parents to get ahead." Home ownership rates among 25- to 34-year-old men have fallen precipitously—from nearly half in 1975 to just over one quarter in 2016.[25]

For millennial men without jobs or decent jobs, lifetime career prospects and earnings almost inevitably decline. And so do a lot of other prospects. The inability to be a provider makes family formation less likely. Adulthood is shortened as prolonged adolescence marches straight into middle age. And the psychic toll for many is incalculable.

YOUNG MEN LIVING AT HOME

One of the more obvious consequences of millennial men's poor economic fortunes, perhaps abetted by aging helicopter parents, has been the great migration back to childhood bedrooms or basements. Although the phrase "boomerang kids" has been in the popular lexicon for some years and the numbers of young women living with parents also have increased, it is rarely discussed that millennial men are considerably less likely to be independent than their female counterparts. The 24 million millennials living with their parents in 2016 were disproportionately male. About 54 percent of men between 18 and 24 and almost a quarter of those between 25 and 34 lived with their parents in 2015, compared with 46 percent of 18- to 24-year-old women and one-sixth of women between 25 and 34. In addition, one in four male 18- to 34-year-olds lived with another relative, with roommates, in dorms, or in prisons. Excluding gay and lesbian couples, young men are about twice as likely as young women to shack up with other guys. In New Jersey the proportion of male "boomerangers" was half again as high as the national average, as California and northeastern states with high housing prices had among the highest percentage of young adults at home. Nationally, among lower-skilled men in their 20s, two-thirds lived with parents.[26]

That leaves about 36 percent living "independently," a term put in quotation marks since many of these are financially subsidized by their parents. Some of them live alone. Twenty-eight percent of millennial men were married or cohabiting in 2014, half the percentage of those their age who were wed in 1960. Among these, about 10 million had become fathers; more than half were unmarried. Bad jobs and bad wages not only deter weddings, they also put a huge crimp in forming families: The average cost of child care for millennials who are employed devours 27 percent of their income, 20 percentage points above what the U.S. Department of Health and Human Services considers "affordable child care." And the 30 percent who are not employed are more likely to father children outside of marriage.[27]

There is nothing intrinsically "wrong" (and a lot "right") about multigenerational households, which were the norm in America during its early history and remain the norm in many parts of the world. In most such families of yore, each adult generation contributed to the support of others and of the household. However, that is much less true of twenty-first-century non- or underemployed young adults.[28]

Yet for the 35 percent of 18- to 34-year-old men living with parents, the shortage of good jobs together with high housing prices is a big reason why they are home. Ben, who is white and in his early 20s, lives with his parents in Maine. He is ashamed and feels like he's "leeching." He said that his parents "scream and yell about what will become of me." The problem, he said, is that "it's difficult to find work, and the jobs that are available are service-related. I'm continually depressed when I work those jobs. I got in a fistfight when one of my friends complained, 'At least I'm not dishwashing,' which was my job." At home, Ben spends his days on the internet, plays the couple of musical instruments he knows, and reads and writes.

Gene, a mid 30s Virginia man who is also white and recently got a job, recalled, "I lived with my parents from age 23 to 31 and it was utterly humiliating, whether I was working, going to graduate school, or unemployed."

But bad jobs are only part of the problem. Surveys have found that millennials not working and living at home are somewhat happier than those who work. Indeed, the satisfaction among some of these nonworking man-boys and their belief that nothing is terribly amiss with their lives is a cultural sea change in a nation that once embodied the Protestant work ethic, and where the Puritans equated work with godliness.[29]

Not so long ago, such men were looked on askance and were seen as American *bamboccioni*. However, in recent years the mid-twentieth-century stigma of living with one's parents has largely disappeared, as the back-to-the-basement movement has made such arrangements permissible, if not desirable.

While Italian *bamboccioni* often work while living at home to build up their savings (one reason why Italy has the world's second-highest level of per capita assets),[30] in contemporary America the circumstances are quite different. These renesters are mostly men without jobs or with low-paying or part-time jobs. Unlike some multigenerational households of generations past, most of these men aren't married.

At an age long considered to be "adulthood," with all its connotations of independence and self-reliance, a lot of these men in their third or fourth decade of life are being served meals by their moms, spending their days gaming and otherwise vegging out. Some don't own a car or have a driver's license since they can borrow Dad's or have their parents open a Lyft account for them. Many of them don't feel any urgency to get a job or be independent. Psychologists say that parents generally don't demand as much of their sons as their daughters—for example, doing housework—and also don't monitor their activities as much, making life easy for young men. Despite their lives of nominal poverty, these men are a far cry from St. Francis.[31]

> Today I don't feel like doing anything
> I just wanna lay in my bed
> Don't feel like picking up my phone
> So leave a message at the tone
> 'Cause today I swear I'm not doing anything
> —Bruno Mars, "The Lazy Song" (2011)

While some diligently look for work, one startling report claimed that 40 percent of late teenagers and young men just don't want a job.[32] Too old to plausibly be "boys," and few even self-identifying as men, many millennial "guys"—an appropriately age-ambiguous term—live in a world circumscribed by PlayStation, social media, pot, porn, and alcohol.

Technology has made unemployment less lonely, as Tyler Cowen, an economist at George Mason University, has said, although there is evidence that young men and women tied to their smart phones and games are lonelier, and these aging boys are more likely to see technology as a suitable substitute for engagement with the world of work, relationships, and responsibility.[33] Indeed, while Alexander the Great had led armies to conquer much of Asia Minor by his early 20s, and Albert Einstein had developed his theory of relativity at a similar age, today 18- to 34-year-old men spend even more time playing computer games like *Alexander* or *Space Invaders* than teenage boys do. Although some male 20-somethings fancy themselves the next Steve Jobs, with half-baked internet businesses despite low-octane entrepreneurial drive, some of them are just another toke away from torpor. Just as alcoholism is up among this population, more than half again as many men as women say they smoke marijuana.[34]

Like Charles Dickens's Miss Havisham, they often inhabit a manse of memories, where time is frozen in their glory days. Those were the days, typically in high school, when they were cool, had buddies, and dreams for the future—at least of starting a rock band and becoming famous. But those days are gone.

Aaron, a star athlete in his suburban Connecticut high school, was smart and easily got into a large state university in the South. Heavy partying led him into the world of alcohol and drugs. One friend committed suicide, and Aaron, who is white, dropped out of school. Without a job or any money, he moved back in with his parents when he was 21. During the next five years, he did little with his life, his identity sustained by the thin psychological capital of his glory days. He saw several friends commit suicide and overdose on opioids or heroin. With help from family and professionals, Aaron got clean and by 29 had a steady girlfriend and an unskilled job that at least enabled him to move into a cheap apartment near his parents.

Many middle- and upper-middle-class parents initially welcome home their adult sons and daughters, happy to see them, ready to help, and expecting the situation to be temporary. However, parents' initial solicitousness can eventually give way to frustration at having to support "children" nearly to the halfway point of male life expectancy. They begin to wonder, Will they ever let go of the apron strings, find a job and a partner, and become adults themselves? And if they don't, what will become of them? Although some renesting guys help with household expenses and chores, others simply *are* expenses and chores.

American women with adult children living at home spend at least eight hours a week caring for them, and parents with adult kids at home spend less time socializing or having sex than those who are living on their own, according to Bureau of Labor Statistics time-use data. Cost estimates are all over the map, but one financial adviser told *Fox Business News* that housing one's adult child for a decade would leave parents with up to $175,000 less in retirement savings. A Merrill Lynch study reported that two-thirds of Americans over age 50 supported a child who was 21 or older in 2013. AARP, writing for its baby boomer members, has published advice columns on how best to deal with returning adult children, not kicking them out but preparing them for a not-too-delayed departure.[35]

"A lot of parents are very stressed," said Irene Caniano, a mother and former teacher on Long Island who started a MeetUp group for parents of adult children living at home. "They never knew how long this was going to take their kids—especially finding the job that fits."[36]

The Baltimore therapist echoed these views: "There's a maladaptive feed-back loop. Parents fret and worry and feel like they have to continue to monitor or help them, further diminishing the male sense of autonomy. The more they do this, the less able [these young men] are to really strike out on their own."

The media have tended to focus on white millennials like Aaron, with upper-middle-class homes to return to, where they can be tended by heli-copters approaching retirement. However, live-at-homes are more common among the working class, and African American and Latino young men are more likely to live with a parent than whites are. Young black men, according to a Population Reference Bureau study, are nearly three times as likely as young black women to live at home.[37] For these young men of color and their parents, life is hard and there are few escape hatches.

ANGRY, ANXIOUS, AND ADDICTED

Despite reports of happy, at-home techno-guys, many know painfully well that something is wrong, and are miserable and angry. "Having to rely on someone else's money sucks," said one 24-year-old white New York man living at home. Among the unrepresentative sample of young men who responded to my online survey, overwhelming majorities said they were "very angry" at the American economic system, the political system, government, and higher education, which many felt accounted for their circumstances.

"So what do these young men have to be angry about?" asks Frederick Marx, director of the documentary films *Boys to Men* (2003) and *Rites of Passage* (2014). "Plenty. The fact that the economy doesn't know he exists and his future career prospects look dim. The fact that he's up to his eyeballs in debt from egregious student loans with few prospects for repayment." They feel they've been sold a bill of goods and toggle between emotions like rage, shame, and depression.[38]

Noah, an articulate but angry political science student at a college near San Diego and a full-time worker, is not happy about the state of young men in America. He thinks the economy has screwed his generation, young white men in particular. Noah is not alone.[39]

He voted for Bernie Sanders in the 2016 Democratic primary and for Donald Trump in the general election. "Trump's election was a massive 'fuck you' to the forces that got us here in the first place, even if they were ticked off in a sort of mindless manner," he said. "The angry Trump voters feel they have been left behind or are heading in that direction. It will only be a few generations before white men are behind Latinos." Noah, who is white, disdains "the anti–white male crony liberal left wing of the Democratic Party," but, like a lot of millennials who are sick of both political parties and much of their ideology, he also damns "the negative effects of toxic masculinity upheld by the American right wing."

When Noah took a gender studies class, he wrote about gender inequality—how men are being shafted. He acknowledged that throughout most of history, "at least through the generation after the baby boom, women had it worse," that men benefited from sexism and segregation, and that "not everything about feminism is bad." But he is quick to rattle off the problems of young white men: lower grades in school, lower college attendance than women, high suicide rates, school shootings and violence, fatherlessness, bad jobs. He also thinks that men's more severe drug and alcohol problems are due to their expectations being dashed more often than women's.

"It's politically incorrect to say that white men have it worse," he readily admitted, "but things have gotten a lot worse for us."

As psychology has long posited that anger and depression are two sides of the same coin, it's not surprising that depression is on the rise. Some of this may be a matter of reporting, since it has been (and still is) regarded as "unmanly" to be depressed. The American Psychological Association reported that millennials on average have the highest level of stress of any generation.[40]

"As men, especially black men, in our society we're told to not express our feelings, and you wonder why mental illness is such a big issue in the black male community," said Jonah, an African American man in his late 20s. "It wasn't until [hip-hop artist and actor] Kid Cudi was like 'Yo, I suffer from depression' that some black men started to open up on social media."[41]

With depression has come the much discussed uptick in drug and alcohol poisonings and suicides, particularly among white men. Although these tragic "deaths of despair" are also widespread among women and older men, young males have been particularly hard hit.[42] From the fading working-class towns I visited in Wisconsin, Pennsylvania, and Massachusetts to the exurbs of Washington, D.C., just a half-hour's drive from some of the nation's wealthiest and best-educated communities, I heard all too many stories of opioid overdoses.

Eric, a young white man who left Pennsylvania's coal country for Boston, told me, "A dozen or more of the people I grew up with died from drug overdoses. One of my closest friends from high school became a heroin addict. The quarterback from the neighboring high school died of a heroin overdose."

One would not expect cases like Travis, a good-looking, outdoorsy, 27-year-old Mormon in Utah with an attractive wife and baby, to suffer a deadly overdose. When one of his friends showed a photo of a clean-cut young white man in a suit, he said, "Does this look like someone with an opiate problem?"

And then there are young men like Chuck, 31, who seemed to have been launched on a good life when he got his master's in engineering, landed an $80,000-a-year job at 24, and was living in an apartment in a Southern California beach town. He was liked at work, and when he told his boss that he was struggling, she told him to go on disability, which meant getting paid 60–80 percent of his regular salary for a year.

After a year, he couldn't go back to work. Chuck had grown up in a middle-class white family in a midsize city one hundred miles from the Canadian border, but he lacked confidence and was on antidepressants by the time he got to college. When he didn't return to work, after ten days in bed, he called his family to say that he needed help. Chuck went to a doctor, who prescribed OxyContin, which, he said, "took the edge off" his pain. Since heroin cost one-eighth the $80 he was paying for OxyContin, he made the switch.

A couple of suicide attempts followed. One day he was about to down a bottle of benzodiazepines, prescribed for anxiety, when someone wrestled the bottle away. Other times he ended up in psychiatric wards for a week or two at a time.

No longer the well-paid young engineer, he had health insurance through the Affordable Care Act, which covered most of his psychiatrists' bills. Then his family helped him get on SSDI, which enabled him to go on Medicare, even though he was only in his late 20s. He qualified for food stamps and other public benefits, but because he often couldn't get out of bed, his recently divorced mother, earning modest pay herself, became his representative. She went to agency after agency because, as she said, many of America's federal, state, and local social welfare programs "don't talk to each other."

Chuck's next stops were rehab programs on both the East and West Coasts.

He was prescribed an opioid treatment drug, which he then became addicted to. At age 30 he hit bottom. After trying to live with and take care of a friend with a degenerative disease, the friend kicked him out because of his erratic, drug-induced behavior. He was on the streets, sometimes sleeping in his car or a homeless shelter. Then he disappeared.

A younger stepbrother tracked him down in the Pacific Northwest and brought Chuck to live with him. The stepbrother had full custody of his own four-year-old because the mother had also become a heroin addict and disappeared. The three males lived together in a small apartment in the desert Southwest until Chuck returned to live with his mother in Maryland. He spent months in a clinical trial at one of the nation's leading research hospitals, but he still wasn't getting better.

THE POST-PROTESTANT WORK ETHIC AND THE SPIRIT OF EGOISM

Despite millennials' low rates of labor force participation, generally poor economic fortunes, and the mass migration home, it is important to remember—as is the case for all men—that most (seven in ten) young men are working. Nonetheless, employers, human resource professionals, and millennials often point to two big, related differences between these men and those of older generations: workers of this generation, especially those with less education, are prone to hop from job to job, showing little loyalty to an employer, and they put in less effort and expect greater rewards.[43]

A 2016 Deloitte survey found that 44 percent of millennials planned to leave their jobs within two years, were cynical about business, and "often put their personal values ahead of organizational goals." Similarly, 71 percent were found to be either not engaged or actively disengaged at work, according to a study published in the *Harvard Business Review*. Young men appear to have a particular ambition deficit; in contrast, more young women than men of the same ages told another pollster that being successful in a career "is one the most important things" or "very important" in their lives.[44]

Yet another survey, of 20,000 human resource professionals, found that newly minted millennial workers believe they deserve more promotions and pay raises "than their experience, ability or knowledge merit." They believe they can set their hours and work remotely from Starbucks. Men in particular have poor face-to-face communication skills, perhaps due to a lifetime of being online.[45] Many millennials' attitudes come across as arrogance, the human resource director of a large public relations firm told me. "A lot of

times millennials struggle at work," she said. "It's the first time they're not getting trophies or getting raises every six months for just showing up."

A midwestern bank president was more circumspect but essentially said
much the same of his younger employees. Some "work differently," he said.
They are more likely to seek "affirmation," "like having flexible options," "get
bored quickly," are frustrated that "boomers don't take them seriously," and
have "poor job tenure."

The armed forces, hardly a setting where such work habits go over well, has
had its share of millennials who say "I don't really want to do this," said Colonel Patrick Michaelis, an army recruiting brigade commander at Redstone
Arsenal in Alabama. He was the one who spoke of a "three in ten problem"—
the fact that only about 30 percent of men who try to enlist have the physical
and mental health, the academic proficiencies, and the moral qualities that
enable the army to accept them.[46]

Master Sergeant Jeffrey Klimek, a recruiter at Redstone, spoke of helicopter parents "softening" boys, leading to less physically active childhoods (the
declining bike-in-the-neighborhood problem again). "We're dealing with kids
who are obese, who can't do math without a calculator, who are still on Rit-
alin for ADHD, have short attention spans, and are multitaskers who rarely
finish what they start."[47]

The stereotypes of the entitled children of helicopter parents and the lazy
slackers seem at least somewhat true in the world of work. Another survey
found half of employers saying that millennials have a poor work ethic and
unrealistic expectations for pay. They "tend to expect that everything happens quickly, leading them to believe that promotions and successful growth
in a company happens at a much faster rate than in reality," Piera Palazzolo,
senior vice president of marketing at Dale Carnegie Training, told *The Street*.
"Operating under this assumption may also lead Millennials to think that
their career success isn't necessarily dependent on their hard work and dedication to their job. . . . Millennials seem to be unaware that their responsibilities go beyond the basic job description."[48]

Among millennials, only about one-third characterized themselves as
hardworking, compared to three-fourths of baby boomers, a 2015 Pew Research survey found.[49] Some who have jobs move on to new jobs within a year
or two. However, many also described themselves as more idealistic and less
materialistic than earlier generations, seeking meaningful—not necessarily
high-paying—work.

BYPASSING THE ALTAR

Just as unprecedented numbers of young men are not working, are living with parents, and have less than committed attitudes toward work, similarly unprecedented numbers are not marrying. As noted, marriage or partnering and having children traditionally have been among the key markers of adulthood.

Despite surveys showing that young people eventually want to marry, they do not see it as a priority. Marriage has been collapsing, especially among less educated young Americans. Just 28 percent of 18- to 34-year-old men were married in 2014, half the percentage who had tied the knot in 1960 and even significantly lower than during the Depression. A big part of this is about postponing, not rejecting, marriage, as the median age at first marriage has climbed from about 22 or 23 for men during the 1950s, 1960s, and early 1970s to more than 29 in 2017, while the typical age for a woman to marry has also gone up by about six years, from 20 or 21 to more than 27. However, Pew has projected that one in four millennials will have never married by the time they reach their mid-50s. Less educated men and African American men are considerably less likely to marry, some of which is due to the higher "unmarriageability" quotient among young black men discussed in chapter 3.[50]

Debates about why young people aren't marrying have a way of getting quite heated. Those on the left argue that it's largely due to economics: too many people are paid too low wages to afford to have a family. Clearly the high poverty rates, declining median incomes, and rising college debt play a major part. One in six millennials say they're delaying marriage because of student debt. Women don't want to marry economic deadbeats, with all the often accompanying pathologies, and men holding traditional views of masculinity frequently don't want to marry unless they can support a wife and family. Since Americans are less likely to marry outside their social class, such "associative mating" means that women see fewer "marriageable" men.[51]

Those on the right variously argue that the decline in marriage stems from secularism and a general moral rot and that much of poverty can be explained by the absence of marriage (even though conservative Republicans more likely represent states where a high number of couples are having children outside marriage). It is true that married couples have significantly higher incomes, labor force participation rates, and assets than two single individuals. It is also true, at least according to one survey, that millennials are far less likely to call themselves "moral" than their parents or grandparents.[52]

"Men at the losing end of male status hierarchies are bad partners," University of Minnesota law professor June Carbone told me. Nonworking men "do less housework, drink more, and engage in more domestic violence. The men who would gain most by committing to a woman lose the most in the form of 'street cred' by doing so."[53]

But in many ways, this is a chicken-or-egg problem: low wages and the dearth of good jobs are associated with a lower likelihood of marriage, but at the same time, not being married is associated with lower incomes.

No one can credibly claim causation, but we need to look at both the huge changes in values and norms as well as the huge changes in the U.S. economy. And while it's hard to argue that low wages and poverty are anything but bad, the cultural changes of the last half century are a big dimension of the polarization of America. In our long-running "culture wars," some call these changes moral decline while others call them liberating.

Back in 1971, at the apex of the counterculture, Joni Mitchell sang, "We don't need a piece of paper from the city hall / keeping us tied and true." Since the 1960s, cohabitation has increased twelvefold, and a majority of millennials at some point live with a romantic partner outside of marriage. Once quaintly called "living in sin," cohabitation had "historically been associated with women's lack of virtue and men's refusal to take responsibility for their partners and children," according to Carbone and George Washington University law professor Naomi Cahn, co-authors of *Marriage Markets* (2014).[54]

Although a number of single or cohabitating millennials will get married by their 40s, many won't. Some may just not find the right partner, but whether it's women who say they "don't need men" or men who are "going their own way," a significant minority of men are openly hostile to marriage. Some of them who have grown up with divorce are put off by how courts adjudicate custody issues. As the young Maine man, Ben, said, "Marriage is dead to me."

The sharp decline in marriage among millennials has had several profound consequences. First, as the number of unmarriageable men increases, desirable men can play the field as never before.[55]

"There are more casual, serial relationships," said Ray, the successful and single tech-company employee in Chicago. "Guys are always going out to hook up. We see that a lot of marriages don't last, and maybe that's influencing us."

"Men care a lot more about sex," added Alex, a middle-class, white, working college student from Kansas. "Those dating apps favor men, providing easy opportunities. They see marriage as a hostile thing. Boys never really become men."

"When it comes to relationships, many young people don't want to feel responsibility or be attached to someone," according to Mauricio, a 30-year-old Latino man who teaches relationship skills to younger Latino and African American men in Washington, D.C. "It used to be different. If you had intimacy, you'd get married. Now marriage involves so many things—money, wellness, kids. People would rather get together than married. They hate commitment and responsibility."

Second, the decline in marriage has been greater than the decline in childbearing. In fact, a majority of the more than 20 million millennial parents in 2014 had their children outside of marriage—55 percent at last count, compared to a quarter of baby boomers who did.[56]

If these couples had stable unions or eventually married, this might not be a problem. Instead, most men, and some women, move on to new partners, and the average cohabitation lasts only about fourteen months. This is very different from more stable cohabitation patterns in western Europe. And here in the States a significant percentage of women and men go on to have children with one or more other partners without marrying.[57]

"It's so common in some communities that it's just accepted that men may father children and aren't expected to live with them," said Isabel Sawhill, senior fellow at the Brookings Institution. "They don't see marriage as something where you struggle together to make ends meet."[58]

In short, as western Massachusetts nurse Theresa Apple, who has worked with a lot of young people, said, "Marriage has taken such a beating. Young people think marriage isn't a necessity. I see a lot of 20-somethings having children—some marry, some never get married, some relationships fail."[59]

MALIGNED OR MALIGNANT?

Millennial men are disproportionately represented among men out. As many as one in three guys between 18 and 34 are not employed, living in or near poverty, and living at home. A great number of employers are at least somewhat down on them. A lot of young men are not marrying or forming healthy relationships, and many are fathering children in nonmarital relationships that won't endure. Drug and alcohol abuse has become more common and more deadly. Depression and other mental health problems are on the rise. All of this has repercussions for the nation's macro economy, politics, and culture. Anger and the misogyny that we saw in chapter 3 are a number of decibels higher than in previous generations. Once again, young men of color and less educated men fare worse, but they are by no means the only millennial men who are struggling or on the sidelines.

In light of these problems, but remembering that the majority of millennials are doing okay and some are doing very well, has this generation been unfairly maligned? Many of those struggling now eventually will find good jobs, have loving partnerships, and be good fathers, but genuine adulthood will start much later for them. Yet the auguries are not good. If you accept the Jesuits' maxim "Give me the child and I will give you the man," a significant number of these 26- to 34-year-old "boys" (approximately America's life expectancy at the time of independence) may never really become men.

What this means for the housing market, Social Security, and fiscal policy, and, more broadly, personal identity, mental health, living standards, and norms for different stages of life is an open question.

Despite some of the happy talk about "Generation Z"—the children of their alphabet-mates, Generation X—as more resourceful, creative, and idealistic, there is little evidence that current economic, social, and cultural trends shaping millennials will not similarly affect these youngest Americans. Aside from the trouble with generalizing about another cohort that includes a quarter of the U.S. population, it's rather ridiculous to talk about today's 5-year-olds in the same breath as those just entering adulthood. Moreover, in the absence of major changes, which do not appear to be on the horizon, circumstances may be worse for Americans born since 1997.[60]

Whether or not millennials (particularly men) have been fairly or unfairly maligned, the troubles that so many are facing may be a malignancy threatening America's future.

CHAPTER 5

Online, Offline

We have to grit our teeth and hang on to the fence and not take it for
granted that the web will lead us to wonderful things. . . . People are being
distorted by very finely trained AIs that figure out how to distract them.
—*Tim Berners-Lee, inventor of the World Wide Web*

The internet is like alcohol.

It has brought psychic rewards and conviviality and connection to billions,
and it is central to early twenty-first-century human culture. But, like alcohol,
it has also brought damage and destruction to tens of millions of lives.

J.C.R. Licklider of the Defense Advanced Research Projects Agency
(DARPA) touted the outlandish idea of globally connected network comput
ing in 1962, but it is only since the late 1990s euphoria—when Marc An-
dreesen, Al Gore, and a horde of venture capitalists didn't see a dot.com they
didn't like—that the internet or web has been widely hailed as the best inven-
tion since sliced bread.

Despite its incalculable economic, informational, and communications
benefits, the digital world is far from being an unblemished boon to modern
life. It has numerous decidedly negative effects, many of which compound
the problems of men out.

Leaving aside the enormous impact of hacking and fake news on politics,
geopolitics, business, and personal lives, and its obliteration of conventional
walls of privacy, the internet has been socially and psychologically changing

how several billion people around the world live, think, and relate to one another.

In few populations has this been so true as among millennial and younger Americans, although young East Asians and northern Europeans are even more likely to be online than their U.S. counterparts. Americans 35 and older hardly have been immune to the obvious and subtle changes that have come in the wake of the "digital revolution."

"Technology" more broadly may be a predominantly male professional arena, but there is gender parity in overall internet use—texting, email, Google searches, YouTube, music, streaming video content, shopping. However, the web is used somewhat differently by men and women. It also generally has had somewhat different effects on each sex.

There are at least four sets of problems germane to our story about men that will be addressed in this chapter. First, young (and many not so young) American men who are not working spend a large portion of their waking hours on the internet, especially on gaming, and there is evidence of a connection between the two.[1] Such prolonged internet use can become addictive, turning men into digital couch potatoes or "zombies" and compromising or destroying their ability to lead productive and social lives. Second, millions of men use the internet for purposes that are harmful to women and influence how men view and interact with women. Third, the internet and social media, often empathy-free zones, make it easy for discontented and angry men to publicly spew hateful political and social beliefs, not to mention personal vitriol, with little interest in or tolerance for other viewpoints and little care for how their virtual and verbal assaults hurt other people. Since much of the internet is fact-free, many beliefs are readily fed by what have come to be known as "alternative facts." And fourth, while overuse of the internet is diminishing women's and men's face-to-face interactions and attendant social skills, it is exacerbating men's personal isolation and disengagement from community and public life.

Violent and reality-blurring video games, pornography, online dating, and the very dark world of hate and terrorism are predominantly a male domain. This is a world of men and aging boys who are alienated, have dropped out, and have retreated from that old standard package of work, family, virtue, and community.

Once again, this fits into the metaphorical Venn diagram mentioned in chapter 1. The males who prowl this world like hungry wolves are not all jobless, without partners and children, and AWOL from public life, but all too many are.

GAMING AND ADDICTION

The image of the man-boy in the basement, transfixed in front of a screen gleaming into the wee hours, has become a cliché. Parents, wives or partners, social commentators, therapists, and employers see the billions of male hours sucked into virtual reality games, first-person shooter games, survival and tactical games, role-playing games, and other genres as being harmful to gamers who are children, partners, workers, and citizens. Others, including numerous gamers, say that only when gaming becomes addictive or "toxic" is it a problem.

Video games have long had a hold on teenage boys and young men in America, Japan, and elsewhere. Beginning with the first Atari in the 1970s and continuing on through several decades of computer and console games, we have progressed to the huge, all-consuming world of online gaming in the 2010s as broadband internet came into wide use. The president and CEO of the video game trade organization, the Entertainment Software Association, was not exaggerating when he said, "Video games are ingrained in our culture," with nearly half of all Americans playing some game at some time.[2]

The average American spent a stunning ten hours and thirty-nine minutes a day in front of a screen in 2016, according to Nielsen, and an Iowa State University study found that the typical American spends similar amounts of time on digital devices as they do either working or sleeping. Millennials devote twice as much of their screen time to smart phones, computers, tablets, and "TV-connected devices," such as gaming consoles, as do Americans 50 or older, who are more likely to watch TV. Teenagers to 40-somethings on average spend about four hours a day on digital media, including about an hour on social media, although a significant number of "heavy users" spend three or more hours a day. The rising generation that was between early adolescence and 22 in 2017 is said to spend six hours a day on digital devices. Young women spend somewhat more time on social media, whereas young men spend much more time gaming, and hours of usage have been going up during the 2010s. Young men who don't work spend a significant part of their days gaming.[3]

These games, as well as Japanese anime, have been vilified for their violence, for their hypersexualized depictions of women, and for isolating players
from other real people, but at the same time, they have been praised by others
for their sophisticated visual imagery, strategic complexity, and the online
communities they develop. Whether played individually or as part of massive multiplayer online games on Nintendos, PlayStations, or Xboxes, video
games have become one of the leading forms of entertainment in contemporary America.

"Video games help me deal with the pressure," said a 20-year-old African
American man in Washington. "They help me forget all the problems and
stuff."

Linc, a 22-year-old in the Midwest, agreed that gaming is a way of "just
unwinding and immersing myself in a different universe so I don't have to
worry about the problems of this one." Although he acknowledged that he
loses sleep by playing until 2 a.m., Linc said that games enhance his critical
thinking skills and his reaction times. In the online multiplayer game *Player
Unknown*, he knew he would be "killed" by one of the hundred other players
surrounding him in an arena if he didn't know how to respond quickly and
strategically.

Linc has also made "a couple of good friends on *Halo* and *Games of War*,"
he said. "We got to know each other, friended each other on Facebook, and
hang out. I just haven't touched them. Hanging out in real life is good, but
you don't really need to see people in person if you're talking with them"
in a game. Yet gaming has also connected many men in online mobs, such
as "Gamergate," that have attacked feminists and "SJWs" (social justice warriors), in the angry argot of a vocal minority of male gamers.

A Pew survey found that most gamers agree with the positive assessments
and are seven times as likely as those who don't play to say that video games
are a better form of entertainment than TV. Male gamers are also much more
likely than women who play and all nonplayers to recoil at the notion that
games are a waste of time or that violent games are related to real-life violence.[4]

However, it's hard not to see the violence, especially in first-person
shooter games, the most popular subgenre of online gaming. These are typically bloody, 3D fights to the death in *Doom*, *Overwatch*, and *Call of Duty*,
often involving hundreds of players in far-flung locations. The one thing that
bothers Linc, and what he believes gives gaming its bad reputation, is "toxic
players."[5] For them, winning is everything, and "they scream and curse and
are jerks just for the sake of being a jerk," he said.

Contrary to Linc's generally positive assessment, Command Sergeant Major Michael Gragg at the army's Center for Initial Military Training in Fort Jackson, South Carolina, said, "We see a lot of young men who are gamers who don't have the attention span as in previous generations. There's a lack of a sense of being a community and knowing how to be on a team. It's so individualistic."[6] The multitasking that devices enable, with their Versailles-like Hall of Windows, for most means rarely finishing any of their fleetingly interesting online pursuits.

Clearly not a fan of dedicated gamers, Gragg, who supervises basic training, added, "It's easy to be strong and brave online. But really being in the army isn't as exciting as playing *Call of Duty.*"

Others speak of addiction. Kimberly Young, a psychologist who founded the Center for Internet Addiction in West Hartford, Connecticut, in 1995, when there was barely an internet, treats young men who spend twelve to fifteen hours a day gaming. "They have poor health and sleep habits," she said. "They typically have dropped out of school, don't have jobs, have no money, and live with their parents."[7]

On-Line Gamers Anonymous, which has been holding meetings in church basements and libraries around the country since 2002, uses the rather hyperbolic, all-or-nothing language of other twelve-step programs like Alcoholics Anonymous: "As game addicts we lost all sight of our best life. Hopes and dreams receded further and further into the background along with all the rest of real life as we sank deeper and deeper into the anesthetizing world of fantasy. Real dreams were exchanged for a hypnotic numbness found in make-believe worlds that gave us the illusion of control, a semblance of mastery or at least a feeling of manageability while our lives careened into chaos due to neglect."[8]

Even Linc admitted that when one of the new *Zelda* survival games was released, he was completely obsessed and wouldn't hang out with friends.

Whether seen as a benign pastime or a dangerous addiction, games are consuming a lot of young men's time. Four out of five 18- to 29-year-old men played video games in 2015, and one in three of these men identified themselves as devoted gamers, compared to one in eleven young women. Although one hears parents of teenage boys complain of their sons' immersion in gaming, it is actually young adult males in their 20s and 30s who fuel much of this $23.5 billion industry.[9]

Hard-core adult male gamers are nearly twice as likely to be lower income (below $30,000 a year) than relatively higher income (above $75,000). They are also more likely to be less educated, single, and not working. During up to three-fourths of the time that nonworking young men might be working, these (mostly young) men are playing video games, according to University of Chicago economist Erik Hurst. Among nonworking men between 21 and 30 with less than a bachelor's degree, daily usage shoots up to 8.6 hours per day, more than double what it was a decade earlier. Particularly troubling, according to Hurst and Princeton economist Mark Aguiar, is that these men tend to be perfectly content with not working, not having a partner, and living with parents. They also report greater happiness than men who are working.[10]

ONLINE PORN, SEXTING, AND, THE "CANDY STORE"

Many online games portray women with "boobs bigger than watermelons, an ass wider than a fridge, with a waist thinner than my pinky," as Linc colorfully but accurately described them. In *Grand Theft Auto*, players can stop at a strip club and "get grinded on" by realistic-looking virtual women, another player said.

As we've seen, for all the cultural trends reinforcing less sexist, more egalitarian male attitudes and behavior toward women, the internet is a major countervailing force.

While pornography has always existed, a Playmate of the Month is tamer than a kitten compared to the limitless jungle of raging lions on internet porn sites. Statistics are understandably sketchy, but different studies have found that as much as 30 percent of the web's content is pornographic, 15 percent of web searches involve porn, and around 70 percent of American men (plus a lot of boys under 18) look at internet porn.[11] As the cast of the Broadway musical *Avenue Q* sings, "The internet is for porn."

Good demographic data are difficult to come by, as the staid BLS Time Use Survey and the U.S. Census hardly ask about pornography use and then run cross-tabs by sex, age, income, or employment status. However, one study found, not terribly surprisingly, that the number of men who view porn and the amount of time they spend viewing it is much greater than for women.[12] Given the connection between nonwork and internet use, it is not a stretch to see online porn abuse, as well as gaming, as part of the larger set of intertwined issues clouding some men's lives.

Here, things get controversial. Many men, and some psychologists and women, would say, "So what?" Sexual images and masturbation have been a fact of life for ages. Overwhelming majorities of young men say there's nothing wrong with porn, and a sizable and growing minority of women are regular porn viewers. Some say it improves sex, while others say that real intimacy can never equal the titillation on screen. Religious and secular conservatives say it's immoral; feminists say that porn is degrading to women, as they have said for decades; and Utah declared it a public health hazard in 2016.[13]

What's different from past debates is the easy availability and prevalence of online porn, its more extreme and violent content, the ability and proclivity of millions to become amateur pornographers, and its effects on male sexuality and relationships. As limits on what is portrayable crumble, sites stoke and try to sate what one Reddit feed described as men's "dirtiest, most nastiest, weirdest sex fantasies," further degrading the very concept of "deviance."

A Kinsey Institute study found compulsive porn viewing among about one in ten men, and an entirely new subfield of psychotherapy and recovery programs, like Kimberly Young's, focusing on porn and other internet addiction has emerged. Headlines speak of "porn addiction." "Recovery" groups like the moderated website NoFap have emerged. Since orgasms release oxytocin, a hormone associated with bonding to another person, Christian biopsychologist William Struthers writes, "If you're viewing pornography, your partner is the screen in front of you." And one British study found that MRIs of the brains of obsessive porn viewers are similar to those of alcoholics. Yet most therapists tend to use the term "compulsion" instead of "addiction."[14]

Whether to boast of conquests, to titillate, or for revenge, many men and teenage males post, text, or email nude or other sexually graphic images of women they have slept with or know without the women's consent. What might once have been "locker room talk" now can be communicated to the world.

Reports on "sexting" found that one fourth of men under 30 sent or received this kind of photo, and a growing number of young women also send unsolicited sexually provocative pictures of themselves to guys they want to hook up with. One in ten women under 30 has either had such photos posted or had them threatened to be posted; so too had more than 10 million Americans of all ages as of 2016. "Revenge porn"—ex-boyfriends and ex-husbands uploading photos and often addresses of their exes on Snapchat, 4chan, or other sites—has become so common that Facebook received 51,000 reports from shocked, embarrassed, and angry women in just one month. Representative Jackie Speier (D-Calif.) has introduced federal legislation to make non-consensual porn a crime, and several states have begun to enact laws against revenge porn. Countless women have been devastated by incidents like one caused by a 38-year-old Minnesota man who created a Facebook page with nude images of his ex and sent them to her family and friends. A middle-age Illinois school superintendent was fired after a doctored video of a woman looking like her was posted by a man who had sexually assaulted the subject in the video and filmed the assault. And reality TV star Rob Kardashian was reported to have posted pornographic images of costar Blac Chyna.[15]

It is common for domestic violence and stalking victims to receive a barrage of online threats from men. A growing number of rapists film and post their crimes.[16]

Social media, and the internet more generally, are also key tools in human trafficking, with traffickers posting women's pictures as a way to sell victims. With the slave trade now online, more than three-fourths of the 20 million annual victims are women and girls, although men out are unlikely to play a role in trafficking.[17]

The pervasiveness of online porn, sexting, and revenge porn has also been seen as harming real relationships and depressing men's physical attraction to nonvirtual women—those whom one sees on the street or at the office, not on the screen.

"You don't know what normal sex is," Kimberly Young said. "You just see graphic, lewd sex. Looking at porn makes people have problems with sexual involvement, and it's a big factor in breaking up relationships."[18] A recent college graduate from Rhode Island said that a lot of his male peers have an unreal view of sex that makes them unable to perform and find that real sex is unable to live up to their expectations.

As a Maryland therapist told me, "It's very daunting to talk with your sexual partner about improving your sex lives, so it's easier to go onto the internet and have your extra needs met. It becomes a substitute for relationships."

Psychologists Philip Zimbardo and Nikita Duncan have ominously argued that male addiction to internet porn and video games is "rewiring" brains to seek constant stimulation. Both are doing damage to marriages, romantic relationships, men's respect for women, and even male libido, a growing body of evidence shows. What one sex therapist, Ian Kerner, has dubbed sexual attention deficit disorder (SADD) appears to be causing heavy users to lose interest in and desire for their partners or any women.[19]

Several recent studies of increasing erectile dysfunction (ED), particularly among men under 40, have found a statistically significant relationship between heavy porn use and ED. Online porn appears to activate the same "reward system" brain circuitry as cocaine and methamphetamines, increasing men's "tolerance," according to Dr. Matthew Christman, a urologist with the San Diego Naval Medical Center who led the research. "Tolerance could explain the sexual dysfunction, and can explain our finding that associated preferences for pornography over partnered sex with statistically significantly higher sexual dysfunction in men." Even soft-core media like *Playboy* and *Vice* argue, in common parlance, that online porn is "spoiling the real thing."[20] ED, one of men's least favorite subjects, doesn't exactly help relationships and is a punch to the masculine gut. It doesn't do much for women either.

It's not surprising that online porn use is increasingly cited in divorce cases and that large numbers of women consider it "cheating." A sizable proportion of divorces are at least in part due to a husband's obsession with internet porn.[21] Two highly educated professional women in a large eastern city told me how compulsive porn use was the nail in the coffin for their marriages.

Describing her ex-husband, who had been out of a job as a lawyer for years, Lisa, a professional woman, told me, "He would always go downstairs late at night, and I thought he was working, but he was drinking, abusing drugs, and looking at porn. I found a gigantic bag of [pornographic] disks."

Her friend Donna described her once high-flying ex-husband, who hadn't been working for years: "He had a lot of time on his hands. Increasingly, he spent it in the solitary world of his computer, mostly looking at porn."

But the internet sex–man out nexus goes beyond porn, sexting, and relationship damage. The line between pornography and online dating is blurring in several ways. Dating sites, from the originally vaguely Christian e-Harmony to Tinder, implicitly if not explicitly emphasize the importance of appearance, and a woman's smiling face tends to be less successful than an alluring pose. Men are more likely to spend their time "browsing" dating sites rather than "finding a companion," in the words of an executive of Liftoff, a mobile marketing app.[22]

"With so much choice, the grass is always greener for guys," said a New York woman who is on Match.com. "They're bombarded with all these beautiful women." However, many of them are bots.[23]

Even AARP has weighed in, reflecting the reality that this is an issue that goes beyond young men. As the organization's relationship guru says, "Men tend to approach online dating like it's a candy store and they're a kid with a bag of dimes."[24]

It may sound like an old feminist rap or a fire-and-brimstone sermon, but this all reinforces the "objectification" of women. One might reasonably respond that men have always done this, many women objectify men, millions of people have found lasting partners online, and millions of "enlightened" men (and women) don't do any of these things (or at least say they don't). Yet it is impossible not to conclude that the internet has made the cauldron of male-female relations and men's views of women boil a good bit hotter.

Internet porn may resemble video games in that one offers "fake love" while the other offers "fake war," as Russell Moore, a Southern Baptist leader, has noted.[25]

ANGER UNLEASHED ONLINE

Which brings us to the next predominantly male issue with the internet: it enables an awful lot of vile things to be said about individuals, groups of people, and, for that matter, the service at a restaurant or one's neighbor's dog.

Whatever one thinks of Hillary Clinton, one of the sorry outcomes of America's 2016 presidential election was the amplification of the Furies of internet misogyny. How many times did words like "bitch," "cunt," and other derogatory characterizations of Clinton as a woman—not as a candidate, a Democrat, a longtime public servant, a liberal, or a not-so-liberal—appear in blogs, tweets, Facebook posts, and websites?

Okay, many Americans have a lot to be justifiably angry about, but, as the methods of Hitler should have taught us, trashing people because they are part of a group (not just women or people of color but the poor, the rich, a particular nationality, religion, age, political party, etc.) is not exactly civilized, humane behavior. But Hillary was only the tip of the iceberg in internet misogyny. One survey found that three-fourths of under-30 women said they had been harassed online, and one in four said they had received violent threats. The anonymity of the internet has defined deviancy down into the most brackish corners of the gutter, where women can be threatened with rape, dismemberment, and death; can have their appearance denigrated while doctored photos are sent to porn sites; and can see their Tinder conversations degrade within seconds from her asking "How's it goin'?" to her match asking for fellatio.[26]

While male politicians, journalists, and other public figures receive their share of online attacks, their female counterparts get frequent threats of rape, are digitally linked to pornographic websites, and are subjected to other gender-based abuse. Amanda Hess, one of a number of female journalists to report threats of rape and murder from angry men who disagreed with her views, wrote that a Twitter account had been created to make death threats against her and that one man wrote, "I'm looking you up, and when I find you, I'm going to rape you and remove your head." Two million online messages using the hashtag #GamerGate, many with graphic rape and death threats, were posted in a misogynistic maelstrom in 2014.[27]

And less educated men are not the only culprits. In a curious inversion in the history of prejudice, many young (and older) men who wouldn't be caught dead calling a gay man a "faggot" feel no compunction about calling women "sluts," "whores," and the rest of the rich vocabulary of woman-hating.

One study found six million uses of "slut" and "whore" on Twitter in a six-week period just after Christmas 2013. Radio host Rush Limbaugh slurred a female law student who called for insurance coverage of birth control a "slut," only to apologize after coming under fire.[28] This is all of a piece with revenge porn, sexting, and "slut shaming" of women whose sexual lives may be as active as those of the idealized macho male. Although women often buy into this denigrating language, it is angry men who do most of the posting, and some female objects of these attacks who subsequently get publicly shamed are fired, assaulted, or commit suicide.[29]

For all the harm that the internet has enabled mostly men to do to mostly women, anyone is fair game for online hatred and anger. The anonymity of the web makes it possible for millions of shadowy figures—mostly angry men—to use words like an Uzi. Racial and ethnic groups, political opponents, bullied children, and almost anyone can be a target. The Anti-Defamation League found 2.6 million anti-Jewish tweets in the year ending in July 2016. Racist memes about former president Obama seem to have convinced about a quarter of Americans that he was a Kenyan-born Muslim. Many Americans' apparent substitution of quality journalism suggests that Trump is right and Daniel Patrick Moynihan was wrong: everyone is entitled to their own facts.[30] It's a lot easier to post on a white supremacist website or hurl swastikas into cyberland than it is to do so in the streets of Boston or Boise. As Command Sergeant Major Gragg suggested, such internet warriors are anonymous cowards-in-hiding, pathetically hateful, wannabe Brown Shirts whose only weapon is *usually* a keystroke.

Websites appealing to angry, disconnected young white men like the *Daily Stormer* pour antisemitism, racism, and misogyny into one noxious stew. Calling for the expulsion of "Jews, blacks, and lesbians," saying "blacks loved slavery" and that "when you give women rights, they destroy absolutely everything around them," the site has called out to "guys" to harass women and Jews and "prepare for the coming race war.[31] Fertile territory for the emergent "alt-right," these sites have become virtual convocations of what the *Atlantic* called the "brotherhood of losers." Christian Picciolini, a former skinhead who founded the anti-extremist group Life After Hate, told the *New York Times* that thousands of young white men every day are radicalized by online white nationalist propaganda that uses recruiting methods similar to those of ISIS.[32]

While the internet lets down verbal inhibitions, online hate speech has been linked over and over to violent behavior, typically by white men. In just the first eight months of 2017, a 35-year-old white, Portland, Oregon, man stabbed Muslim women after putting pro-Nazi posts on Facebook; a 23-year-old Maryland white supremacist on the Facebook site "Alt-Reich: Nation" fatally stabbed a black army lieutenant; a white, 66-year-old Minnesota member of a "Terminate the Republican Party" Facebook site opened fire on GOP members of Congress playing baseball; and a 20-year-old Ohio man, also white, with Facebook posts praising Nazis, Syrian dictator Bashar al-Assad, and white supremacists, drove his car into a crowd of antiracism protesters in Charlottesville, Virginia.[33]

If this isn't dark enough, darker things can be found on the so-called dark web. Here, thanks to special browsers like The Onion Router (TOR), roam hackers and extortionists, drug dealers, money launderers, fascists, and other assorted criminals whose sophistication leaves the gun toters in the dust. Terrorists also roam on this dystopian virtual range. The line is vanishingly small between other hate websites on the "surface web," including social media like Facebook, and ISIS or al-Qaeda recruitment sites in those parts of the internet that cannot be accessed by standard search engines. The target demographic is similar: young white males. Charleston mass murderer Dylann Roof was caught up in "internet evil," his stepmother told NBC. The Newtown, Connecticut, school massacre was committed by a guy who holed up in his mother's basement playing *Call of Duty*. From these lonely, perverse, and dangerous corners of the internet emerge what have come to be called "white male terrorists," who have caused more mass carnage than any other demographic group. Following the logic of racial and other demographic profiling, nonworking, isolated young white American males should be strip-searched and the first to be deported by Homeland Security agents.[34]

Some of this is inchoate, free-floating anger. Some comes from self-loathing. Some of this anger would have been bottled up a few generations ago—perhaps one benefit of traditional masculinity. Men are not uniquely angry, but in this virtual cesspool, it is generally men who associate anger with toughness, which in turn is linked to masculinity. Men are also more likely to have hair-trigger anger, even if (or perhaps because) they typically have been culturally brought up to be less able to talk through their feelings.

ANTISOCIAL MEDIA AND MEN

Which brings us back to that image of young males glued to their screens. They aren't alone. Most Americans are glued to screens. It's just that younger people are more tied to digital devices than older Americans. Younger men spend this time differently than women, transfixed by gaming and websites that can't be rated with enough Xs. And less educated, nonworking men clock huge amounts of screen time.

Video games, social media, texting, and online dating have a putatively social component, yet all four largely involve individuals acting alone. Women tend to use social media and email more to keep in touch with friends and families and are likelier to write longer missives and share photos than more typically terse men.[35] While these services—from Facebook and Instagram to Google Messenger and Match.com—vigorously claim they are all about bringing people together, they mostly do so electronically. It's true that they do connect people, but what is the trade-off? As parents, partners, employers, teachers, and other users say, smart phones, the internet, and all the candy in the digital candy jar also take users away from families and friends, real-world communities, and productive work. Certainly the internet has made being alone seem less lonely.

This, too, is a set of topics that elicits quite divergent responses.

As Command Sergeant Major Gragg told me, "Technology has changed social norms. This generation doesn't go outside for entertainment. They communicate with social media rather than meeting under the streetlights to ride bikes." This echoes how the Vietnam veteran in Pennsylvania, the nurse in Massachusetts, and others described the antisocial effects of the internet.

Even Trevor, a 20-year-old man from Missouri, waxed nostalgic for a childhood before iPhones. "Growing up when I didn't have a phone, kids were always outside playing, and their parents were on the front porch," he said. "But now kids are inside, they're on their iPads, they're watching TV, that sort of thing. It just disconnects people. My generation really isn't able to foster the sense of community that our parents or grandparents were brought up on."

Beyond addiction or compulsion, misogyny, and anger, the other big downside to the digital world is its effects on relationships with people—

individuals and the community at large. We heard Linc essentially say that, if you have a "friend" online in a game or even on Facebook, who needs to have friends you see in person? One survey found that two in five millennials spend more time on smart phones than with real people. Many believe that digital usage is even higher among the post-millennial generation.[36]

Replacing face-to-face or even telephone communication has been implicated in real-life problems ranging from isolation and its psychological consequences to social awkwardness and being less able to work collaboratively. On social media or in a game, one can't read body language or get facial or vocal cues. Emojis are a long way from the subtleties and endless varieties of real emotions. And the internet is anything but the agora, much less a cocktail party, a bus stop, or a bar. It tends to segregate people in that users interact with those who share their points of view and interests.

Because online activities are sedentary, they also have been identified as increasing obesity. Similarly, since users flit from one app or message or window to another, the internet has been blamed for conditioning users to have shorter attention spans. Excessive use of digital media can have "negative health effects on sleep, attention, and learning; a higher incidence of depression; exposure to inaccurate, inappropriate, or unsafe content and contacts; and compromised privacy and confidentiality," according to the American Academy of Pediatrics.[37]

So-called Facebook depression is said to ensue from users comparing themselves to others' photos, posts, and number of "friends" and the consequent belief that others have better lives. This can lead to an anxiety-producing de facto arms race to promote one's own wonderful life and self. Welcome to the cultivation of narcissism. It's all about me.[38] With the selfie and the smart phone's multi-gigabyte capacity to take photos and share them far and wide, an individual is able to say, "Look, world, here I am with a celebrity, on the most beautiful beach, hanging out with my many friends, in my new car. I'm interesting. I'm cool. I'm successful. I'm popular."

It's not surprising that real-life social skills can deteriorate. It has become easier and preferable among some men and women to text, email, or use other digital communications rather than to meet someone in person or call them on the phone. Employers report that younger, tech-tethered workers often are less proficient in serious conversation. "Having grown up on social media, we don't know how to talk to each other face to face," as On-Line Gamers Anonymous proclaims.[39]

Adolescents and young adults are much less likely to see friends than they were at the turn of the twenty-first century, and they are more likely to feel isolated or depressed. Is this "the worst mental health crisis in decades," as psychologist Jean Twenge asserts? Are iPhones and Androids becoming the public health hazard that cigarettes were becoming in the 1960s? Are video games eroding the work ethic and hurting individuals' and the nation's economic fortunes?[40]

"So while we're communicating more, we may not necessarily be building relationships as strongly," DePaul University communications professor Paul Booth has argued. We're also rude and distracted as we text or otherwise use smart phones while we're with other people. Such "thubbing"—even texting another potential date while on a date—is not uncommon among women and men. To invert the old Stephen Stills song, Love the one you're not with.[41]

"Young users are particularly likely to use a smartphone to avoid boredom— and ignore other people," the Pew Research Center reported.[42] But a lot of hard-core users, like Peter, a gamer and college student from Indiana, strongly disagree. "It doesn't cut down on the time I spend with friends," he said. "I just put the game on pause if I want to see them. It hasn't affected my social life in a negative way."

Whether or not technology expands or enhances relationships, social skills, and social ties more broadly, or constricts them remains a matter of debate. Some would say that communication is merely changing with new technologies, just as happened with earlier technologies such as the telephone. Given the amounts of time that the typical American, much less heavy internet and digital device users, spend wired, what is happening in the 2010s is much more totalizing than the advent of Ma Bell. The digital age has its pros and cons, and many of the downsides are deeply troubling.

To the gendered question of different uses by, and effects on, men and women, it is clear that men are much more likely to be immersed in violent games, look for sex, and use online communications in hostile ways. The traits that underlie such behavior to varying degrees can be considered traditionally masculine and long predate the digital revolution. However, these traits, and the accompanying attitudes and behaviors, are ones that largely fall into the realm of "toxic" masculinity.

Taking this a step further, toxic masculinity tends to be more characteristic of American men who feel threatened or sidelined. Heavy technology users also tend to be people with time on their hands. The internet has squeezed time away from women and men of all backgrounds for all manner of activities—from reading, spending a romantic evening with one's partner, working, and appreciating nature (without one's smart phone) to studying, volunteering, critical thinking, and having dinner parties. For those who work and have children and partners, there is less time to be squeezed out, although we've seen that highly wired people may have poorer work habits and be more likely to divorce or have short, casual relationships.

For those who don't work, it's a different story. Whereas nonworking women typically spend much more time on care activities, for nonworking men, gaming and other digital activities devour time that could be spent on the job. Similarly, single and unpartnered men appear to spend more time online, and in fewer social activities, than either women or men who are married or have partners.

So we're back to the chicken-and-egg conundrum: does excessive non-work-related internet use contribute to men being "out," or is it a symptom? Either way, it is a piece of the puzzle, a segment of that Venn diagram. And it is a problem.

CHAPTER 6

Marriage and Husbands 2.0

We don't need a piece of paper from the city hall keeping us tied and true.
— *Joni Mitchell, "My Old Man," 1971*

Oh, Romeo, Romeo! Wherefore art thou, Romeo?
— *William Shakespeare*, Romeo and Juliet

Jay, a 50-year-old nonworking white man living in a coastal southeastern town, was long given cover by his wife, who would tell neighbors what a wonderful father he was to their three boys. His parents, who were comfortable enough to own a second home, had sent him to college, but he never took a job any more intellectually taxing than mowing lawns. And he did that for barely a year. His wife would say, "He's really trying to find something he's happy with."

He started smoking pot when he was young, and in middle age the smell of marijuana would waft out of his basement by midday as he played his guitar. Their home fell into ever greater disrepair, as nothing was fixed after several floods, and the driveway became unusable after the roots of a nearby pine tree split it wide open.

When Jay's sons were about 10 and 13, his wife left him. There was no drama about it, but friends say she was tired of his not doing anything. His own kids called him lazy.

At that point Jay took a nosedive. He drank and got high virtually around the clock. Beer bottles piled up in his SUV. When he came out of the house, he had a pistol and knife visibly attached to his waistband. He said he needed them because he was afraid that the police would get him.

Emerging from his depression, Jay hooked up with an old girlfriend, who waited tables. The woman and her teenage son moved in, ushering in a short-lived period of stability. Jay tried to start a business on the docks, but that too didn't go anywhere. He would occasionally complain to neighbors that his girlfriend was having an affair with a couple, but she paid the bills. He may have sold drugs or gotten public assistance, and his aging mother paid his mortgage, but he had no other source of income.

There are a striking number of Jays in America—husbands who don't work and thereby destroy their marriages.

Ben, the young Maine man who lives with his parents and works odd jobs, said he gets along with women, but "a long-term relationship is not worth my trouble." He loves children and finds "great joy to see them playing and hear their laughter," but he's afraid to get too close for fear of being labeled a pedophile. He is certain that "feminism is bad for men," because "women reap the economic benefits of a social and justice system that is skewed toward them, even though they continue to cry out about oppression."

There are also a striking number of Bens in the United States—men who don't work and expect never to marry.

Martha, the ex-wife of fifteen-years-out-of-work Bill from chapter 1, said, "He somehow seemed to feel like he didn't need to contribute and it was unfair for me to demand that. I was seen as a meal ticket."

In fact, the number of husbands not in the labor force rose from 2.8 million in 1996 to 4.6 million in 2016, a 64 percent increase, even though the number of married couples grew by only 13 percent.[1]

Laura, a white professional woman in the East who divorced her husband after he spent many years out of work, had similar comments about his lack of "resilience and grit," attributes that she saw in her father. "When I saw that he couldn't arrange kid activities or do regular daily tasks, I thought, 'How is he going to succeed at a job that is reasonably paid?'"

America also has many Marthas and Lauras—women who left husbands or partners in large part because their men stopped working or never did much work to begin with.

But there are also men like Louis, a well-educated white man in the Pacific Northwest, who stayed home to care for his children while his wife, with greater earning power, was the principal breadwinner. The ranks of these men are also increasing.

In 1964, when the Dixie Cups released "Going to the Chapel," nearly every American was married by their late 20s and more than three quarters of those marriages lasted a lifetime.[2] A diamond was forever.

"Goin' to the chapel and we're gonna get married" was the happy culminating refrain of romantic love and one of a few normative points of embarkation for responsible adulthood. Not too different from four decades earlier, when sociologists Robert and Helen Lynd observed, "In each of Middletown's homes lives a family, usually consisting of father, mother, and their unmarried children," with women wanting husbands who can "provide a good living" and women being homemakers.[3]

My, have things changed.

Marriage remains a goal for most Americans, and millions of straight and gay couples are happily married. Yet only half of U.S. adults in the mid-2010s were married, as divorce, cohabitation, delaying marriage, and remaining single have driven this percentage to a historic low. In 1967 seven out of ten adults were married, although marriage rates were lower (but not as low as today) around the turn of the twentieth century. The share of never-married adults age 25 and older has risen from 9 to 20 percent during the last fifty years, with that number climbing to 36 percent of adult African Americans and 26 percent of Latinos. And the gender difference for all Americans is significant: 23 percent of men had never married in 2012, compared to 17 percent of women. The differences by education, employment, and income are even greater. Some demographers think that if the current trajectory holds, an ever larger proportion of the population will never marry.[4]

In short, something is rotten with the state of marriage, at least among a sizable proportion of Americans. While gay men and lesbians fought hard for the right to marry, a lot of heterosexuals are backing away from marriage. This is in spite of the eloquent words of Supreme Court Justice Anthony Kennedy in his opinion supporting marriage equality: "No union is more profound than marriage, for it embodies the highest ideals of love, fidelity, devotion, sacrifice, and family. In forming a marital union, two people become something greater than they once were."[5]

Of course, women and men are both part of the equation, but there are a number of ways that the sidelining of millions of American men is a cause and consequence of falling marriage rates and marital discord. We saw in chapter 2 that in numerous heterosexual couples, women are the primary or sole earners, that unmarried men are less likely to work than guys who are married, and that nonworking (as well as working) husbands tend to put in far less than their share of time and effort taking care of children and the household. In chapter 3 we saw that misogyny is on the rise and that some straight men want little to do with women beyond sex. In chapter 4 we saw that many millennials are not marrying or are postponing marriage, and that less educated, out-of-work millennial men who may have still other strikes against them are not exactly the pick of the litter in the contemporary American marriage market. And in chapter 5 we saw that some men hole up in dark, virtual man caves, gaming, looking at porn or sexting, or browsing dating and hookup sites. In chapter 9 we will see that women often automatically rule out the sizable numbers of formerly incarcerated men as partners. None of these characteristics and lifestyles are what most women would say they're looking for in a male partner.

This is not to say that many men don't have legitimate complaints about existing or potential female partners. As we've seen, women often send mixed signals that they want a "manly" man who is egalitarian and not sexist yet who finds them attractive and sexy. Some women are as likely as men to "ghost," "thub," or otherwise unceremoniously blow off a guy. Many able-bodied women who aren't taking care of children don't work, or else they have husbands who share in childcare and home care. And many women, as well as men, cheat, lie, drink, and generally behave like characters out of an old Hank Williams song.

In one sign of positive changes in ideas about male roles is the evidence that growing numbers of men are comfortable with—nay, actively seek—egalitarian marriages and involved fatherhood. Younger fathers are especially likely to say that being a hands-on caregiver is as important as career success, and men want work-life balance as much as women. The number of single fathers is at least two million. A Pew Research study found that about two million fathers are nominally "house husbands," at home with their minor children.[6]

However, the change isn't as great as some liberals in well-heeled enclaves in large metropolitan areas might like to believe. Pew says that only about 20 percent of these house husbands stay at home intentionally to care for their children. The U.S. Census Bureau puts that number at just over 10 percent. And the U.S. Bureau of Labor Statistics (BLS) puts the ten-year increase at a whopping 0.3 percent of working-age men. For those who think the egalitarian utopia is around the corner, about twelve times as many 25- to 54-year-old women as men said they stayed home to take care of children and household tasks in 2014. The BLS's time use surveys indicate an uptick in husbands' involvement in food preparation and cleanup, yet they also show that wives spend three times as much time on household activities as their husbands.[7]

Many men's desires for more egalitarian marriages may be stymied by culture and law, argues Katherine Gallagher Robbins, with the progressive Center for American Progress. "Because of the way that we structure work, and the difficulties of managing caregiving and work responsibilities, it can lead one parent in two-parent families to specialize in one and one in the other," she said. Moreover, "men are too often an afterthought in conversations about working parents and workplace flexibility," Karyn Twaronite, global diversity and inclusiveness officer for Ernst and Young, told the *Washington Post*.[8]

Men and marriage also appear to be hurting due to the rising number of women who are the primary earners in marriages. Higher-earning women are less likely to marry in the first place, and women of all socioeconomic backgrounds are hesitant to marry men who can't hold a job. Higher-earning women characterized 29 percent of married couples in which both spouses worked in 2015 but 38 percent of *all* marriages, given the number of men who don't earn anything. Undoubtedly, this is an affront to the masculinity and self-esteem of some of these men (although some clearly have no compunction about being on their wives' meal ticket). A University of Chicago business school study found that when the wife earned more, couples reported being less "happy" and were more likely to have discussed separating, although husbands who are the sole breadwinners are less happy than men whose wives also work. Another study reported that men who are financially dependent on their wives or girlfriends are significantly more likely to cheat on them.[9]

Gender-role stereotyping may be hindering men's ability to be househusbands and primary caregivers, but the reality is that the number of stay-at-home dads by choice remains small enough to fit these rare creatures into a handful of football stadiums.

THE (CLASS-BASED) DECLINE OF MARRIAGE

While almost all Americans still profess to want to marry eventually, in practice a record 50 percent of adult Americans, or about 111 million men and women, were not wed in 2016.[10] There are basically five ways for heterosexuals not to be married: (1) they can postpone marriage, (2) they can never marry, (3) they can cohabit, (4) they can divorce and not remarry, or (5) they can be widowed and not remarry.

It takes two to tango, but why have both women and men stepped off the dance floor? In some ways, it's good to be older and more mature before marrying, divorce is more available to end bad marriages, and the moralistic proscriptions on living together have fallen. As one progressive woman said, "The divorce rate in Syria is probably zero." Yet cohabitation is fragile in America, divorce causes psychological pain for spouses and children and increased academic and behavior problems for boys in particular, and the share of children born to unmarried mothers has skyrocketed from 5 percent in 1960 to 40 percent in 2016.[11]

It seems impossible to "put the marriage genie back in the bottle," as Isabel Sawhill, one of the nation's leading scholars on marriage and family issues, has concluded.[12]

The unspoken, dirty little secret about the collapse of marriage is that it has become largely a class-based and racial phenomenon. While well-educated whites have been postponing marriage, the most severe problem is among less educated, less well-to-do, nonwhite Americans. Marriage has held up pretty well among the educated upper-middle class but has been in free fall among the poor and working class.

Whereas in 1960, Americans of virtually all socioeconomic backgrounds were equally likely to marry, by 2013, 83 percent of those in their late 30s in the top income quintile were married, compared to just 33 percent in the bottom two quintiles. Well under half of those without a college degree were married, compared to nearly two-thirds of college graduates. In the words of Jonathan Rauch, a Brookings Institution senior fellow, marriage is becoming a "gated community for the baccalaureate class." Some studies suggest that a portion of America's rise in economic inequality is associated with the class-based decline of marriage.[13]

"There are relatively few relationships that are more fully documented than those between economic well-being and marriage," according to Ron Haskins, the author of numerous papers on marriage and another senior fellow at Brookings. However, the nature of this relationship is hotly debated. Married people have higher incomes, greater wealth, and are healthier and happier than those who are divorced or cohabit. While the correlation is well established, is this a causal relationship, and, if so, which is the cause and which is the effect? Does marriage make people economically better off, or are the affluent simply more likely to marry—or a bit of both?[14]

Hardly anyone would call marrying at 28 or 30 or having children in their 30s "delaying" these days, and an increasing number of Americans don't marry for the first time until their late 30s or 40s. The proportion of married 18- to 34-year-olds has halved since 1980. More than two-thirds of men in their late 20s and 27 percent in their late 30s had never married in 2015. These shifts away from marrying in one's early 20s may have emotional and financial benefits, but one consequence is that "later" is increasingly turning into never. Mr. or Ms. Right never appears. Careers take precedence. Some are happier with a single life—what used to be quaintly called "confirmed bachelorhood" (with the more negative "spinster" label hurled at women). And as online dating has become like shopping on Amazon, the profusion of choices can either seem like a candy store or create anxiety and paralyze decision making.[15]

Divorce is probably the best-known factor in the decline of marriage, but it is not the only one. Largely driven by the feminist push to liberate women from bad marriages and the counterculture rebellion against marriage and ethos of individual self-actualization, no-fault divorce began in California in 1969 and rapidly spread throughout the nation. National divorce rates, which skyrocketed in the 1970s and then leveled off and have dipped since the early 1980s, have been rising among middle-age couples. In fact, the incidence of divorce among over-50 couples doubled between 1990 and 2012. As a result, about one-third of children under 18 have a stepparent in their lives. At the same time, many who have divorced, particularly women, aren't interested in remarrying. About 26 million divorced Americans were not remarried in 2015.[16]

Adding together the divorced, separated, and never married (plus the small number of widowers), about 38 percent of middle-age men weren't married in 2016. This is startling for a country where the normative image of a 45-year-old man is someone who is working, married, and with children at home. This figure is clouded somewhat by cohabitation, which is primarily the province of the young but has become more common among over-50 Americans, and the phenomenon of "living apart together" (LAT), self-identified couples who live in separate households. About 18 million unmarried men and women live together, and about one-third of adults who are not married or cohabiting are in LAT relationships, although some of these are simply dating, without a long-term commitment.[17]

WHY NOT MARRY?

The fact that large numbers of Americans are delaying marriage, not marrying, divorcing, cohabiting, or LATing accounts for the high numbers, but it doesn't answer the question of why they aren't getting married. Nor does it say anything about the consequences, the class differences, and how being unmarried may affect men and women differently. In broad brush, the reasons fall into three buckets: changed cultural norms, individuals' families of origin, and economics.

There are many ways that cultural changes appear to have been associated with the decline in, and declining appeal of, marriage. This is borne out by the U.S. Census survey that found that more than half of under-35 Americans believe marrying and having children are not very important in order to become an adult.[18]

Nonmarital (in the more innocent late twentieth century, it used to be called "premarital") sex and cohabitation, historically considered sinful, whispered-about abominations, have become widely accepted during the last four decades. They represent "the deregulation of adult relationships," in the words of professors June Carbone and Naomi Cahn, who have studied "marriage markets."[19] As we have seen, the technology and the hookup ethos have made nonmarital sex easy, if not appealing. The cultural revolution of the late 1960s and 1970s largely began with the upper middle class, but its greatest impact in the twenty-first century—when it comes to marriage, cohabiting, and childbearing—has been on the working class and poor.

"Living together" may sound liberal, tolerant, and hip, but it is a much more fragile arrangement than marriage, typically lasting little more than a year. While some cohabitations are seen as "trial marriages," an idea first floated in the 1920s, most of America's millions of cohabiters are unrealistically optimistic that they will eventually get married, and they tend to have a series of live-in partners. Cohabiters—particularly those in their 20s and 30s—are likely to have lower incomes, less education, and poorer health than married couples, but the biggest problems occur when children are born of these unions.[20]

"In a lot of cohabiting relationships, couples say they're basically married," said David Lapp, a writer studying working-class couples in Ohio. "But when that relationship ends, you have a divorce with no name. And you often have children involved." At least half of the 1.6 million children born outside of marriage in 2016 were born to cohabiting couples. Three million cohabiting couples have children living with them, and about half to two-thirds of these couples will have split up before their children start kindergarten. Some don't marry because of the perverse disincentive that mothers could lose some public benefits. Among all unmarried relationships in which a child is born, the vast majority of them dissolve.[21]

The effects of cultural change on marriage go beyond cohabitation. "Liberal tolerance of single parenthood, and ignoring marriage and family structure have made the problem worse," said Brad Wilcox, director of the National Marriage Project at the University of Virginia.[22]

Polarized, holier-than-thou politics have stymied much productive dialogue on this set of issues, which hurts women, children, and men. The Christian evangelical right popularized the motto "family values" in the late twentieth century, and the George W. Bush administration poured money into marriage promotion efforts that largely failed. On the left, it's politically incorrect to criticize single mothers, and some fear that promoting marriage plays into a right-wing agenda. Talk of "marriage" as a public policy issue makes many progressives squirm because it seems to have the bad odor of opposing women's rights and freedoms, castigating single moms, and acts as a distraction from looking at the "real" issues of economic justice.[23]

While it's hard not to sympathize with most single moms and unfair to damn most single fathers, children suffer the most. Nevertheless, many conservatives are more interested in blaming the parents, and most liberals are more focused on addressing the needs of poor children than on the circumstances of their birth.[24]

Back in 1993, after Vice President Dan Quayle criticized the TV sitcom *Murphy Brown* because the main character was a single mother by choice, cultural historian Barbara Dafoe Whitehead asked in the provocatively titled article "Dan Quayle Was Right," "How can we square traditional notions of public support for dependent women and children with a belief in women's right to pursue autonomy and independence in childbearing and childrearing? How do we uphold the freedom of adults to pursue individual happiness in their private relationships and at the same time respond to the needs of children for stability, security, and permanence in their family lives?"[25]

"So many people have trouble dealing with marriage as an issue and what should be norms" for marriage and raising children, said New York University political scientist Lawrence Mead. "The public isn't willing to disapprove parenthood with marriage, and we're more tolerant of alternatives to marriage."[26]

While we have alluded to the "I don't need a piece of paper" values of the counterculture, this belief elided with the rise of the singles culture in the 1970s. After the first TGI Fridays opened on Manhattan's Upper East Side in 1965, singles bars emerged across the country.[27] Movies like *Annie Hall* (1975), *Looking for Mr. Goodbar* (1977), and *An Unmarried Woman* (1978) etched the trials and tribulations of singles' life into the national consciousness.

We have also mentioned another counterculture spinoff or corollary: humanistic psychology emphasizing self-actualization and the individualistic notion of human potential. From Esalen to suburbia, it became fashionable to "find" oneself, a quest that put less emphasis on the "we" of marriage or civic life and more on the "me" in what Tom Wolfe famously called the "Me Decade." Historian and social critic Christopher Lasch, in *The Culture of Narcissism* (1979), asserts that these "new therapies spawned by the human potential movement" made the individual paramount and actually deepen the "isolation of the self."[28]

The increased availability of real and virtual sex is another cultural factor that may be making marriage less attractive to some men. Feminism, the human potential movement, and other psychological, social, and cultural currents of the late 1960s and 1970s also led a substantial number of women and men to expect more out of marriage. If it didn't provide fulfillment, didn't offer equality, didn't bring together "soul mates," and didn't include great sex, among other things, why not pass or keep on looking for such a perfect partnership?

Wilcox points out further evidence that culture matters: although there is a strong correlation between social class and marriage and family stability, he has noted that—holding economic and educational variables constant—Idaho, with a large Mormon population, has greater family stability than states like Louisiana or New Mexico.[29]

In addition, when we talk about "culture," let's not forget that one of the most powerful signifiers of traditional masculinity is the ability to provide for one's family. For the still large numbers of men and women who have more or less internalized this norm, the inability to provide can be a big deal-breaker. Women don't want this kind of "unmanly" man, and men who don't work or have only intermittent or low incomes may compensate for their feelings of inadequacy by trying to prove their "manhood" in other ways that are less productive than being a spouse-provider (or, at least, co-provider). When Wilcox made a YouTube video called *Be a Man: Get Married*, he got a lot of views but also a lot of pushback: You don't need marriage for sex. You abandon fun and adventure. You lose personal freedom. Monogamy is "uncool." "Radical feminism teaches that men are the enemy," wrote one respondent. "So is it any surprise that more and more men are checking out of marriage and relationships and are joining the sexodus?"[30]

Another reason that some young people choose not to marry stems from the trauma and pain they felt in their own family lives growing up. The ongoing Fragile Families and Child Wellbeing study, which has followed the children of 3,600 unmarried parents and 1,100 married parents since 1998, found that unmarried fathers are more likely than married fathers to have grown up without two parents present. Children of divorced or single parents may be more prone to divorce, and in some cases the divorce-boom generation may be warier of marriage, not wanting to recapitulate their parents' perceived failures.[31] However, in this effort to avoid inflicting the kinds of pain they felt with divorcing parents, they may be causing an even more problematic set of circumstances.

By cohabiting or having unprotected casual sex, they too often become the parents of the 40 percent of babies being born to unmarried couples, with more than half of these parents having additional children with at least one other partner. The number of cohabiting couples with children doubled in the twenty years after 1996. Two-thirds of fathers under 29 have had children out of wedlock. The ranks of unmarried parents have been further pushed up by the fact that many gay and lesbian couples have children (although at least one study shows that their children generally do quite well). The proportion of white mothers who are unmarried has shot up to 29 percent (several percentage points higher than for white fathers), and the share of black mothers who aren't married has increased to 70 percent. The Fragile Families longitudinal study has revealed that most of these children were born to couples in relationships, and Princeton sociologist Kathryn Edin has reported that most of these couples want the relationship to endure, dispelling the "hit-and-run" stereotype. Most are born to parents in their 20s or early 30s, as teen pregnancy rates have declined. But they are called fragile for a reason. As noted, they break up. In addition to fragmented families from cohabitation or longer-term relationships and families broken by divorce, there are also children born of liaisons that never lead to any kind of family formation. In addition, one or both parents often have children with new partners. Sometimes there are many children by many partners, and parents'—especially fathers'—attention tends to focus on the most recent offspring. For children it means navigating stepparents, girlfriends or boyfriends, half-siblings, sometimes parents who have become gay or transgender, and a cast of characters so large that they might as well wear name tags. Thus is born the so-called complex family.[32]

Neville, who has lived in various cities on the East Coast during his 43 years, has had seven children with five different mothers. His circumstances make for a very complex family and are an extreme version of the experience of one in seven American fathers who have had children with more than one woman.[33]

Neville's children range in age from 3 to 28, few are emotionally close to each other, and they are scattered up and down the eastern seaboard. Just one, his 3-year-old, lives with him and his partner. Four of the others live with an aunt and two mothers, although one daughter lives on her own, as does a son, who was kicked out before he turned 18.

Neville, who is African American, has good relationships with a few of his children and insists that he wants to make things last with the mother of his toddler. He especially regrets not being closer to his eldest son, recognizing that "I was just a child when he was born."

He acknowledged that he has "made poor decisions." He attributes some of it to drinking, which he has since given up. But, he says, "I also kind of blame their mothers, because they had the children" and didn't always tell him they were pregnant. Men are often the ones demanding an abortion, even though it's women whose bodies and beliefs have to deal with the damage, but those cases in which women have babies from unplanned pregnancies against men's wishes led one men's rights advocate to provocatively ask "What about men's bodies, men's choices?"

Neville has been in and out of jobs but now works more than full-time as a barber. When he has worked, he kept up with child-support payments, even though they devoured 60 percent of his gross income, leaving him with the equivalent of a subminimum wage. He lived with his grandmother for a number of years when his children and their mothers weren't with him.

Cultural changes and childhood experiences have played a big role in the decline of marriage, but economics is at least as important a factor. As suggested, the relationship between economics and marriage is controversial, complex, and multidirectional. Declining wages, low incomes, unstable jobs, and not working have led a lot of especially less educated young people to conclude that they can't afford to get married. At the same time, declines in marriage appear to have led to declines in work.[34] Remember the millions of millennial men living at home. As in times past, many say they want to get on their feet before tying the knot. The difference between the 2010s and the 1960s is that it either takes a good bit longer to find one's footing or it is impossible to do so.

Not working, if not a predictor, is correlated with not being married and not having children. In 2016 only 34 percent of prime-age men not in the labor force were married compared to 58 percent of prime-age men in the labor force who were married. Looked at another way, married men are more likely to work than those who are unmarried or divorced. Just over 71 percent of married white men 25 and older were employed in 2015, compared to 62.7 percent of divorced men and 65.4 percent of all unmarried men. Black married men have almost identical employment rates as white married men, but the falloff is much more dramatic for those who haven't married: 52.2 percent of divorced men and 56.5 percent of all unmarried men in this age group aren't working. Similar patterns can be found among married Latino and Asian American men, although employment rates among these groups were 5 to 8.5 percentage points higher than for white men. Married men with children had still higher employment rates among all groups.[35]

But this is yet another example of the complicated cultural-economic nexus. The U.S. marriage rate started its long fall between the mid-1970s and 1980, when wages began to stagnate and decline for working-class and poor men and when the norms of the counterculture and the "Me Decade" gained traction. "Women's liberation," higher expectations for marriage, and the greater ease in changing partners also made it easier to dump a spouse or potential spouse if he did not work and have income.[36]

Conservative scholar Charles Murray bluntly has said that "single prime-age males are much less industrious than married ones." Melissa Boteach, vice president of the Poverty to Prosperity program at the liberal Center for American Progress, counters: "The word 'culture' when applied to working-class people is often used as a code word to suggest that struggling families don't value marriage. The reality is that, if anything, people with lower incomes have more traditional views on marriage than those with higher incomes, and very much desire stable and healthy families." Like Boteach, historian Elaine Tyler May argues that family fragmentation is a symptom of economic hardship.[37]

Economics matter, but in the context of culture, according to David Blankenhorn, the liberal founder of the conservative sounding Institute for American Values and author of several books on marriage and fatherhood. "There's no question that middle-class blue-collar jobs have declined and that it's a contributor" to the class-based decline of marriage, he said. "But things get baked into the culture. If zillions of good blue-collar jobs came back, it wouldn't solve this crisis."[38]

WHO'S TO BLAME?

These cultural and economic factors have changed the landscape of marriage, and one can toggle between calling them "causes" and "effects." They also exacerbate other widespread and unsavory male proclivities. Men are more likely to commit the most violent acts of sexual and spousal abuse, but there's evidence of gender parity when it comes to less severe, nonsexual domestic violence. Men are somewhat more likely to have affairs, but there is also evidence that this is primarily true among over-40 men and, as a Maryland therapist drily put it, "Monogamy is being examined more fluidly." Nonworking and unmarried men are especially prone to these behaviors.[39]

But can one apportion the preponderance of "blame" to men or women?

The old line is that men don't want to make a commitment, but it's divorced women who don't want to get remarried, and a lot of never-married women aren't in any great hurry to marry. Women tend to be less satisfied than men with marriage and initiate nearly 70 percent of all divorces, a proportion that has barely changed during the last century.[40]

On-the-make, commitment-averse men with at least some desirable attributes "play the field," in which the sexual odds are in their favor. At the same time, in a striking reversal of the still very real phenomenon of successful older men with young "trophy wives," older successful women, so-called cougars, now have young studs on their arms. Many a successful 50- or 60-year-old woman has a gleam in her eyes when talking about the 25-year-old guys propositioning them. And growing numbers of women are "players."

But men who are married are generally the lucky ones, economically, psychologically, and in terms of health and self-esteem.[41]

With the increase in assortative mating—Ivy Leaguers marrying Ivy Leaguers and high school grads shacking up with high school grads—well-educated women play a game of musical chairs, in which they always outnumber men who are their "equals."[42] As a chair is pulled away when one of these "good catches" goes off the market, they are left standing. While there are still more men than women with six-figure incomes, by age 27 there are one-third more women than men with bachelor's degrees, and 30 percent of wives have more education than their husbands.[43] For "good" men, the odds are good. Thus, women with at least a college education have three choices: compete for the successful guys (which may require downplaying their success and donning a little black dress), marry down, or drop out in frustration, often rationalizing that they don't "need" the hassle of men.

Some men out who are not top-drawer husband material feel cowed and outclassed by women. Men who are living at home or jobless or those with less education or lower incomes than women—hardly the catch of the day—often feel intimidated by women whose expectations they can't hope to live up to.

Others roam from one sexual liaison to another, as the internet has enabled much greater efficiency in such pursuits than the increasingly anachronistic singles bar.

If some men are sexually predatory cads, others simply do not make the cut. Even among those who do marry, with more and more wives outearning their husbands, many men find it hard to adapt to the role of economic dependent. Then there are those who find it all too easy to become dependent, losing or quitting jobs not to become stay-at-home dads but to turn into economic parasites. They rely on their wives not only to take care of the kids and put meals on the table but also to provide the family income, health insurance, and the mortgage payments. Such men, in the upper-middle class as well as among lower-income households, while away their time pretending to work, watching TV, yoked to the internet, and ready to hit their first beer just hours after slouching out of bed. These men have become prime divorce candidates. Forget "for richer, for poorer."

Rob, a 60-year-old white New England man who had a career in the media, gradually started losing clients about fifteen years ago and now rarely works. His wife worked ever harder, and "his contribution became less and less," she said.

With a family and a mortgage, he became withdrawn and depressed, and instead of trying to drum up new business, he spent his time watching sports on TV and surfing the web. He got in rages and physically threatened his wife countless times, all the while expecting her to work harder and take care of their two teenage children. Rob claimed he was spending more time with the children, but according to their mother, he was brutal toward them, yelling at them over small things he didn't like.

Rob was providing almost nothing to the family's income and getting increasingly angry toward his wife, neighbors, and kids; his wife finally left him. Alone, having moved from a big house to a small apartment, he does occasional work, but his children almost never see him, and his health has deteriorated.

When men can't assume their culturally prescribed role as providers, such apparent laziness and irresponsibility is often a function of depression and shame, according to Cabrini University psychologist Mark Kiselica, who is a former president of the Society for the Psychological Study of Men and Masculinity. "Shame affects self-esteem and identity as a male," he said. "It's not just a career issue. They tend to feel like complete failures."[44]

Nonworking husbands not only may experience shame, but they often feel unneeded. They may feel like they've failed, but the consequences of such feelings can result in depression, hopelessness, substance abuse, and suicide. And the regrets pile up.

Such feelings also can lead to anger, blaming their situation—rightly or wrongly—on immigrants, women, or other groups, the government, Wall Street, or the economic system. Or the shame can spur them to show their families and the world that they aren't failures by persevering until they're back on their feet.

When Ed went to the dog park in his affluent New York suburb, he knew that the men there were out of work, and the women were married to men with high incomes. "There's more shame for men who aren't working," he said. "We feel we're to blame, and many women think that men should provide the support."

Ed, a white man in his early 60s, has an MBA and had long worked for a major New York publishing company. He felt secure in his job until another company bought his employer in the early 2000s, shifting its focus to become more technology-oriented.

"I didn't think I was getting older, and my declining value because of my age and lack of technology skills didn't occur to me right away," he recalled. When he lost his job in his late 40s, he and his wife and their children moved in with Ed's mother. "There was a lot of collateral damage." He cashed in his retirement savings to keep paying off his house. Ed spent thousands in legal fees to try to stave off foreclosure. He lost, and his house was gone.

The "collateral damage" continued. Ed's wife, who, he said, "had the capability to earn good money," stayed home. After thirty-three years of marriage and several years of hard times, Ed's marriage ended.

Yet he hardly gave up. Not only did he look for jobs every day, but he formed a support group for people in his position. He took a "grunt job," working at a local supermarket. But even there he has been on a short-term contract, with no job security. "I don't have any savings, and I'll have to work until the day I die."

Ed is bitter but hardly a quitter. He sees the depression and alcoholism of others in his group, hates politicians who say that people like him "are living beyond their means," and is angry that there seem to be more jobs programs for "special-needs populations" such as ex-offenders and African Americans. But he said he can't understand men who give up and stop looking for work. Ed keeps trying—both for himself and to help others who don't have jobs.

WHY BREAK UP?

"Breaking up is hard to do," sang Neil Sedaka back in 1962. It may have been harder then.

Financial issues always have been a cause of divorce, but the simultaneous growth of an economically insecure "precariat" and of cohabitation have made the state of America's unions extremely brittle.[45] Not only do cohabitations and unmarried parental relationships crumble easily, but the likelihood of divorce for struggling couples is high.

Again, there is a gendered dimension to how economic adversity, particularly nonemployment, affects marriages. Women are more likely to be in low-wage occupations and jobs, but mothers (single and married) are also more likely to take and endure bad jobs to keep their children fed. This is not to say that most men don't provide, or try their best to provide, for their kids, but the toxic combination of the masculine prescription to be the provider and the growing absence of work among men has sounded the death knell of many a marriage across the socioeconomic spectrum.

There is also a gendered dimension to how divorce and breaking up other unions affect men. Because of the long-standing presumption, now changing, that mothers should be given primary custody of children because they have been culturally deemed the more "important" parent, men often lose some or all contact with their children. Some men may skip town, but most fathers have just as strong, albeit different, bonds with their children as women do. As the Fragile Families study, surveys, and divorce lawyers say, and as we will see in the next chapter, many men are shut out of their children's lives because of this cultural and legal bias, because of ex-wives or ex-partners' "gatekeeping," and because of the enormous legal costs of fighting for their rights.[46]

Lisa, the manager of a fast-food restaurant in Ohio, and Jessie, who had thousands of dollars of debt, married after living together at a friend's apartment. She encouraged him to get a job, but she loved him enough to marry anyway. Not long after they married, she discovered that he was being prescribed drugs for mental health issues and she suspected that he was abusing them. One day Lisa got a call from the cops, telling her that Jessie had overdosed on heroin. They divorced. "All my life, I always said it didn't matter how much money a man had, but after my divorce, I have to have higher expectations for a man financially," she said.

If Lisa and Jessie were in the twentieth percentile in America's income distribution, Donna and Mark, both also white, were easily in the top first or second percentile. Everyone had thought of Mark as a genius when he was young. After being on law review, he was hired by one of New York's most prestigious law firms. An idealist, he took a job with a progressive nonprofit in Washington, D.C. Before he was 30, he had become an aide to President Bill Clinton. He was often invited to fancy Washington events with political celebrities from both parties. Often described as "the life of the party," he charmed Donna, the professional woman we met in chapter 5, into marrying him.

But Mark's glide path to success ended after Clinton left office. A Republican friend helped him get a good private sector job, which he lost within a year. A leading figure in the Clinton administration then helped him get another job, which he also was fired from in less than a year.

The couple had two young children, and Mark's wife had left her job just before his second layoff. "There was a tipping point after three to four years out of how long I could stay out of the workforce," she recalled. "So I was forced back to work."

One day Donna found evidence that Mark was "leading a double life." He would often drink two bottles of wine in a night, but that was the least of it. The alcohol would be paired with long late-night sessions looking at pornography and texting women for sexual liaisons. When Donna discovered this, she filed for divorce. Mark—not working for much of the twenty-first century—is fortunate to have the economic cushion of a big inheritance from his parents, but the glory days of D.C. in the 1990s are long behind him.

Economics in general, and men not working in particular, clearly is a factor in divorce as it is in not marrying and the dissolution of cohabiting relationships. However, during the severe economic disruptions of the Depression in the 1930s, there was no increase in divorce.[47] So we return to the fact that changes in the culture and in the economy are reinforcing each other, with devastating results for countless marriages, relationships, and children.

Hidden from bustling offices, shops, and industrial plants and far from neighborhoods where moms and dads walk their kids to the school bus each morning are millions of American men who are neither working nor married and often are missing as fathers. Although women and children who have felt deeply disappointed by them, as well as some social scientists and marriage proponents, talk about them, they are like the oddball aunt or the family black sheep. They are a subject that most of America avoids talking about.

They are part of that Venn diagram of men out. Some also may be internet addicts or ex-offenders. Some may be millennials or people of color. Many have health problems or trouble with what it means to be masculine. Many never get a college degree and many are isolated.

If one believes that marriage or at least stable families are good, one can rail at these men and try to promote different values and norms or a more broadly prosperous economy.

While more than three-fourths of men will marry at some point, Husbands 1.0—those responsible, somewhat mythical men of *Father Knows Best* and *Leave It to Beaver* days—aren't going to be the near-universal norm that they were in the mid-twentieth century. As Sawhill said, the marriage genie is out of the bottle.

And as the great anthropologist Margaret Mead said many decades ago, "As the family goes, so goes the nation."[48]

CHAPTER 7

Fathers without Children

Every known human society rests firmly on the learned nurturing behavior of men.

— *Margaret Mead*, Male and Female, 1949

Too many fathers . . . are . . . missing—missing from too many lives and too many homes. . . . And the foundations of our families are weaker because of it.

— *Barack Obama, Father's Day speech*, 2008

Single moms elicit widespread sympathy, with an undercurrent of ambivalence. "Deadbeat dads" are universally denounced. Children of divorce and their parents are seen as significantly disadvantaged and have been extensively studied. "Enlightened" caregiving and stay-at-home dads have been spotlighted by numerous progressives, men's groups, and the media. Custodial fathers receive little attention.

However, the story of America's crisis of missing fathers is a good bit more complicated. It involves a long list of more nuanced issues, including the following: (1) traditional and new norms about fatherhood, (2) men not working, (3) masculinity, (4) poverty and bad jobs, (5) nonmarital births, cohabitation, and fragile and "fragmented" families, (6) child custody and child support laws, (7) perverse government policies that make it more difficult for poorer men to see their children, (8) mothers "gatekeeping" to keep fathers away or alienating their kids from their fathers, (9) men and women having children with more than one partner, (10) public lack of attention to the problems of missing fathers, (11) mass incarceration, (12) men's sadness at being separated from their children, and (13) many fathers' anger at being treated like second-class parents.

Although we will discuss the risk factors and harm done to children without fathers, let's point the looking glass in the other direction: What is the state of *fathers without children?* How are men—as well as their children—harmed by being without their children, and how can a man being without his children contribute to his being sidelined?

Jemal has had four daughters with two women—two daughters in their 20s, two in preschool—but is living with none of them. A thoughtful 47-year-old African American man in a large eastern city, he knows he "made mistakes" and said, "I don't want to repeat them with my younger daughter."

Jemal is among the more than one in four American fathers who do not live with all of their children under 18, and his minor children are among the one in three who are not with their father on any given night—compared to one in nine children in 1960. He is also among one in seven U.S. fathers who have had children with more than one woman. The nearly 25 million children who lived in single-parent families in 2015 were disproportionately poor and born to parents of color, but there are millions of white and better-off fathers (and also some mothers) who live apart from their children. A majority of U.S. children spend some portion of their childhood with only one parent, and less than half the nation's children live with two married parents who are in their first marriage.[1]

Of the nation's roughly 36 million fathers of America's 74 million under-18 children, about nine million to ten million dads do not live with all of their minor children most or all of the time (including about one million incarcerated fathers), and several million more see their kids at least once a week, although the proportion has been rising. In addition to ten million single mothers, there are more than two million custodial single fathers. Nearly half of African American children, one quarter of white and Latino children, and one-eighth of Asian American, American Indian, and Alaska Native children live without their fathers. About 2.8 million children live with neither parent.[2]

Jemal hardly had good role models for parenting. He grew up in a poor African American neighborhood of Brooklyn, and his mother died of cancer when he was seven. He lived with his dad, who had several women in his life even before his wife died. "I don't doubt that he loved me, but he didn't know how to be a dad, because he didn't have a great dad," Jemal reflected.

Jemal ran with the "wrong people" in his early 20s and knew he'd "end up in jail" if he didn't leave town and leave behind his old identity. When he was 24, he met a woman and got married. They had two daughters, and after they split in 1999 he gained custody of both because their mother had legal and emotional problems that led their children to have an "adverse opinion" of her. Jemal always made sure that his daughters saw their mother.

But despite his work experience in IT, he lost his job and then lost his house during the global recession and thought it was best for his daughters—then in seventh and ninth grades—to live with their mother. They felt rejected, a feeling they still hold on to years later, Jemal believes. He also fears that they only value him for his income. He has continued to try to reconcile with them, but in the meantime, in his early 40s he met another woman, fifteen years younger, with whom he has had two children. He believes that one of his older daughters feels that " 'I wasn't important to you when I really needed you, because you had other women.' "

Jemal has had a volatile relationship with the mother of his preschool daughters. She wanted marriage, then left him to live on a $13-an-hour job, food stamps, and the earned income tax credit (EITC). He entered an employment and fatherhood program. He said, "I absolutely love her and would marry her" and take care of their kids and the three children she had with another man. But she wasn't interested the last time I spoke with Jemal.

While he agonizes about reconciling with his older daughters, he has tried to be the best dad he can be with his younger ones. He reads them Dr. Seuss at night, checks out dozens of books at the library for them, and buys them Legos and Mega Bloks. "I'm committed to being a good father to all four of my daughters," he said, "but we have human frailties, and I need to make a concerted effort."

Then there are men like Matt, a white professional in the Carolinas who essentially became his three children's full-time parent after his ex-wife went in and out of relationships with men. Having started his own business, he used his flexible hours to be there for his children when they needed him. He took his sons on overseas trips to see top-ranked European soccer teams, and to a presidential inauguration. He tried to make sure they saw their mother, but she moved so often for the men in her life and sank ever deeper into debt that she couldn't really take care of them. For guys like Matt, "father" is a verb as much as a noun.

On the one hand, the numbers of very involved fathers, stay-at-home dads, male-headed single-parent households, and gay fathers are increasing rapidly, although they remain low. On the other hand, the overall proportion of adult men who are fathers has fallen sharply in recent decades. Including fathers missing from their children's lives and men who have never had children, barely half of America's 40 million 25- to 44-year-old men live with a child, with the proportion falling to one quarter among African American men.[3]

And as many of the men we've met in this book illustrate, a significant minority of fathers have played a less than stellar part in their children's lives, and some have even dishonorably disappeared. Some mothers also fit this bill, but their numbers are far exceeded by those of fathers. There are also the men who demand abortions of women they impregnate.

Yet for virtually all of human history, the vast majority of men became fathers and women became mothers, and they did their best to raise their children. It was a given. It was not a choice. While the term "missing fathers" is used to refer to fathers who spend little or no time with their children, recent decades have seen another form of missing fathers (and mothers): the growing numbers of adults who never have children by choice.

The nature and norms of fatherhood have varied considerably throughout history and across cultures. For all the loose talk about patriarchy today, the United States was truly a patriarchal society until the early twentieth century: fathers controlled all decisions in the family, including those relating to childrearing (even if they played a less than active role). While women have worked at least as much as men throughout history, the Industrial Revolution led to a de facto division of labor—men as wage-earning fathers, women as nurturing mothers in what historians have called the "cult of domesticity" (or "true womanhood"). Although wives continued to be denied many equal rights into the mid-twentieth century, moms were both celebrated and criticized as the architects of childrearing. Mother's Day quickly was proclaimed a national holiday in 1914. Despite simultaneous attempts to create a Father's Day holiday, it did not become official until 1972.[4]

Fathers were in the background in their children's lives. Ward Cleaver, in *Leave It to Beaver*, went off to work each day, June stayed home to care for the children, and the most notable aspects of Ward's role as father were that he was his boys' buddy and the problem solver when Beaver got into trouble. The often idealized twentieth-century "nuclear family" was not always the idyll of family meals and station wagons filled with two parents and two or three kids on road trips, their smiling faces memorialized in Kodak moments. The stable father–working nuclear family of post–World War II lore was really a historical anomaly, as sociologist Andrew Cherlin points out in his 1981 book, *Marriage, Divorce, Remarriage.*[5]

Gender roles were sharply defined, with fathers "knowing best" and most mothers consigned to housewifery—daily chores and the expectation of looking pretty for their husbands when they came home from work. In keeping with traditional codes of masculinity, men were implicitly told not to express their feelings and not to be too nurturing to their children. Often fathers had little involvement with their kids, given a sharp gender-based division of labor that made mothers the principal caregivers and, in the process, wasn't great for either fathers and children or mothers. Strictures against divorce led to a lot of unhappy marriages, whose effects rubbed off on millions of children. Then, as divorce rates spiked upward in the 1970s, even fathers who wanted to be engaged with their children were generally denied custody, given the presumption that mothers were intrinsically better parents.[6]

Since definitions of the normative father and mother are culturally and historically specific constructs, how did this mid- to late-twentieth-century role develop? Ideas about masculinity and femininity and the sexual division of labor were reinforced in laws, novels, and popular culture.

Hollywood has presented particularly disparate views of fathers since the mid-twentieth century, ones that have mirrored and shaped reality. Fathers have been either the emotionally distant provider, the authoritarian patriarch, the loser, or the heroic and sensitive father, who is typically widowed or divorced. Good, strong, sensitive fathers ranging from Atticus Finch to Andy Griffith and Marlin in *Finding Nemo* (2003) have been widowers, and Andy had Aunt Bea to play the requisite adult female. In *The Cosby Show* the father and mother played both parenting and professional roles, yet the mother was usually right. In *Star Wars: Episode V—The Empire Strikes Back* (1980), Darth Vader is evil incarnate, only to be redeemed as Luke Skywalker's father. Homer Simpson is the archetypal dumb, lazy, crude, yet buffoonishly lovable father. Psychologist Ross Parke at the University of California–Riverside has argued that the overrepresentation of single fathers on TV shows, mostly sitcoms, since the 1960s has been because "fathers provide a facile and nearly endless source of humor."[7]

Enter the New Involved Father. He is emotionally expressive and nurturing from the first diaper on. He provides a somewhat androgynous mix of rough-and-tumble play, hugs, and hours of reading to his child in bed and talks about feelings, schoolwork, and the world. He is the ideal of countless "liberated" men and women ("Moms think good dads are sexy," according to Doyin Richards, a fatherhood blogger), and at least one study has found that more egalitarian marriages are happier. However, he can be resented by some women for intruding on their perceived turf and looked down on as "unmanly" and a problem by many employers and a large segment of the population. But at least as big a problem is that the norms of the New Involved Father run up against traditional masculine norms. More than a few men feel torn between wanting to cuddle, bathe, and read to their kids and facing social pressure from other men, women, and older generations who tell them that such behavior isn't "masculine." As a result, and despite his much-hailed emergence in the early 1980s, this thoroughly modern dad still represents a small minority of America's fathers, whether in married, partnered, divorced, or otherwise broken families. Data on fathers' time use and true stay-at-home dads, and women's widespread and mostly valid complaints that they have to do everything, point to this being a pretty rarified, if leading-edge, phenomenon.[8]

At least since the fatherhood movement emerged in the 1990s, if not as far back as Daniel Patrick Moynihan's controversial essay "The Negro Family" (1965), issues of father involvement, father absence, family breakdown, single parenthood, and fathers' roles have been the subject of considerable research and debate. The alarm bells started to sound about missing fathers in the 1990s as the percentage of unmarried white parents surpassed that of unmarried African American parents in the early 1960s, when Moynihan called it a "crisis." Robert Lerman, Institute Fellow at the Urban Institute, and Theodora Ooms, a social worker and consultant to the National Healthy Marriage Resource Center, published the first comprehensive book on absent fathers of all races in 1993.[9]

There are very notable exceptions—think Bill Clinton and Barack Obama—but, generally, growing up without a father is a recipe for failure. Although a good bit of liberal versus conservative mudslinging exists on whether economics or culture is principally to blame, the reality of the problem is one issue that conservatives and liberals, Bible Belt Christians, and civil rights activists agree on. Conservative "family values" proponents constantly beat this drum. Some of the nation's leading social scientists have made this their life work.

Family fragmentation is the "overwhelming social disaster of our time," historian Stephanie Coontz has said. As we've seen, Louis Farrakhan and Promise Keepers brought hundreds of thousands of men to the National Mall in Washington, D.C., in 1995 and 1997, urging them to dedicate themselves to their families. President Ronald Reagan, in his 1986 State of the Union address, said, "In the welfare culture, the breakdown of the family, the most basic support system, has reached crisis proportions: female and child poverty, child abandonment, horrible crimes, and deteriorating schools." President Obama (before becoming president, as a senator) tried to address the crisis but made little headway.[10]

The problem is that the issue generally has been defined narrowly, missing a key ingredient. The effects on children and on single mothers deservedly have received much attention. But the facile assumption has been that missing fathers are the bad guys. Aside from a number of exceptional studies, neither the public, nor policymakers, nor the advocacy community pays much attention to missing fathers themselves. Who are they? Why is this happening? In what ways are they "doing the best that they can," as Princeton University sociologist Kathryn Edin has written? How are most of these dads harmed and hurting by being out of their children's lives?[11]

CHILDREN NEED THEIR DADS, BUT FATHERS ALSO NEED THEIR CHILDREN

Despite the long-standing notion that pregnancy creates the ultimate bond between a mother and her child, research has shown that the overwhelming majority of fathers develop similarly strong bonds with their children and relish the very idea of being a dad. Becoming a father can dramatically change a man, leading him to "reorient" his values and behavior toward tenderness and caregiving.[12]

"People think they don't care, but we know they do," Joseph Jones, president of the Baltimore Center for Urban Families, has said. "We see how dads are fighting against the odds to be engaged in the lives of their children."[13]

"They may adhere to traditional masculine ideals, have no jobs, done drugs or been in jail, had fathers who were bad role models, but so many want to be nurturing and loving," according to Sonia Molloy, a professor of human development at Penn State who has studied mostly poor white fathers in Appalachia.[14]

Having a baby can strain partner relationships and be a big adjustment for some men, yet fathers—especially but not exclusively those who live with their children—report greater meaning in their lives than men without children. Perhaps in part because of the still disproportionate workload and consequent stress that moms typically experience, multiple studies have found that being a father brings greater happiness to men than being a mother does to women, although others indicate that women more often provide ongoing *care* for their children than men do.[15]

Fathers, as well as mothers, play an essential role in children's development. Love and nurturing are important for both parents, but fathers have been found to generally play a bigger role in promoting their children's cognitive development, regulating their behavior, stimulating creative play, and developing their identity and social competence.[16]

Contrary to widespread opinion, most unmarried men don't want to abandon their parental responsibilities when a child is conceived. In fact, when they become parents, even the poorest men "are suddenly transformed" and try to get a decent job and be there for their baby. As Vernon Wallace, program manager of Baltimore's Responsible Fatherhood Project, said of the African American fathers in his program, "They may seem like super-tough street guys, but they sit down and bawl when talking about their kids and fathers. The faucets come on. No man wakes up thinking 'I want to have kids and don't want to take care of them.' These dads aren't perfect, but they want to be with their child."[17]

Possibly because society cuts off more avenues to professional identity for people of color, African American men—both those who live with their children and those who do not—are somewhat more involved with their kids in activities such as bathing and reading than white or Latino fathers.[18]

For large numbers of poor men, "children are not millstones but life preservers [and] saviors," according to Kathryn Edin and Timothy Nelson, authors of *Doing the Best I Can: Fatherhood in the Inner City*. They invest their identity in their kids, consciously or unconsciously knowing that the alternatives, such as prison, drugs, and death, are bleak. Unfortunately, these ideals too often don't translate into reality.[19]

SINGLE MOTHERS

Thus, as we saw in chapter 6, millions of American children spend a good chunk of their childhood with little or no connection to their fathers. Half of U.S. children will spend at least two years living in a one-parent home.[20] Some will never or barely know their fathers, while some of these fathers may see their children anywhere between very infrequently and very often. Why this happens and which of these circumstances occurs matter tremendously not only to children but to fathers as well.

Because five out of six single-parent households are headed by women and the percentage of kids living only with their mothers tripled between 1960 and 2016 to 23 percent, the nation's 10 million single mothers, who care for more than 20 million children, have received a great deal of attention. Their plight has been highlighted by progressives and feminists, because they are much more likely to live in poverty. They bear the burdens of rearing these children singlehandedly, often with the near-impossible balancing of work and kids. They also have been derided by conservatives who hold on to Ronald Reagan's image of the "welfare queen" and blame the pre–welfare reform Aid to Families with Dependent Children (AFDC) program for making it okay to be a single mother.

Single mothers range from young, white, and rural; to poor, early middle-age, urban, and black; and to high-powered professional straight and gay women who have chosen to have children without a male partner. Yet on average they are poor, surviving on low-wage jobs, government support, and child support. For many poor young women, as for some poor young men, early childbearing gives their lives meaning. One-third of single mothers lived below the poverty threshold in 2015, and they are twice as likely as other women to be in low-paid occupations such as health aides, child care, food service, and housekeeping. Welfare reform in 1996 cut cash support, ending the AFDC program, which supported about 13 million single mothers, and replaced it with the Temporary Assistance for Needy Families (TANF) program, which in 2016 provided temporary aid to about 3 million women until they found work. While a good number of single mothers did get jobs, many of them were low-paying, and nearly 2 million desperately poor single mothers neither worked nor received government aid in 2015.[21]

Many are like Kamica in East Oakland, California, a black woman who works part-time caring for other people's children and part-time as a cashier at 49ers and Giants games. She earns about $11 per hour without benefits to support her own five children, who are looked after by her uncle.

Meanwhile, missing fathers have come in for attack from all sides. As J. D. Vance suggested in *Hillbilly Elegy*, it's hard to have sympathy for a "man who can find the time to make eight children but can't find the time to support them." Yet the 3 million children living with at least 2 million single fathers, a figure that has quadrupled since about 1980 from 1 to 4 percent, are not often talked about.[22]

WHO ARE THE MISSING FATHERS?

The prevailing assumption is that these poor single mothers have been abandoned by good-for-nothing men who got them pregnant, disappeared, don't pay child support, and have moved on to other women. As William J. Bennett, George W. Bush's secretary of education, said, "It is unmarried fathers who are missing in record numbers, who impregnate women and selfishly flee."[23] This stereotype often comes with a generally unspoken racial (i.e., racist) dimension.

Even former president Obama, often cited as a model father, said in 2007, prior to his presidency, "There are a lot of men out there who need to stop acting like boys, who need to realize that responsibility does not end with conception, who need to know that what makes you a man is not the ability to have a child but the courage to raise one."[24]

The problem with this narrative, despite elements of truth for some men, is that it misses the several nuanced reasons why men become missing fathers. Like other scapegoating endeavors by racists, anti-Semites, and others, the blame-the-man trope is facile, hateful, and largely wrong.

The most common reasons that "missing" fathers don't see their children have to do with feelings of loss, made worse by occasional visits. They feel shame over the break-up with the child's mother and their inability to provide economically. They are uncomfortable around stepfathers, feel two- or one-way hostility with their children's mothers, and face custody orders and mothers preventing fathers from seeing their children.[25]

According to the social policy research organization MDRC (formerly Manpower Demonstration Research Corporation), "Low-income noncustodial fathers are a disadvantaged group. . . . Many live on the edge of poverty and face severe barriers to finding jobs, while those who can find work typically hold low-wage or temporary jobs. Despite their low, irregular income, many of these fathers are quite involved in their children's lives and, when they can, provide financial and other kinds of support."[26]

What is true is that, unlike a generation ago, the majority of circumstances in which fathers and children are missing from each other's lives are now a result of nonmarital childbirth. In addition to speaking of "family breakup," social scientists now focus on the lack of family formation.[27]

If missing fathers aren't roundly blamed for the plight of single mothers and poor children—not to mention the demise of the family—they're ignored. As early fatherhood movement leader David Blankenhorn wrote in 1993, "Our public debate on the family focuses almost exclusively on the roles of women and the plight of children, as if the male role in family life were somehow secondary or even irrelevant."[28]

A plethora of fathers' rights groups advocate for the idea that fathers are just as important parents as mothers, for equal rights for fathers in family law, and for men to be more responsible, caring, engaged fathers. "Responsible fatherhood" has gained an official imprimatur with the federal grant program of that name run by the Administration for Children and Families of the U.S. Department of Health and Human Services.[29] They have made some gains in all three arenas, but it is still a long, uphill struggle.

In keeping with the findings from the Fragile Families study and Kathryn Edin's research that the vast majority of such men deeply want to be involved in their children's lives, Ronald Mincy, a Columbia University professor of social policy and social work and director of its Center for Research on Fathers, Children, and Family Well-Being, has argued that most try to see their children regularly, despite economic, legal, and ex-partner barriers. If these poorer men had better social and economic supports, including jobs, they would be able to contribute much more to their kids.[30]

At the regular Tuesday night meetings of Baltimore's Responsible Fatherhood Project, thirty to forty men gather to talk about how much they miss their kids, how their ex-wives or ex-partners block them from seeing their sons and daughters, how they've made mistakes but want to recommit to their children, and how hard it is to be poor and black and an unmarried father. Some wearing old fedoras or hoodies, some in their 20s, and some in their 50s, these men have lived tough lives, but they're as soft as pussycats when it comes to talking about their children.

Further up the class ladder, in an affluent, white eastern suburb, George is virtually in tears when he talks about not seeing his children. Although he obtained joint custody, his ex-wife has kept their kids from him and even blocked their smart phones and emails so that George cannot connect with them online.

Scholars like Blankenhorn and Ron Haskins acknowledge that a large proportion of men may have powerful feelings for their children and want to be involved, at least in the early stages of their kids' lives. Yet the fact is that the men are not there.

Most of the nation's ten million missing, or "nonresidential," fathers were not married when they conceived their children, unlike two or three decades ago, when the majority were divorced. These men are disproportionately non-white with a high school diploma or less, and they often have a felony record.

They are also generally younger and poorer than married fathers, have little or no attachment to the labor force, and are much more likely to have grown up in single-mother households with their own fathers missing. Frank F. Furstenberg Jr., emeritus professor of sociology at the University of Pennsylvania, says, "'Good' dads, men who play an active, consistent, and nurturing role in their children's lives [, have] become scarce in the bottom strata."[31]

It's not as if most of these men are going from sex partner to sex partner. Rather, they meet and form relationships with the women in their communities, just as people in Beverly Hills or Cambridge, Massachusetts, do. These men and women are poor, but they generally want to stay together, marry, and bring up their children together when they have the economic stability that never comes.

Many poor younger missing fathers are like Thomas, a nonworking white man in his mid-20s who lives with his grandmother in West Virginia. He had been going out with a woman, perhaps one of several, and she got pregnant. The mother had enough of him and moved in with another man, taking her baby. Thomas tried to go to court, using his grandmother's money, but he had to settle for seeing his child every other weekend. The mother's mother, who tries to support her own daughter and granddaughter, has little sympathy. "He should get off his butt and get a job," she said.

For most of these men, pregnancy was anything but planned, because birth control is all too often not used. Their relationships are not casual, and pregnancies tend to bring the couples closer together rather than drive men to flee—at least, for a while. Unlike middle-class families, in which pregnancies generally follow from long-term relationships and marriage, in poor white and black communities a stab at a real relationship often follows from the pregnancy.[32]

In some cases the father wanders, having sex with new women, in others the father may feel angry at the mother for her expectations that he should work and make money. However, in some cases it is the mother who decides that she doesn't want to be with the father and finds another man, who may have children and with whom she is likely to have additional children.[33]

Studies have found that a large majority of unmarried mothers have a child with a second man, and about half have children with three or more men. Complex families—ones including stepparents, unmarried partners, and children from different marriages or relationships—are generally a vicious cycle. The mothers, with their gaggle of children and children's fathers, become unmarriageable, and the fathers get cut off by the mothers and their new boyfriends. These new men in a household are often culprits in child abuse.

Meanwhile, as unmarried fathers have children with additional women, they tend to drift away from children from their earlier liaisons and become more unable and unlikely to pay child support, although they tend to maintain relationships with at least one child.[34]

Neville, the former New Yorker, is a good example. He is very involved with the 2-year-old he had with his current partner, and he tries to give money or pay child support for several of his somewhat older children. Yet his relationships are tenuous at best with most of his seven children.

Stepparents sometimes can play a positive role, but as more and more bit players come on stage, as Moynihan long ago said, a society of unattached males leads to "chaos."[35] Other men—uncles, neighbors, strangers—may step in and provide some support for children, but that, too, can be short-lived. In the sensitive recent Oscar-winning Best Picture, *Moonlight*, a young boy named Chiron lives with his drug-abusing mother, and his birth father is nowhere to be seen. Juan, an Afro-Cuban drug dealer, rescues Chiron from bullies, gives him sanctuary in the house where he and his girlfriend live, teaches him how to swim, mentors him, and tells him it's okay to be gay. Despite the movie's (relatively) happy ending, Chiron grows up to be a drug dealer, Juan dies, and Chiron's mother is committed to a drug treatment facility.

THE CUSTODY WARS AND ENFORCED EXILE

Talk to a lot of divorced men and women with minor children, and you'll feel like you've stepped into Akira Kurosawa's classic film *Rashomon* (1950). The stories for the same couple can be as different as night and day. Women will say their ex-husbands were emotionally volatile, shiftless, philandering scum who did little to help raise the kids, while men will say their exes were selfish, haughty, and deceitful, naturally assuming that they were the "primary" parent and employing every dirty trick in the book to keep the fathers from their children after their marriages dissolved.

Condemned to live in an age of relativism, both narratives have varying degrees of truth value. Nonetheless, probably the most frequent complaint that men—even never-married ones without children—have against women is that many talk a big game about equality, but when it comes to child custody, all too many women naturally see themselves as superior to the other parent.

"Feminists, who talk about wanting 'equality,' continue to fight for women to get custody of their children because they have vaginas," one man wrote to me. A lot of men see the courts as irrefutably biased against them in custody cases.[36]

Until the late twentieth century, when a number of states adopted laws that stipulate a rebuttable presumption of joint custody,[37] women in the United States almost automatically got custody of children in divorce cases. While this "presumption" started to come onto the books by the 1980s, supplanting the "tender years" doctrine dictating that mothers be given sole custody of younger children, judicial practice changed little until the twenty-first century—and significant numbers of people would say that it still hasn't really changed.[38]

This sotto voce assumption that mothers are innately better parents has not only been a guiding principle of family law since the mid-twentieth century, but it also remains powerfully ingrained in public beliefs. Philip Wylie, in his 1942 best seller, *Generation of Vipers*, called it "momism." For generations, some psychologists and feminists, Hollywood, and even children's books have tended to portray fathers as biologically unfit, dangerous, lazy, or useless. A recent Pew survey found that 45 percent of Americans think that mothers and fathers do an equally good job as parents, but 53 percent believe that mothers do a better job, while only 1 percent believe that fathers do better.[39]

Many a man has come home to find that his wife has filed for divorce, taken the kids, and filed for sole custody and generous child support. The icing on the cake is the domestic abuse charge she's filed and protection order she's obtained. "This is the nuclear option," one divorce lawyer said. "Attorneys tell wife clients, 'If you have any fear for your safety, fill out a form and an order of protection will be issued.' The man comes home and a police car is there. The officer says, 'Get your shaving kit and I'll escort you off the property.' With no evidence, this guy is sleeping in a motel or on his parents' couch. It's embarrassing, humiliating, and your career can be over."[40]

With divorce attorneys charging upward of $400 an hour, only affluent, legally savvy, dedicated fathers are able to fight the battle. And many ex-wives, like adversaries in wartime, are quick to pull out the guns, calling these men crazy or dangerous. Some are, but most just want to be involved fathers.

The rest are forced to capitulate and join the ranks of the "missing fathers." African American fathers may be further deterred from even seeking custody out of fear of racial profiling, according to Donald Gordon, executive director of the Oregon-based Center for Divorce Education.[41]

Hardly a wild-eyed radical, Jonathan, a middle-age working-class white Ohio man, said:

> My youngest boy had another child by a girl earlier on. He wanted to be the dad. He petitioned the court to find out if he was the dad. The

court slapped a huge fine and said he owed a year in child support. He's still in arrears. He ended up giving up custody. He tried to bargain so that the baby's mom would take custody and the arrears would go away. She didn't want the money or the child support. The courts said no. They took his driver's license and he's been in and out of jail for child support. He's $13,000 in arrearage.

"Society has criminalized being a father if you can't pay child support," he added. "The men are always having the children used as a tool against them, and some mothers keep the child away from the fathers. They have been taught that they can use the child against the father." He paused. "Then there are also the dads who are totally worthless and tell them they don't want anything to do with their children."

Certainly there are men who don't want to pay to support their kids—some feeling that it is cruelly unfair to pay to support their children and their mother while they are given little opportunity to see their kids, some because they think that supporting a child is "the woman's job," and some because they are irresponsible and don't want to obey the law.[42]

Among the latter are men like Bob, a white roofer who works seasonally in Cascade Mountain towns that look like the settings for *Twin Peaks*. He avoids paying child support for a son from an earlier marriage by getting paid in cash that isn't reported to the government. He has had four more children with his unmarried partner, but he is abusive to them and their mother. With only a high school education, little ambition, and undeclared income, he gets food stamps, still leaving both of his families in poverty.

Far from the struggling or deadbeat "missing" fathers in Baltimore, Ohio, or Washington state, in the comfortable St. Louis law offices of Cordell & Cordell, a divorce law firm for men, with one hundred offices around the country and in the United Kingdom, founding partner Joseph Cordell has a lot to say on this matter. "We regard it as a basic truth that the father-child relationship is as important as the mother-child relationship and that gender-based discrimination in family court is unconscionable," he said. "You're up against the stereotype that women are the primary caregivers and men are the primary breadwinners. Today those stereotypes have more exceptions than they did twenty years ago."[43]

Nonetheless, the all-too-common scenario, according to J. Steven Svoboda, executive director of Attorneys for the Rights of the Child, remains. "If you're getting a divorce, a woman accuses you of domestic violence, a protective order goes over, and you don't get your kids." Most men don't have the tens of thousands of dollars to pay for a lawyer to fight for their children in what has typically been a losing battle. And unmarried fathers are "really shafted by the courts, which often don't even adjudicate custody," Kathryn Edin said. The vast majority of noncustodial parents are men.[44]

So kids generally "live with" their mothers, while men get "visitation," a demeaning term suggesting that a father is like a visiting uncle. The term has been attacked by fathers' rights groups (which some call "the mad dads") such as the Family Research Council, which promotes the Friday before Father's Day as National Fatherless Day. "Visitation is for criminals behind bars—not for parents and their children. . . . Deny a child the joy and memories of being with the other parent is an act of pure evil." As Warren Farrell said, "If we talked about women 'visiting' the workplace, it would sound so Neanderthal." Yet one Nebraska study found that 72 percent of noncustodial fathers saw their children an average of 5.5 days per month, indicating that fathers are usually little more than visitors, and many of these dads resign themselves to the role of being, at best, pals or "big brothers."[45]

Cordell takes the argument further. "This is a civil rights issue," he said. "What civil right is more important than the role that a parent plays in a child's life? But this civil right is in the dark corner of the room. It's an orphan. Most people are not particularly disturbed by it. There are no powerful voices."[46]

At least one voice has been that of the American Psychological Association, which issued a resolution in 1977 saying, "It is scientifically and psychologically baseless, as well as a violation of human rights, to discriminate against men because of their sex in assignment of children's custody [or] adoption."[47]

Longtime men's rights advocates like Farrell, who was an active feminist until the late 1990s, are especially angered by the apparent hypocrisy of feminist groups like the National Organization for Women (NOW), which came out against the legal presumption of joint, or shared, custody more than thirty years ago. "I couldn't believe the people I thought were pioneers in equality were saying that women should have the first option to have children [and] that children should not have equal rights to their dad," he said.[48] NOW, which continues to fight state joint custody laws, posts lurid stories worthy of the British tabloids, such as "California Family Courts Helping Pedophiles, Batterers Get Child Custody," to not so subtly back its position.[49]

As noted, a prominent grievance among the men I surveyed for this book was the injustice of custody laws. As one man simply, and plaintively, said, "Dads are parents too." These complaints often became the launching point for some men to attack "radical feminism" and others to go on misogynistic rants. On the other hand, divorced women frequently say that men don't do their fair share, and studies have shown that women are more likely to be impoverished by the breakup of a marriage.[50]

Divorce lawyers often take the reasonable position that custody should be decided on a case-by-case basis, which is what a rebuttable presumption would enable. Divorcing parents would share physical as well as legal custody unless one parent was clearly shown to be unfit. Given the countless studies showing that children do better with a father in their lives, a few feminists such as the late Karen DeCrow, former NOW president, have argued for feminist consistency: if women want to achieve equality in the workplace and other realms, it is essential to get men more involved in parenting.[51]

Whether it is a function of bias, the "nuclear option" of alleging abuse, poorer men not being able to assert their rights, or men disappearing, the reality remains that most children of divorced parents, like most children of unmarried parents, live with their mothers or, sometimes, with their grandparents.

Custody laws and decisions are only part of the problem for fathers who want to be involved with their children. While ex-spouses and ex-partners all too often badmouth each other, some divorced and unmarried mothers with custody go further, becoming "gatekeepers," like George's wife, who actively keep fathers from seeing their children. They may have new boyfriends, have moved a considerable distance away, or out of fear, loathing, or spite want to keep their exes away. Some fathers can be dangerous, and men can trash the mothers of their children at least as well as women trash the fathers, but women have the greater opportunity to keep fathers away, and they can call the police and get a protective order if need be. One-fifth of the 5.6 million custodial mothers who did not receive child support in 2013 told the U.S. Census Bureau that they didn't file for support because they did not want their child to have contact with their father.[52]

CHILD SUPPORT

Federal laws from mid-1970s to 1996 establishing child support guidelines had the well-intentioned goal of trying to maintain children's predivorce standard of living, withholding (mostly) men's wages to guarantee payment. All told, $32 billion in child support was collected in 2015, supporting 16 million children. Unfortunately, these laws often fail to achieve their goal, are unsuited to present circumstances, and have had perverse effects. Designed when fathers worked and women stayed at home, these laws don't fit a society where many mothers work and many fathers don't. They also have a hard time addressing never-married parents, impoverish already poor and incarcerated men, and can disincentivize men from working so that they don't pay child support.[53]

"When people have orders that they can't comply with, it doesn't motivate them to work and pay," a Maryland child-support official said. "It does the opposite," leading many men to quit jobs, turn down promotions, or go underground when courts set child support orders that are impossibly high.[54]

About 5.8 million mothers and 740,000 fathers were due child support averaging $5,774 per year in 2013, although only about two-thirds of that amount was collected, and about two-thirds of all single mothers receive no support. While up to three-fourths of fathers owing support pay something, only about half pay the full amount. Unmarried fathers are less likely to pay support and pay less than divorced dads. Most don't pay because they are devious deadbeats but because of the reality that they earn less than $10,000 a year, don't work, or are incarcerated. As advocates have pointed out, "deadbeat" is not the same as dead broke.[55]

Neville, the father of seven children, told me he pays 60 percent of his income in child support and has been thrown in jail briefly several times in different jurisdictions for being unable to pay. Then there's the son of the Ohio man who owes $13,000 in back payments. One study found that child support orders for low-income nonresident fathers accounted for 21 to 61 percent of their income.[56]

Basically, low income fathers are required to pay low-income mothers child support or face going to jail or losing their driver's license. If they can't pay and arrears build up, they can be rearrested. In these circumstances, child support may marginally reduce poverty for children but increase it for men. And some incarcerated fathers, paid pennies for prison work, are perversely ordered to pay child support, as fourteen states consider prison to be "voluntary unemployment." "You can't get blood from a turnip," says Cynthia Osborne, director of the Child and Family Research Partnership at the University of Texas. "We have been setting court orders for noncustodial parents, usually fathers, who have no ability to pay because they are chronically unemployed, disabled, and incarcerated."[57]

One can rightfully say that children matter more, especially if these men fit the caricatured stereotype of "hit-and-run" guys who barely work, impregnate women, and then disappear. As we have seen, the story is usually much more complex. And to be able to pay support, these men need supports themselves—including jobs, training, and access to benefits like the EITC or Women, Infants, Children (WIC), which are essentially unavailable to non-custodial fathers. Subsidized government housing is also usually off-limits to fathers who have a felony record, even if the mother of their child lives in public housing. Since children don't see where the mother's money is coming from, they may feel that their fathers don't support them, and more visible aid, like a dad buying shoes or games for his child, is not counted as formal child support. Then if the mothers don't let fathers see their children, fathers are understandably angry and refuse to pay. If up to 65 percent of wages can be garnished, it's not surprising that studies have shown that child support orders for poor men modestly decrease the likelihood of their being in the labor force.[58]

Despite some women who say they don't need the man who fathered their child—that they can do it all—children need their fathers. They benefit not only from spending time with their dads but also from the ongoing presence of both parents, if they are committed to coparenting. If poor fathers can get jobs and the supports to be able to work, they can pay child support, live without the fear of being sent to jail, and even establish less hostile relationships with the mothers, who may then be less reluctant about their kids seeing Dad, as a former Texas child support official said.[59]

Child support also can be twisted in other ways. As with custody, it can be used as a bargaining chip: a mother may drop real or contrived domestic abuse charges or "allow" fathers to see their children more in exchange for child support. In addition, it is consciously or unconsciously used by some ex-wives as a form of spite. Although one may have little sympathy for a divorced man with a six-figure income, there are men whose high support payments are based on a prior job in which he made even more money, and there are women who receive child support even though they have six-figure incomes at least as great as their exes. And the reservoirs of misogyny deepen.

When it comes to custody and child support, to paraphrase Chairman Mao, divorce "is not a dinner party."

WHEN FATHERS DON'T WORK

Fathers who do not work are much more likely to be physically or emotionally absent from their children's lives. And men who are fathers and married have the highest employment rates.

Jenny, a 20-year-old white college student, grew up in Arkansas with her father out of work for a decade. "Losing his job did a number on his self-esteem and contributed to his depression," she remembered. Although her dad has taken a few small construction jobs over the years, "none made a lot of money."

Her mother "was always the one with a steady, well-paying job," but Jenny's mom often had "outbursts," leading her father to "shut down" or become "passive-aggressive." This was a vicious cycle throughout her childhood—mom's anger, dad's silent, depressed passive-aggressiveness. "I was an only child, so without either parent to talk to it got lonely, and I started irrationally blaming myself for these occurrences," she recalled.

Jenny's dad didn't talk to his brother, who not only didn't work but also "remarried so many times that I have lost count" and got violent with each wife. "The problems in my family, especially the men, worry me," she said.

Whatever the case, Jenny was scarred by her father's being at home and being depressed most of the time. "I have seen a lot of behavior, especially from my dad, that makes me not want to have children," she said. "I would not wish my parents' depression issues on anyone."

A large number of fathers and mothers are out of work for some period while their children are growing up, yet we've seen that nonemployed noncustodial fathers who are unable to support their children are less likely to see their children, whether due to the father's irresponsibility or the mother's gatekeeping. Among nonworking men, only 28 percent lived with children under 18. These kids tend to be handicapped in their chances for success. In intact families, one study found that a father's being without a job can have more adverse effects on children than a mother's being out of work (or at work). Nonworking men do not spend appreciably more time caring for a child or other family member than men who are working.[60] Many women have run out of patience with male "partners" who simply aren't very good at either bringing home some bacon or at least occasionally taking care of the kids.

In addition to lower family income, household anxiety levels rise. Children's educational achievement suffers, as the likelihood of a child repeating a grade or dropping out increases; conflicts between teenage boys and fathers escalate; and long-term economic prospects for children deteriorate, according to Gail Melson, a professor of child development at Purdue University. With high joblessness among African Americans and the sharp rise in black male incarceration rates since the late twentieth century, the problems associated with nonworking fathers are more pronounced among black children.[61]

Middle-class children, like Bill's son, often are ashamed and alienated from their nonworking fathers. Or they don't learn how to be Dad the provider, as was the case with Jemal, whose father was a poor role model. And then there are more ambiguous cases. What about the children of Yates, the once practicing lawyer who became an "ideal stay-at-home dad" by day but drank, self-medicated, and trolled the internet for women while his wife and kids slept? Did they ever know, or will they discover, this side of their father? And what will that do to their opinions, feelings, and relationship with him?

THE REAL LOSERS: CHILDREN

As discussed in chapter 6, the rise of divorce and nonmarital unions can be attributed to cultural factors, such as the neohippie, self-actualizing "culture of narcissism," and economic factors, such as the increased number of women in the workforce and declining or stagnant male wages. However, as Isabel Sawhill has said, "You can divorce a spouse, but not a child."[62]

One can debate whether mothers or fathers are hurt more by divorce or the degree to which families are harmed by fathers not working, but there is no question that, on average, children are the real losers from father absence. Not having a father present is "an injury," as Robert Bly, the mythopoetic men's guru, wrote in *Iron John*. Reams of evidence have demonstrated that father involvement positively affects cognitive development and academic achievement and reduces behavior problems in children. Even in divorced or unformed families, children who spend at least 35 percent of their time with each parent, rather than live with one and visit the other, have better relationships with their fathers and mothers and do better academically, socially, and psychologically.[63]

Neville hardly lived a life or in a milieu that made things easy for kids. His are the kind of children that any social worker would be quick to classify as being "at risk." Their chances of getting good parenting, living in an economically stable environment, going to good schools, making it to college, and finding good jobs are very low compared to children of high-earning professional married couples.

Hank, the southeastern man who often told his son how worthless he was, left lasting damage to his son's self-esteem. The millions of fathers who have been in prison rarely have been good for their children.

Study after study has shown that children without fathers are significantly more likely to live in poverty, have a range of emotional and behavior problems, do less well in school, have a less safe home environment, become substance abusers and commit crimes, and not work and remain poor as adults. Boys, perhaps not surprisingly, tend to do worse than girls in numerous ways when their fathers are absent and they experience multiple family transitions.[64]

Children with missing fathers are about four times more likely to be poor, twice as likely to drop out of school and engage in criminal activity, and many times more likely to spend time in prison. Ninety percent of homeless and runaway children are from fatherless homes. "A community that allows large numbers of young men to grow up in broken families . . . never acquiring any stable relationship with male authority, never acquiring any rational expectations about the future—asks for and gets chaos," as Daniel Patrick Moynihan put it.[65]

The psychological harm is significant, with too many children feeling abandoned, hurt, and angry. Boys lack good male role models and fail to develop what Lawrence Mead calls "the male virtues." Children with missing fathers are twice as likely as other children to be treated for mental health issues. Thoughts about suicide are more common. Fatherless children are twice as likely to commit suicide, and 63 percent of youth suicides occur among these children. New boyfriends of single mothers can sometimes be supportive but are often new sources of conflict, especially for boys.[66]

In school, children in single-parent families are one-third more likely to drop out of high school and roughly twice as likely to be suspended or expelled. They tend to score lower on standardized tests and receive lower grades in school. Strikingly, father absence may depress academic performance more than poverty does, as children from low-income, two-parent families outperform students from high-income, single-parent homes.[67]

The risks of behavior problems and getting in trouble with the law go up sharply. In a longitudinal study of 1,197 children beginning in fourth grade, researchers observed "greater levels of aggression in boys from mother-only households than from boys in mother-father households." Boys in mother-only households are almost three times as likely to carry guns and deal drugs, and substance abuse is far more common. Nearly three-fourths of adolescent murderers and 60 percent of rapists grew up without fathers.[68]

Girls, too, are hurt when their fathers are missing. Girls (and boys) are more likely to be abused either by their parent, stepfather, or a mother's boyfriend. Daughters of single mothers are more than twice as likely as girls in intact families to have children outside of marriage and about 90 percent more likely to divorce.[69]

The effects of being raised in a single-parent home continue into adulthood. These children are 50 percent more likely than kids with married parents to be poor and to have mental health problems as adults. They don't benefit from the counsel or the soft nepotism of a father helping them find a job. When families of the same race and similar incomes are compared, children from broken and single-parent homes have three times the incarceration rate by the time they reach age 30 than children raised in two-parent families. Young men from all socioeconomic backgrounds with little or no contact with their fathers during childhood are less likely to be employed, according to economist Raj Chetty, thereby perpetuating the cycle.[70]

Nonwork among men is more than a labor market or moral issue. It is also a child welfare issue, as Melson said.[71]

Although the circumstances of missing fathers are more varied, complex, and tragic than the get-'em-pregnant-and-disappear stereotype, many of these men bear responsibility for hurting their children. The majority of missing fathers crave being with their children or regret their mistakes, yet those who are missing can permanently scar their kids.

It is widely known that children, mothers, and our society and economy are harmed by fatherlessness. In 2006 the National Fatherhood Initiative conservatively estimated that the federal government alone spent at least $100 billion assisting father-absent homes, a total that not only has increased but also excludes the costs associated with poor outcomes for children with missing fathers.[72]

Yet it bears repeating that most of the 10 million fathers who are missing or shut out from their children's lives also are hurting. Rather than damn most of these men, we should recognize that they often ache for their children. A lot of them feel emasculated that they cannot play their roles as fathers. Many are depressed, have alcohol and drug problems, have had run-ins with the law, are poor, and are not working—sometimes because America's child support and tax laws don't make it worthwhile for them to hold low-paying jobs. The problems caused by and afflicting most missing fathers need to be seen as part of the larger phenomenon of sidelined men—men out.

CHAPTER 8

Male Sickness and Sadness

Nearly half of prime age not-in-the-labor-force men take pain medication on a daily basis, and in nearly two-thirds of cases they take prescription pain medication. . . . Prime age men who are out of the labor force report that they experience notably low levels of emotional well-being throughout their days and that they derive relatively little meaning from their daily activities.

—*Alan B. Krueger, "Where Have All the Workers Gone?"*

I used to consider [my body] as my servant who should obey, function, give pleasure. In sickness, you realize you are not the boss. It is the other way around.

—*Federico Fellini*

Pain. Rising mortality. Opioids. Depression. Isolation. Disability. Anger. Obesity. Suicide. The United States is in the midst of a silent, spreading epidemic of middle-age men in poor physical and psychological health. Both physical and mental health issues are causes or consequences, or both, of millions of men who did, could, but do not play a productive role in contemporary America. Many of these health-damaging issues affect women and younger men, but the incidence among middle-age men is particularly striking.

We've seen Rob in New England, whose health is failing; Hank in the southeast, who was so angry he shot his dog; Mark, the D.C. lawyer with the porn addiction; Neville, the father of seven who "made poor decisions"; Ed, who feels "shame" when walking his dog midday in a suburban New York dog park; Randy, the upper-middle-class, well-educated L.A. man approaching middle age who feels "unsettled"; Chuck, who has been addicted to opioids for a quarter of his life; and all the Bills and Yateses and Michaels and Jameses whose wives left them. Ben and others have expressed their loneliness. These guys are surviving, but they are not healthy or happy. Beyond the raging misogyny and seething online fury, there are the mass murderers like Stephen Paddock in Las Vegas, or Dylann Roof in Charleston, or Nikolas Cruz in Parkland, Florida.

This chapter only begins to discuss the largely silent and growing men's health crisis in America. The rising incidence of physical and psychological ill health, particularly among men over 50 and young men, is at once a consequence and characteristic of, and a contributor to, men's being sidelined.

Martin has been in failing health for many years, but that isn't why he hasn't worked in decades. Now about 70 years old, he lives alone in a small, bedraggled house in a virtually all-white community in the Midwest. Severely overweight, he rarely gets out except to go to church, where he is friendly with men well into their 80s and 90s.

He has both a B.A. and an advanced degree from a major public university, but his last job—back in his 40s—was working as a clerk at Walmart. It's hard to tease out why. He's shy. There is probably some moderate mental illness. He never really had career aspirations, at least as he tells it today.

A sweet man, Martin never married and lived with his mother until she died a few years back, when she was more than 100 years old. He still lives in that house, where the décor looks like it was frozen in the 1950s. There's not much room to sit amid the clutter, and the yellow aluminum siding and dirt driveway have seen better days.

A good number of his baby boomer classmates protested against the Vietnam War, went to grad school, got good jobs, got married, and had kids. Now they have retired and have grandchildren, but Martin is alone, in poor health, with no career to look back on, no partner, and hospital visits and uncertainty lying ahead.

Rick's situation is very different. He had worked for a Wall Street ratings agency for nearly twenty-five years, making good money, when he was laid off at 50. As with many other middle-tier workers in the financial industry, the global recession was hard on him. As he noted, the industry's executives received virtually no punishment for their role in the crisis, and their eight-figure earnings are higher than ever. For him, life is ringed with frustration, shame, ostracism, and cynicism.

"Emotionally, it really takes a toll," he said from his New Jersey home. "You're hitting middle age and you're out on the street. It's nothing like you thought it would be. It makes you feel like a piece of crap."

"I'm frustrated," Rick added. He applies for jobs but feels like applications "go into a black hole." He gets up at six every morning, drives his children to school, and then spends much of the day looking for work until he picks up his kids and goes to evening networking meetings. He says the endless hunting gets depressing. So he goes down to the basement and works on Thomas Kinkade jigsaw puzzles to take his mind off things.

"I fear that I may not be able to get back into my career and that I'll have to work another twenty years when I get a job," Rick continued. His father, at 78, is still working. "It hurts when your wife, who was working two days a week at a school, has to become the breadwinner. Neighbors don't even ask. It's a stigma. A lot of people won't associate with people who aren't working. It's like they think it's going to rub off on them and they'll be next." Rick, who is white, is cynical about employers and government, disappointed in family and friends, and resentful of people who are doing well. He mentions a cousin who no longer talks to him and a neighbor who is always going on private boats or skiing.

Martin and Rick, and others we've met, are part of the army of middle-age and young men who are emotionally and physically suffering. They don't put on suits and ties in the morning. They don't drive to an office or any other workplace. There are no business meetings. No co-workers or colleagues. And no "bringing home the bacon." They may not be married or in the game as fathers. They are men in the prime of their lives who have become marginal to American society. Many are hurting physically and emotionally. And there's an increasing brokenness to their bodies and psyches.

This army also includes men like Maurice, a divorced African American man in Maryland who makes less than $20,000 a year from occasional jobs. "Being out of work is disheartening and has made me seriously question what's really wrong with me," he said. "I have no criminal background or chemical dependencies, yet my employment situation has been tenuous at best for the last five years."

"My lack of work has greatly strained my personal relationships," he added. "Paying bills has become a nightmare. Going to the mailbox and answering the phone cause me a lot of anxiety. I want to provide, as I have in the past, but being unable to has called into question my manhood—even if I'm the only one doing so."

THE PHYSICAL TOLL

Few National Academy of Sciences papers have created more buzz in recent years than a 2015 report by husband-and-wife Princeton economists Anne Case and Angus Deaton indicating that mortality rates among middle-age American whites had been increasing by approximately 2 percent per year between 1998 and 2013 while declining at a similar rate in Europe, even among those with less education. Beyond this rise in what they have called "deaths of despair," morbidity, pain, and other ailments of the body and mind have also been on the increase. Initially cautious to discuss causes, in 2017 they spoke of "accumulating despair"—years or decades of economic misfortune and social dysfunction. While age-adjusted mortality was rising for men without a B.A., from 762 per 100,000 in 1998 to 867 in 2015, it fell for those with at least a bachelor's degree from 349 to 243. Joseph Stiglitz, like Deaton a Nobel Prize winner, bluntly said that "inequality kills," noting the parallel rise in income inequality and mortality in America. Case and Deaton and others expanded research on this stunningly tragic reversal of generations of improving health, finding mortality increases for whites in every age group between 25 and 64. Their Princeton colleague Alan Krueger put forth compelling data to suggest that these disturbing health trends could be a major factor in the declining number of men working.[1]

Society-wide health data for men are troubling and reflect why American men, on average, live five years less than American women; male life expectancy fell by more than two months in 2015 and 2016. A century ago, the difference was one year. African Americans have a considerably lower life expectancy. Men are somewhat more likely than women to be obese and to smoke and more likely to drink heavily. Reflecting, perhaps, an artifact of traditional masculine norms of stoicism and self-reliance, fewer men than women get preventive care, like flu vaccines, and fewer have a regular place to go for medical care. Even among 25- to 44-year-olds, 71.3 percent of men have a usual place for care compared to 78 percent of women. Men's rights activists point out that much less is spent on research on the health problems of men than those affecting women.[2]

Male mortality also takes a toll on women and children. In addition to the pain resulting from fathers dying young, which is more common than mothers dying while their children are still minors, widowed women are considerably more likely than married women to live in poverty.[3]

In addition, as the Case-Deaton data suggest, a number of health statistics for men have been moving in the wrong direction in the twenty-first century. Mortality rates have spiked upward in rural areas while declining somewhat in large metropolitan areas. The proportion of men between 45 and 64 with at least two of nine chronic conditions increased by one-third during the first decade of this century. The incidence of hypertension among adult men went up from 26.4 percent in the early 1990s to 31.0 percent in the early 2010s, and high cholesterol, once more common among women, is now more prevalent among men. Men account for as many as nine out of ten accidents and injuries. ADHD, a condition that continues into adulthood, has increased sharply among boys, from 9.6 percent of 5- to 17-year-olds in the late 1990s to 14.1 percent in the early 2010s. Diabetes has increased among both men and women since 1990.[4]

The only silver lining amid this profusion of gloomy health statistics is that life expectancy and physical well-being continue to increase for African Americans, Latinos, and well-educated and well-to-do whites and Asian Americans. And—hardly something to celebrate—men are doing less poorly than women on a few indicators.

Men who report being in the best health tend to be working, married, and have working spouses. Married men are more likely to seek preventive health care services.[5] They probably also have children they are close to and who don't while away the hours on video games or social media, among other things.

Case and Deaton, Krueger, and public health experts also have found a dramatic increase in individuals saying that their health isn't great and that they experience frequent or chronic pain. Among 45- to 64-year-old men, reports of headaches, severe migraines, and lower back pain also increased significantly between 1997 and 2014; although these and other conditions such as osteoarthritis and fibromyalgia remain more common among women. About 25 million adults reported severe daily pain in 2012, and half of the nation's adults said they experienced some pain during the last three months.[6]

Forty-three percent of nonworking 25- to 54-year-old men reported that their health was poor or fair, compared with just 12 percent of those who had jobs. One in five have trouble walking or climbing stairs. Self-reported pain is 88 percent higher for nonworking men than for men with jobs, and 44 percent of nonworking men take daily medications for pain. Another study found that the ten counties with the highest male mortality rates had average male labor force participation rates (for ages 25–54) that were 15 percentage points below the national average. Yet a better-educated man working at a desk is obviously more able to do his job than a less educated guy in a distribution center or big-box store where workers are on their feet and lifting all day. Again, one can argue about cause and effect.[7]

Rising levels of pain have mirrored the sharp increase in the use of prescription painkillers in the United States since the late 1990s. The extent to which this has been driven by demand- or supply-side factors is an open question, as the pharmaceutical industry began aggressively marketing drugs like OxyContin, Vicodin, Percocet, and other prescription opioids, and well-meaning groups like the American Geriatric Society encouraged their use. By the mid-2010s 100 million or more Americans, or one-third of the population, used pain-relieving drugs. Perdue Pharmaceuticals made $31 billion from the sale of OxyContin between the end of the 1990s and 2016.[8]

The tragic story of America's opioid epidemic is all too well known, as about a quarter of a million people died from prescription opiate overdoses between 1999 and 2017. Prescription opioids have opened the door to a surge in the use of heroin, which has become less expensive, and extremely potent drugs like fentanyl. About 660,000 Americans died from all types of drug overdoses between 1999 and 2016, with 116,000 of these—including more than 74,000 men—dying in 2015 and 2016 alone. Male death rates from drug overdoses are twice as high as the rates for women.[9]

Stories of opioid overdoses were widespread in the declining small towns in Pennsylvania and Wisconsin that I visited. But they were also disturbingly common in the Washington, D.C., exurbs and western Massachusetts. Then there was Travis, the clean-cut, outdoorsy 27-year-old Mormon man in Utah who no one could have imagined would die of an overdose.

Despite the somewhat greater reported incidence of pain among women, men have overwhelmingly born the brunt of the country's opioid and heroin crisis. About 55 percent of America's 9–11.5 million opioid abusers are men, with rates about 60 percent higher among gay men than among heterosexuals. All told, men are about twice as likely as women to have substance abuse disorders, with 12.7 million men afflicted in 2015. More dramatic differences are seen in the death rates of each sex: heroin abuse is twice as common among men than women, but the number of deadly heroin overdoses was nearly four times higher among men in 2013. Drug overdose death rates among white males have tripled between 2000 and 2014, with a fourfold increase in opioid deaths and a sixfold increase among younger men. Although these "deaths of despair" are rampant among millennials, Americans over age 45 account for more than two in five opioid overdose deaths, and opioid deaths among 55- to 64-year-olds increased by about 800 percent between 2000 and 2014.[10]

Rising drug abuse has led many potential job candidates to fail drug tests, employers report. Drug use is one of a handful of reasons that 71 percent of America's 34 million 17- to 24-year-olds do not qualify for military service, according to Andrea Zucker, chief of consumer market research for the U.S. Army Marketing Research Group.[11]

Although alcoholism and alcohol abuse have long been more common among men than women, extreme drinking has increased markedly among men in the twenty-first century, notably in middle age. While overall alcohol use and alcoholism rates have not changed significantly in this century, and use among teenagers and young adults has declined, binge drinking and heavy drinking have shot up. On almost every metric, men are twice as likely to abuse alcohol as women. About 4.7 million men, compared to 2.8 million women, were alcohol-dependent in 2015. Nearly a quarter of adult men report binge drinking—variously defined as five to eight or more drinks in a day—nearly double the proportion of women who binge. Men are also twice as likely to be heavy drinkers, downing fifteen or more drinks per week or bingeing at least five times a month. Bingeing and alcohol disorders among men over 50 and over 60 have risen by about 20 percent since 2000, although rates are also going up among middle-age women. The dramatic increases among middle-age and older men, and the discrepancy between men and women, contrasts with the fact that men born after 1980 have only slightly higher rates of heavy and binge drinking than women their age.[12]

Estimates of the combined economic costs of opioid, heroin, and alcohol abuse go as high as $350 billion per year, including the $35 billion treatment industry. This includes workplace productivity but excludes the costs of declining labor force participation. Krueger has argued that about one-fifth of the decline in male workforce participation between 1999 and 2015 is related to rising opioid addiction. Binge drinking and alcohol poisonings, as well as heroin overdoses, also appear to be linked to nonwork. Both economists and psychologists have taken note.[13]

Once again, is the absenting of men from work, families, and society a cause or an effect of rising pain and substance abuse? And how can one tease out the psychological distress that is also part cause, part consequence from cultural factors—notably, change, ambiguity, and dissonance in norms for masculinity?

THE DARKENING SOUL: THE PSYCHOLOGICAL TOLL

I coulda been a contender. I coulda been somebody, instead of a bum,
which is what I am.

—*Terry Malloy (Marlon Brando)*, On the Waterfront, 1954

"There is at least as much hopelessness among men as women, and men tend
to have fewer friends or best friends with whom they want to share personal
feelings or problems," according to Andrew Smiler, a clinical psychologist in
Winston-Salem, North Carolina, and author of *The Masculine Self*. "Part of
the reason for these high alcohol and other substance abuse rates is that men
are supposed to prove their worth and provide for their families, but if they're
not working or in a low-wage job, they're failing at one of the central tasks of
masculinity."[14]

Many men—and many Americans—are less happy and less psychologically fit than they once were. Aside from the increasing headaches, back pain,
hypertension, and substance abuse problems, as well as anger, that bespeak
psychological problems, there also appears to be increased depression, anxiety, and feelings of failure. Suicide rates have gone up, and isolation, or loneliness, may be the nation's "biggest public health problem," in the words of
former surgeon general Vivek Murthy. As noted, these problems are more
acute among young and later-middle-age men as they drift ever further from
work, partners, and children.[15]

John left the nonprofit he had been working for in 2008, when he was in
his mid-40s because of what he calls the organization's "dysfunction" and "ir-
rational" management. With an MBA from a top business school, he thought
it would be easy to find a new job. He can't count the number of interviews
he's had, having made it into the final round numerous times. But there have
been no offers. He networks, does volunteer board work, and has taken and
taught job-training courses.

A gay Asian American man in a liberal western state, John says he feels
the most discrimination because of his age and the stereotype that Asians are
hardworking and successful. His partner and family have been "wonderful
and supportive," but years without a full-time job have left him worried about
his future.

He feels ashamed in social situations when people ask what he does. "I
wonder what they think when I say that I'm self-employed." Some friends and
family no longer ask, and he said, "I wonder if they're embarrassed for me."

"Everyone knows I left a good job," he said, "so I start thinking that I fucked up somehow." John does not have physical health problems or addictions, but he feels the shame, self-doubt, worry, and depression that dog the psyches of many men out.

Nolan, a mid-50s white California man who lost his job with a "once great company," describes himself as "often sullen and moody." Soon after his job ended, his "marriage was effectively over," and he moved in with his elderly father. He finds it strange and depressing to "scrimp as much as we can while everyone else in town is a millionaire."

Men don't like to talk about their feelings, especially ones that express vulnerabilities, or so the traditional man code has dictated. Yet in their hearts a lot of them feel like John, that they "fucked up."

Psychologists and men's health professionals think that the long-accepted idea that psychological distress is more common among women is distorted by this male tendency to deny, underreport, and eschew treatment for such problems. "Given men's tendency to minimize expressions of sadness, the epidemiology behind this is flawed," University of Pittsburgh psychiatrist Pierre Azzam writes. For example, women are two and a half times more likely than men to see a psychiatrist and receive treatment for major depression. But that doesn't mean that they are necessarily more likely to be depressed.[16]

"Masculinity hates vulnerability," said Daniel Singley, a San Diego psychologist who headed the American Psychological Association's division focusing on men's mental health. "Men will do all kinds of stupid crap to avoid feeling shamed."[17]

Many masculine norms, as we've seen, contribute to, disguise, and hide mental health issues with men. Studies have regularly found that "traditional" men are more likely to cut themselves off from intimate friendships, avoid expressing their true feelings, resist seeking help when they need it, experience depression, and think frequently about suicide.[18]

"Society tells men to not express ourselves—especially black men," said Daryl, a 30-year-old African American man in Washington, D.C. On the one hand, depression and anxiety are killing black men, he said, but black males think that "it's not okay to go to therapy, because there's nothing wrong with us."

Allan, an early 60s white California man with a Ph.D., who hasn't worked in a decade, spoke of "plenty of darkness and frustration." He had sold his stake in a midsize business, thinking he could move seamlessly into a new career. It hasn't happened. Despite family support and "cobbling together a life" of volunteering and other activities, he has felt cut off from the world and depressed.

The proportion of men reporting that they were "not very happy" rose from 9 percent in 2002 to 14 percent in 2015, according to the General Social Survey conducted by the National Opinion Research Center. (That brought men to parity with women, whose incidence of unhappiness remained essentially the same.) Not surprisingly, nonworking men are especially likely to be depressed, according to economists Justin Pierce and Peter Schott. There were not significant gender differences in self-reports of frequent "poor" mental health (15–20 percent) and feelings that life is "routine" or "dull" (about 50 percent), although we come back to the problem of men often not reporting emotional vulnerability.[19]

Not only are men less likely to acknowledge the storms in their souls, but they also tend to experience depression somewhat differently than women. They are more apt to be tired, irritable, and angry and lose interest in their work and family, according to the National Institute of Mental Health. Indolence can lead to fantasies and obsessions. They are also more likely to let their depression express itself as anger, blaming their situation on immigrants, women, other racial or ethnic groups, government, employers, or the economic system. Sound familiar? Men are less likely to seek help for psychological problems. Yet a study led by Dr. Brian Sites of the Dartmouth-Hitchcock Medical Center found that all Americans with depression and anxiety are more than three times as likely as the general population to use prescription painkillers.[20]

If one accepts the long-standing idea that depression is anger turned inward, the considerable evidence of widespread male anger suggests a lot of undiagnosed depression. Beginning in childhood, when boys are more likely to be rowdy, get in fights, and be diagnosed with conduct disorder, this anger morphs into violence, crime, run-ins with authority, and lying in adulthood. Men also appear to have their hearts broken more often from divorce and breakups than women do, although these feelings may be cloaked by anger and bravado. Since sleep disorders can be another sign of depression, it may be noteworthy that men who don't work sleep about seventy minutes more each day than men who do work (or it could be that they just have more time on their hands).[21]

Another possible sign of depression or anxiety is the rising rate of erectile dysfunction, especially among men under 40, as we have discussed. The "sexodus" we've heard about may stem from both a flight from intimacy and a failure to perform.[22]

The grimmest sign of growing male despair is the sharp increase in suicide since the twenty-first century began. More than 33,000 American males killed themselves in 2014, 10,000 more than in 1999. Although women are more likely to contemplate and attempt suicide, men are more than three and a half times likelier to kill themselves, and men's rates of "suicidal ideation" rapidly increased in the early 2010s. White men, younger men, and late middle-age men have the highest risk for taking their own lives. After a divorce, men are many times more prone to suicide than women. Suicide was the seventh leading cause of death among men in 2015, with guns and hanging the preferred methods, while suicide was not among the top ten causes of death among women. Among 45- to 64-year-old white men, the incidence of suicide spiked upward by 59 percent during the same years. These middle-age white men now are more likely to kill themselves than American Indians and Alaska Natives (AIAN) of the same ages, although overall AIAN suicide rates remain the highest for any ethnic group. Suicide is far less common among people of color, and rates declined for African American men in the early twenty-first century. The youngest millennial men, between 20 and 24, had more than six times the suicide rate as women in their age group in 2011.[23]

Men who aren't working are about three times more likely to kill themselves than men in full-time jobs, according to government data. Both suicide and deadly drug and alcohol poisoning rates for men are higher in areas with low male labor force participation.[24]

Homelessness, which can be accompanied by mental illness, also exhibits another grim gender disparity. Unmarried men are almost three times as likely as single women to be homeless. The National Coalition for the Homeless attributes this to "men's greater likelihood of being veterans, or the tendency of men to not seek treatment for their mental illnesses and substance abuse."[25]

RISING DISABILITY RATES

Increasing physical and psychological ailments appear to account for the rising rolls of Americans on federal and state disability programs since President Reagan relaxed the rules for claiming disability. A politically charged topic, some policymakers and economists have pointed to this as evidence that nonworking men are lazy, while others argue that beneficiaries have few other ways to support themselves.[26]

The proportion of 25- to 54-year-old men claiming SSDI benefits rose from 1 percent to 3 percent between 1967 and 2014. Those claiming disability are much less likely to work than those who aren't disabled. In addition to the 10.4 million Americans on SSDI in early 2018, another 4.8 million 18- to 64-year-olds received benefits from the SSI program, and the military paid disability to 4.5 million veterans in 2017. These benefit programs also impose a huge cost on society; SSDI and SSI were expected to pay about $210 billion in 2018, 5 percent of the federal budget. Women are well represented on the disability rolls, but these men and women are only a subset of the estimated 30 million 16- to 64-year-old Americans counted as disabled in 2015.[27]

However, the many types of increased male health problems and substance abuse suggest that they truly are disabled and can't work. Census data indicate that the highest disability rates for nonworking men—40 percent or more—are among whites who are 40 to 54 years old or have less than a college degree. Since nearly 18 percent of people on disability were working, albeit more likely part-time, and 10.5 percent were unemployed in 2016, they are considered part of the labor force.[28]

Yet for those ready to point to disability as a "hammock" (as opposed to a "safety net") or a cause for the increase in men not working, the 2 percentage point rise in disability claimants over a 47-year period and the facts that nearly two in seven are in the labor force and almost half are women strongly suggest that SSDI is not a major cause of the decline in men's work. Nonetheless, the reality of worsening physical and mental health and skyrocketing substance abuse does demonstrate that there is a relationship between health and work.

Yet the question dangles: Why are the health and work problems (not to mention the family and parenthood and internet addiction problems) worse among men than women? We all live in the same culture and economy with the same political system.

ALL THE LONELY MEN, WHERE DO THEY ALL COME FROM?

As former surgeon general Murthy said, isolation or loneliness is perhaps America's biggest public health problem, and it is one that is growing. It is particularly acute among the unmarried, those in middle age, and men. The proportion of 15- to 64-year-old men living alone has risen by a startling 50 percent between 1970 and 2012—to just over one in three men—while the proportion of women living alone has remained the same. At first glance puzzling, this change is almost entirely attributable to fewer and fewer men living with children. People—men in particular—who are isolated are much more likely to die during any given time frame than those who are socially connected, with studies even finding that loneliness can be as much of a long-term risk factor as smoking fifteen cigarettes a day, obesity, or heavy drinking.[29]

While the Beatles lamented "all the lonely people," loneliness has become increasingly gendered, and these days men are more likely to be isolated than women.

Before turning to the data, one fact that struck me when talking to divorced men and women was the striking postdivorce social difference between the sexes. Whereas men felt greater urgency to find a new partner, women had much more extensive and deeper support networks. In one eastern metropolitan area, I found a tightly knit "divorced moms" group of seventy-five women living within about a mile's radius of each other, whereas men generally had no such network. One of the rare divorced fathers' groups had less than a handful of men, and they participated irregularly and lived far apart.

With the doubling of after-50 divorce rates since 1990, the ranks of older, isolated, divorced men are growing.[30] We've heard a number of men whose marriages fell apart express their sense of isolation. Santiago, a 40-something Latino man in California with a professional degree, a low-wage job, and a wife who left him, simply said, "I don't have any friends or family."

Even among married men, when asked, "Who's your best friend?," a good number would say "My wife" and have trouble coming up with a male name. Although some adult men play on sports teams, as men generally need activities to hold them together more than women do, women jog and do yoga classes with other women, take trips with longtime girlfriends, join book clubs, talk on the phone and use social media more, and meet up for drinks with their pals. As David Figura of the Good Men Project writes, "Check the family calendar on the refrigerator. . . . All the kids' activities and the wife's book club and the next girlfriend getaway are written down—and there's nothing for you."[31]

A big part of the problem gets back to men developing less of an emotional repertoire than women, as they are told not to reveal their sorrows or dreams, other than maybe to their wives. And the masculine code tells males that expressing negative feelings like hurt, loss, defeat, and loneliness itself is "whining," and whining isn't manly.

Men, especially after their 20s, have more trouble making friends than women do, although they tend to be somewhat better at making "contacts." The friends they have tend not to be confidants—other men who they can talk with about their difficulties and worries—as much as they are beer buddies or guys they meet up with on the basketball or racquetball courts. Without close friends or strong real-life social networks, and fewer family ties than women, these men "can go down the rabbit's hole without anyone even noticing," Azzam said. Many men and men's advocacy groups sadly and correctly bewail the dearth of male friendships.[32]

"I am 42 years old and have no friends," one man plaintively posted on the internet. "What are some ways I can forge relationships so that I don't feel so alone? I used to have friends, but they were friends I made when I was a teenager and I've moved around a lot since then. Now I find myself middle-aged and alone. I feel this makes me less attractive to the opposite sex and more likely to grow into a crazy old man." Some dating advice columns concur, saying that men without friends or a social life tend to be ignored or rejected by women.[33]

A Red Pill podcast declared, "We talk a lot about lifting and self-improvement and game and women, but let's not forget about that other core tenet of The Red Pill—having male friends." The more moderate *Men's Journal* asked in a headline, "Do Men Suck at Friendship?"[34]

While there are exceptions to this portrayal, men who aren't working or partnered or involved fathers are cut off from key people in their lives. Loners, they tend to be disengaged from, or angry toward, their communities or country. Isolation begets, and is reinforced by, internet and pornography addiction, not to mention alcohol and drug problems. In a vicious cycle, these problems make it harder for men to get and hold jobs and have good relationships with a partner and children. Pain and illness make life more difficult. Financially more insecure, they fall into poverty, possibly crime, and dependence on the government. Children and many wives and partners suffer. And the cascade of ill effects goes on.

HORICON, WISCONSIN

PORTRAIT OF A TOWN

Horicon is a small Wisconsin town about forty miles north of Madison, anchored by what started as a farm machinery factory in the nineteenth century and surrounded by farms and the scenic Horicon Wildlife Area, where tens of thousands come to watch flocks of migrating Canada geese, go duck hunting, canoe, and hike.

Early twentieth-century wood-frame houses, some with cupolas and other flourishes, are interspersed with post–World War II split-level and ranch homes with vinyl siding in the compact, tree-lined streets of "downtown." A lot of them are well tended, although the paint is peeling on others, with yards cluttered with toys, tools, and plastic deer. The American flag flies every day at many homes. Modest, newer two-story apartment buildings are clustered near the site where the town's last grocery store stood. Trailer parks are scattered on the outskirts.

The Rock River winds through town, with the giant John Deere factory dominating one side and a small International Association of Machinists union hall and park on the other. The Horicon Marsh, half again as large as Manhattan, includes more than thirty-three square miles of state and national parkland. Farmhouses and granaries are still dotted along Route 151 coming into town from the west.

When I last went to Horicon to see the town where my mother grew up and I spent many childhood summers and holidays, a TV documentary was being screened at the high school, promoting the marsh, the boat tours to see more than three hundred species of birds, Horicon's "great employers," and the town's "family environment."

It could be a Norman Rockwell image of the idylls of mid-twentieth-century small-town life. But there are cracks in the picture, including an all but deserted main street, a factory that pays its workers less in real-dollar wages and benefits than it did thirty-five years ago, churches whose congregations have dwindled, a multipronged public health crisis of opioid overdoses and widespread obesity, an aging population, numerous nonmarital births, many men feeling marginalized, and a waning sense of neighborliness, sociability, and trust.

"There's a defeatism, and people in Horicon are defensive about how well it was doing in the old days," one city official told me. "If not for Horicon Works"—the name of the Deere plant—"there'd be almost no jobs."

One longtime Horicon resident recalled that back in the early 1980s, the main street "had a couple of bakeries, two pharmacies, the Ulrich clothing store, a few hardware stores, Curry's grocery store, four gas stations, three car dealerships, more than half a dozen taverns, a railroad business, the *Horicon Reporter* [newspaper], and two feed mills supplying the farmers. All gone." Horicon's movie theater had closed around the time of *The Last Picture Show* (1971).

There are other signs of decline, several linked to the deterioration of a once thriving male working class. While the troubles of small-town America are a much larger, more complex story, it is notable how many indicators of regression circle around the waning fortunes and problems of men. Men can't support a family on their own. Men are not hanging out together or active in community life. As elsewhere in the country, men are more likely to die of drug overdoses. Some fathers who have children out of wedlock disappear. The outdoorsmen—the guys who went hunting, fishing, and boating—are fewer and older, while isolated indoorsmen watching TV and playing video games are more common.

Horicon still had about 3,655 residents in 2016, down just 5 percent from its 1990 peak. More than 95 percent of its residents are white, largely of German ancestry, and the median household income was about $60,000, almost exactly the same as the nation at large.[1]

Nonetheless, all is far from well when it comes to wages and living standards. On the one hand, John Deere recently expanded its production and raised its hourly wage by a dollar because it is having a hard time finding workers who are both qualified and can pass drug tests. Horicon Bank has also expanded throughout the middle tier of the state. Gardner's Manufacturing still employs about sixty people. And a few smart young men, like the local chiropractor, have come back to work in their fathers' businesses.

On the other hand, according to a retired veteran of Deere, "The jobs pay less than I was making thirty years ago. Benefits, which didn't cost me anything, have dropped and workers have to pay part of their benefits." Wages now average about $14–$18 an hour, compared to about $18–$25, in constant dollars, back then. A 96-year-old Deere retiree and another thirty-five-year veteran of the company count themselves fortunate to be receiving monthly checks from Deere's old defined-benefit pension plan (replaced, as at other companies, by a riskier defined-contribution plan).

"It's moved the Deere worker from middle-to-upper income to low-to-middle income," Horicon's mayor said. "Today's wage doesn't buy a house. It used to be that husbands could support a family. Now it takes two incomes. Some people don't take pride in their homes and don't care what they look like."

And this is in a town where three- or four-bedroom houses sell for $100,000–$150,000. Another retiree in his 80s, a local history buff and long a part-time writer for the town's former newspaper, recounted how the Van Brunt Company, which Deere bought out, gave employees $1,000 or more in the 1930s to help them build a house in Horicon. Moreover, Deere's work-force, which was once drawn heavily from the Horicon area, now counts only about one-third of its workers from the town.

New Hampshire Industries completed its Horicon plant shutdown in December 2017, laying off thirty-nine workers. Eberle's, one of several former cheese factories in the area, is now a produce store. And the main-street shops have closed because people now drive to Walmarts or supermarkets nearly fifteen miles away in Beaver Dam. Among the few downtown businesses left are a tawdry tattoo parlor and a smoke shop. Few pedestrians walk down Lake Street anymore, and eighteen-wheelers whiz in and out of the Deere plant.[2]

Horicon leans more to the right than it did a few generations ago, yet there is an undercurrent of resentment about "corporate greed" and the attack on unions. Although a lot of the homes are modern and comfortable, and had Easter decorations in the window when I visited, more than one resident described Horicon as "slowly dying."

For young adults, economic circumstances aren't good, as is true in other parts of the country. As a result, they are either leaving town for work or often don't work and live with their parents. With younger families moving away for better opportunities and amenities, the city's public schools have been combined into one building for 5-year-olds and 18-year-olds alike.

Of those who remain, fewer marry, stay married, and have children. Another indicator of how young Horicon families are faring is the fact that about 40 percent of the town's high school students qualify for free or reduced-price meals, according to the former president of the school board. The percentage increases to about 55 percent for children in elementary school.[3]

School enrollment has fallen from about 1,000 to 720 since the 1990s, truancy rates are well above the state average, and the high school had to combine its football team with one from a nearby town in 2016.[4] The "Marshmen," who generations had rooted for, are gone. Like elsewhere in America, many residents bemoan the disappearance of boys playing army or baseball, opting instead for computer games or activities organized by their parents.

Horicon residents speak of a disturbing rise in divorce, nonmarital births, and greater tensions between the sexes. "As men are less the head of the home than in earlier times, they've lost some degree of their sense of manhood," the president of Horicon Bank told me. "Wives, because of their increased financial freedom, may respect and rely on them less, which diminishes their self-esteem."

Teachers report more children with only one parent in the home, the recent school board president said. Too many guys are "jerks," one older resident said. "They get women pregnant and disappear. Sometimes the girl takes off and parties. I know a number of grandparents who are raising the kids because the parents are drunk or in jail."

One Horicon grandparent has been doing just that, and older people, like a man who has written a history of the town, are upset: "Having babies out of wedlock I don't agree with. Get married. Give that child a name, a father. They know they can get help from the state if they're not married."

Many young men are immature, insensitive, and lacking in basic values. "I'm ashamed they're guys," one man said. "You used to treat a girl with respect."

OxyContin, heroin, methamphetamines, and other drugs have come to town, taking their deadly toll. Obituary notices for overdose deaths of men and women in their 20s, 30s, and 40s invariably use the euphemism "passed away unexpectedly." An EMT worker said they are always on the lookout for meth labs, which he has found in the homes or garages of townspeople of all ages. Between drugs, obesity, and deadly high-speed car chases, often linked to heroin, Horicon was unofficially deemed an "unhealthy community" when it was included in the Blue Zones Project, a global initiative to get people to lead healthier lives.[5]

One of the most frequently heard regrets about contemporary Horicon is the decline in civic life. Men no longer take the leadership roles they once did. With considerable nostalgia, one resident I met remembered a time when people knew each other, socialized, and could be trusted.

John Deere, which once sponsored celebrations like Marsh Days, itself has become less involved with the town. "A tier of middle managers no longer work at this great company in Horicon, and this change has impaired many aspects of community life," said the still very active 74-year-old bank president. "It's hard to sustain our civic clubs, our golf course, and even our schools."

The Rotary, Elks, and American Legion have hemorrhaged male members and are barely kept afloat by the women who have joined. No one shows up for the open city council meetings that the mayor chairs. School board meetings are sparsely attended.

Attendance has plummeted at the United Methodist and United Brethren churches, where one elderly member said, "We're lucky if we get seventy people out of our four to five hundred members." The 160-year-old Presbyterian Church has virtually shut down, holding on to a membership of barely twenty that was nearly 90 percent female and 90 percent over 65 in 2015.[6]

The newspaper, which covered townspeople and events, also provided a sort of social glue, the 86-year-old former editor said. Founded in the late nineteenth century, it stopped publishing in 2009. The editor lives in a mobile home adjacent to twenty-nine others in a park on the edge of town.

Horicon once might have vied for the distinction of having one of America's highest number of bars per capita, as it had ten taverns, mostly on the main street. Men would flock to them after work for a Pabst or a Schlitz and conversation. There was Fat's, which bought uniforms for school sports teams. At Metzdorf's there were thirty barstools, and men would have their regular stools. "My dad occupied number twenty-nine," the town historian recalled. "After work, that was where men caught up on what was happening in Horicon and in the world. Many would come back after supper." While the old taverns may have been all-male, they were a place for men to socialize. By contrast, of the two or three bars that remain, one third-generation resident said that at least one of the bars has become rougher, catering to the young, with heavy-metal music blaring. "It's the type of place you walk in and don't feel welcome," he said. Incongruously for a state that was once a very Germanic beer capital of America, the new bar styles itself as an "Irish pub," which one Yelp reviewer called a dark, "rowdy . . . dive."[7]

Another staple of male camaraderie—hunting—has also been in decline. "It's not something that men do as much," a local official with the state's Department of Natural Resources said. In an effort to attract younger men, the DNR is offering "Learn to Hunt" classes.

Horicon residents often say that people don't socialize as much as they did years ago. "There's a liquor store that didn't exist ten years ago," a man in his mid-40s said. "People just buy stuff and go home. I remember families going out to the Wooden Shingle or the Pyramid restaurants, where there was sort of a supper-club feeling."

Now people don't go out so much. Some attribute it to the economy—not enough money to spend. Others blame the internet—"that impersonal computer" that has meant a lot of people "don't know how to interact," as one middle-age man put it. Still others say that people just aren't as friendly. The 96-year-old recalled, "People used to know everyone in town. Not anymore."

The history buff fondly recalled when the town was "like a family." Now, he added, "you don't know who your neighbors are or what they're like. It affects trust."

Horicon is better off than some other small towns in contemporary America, and many of its problems have roots in economic forces that sweep beyond the city limits and even the nation's borders. The changes and difficulties of 2010s Horicon affect all residents, and, like all social change, they are multifactorial. Yet swirling through this story is a significant (and also multifactorial) story of the countless men who are struggling and have lost their way.

CHAPTER 9

Locked Out

Formerly Incarcerated Men

Surveillance is permanent in its effects, even if it is discontinuous in its action.

Michel Foucault, Discipline and Punish, *1977*

It must surely be a tribute to the resilience of the human spirit that even a small number of those men and women in the hell of the prison system survive it and hold on to their humanity.

Howard Zinn, You Can't Be Neutral on a Moving Train, *1994*

It's a Tuesday night at "the Castle," an ornate former Catholic girls school in West Harlem that has become home to the Fortune Society, a residential reentry, social services, and advocacy organization for formerly incarcerated men.[1] Men like Philip and Jack, the first African American, the second white, both in their early 50s, live in the Castle's spartan rooms that accommodate from one to five people.

Both men join a crowd of sixty to seventy men and a few women for an evening of talk facilitated by three moderators. One white man had just been released that day, as is typical, with little more than his clothes, two $20 bills, and subway fare. A few ex-felons come from all over New York City just for the meetings. Others have spent months living at the Castle, getting meals, help obtaining health care, and looking for jobs and other supports.

At least two-thirds of the men are African American, but the demographic fact that stands out nearly as painfully is that these men are old or look old beyond their years.[2] Since many of them have spent twenty, thirty, even forty years in prison, they are balding or have gray beards. They also have scars and canes, and some are in wheelchairs. Most wear sweats or running pants, although a few arrive dressed in suits and ties. Caps are ubiquitous—skull caps, baseball caps, ski caps, old felt hats.

They talk about how hard it is to reintegrate into society, work, family, and relationships, and about their goals. Some are haunted by prison memories and are bitter, while others talk about their battered self-esteem. On this Tuesday night, as the conversation bounced around the room, one black man who had been at Attica during the 1971 riots said, "Many of us have attitudes." Another said, "You hear negative things about yourself all your life, it's hard to think good things."

But it isn't all doom and gloom. A lot of them talk about how they are striving for "a better direction in life" and are determined to "get their shit together." While the discussion is often intense, with thoughtful and self-reflective comments, it is also leavened by laughter at periodic jokes.

After several hours of talking, the group gathers for a memorial service and remembrance for a Fortune member who had recently died. He had spent the majority of his 83 years behind bars.

"We have a society that says it believes in second chances, but that hasn't panned out," says Ronald Day, associate vice president of the David Rothenberg Center for Public Policy. (Rothenberg, who founded Fortune in 1967, is still active with the society.) "People are struggling, and communities aren't prepared to welcome them home and can't handle them."[3]

"You're judged," said a 60-year-old black man in Ohio who had spent time in prison. "There is discrimination that means you don't get the interview. If I committed a crime, it's what I did, not who I am. There is a scar on me, as though I've not changed since then. I *have* changed since then."

Between 70 million and 80 million Americans have criminal records, including some 20 million with felony convictions. About 90 percent are men. Incarceration rates more than quadrupled during the half century since 1970 and were about seven to nine times higher than in France or Germany, as 2.2 million Americans were in prisons or jails and another 4.7 million were on parole or probation in 2015 and 2016, even though incarceration rates started to fall around 2010. These are the statistics behind America's much-discussed mass incarceration problem. Of course, for every violent criminal or burglar or thief, there are victims—5 million victims of murder, rape, assault, robbery, and other violent crimes and 14.6 million victims of property crimes in 2015.[4]

This chapter addresses how America's mass incarceration policies of recent decades have left millions of formerly incarcerated men locked out of work and economic success, family, and society.[5]

Crime rates in the United States dropped between the early 1990s and mid-2010s, with an uptick in recent years, but more and more men—particularly men of color—have been thrown behind bars. Tougher penalties have been imposed for minor crimes, and "three strikes" laws enacted since the 1990s have led to longer sentences. Incarcerated men are not included among the unemployed or in the denominators of the labor force participation rate or the employment-to-population (e:p) ratio, even though they account for about 2 percent of adult American males.

These men—the incarcerated, the twice as large population on parole or probation, and the ten times larger population of those formerly incarcerated with felony records—are also among the ranks of *men out*. Counted in the e:p ratio and, if they're actively looking for jobs, in the labor force participation rate, men who have been in prison experience much higher rates of nonwork, sporadic work, low-wage work, and poverty than the general population of men. They also are much less likely to be married or partnered and have children in their lives and much more likely to have physical health and mental health problems.

Jack is one of countless men who try very hard to turn their lives around after getting out of prison. After a total of fifteen years of incarceration for drug-related burglaries, he was released at age 51 and has been trying to start a mobile dog-grooming business.

Life was difficult for Jack before he went to prison, and it's been difficult since his release. His father died of cancer when he was 5, and his four siblings, he said, "flew the coop at young ages, leaving me to deal with my mother's insanity." They were among the few people in the projects who were white. Men cycled through their apartment, and his mother "allowed sexual abuse by some of her boyfriends and 'uncles,'" he said. "I was used to being beaten at home, so I got used to being beaten and stabbed in prison." However, "it was the emotional pain I couldn't deal with, so I gravitated toward drugs to dull the pain."

While in prison, Jack wrote poetry, fiction, and children's books; tried to dissuade fellow prisoners from joining gangs; and took college courses but feels he was unjustly thwarted in getting a degree. The drug treatment programs he attended were "a farce," so he got clean before he was reincarcerated.

Jack is ashamed of the crimes he committed and wants to make amends, but he is bitter about the prison system and how ex-felons like him are treated.

"The system is corrupt," he said. "They lock people up for being homeless and being an eyesore to tourists," or "they get men for trumped-up sexual assault charges. It's all to keep the prison-industrial complex running." Reflecting on how dozens of new prisons were built in New York state alone during the crack epidemic, he remembers former New York governor Mario Cuomo calling prisons a "family employment industry" for rural communities with few other jobs. Half a million Americans work as correctional officers.[6]

Since leaving prison, Jack has gone on a number of job interviews where the bias against hiring people who have done their time comes out. "Some say, 'You have a criminal record so we can't have you here.' Some try to soften the blow and say, 'We're not really looking for anyone,' even though they had posted a job." Community-based organizations are better, but "some take advantage of you," he said. They say they'll help him to find decent jobs, but all they've done is to send him out on short-term work, picking up trash in housing projects or salting the roads.

Being an ex-convict is not the only strike against him. He feels that he is too old to do the physical labor that he once did and that younger men can do. Because technology changed so much while he was incarcerated, he didn't know how to fill out an online application.

Jack said he would "love to get married and have someone else in my life," but most women see him with "three big Xs tattooed on my face, and they say 'ex-offender.'" Afraid to date, he says he would feel safer seeing a prostitute.

Nonetheless, he said, "I feel confident that I will succeed." He recounted how he was unexpectedly influenced by a "black militant who hated white people" and was sentenced to life. "We would play chess and, knowing that he would never be free, he would keep saying to me, 'You have a chance.' It opened my eyes." However, when I last spoke with Jack in early 2018, he was facing another sentencing.

THE PRISON STATE

Perhaps the result of endless crime and police TV shows and movies and lurid news coverage of murders, kidnappings, and other "sensational" crimes, Americans and others have an almost perverse fascination with crime. "There's a criminal mystique," a clinical social worker involved with former inmates in New York, said. "Maybe it's what people fantasize about but don't

have the heart to do. It makes an ex-offender an interesting object out there,"
someone different and most likely feared.

Needless to say, the reality is not like on TV, and the enormous subculture
of inmates and the formerly incarcerated is not what most Americans want to
see. Without overly rehashing the history and consequences of tougher sentencing laws and mass incarceration, it is worth taking a quick statistical tour
of America's prison state. The United States has more than 1,800 state and
federal prisons, over 3,200 jails, and roughly 900 juvenile detention facilities,
and these don't count immigration detention centers and military prisons.
Incarceration directly costs government $80 billion a year. The total costs to
society could be as much as $1 trillion if one adds in lost wages, the likelihood
that imprisonment will lead to future criminality, and the social welfare costs
for programs supporting former prisoners. Many prisoners are forced to work
for nothing or as little as 12 cents an hour, producing goods and providing
services for dozens of well-known companies such as Victoria's Secret, AT&T,
Starbucks, and Walmart and working on prison farms that supply major grocery chains.[7]

Eleven million Americans are put behind bars each year, although most
sentences are brief; thus the 2.2 million rolling average of people in U.S.
prisons and jails. Of the nation's two million male inmates, half are under 34.
Roughly 40 percent of all those who are incarcerated are black, and a similar
percentage are white, but incarceration rates for African Americans are about
five times higher than for whites. On any given day, 4 percent of all 18- to
29-year-old men, and 11.5 percent of high school dropouts in this cohort are
incarcerated. About 640,000 people like Jack and Philip are released from
prisons and another nine million are sent home from jails each year. As many
as one-third don't have a home to go to.[8]

Some of these men have been locked up for drug or other relatively minor
offenses, yet half are in prison for violent offenses, even though violent crime
rates have fallen sharply since the early 1990s.[9] However, their criminal records stay with them, generally keeping them out of jobs, making them less
appealing partners, and preventing millions of them from voting. For those
who don't return to crime, most are unemployed or underemployed and
struggling.

More than half of incarcerated men are fathers, with a majority of them
unmarried. About 1.1 million incarcerated fathers (and 120,000 mothers)
have some 2.7 million children, half under 10 years old. These include one
in nine African American children and one in fifty-seven white children. All

told, five million to ten million kids have a parent behind bars at some point during their childhood. One quarter of black children and one in twenty-five white children had a father in prison by age 14. Most do not see their dads in prison. An older study found that two-thirds of parents were handcuffed in front of their children. In one-fourth of parental arrests, children saw guns drawn. These kids often have experienced symptoms of posttraumatic stress. They tend to have significantly higher levels of anxiety and depression and lower academic achievement, and they generally live in poverty. Single mothers left behind are often traumatized, further impoverished, and suffer from addiction and other health problems.[10]

For many incarcerated fathers, the broken bonds are devastating. As one man told government researchers, "Being away, not being able to be a dad. Not being able to be there and protect my daughter from anything. Like, just being a dad. That was the hardest thing for me."[11]

LIFE AFTER PRISON

Philip, whom we met at the Fortune Society, spent the prime years of his life, between 20 and 50, in prison. Although he had recently been released ("I was placed on the bus and told 'see you later'"), Philip has had unusual successes and several typical failures of formerly incarcerated men.[12]

While in prison, he wrote a play, *The Nigger Trial*, that was produced, performed at a major university, and filmed. He also wrote articulate essays on the horrors of prison life:

> Justice is blind and swift—an icepick in the stomach or eye when stepping out of the shower, a knife in the head or neck on the way to the yard. . . . So I accepted the fact that many more would die in dimly lit corridors, bereft of the humanity that their very existence cried out for. And after each time, I'd stand around those yards and corridors with everyone else, feigning indifference and philosophical detachment, and I would console myself with life-sustaining irrelevancies. "It wasn't my fault; he probably brought it on himself; I don't even know that mother—."

Philip recalled that he was taught "good values" as a child, but he "wanted to go my own way" and became addicted to crack cocaine and committed a violent crime. "The hardest part was not serving the time, but the guilt and shame for doing what I'd done," he said.

The local government has paid his $215-a-month subsidized rent in exchange for participation in parole and reentry programs. He reconnected with the mother of his children, now in their 30s, and her children from another relationship. "When I contacted her, I was expecting animosity, but she offered forgiveness," he said. "I do things with my daughter and she's very understanding, even though I went to prison when they were babies." Finding a job and "making ends meet" seem out of reach, yet he is grateful for the family that has given him "a rebirth into a whole new world."

Philip, hardly thriving, has done better than most formerly incarcerated men. He found a reentry program, has some supportive family members, and cultivated his writing talents during the thirty years that he was imprisoned. Yet he is in 50s, has virtually no work experience, not a lot of good prospects in the dozen or so years before normal retirement age, and is dead broke, without much chance of amassing even a small fraction of the assets that retirement planners tell clients that they need.

"Returning to the community from jail or prison is a complex transition for most offenders, as well as for their families and communities," the National Institute of Justice reported, with all the bloodless understatement of a government agency. "Upon reentering society, former offenders are likely to struggle with substance abuse, lack of adequate education and job skills, limited housing options, and mental health issues."[13]

These men are lucky if they make it out of a homeless shelter, a government or nonprofit agency offers support, and they don't end up back on the streets selling drugs because they can't get a job and go back to prison. Those who find companionship and aren't deeply psychologically scarred, angry, abusing drugs or alcohol, and alone are the fortunate few.

For most, it's the "see you later" line.

A number of states stipulate that those being released from prison have some "reentry case plan," identifying health, work, and other needs, as well as providing help with a place to live. While a few cities like Los Angeles and New York are experimenting with one-stop reentry centers for rapid assistance, most efforts are halfhearted, underfunded, and unsuccessful, according to many formerly incarcerated men and practitioners in the field.[14]

The vast majority of these men face a seemingly insuperable array of barriers to a decent life and being reintegrated into the putative America of "second chances." "A person coming out [of prison] trying to get a barber's license was denied because of his criminal conviction," Ronald Day said. "You name it. There are any number of barriers."[15]

Men who were formerly incarcerated are often barred from public housing, even if their children are living there. It is more difficult to get public benefits such as Medicaid, food stamps, or subsidized access to education or job training. More than six million are disenfranchised for life, with a dozen, mostly southern states—notably Florida—denying them the right to vote. Employers don't want to hire them, and a lot of occupations are de facto off-limits, although the movement to "ban the box" requiring former convictions to be disclosed in job applications is starting to make a difference. Most women don't want to date them, although this is less true in the high-crime 'hood where many of these men came from. Reestablishing relationships with children, other family, and pre-incarceration friends is extremely difficult. Finding a place to live that is affordable and where neighbors aren't trying to keep them out is another major challenge. Then there are the indignities of being looked down on and under constant scrutiny, especially if one is on parole or probation. African American men face the additional consequences of racism.[16]

Sylvester, a 60-year-old African American man in Wisconsin, was first convicted in 1983. Since being released from prison, he has had to wear a GPS monitor on his ankle and must continue to do so for the rest of his life. He has been picked up and thrown in jail for several days at least eight times because the GPS signal couldn't be detected. One of these instances occurred when he was taking an English class at the state university in Madison. "I'm consistently encountering problems," he said. He hopes that he is "able to continue to withstand this."

NO WORK HERE

Nonetheless, the greatest barrier for formerly incarcerated men to get back on their feet is in the job market. Three-fourths of these men are out of work a year after their release, according to the Department of Justice. A survey by the Ella Baker Center for Human Rights found that two-thirds of them were without work or underemployed five years after being released. Three-fourths said that finding a job after being released was difficult or nearly impossible. Looked at from the broader perspective of nonworking men, one report suggested that as many as one-third of men without jobs had criminal records.[17]

A criminal record becomes a "credential," says Harvard sociologist Devah Pager. "The 'credential' of a criminal record, like educational or professional credentials, constitutes a formal and enduring classification of social status, which can be used to regulate access and opportunity." It also reinforces inequality, denying generally poor and poorly educated men the chance to get ahead.[18]

It's no surprise that most employers don't want to hire men with prison records, thus stereotyping job candidates out of fear for other workers' safety, concerns about men's "character," worries about hassles with parole officers and the criminal justice system, and the sense that such men aren't like us (the "interesting objects" to be observed but not gotten too close to). Some concern—particularly for applicants with a record of violent crime—is reasonable. But since most men who are released weren't in for the most heinous offenses, and with the sharp increase in nonviolent drug-related arrests, much of the worry is not so reasonable. It's profiling and it's bias.[19]

Employers have routinely asked, "Have you ever been convicted of a crime?" A yes is often a disqualifier. In recent years, ten states and scores of cities and counties have adopted "ban the box" laws that forbid prospective private- and public-sector employers from asking that question, and President Obama banned it for many federal jobs. Yet it is relatively easy to find such information online, and more than two-thirds of employers surveyed by the Society for Human Resources Management said they do criminal background checks. Former prisoners often feel embarrassed to talk about their past, and employers often find excuses not to hire or simply to deny a job to a man who is out of prison.[20]

A Justice Department study in liberal New York City found that a criminal record reduced the chances of a job applicant getting a callback by 50 percent. Negative effects were greater for black applicants. Even though those who got face-to-face interviews did somewhat better, one black tester in the study recalled: "As she looked over [my résumé] I could barely hear her say, 'Oh, I see.' I don't know what it was in response to, but it was pretty quick so I would guess it was my conviction. She then just looked up at me and said, 'I'll give you a call.' It seemed like she ended it a bit abruptly."[21]

Even those who were arrested but never charged or convicted, as well as those who are later found to be wrongly convicted, still have strikes against them. They tend to earn less and are less likely to own a home, and it is often a Kafkaesque process to get their records expunged.[22]

Most formerly incarcerated men are further handicapped because they have little education or work experience, and typically have lost nearly six and a half years of potential work life in prison. Moreover, few prisons offer much in the way of job training, generally providing what some prisoner rights activists have called "slave labor."[23]

Some get jobs, but many don't pay a living wage or are in temporary jobs like construction. A few organizations, such as Goodwill Industries, make a point of giving these men jobs. Others work off the books in the underground economy.[24]

"So many people are desperate for jobs," Jack said, "so they wind up selling drugs." More than 55 percent of formerly incarcerated men are rearrested within the first year after release—some for new crimes, like Jack; others, like Sylvester, for technical parole violations. Seventy-five percent are arrested again within five years, according to a Justice Department study. Lack of a job, substance abuse, and mental health problems increase the likelihood of recidivism. So do very low wages. The high recidivism rate is sadly understandable, given the lack of social supports and jobs, which are on top of the host of problems with housing, health, relationships, and family. So the vicious cycle continues.[25]

Jared is not who most Americans would picture as an ex-convict who has served two terms totaling fourteen years. A white Jewish former journalist in his late 60s, he's been out of prison for more than a decade, but he lives in the equivalent of a homeless shelter in the basement of a New York yeshiva.

Before going to prison in the 1980s, Jared lived the life of a colorful prankster. He and former colleagues at the radio station where he worked made the news when they took over a prominent building and outwitted the authorities while continuing to broadcast. Jared described himself as a onetime "professional party-crasher," meeting Hollywood and Washington celebrities.

Life has been hard since he got out of prison in his mid-50s. The room he rents, above a school, has people sleeping in the halls and showers. He has been appealing his convictions for years. Very much alone and his diabetes "out of control," his only saviors have been a primarily African American organization for ex-offenders, which he was connected to by a well-known politician he knew from the olden days. Jared's been looking for a job and friends, without much success, and feels that he is a *shanda*, a Yiddish word that he translates as "an embarrassment to the race."

Diabetes, as well as high blood pressure, AIDS, hepatitis C, mental health problems, and substance abuse, is more common among ex-offenders than the general population. Then there are the wounds from the stabbings and other violence of prison life that Philip described. One study found that ex-prisoners were thirteen times more likely than a comparable sample of the general population to die of a drug overdose within two weeks of release. Mortality rates for those released from Washington state prisons were three and a half times higher than for other state residents. In addition to over-doses, death rates for homicide, liver disease, motor vehicle accidents, and suicide were notably higher. The *Baltimore Sun* produced two maps of the city's neighborhoods, color-coded for low to high incidence—one for rates of HIV and one for incarceration rates. They look virtually identical. Formerly incarcerated men do better in states that have expanded Medicaid, yet health services can be catch-as-catch-can and far from high quality. During the two years after Maryland expanded Medicaid in January 2014, only about 15 percent of released prisoners had signed up for the program, even though about 90 percent were eligible.[26]

LOCKED OUT OF FAMILIES

Most formerly incarcerated fathers have little or no connection with their children. A lot of them find their minor children living with their mother and her new partner. Often children whose fathers were imprisoned when they were infants or toddlers have no memory of their dads. If fathers' relationships with the mothers aren't good, they have less contact with their children. The rare men with short incarcerations, who had formed prior bonds with their kids, who had stable housing, and whose partners welcomed them back, or former partners who wanted their children to see their dads, were best able to reestablish relationships. "Living with housing insecurity, often in the grip of addiction, and managing time and relationships with several partners are objective barriers to positive parenting for even the most committed mothers and fathers newly-released from prison," according to Harvard sociologists Bruce Western and Natalie Smith.[27]

Most formerly incarcerated men aren't married, including nearly five out of six fathers. Most are not seen as desirable mates by women, despite there being ten women for every six men in high-crime areas of Washington, D.C., for example. As one woman on one of the "dating is hell" websites sarcasti-cally said, after meeting a formerly incarcerated man, "I learned that in the future it may be a good idea to ask potential suitors about their prison records before meeting them." On the other hand, as noted, some women in these men's old neighborhoods are more accepting.[28]

"There are a lot of women who wouldn't mess around with people who were formerly incarcerated," Rafael, a Hispanic New York man, said. "Personally, I've been out twenty-two years and I've had three failed relationships. For me, one of the hardest things for me to deal with, and I have PTSD [post-traumatic stress disorder], is a sense of unfairness in the relationship. In my last one, after the children were born, I was discriminated against because of my background."

It's hard to get around the fact that formerly incarcerated men are among the most marginalized American men. Some policymakers, social service agencies like the Fortune Society, and academics are trying to address their myriad problems. Clearly, most need a lot more help with jobs, housing, health, and other challenges of reentry than they are getting.

Tyrone, an African American man who had spent thirty-two years in prison when he was released in 2014, is among the more fortunate—although that is not saying a lot. He has an advanced degree, a job, and a girlfriend, although his housing situation is precarious.

His childhood was "dysfunctional," as he grew up in a house where people gathered to illegally play the numbers, and, as a child, he would be sent to collect money from neighborhood bettors. Tyrone felt "distrust and disdain toward police officers from an early age," having seen cops beat a man to death for a traffic violation. However, some of his best times as a youth were when he participated in the local Police Activity League.

His father always had a job, even though his education ended after third grade because he was needed for farm labor in the South. Yet his dad insisted that Tyrone finish high school and enroll in college. This did not go well, and he got involved in a petty crime with friends that tragically turned violent. Tyrone was convicted and "sent upstate" just six months after he became the father of a baby girl.

In a number of ways Tyrone was a model—and fortunate—inmate. He received his master's degree and was able to work in prison for nineteen years facilitating domestic violence and parenting programs, as an academic assistant, and writing fundraising proposals for several nonprofits serving prisoners.

"I came out with the skills and attitude that crime was no longer an option," he said. "And it made it easier to get a job." He got little help from local government social services agencies, and—like most formerly incarcerated men—had to fend for himself. He found a room where he could live and a job with a prisoner reentry program, helping formerly incarcerated people with illnesses and with getting access to health care. After making appeals to ten parole boards, he finally was released from parole.

Tyrone knows he is unusual among formerly incarcerated men. Aside from the education he got and the work he did while in prison, he built up an extensive roster of contacts from his work, and his ex-wife, father, sister, and even his daughter have been supportive.

He has seen many men who never get jobs, and recounted the story of one man who had been out of prison and "clean" for twenty years who was about to be hired until his prospective employer reconsidered at the last minute. In general, he saw that only younger men who served short sentences could get jobs in a limited number of fields, such as construction. Referring to ex-felons as "the least of them," he knows that they're far from policymakers' top priority, "since so many other people and issues come ahead of them." Life has turned around for Tyrone, who was making dinner for his girlfriend when I spoke with him.

America's 17–20 million formerly incarcerated men overlap with the nation's 20 million nonworking men, the nearly 10 million men not spending the night with their minor children, the millions who are not married or in relationships, and those who are dependent on parents or government, or who suffer from health and mental health problems.[29] But they are not all the same men by any means. Tyrone is working. The upper-middle-class man in the New Jersey dog park is not. The millennial men living at home and playing video games are generally not among the formerly incarcerated. Most of the fathers cut off from their children never went to prison. Some ex-prisoners struggle with their masculinity; many have more immediate concerns. And though some of their struggles are different, the reality is that they still intersect in so many ways, suggesting the need for an overarching, multipronged strategy for the nation's *men out*.

Again, this is not to argue with the fact that more women than men are struggling, though in different ways and to different degrees. They tend to have lower wages, bear the burden of single parenthood, and are the objects of misogyny and harassment. Yet women also are far less likely to have been incarcerated, are better educated and more likely to be independent, and are in better health. It isn't a competition for who's better off—or worse off.

CHAPTER 10

Civitas Sundered

We must delight in each other, make others' conditions our own, rejoice together, mourn together, labor and suffer together, always having before our eyes our community as members of the same body.
—*John Winthrop*, "City on a Hill," 1630

Americans of all ages, all conditions, all minds constantly form associations. Not only do they have commercial and industrial associations in which all take part, but they also have a thousand other kinds: religious, moral, grave, futile, very general and very particular, immense and very small; Americans make associations to give entertainments, to found seminaries, to build inns, to raise churches, to distribute books, to send missionaries to the antipodes; in this manner they create hospitals, prisons, schools.
—*Alexis de Tocqueville*, Democracy in America

It almost feels obligatory to begin a discussion of civic life in the United States by citing both John Winthrop's "City on a Hill" and Alexis de Tocqueville's 1835 masterpiece, *Democracy in America*.[1] What the great French writer captured about the genius of American democracy—notably the widespread engagement in associations dedicated to causes, which brought citizens together—remained one of the country's great strengths throughout much of its history.

The decline of civic engagement, distrust of institutions, the deterioration of formal and informal associations, mistrust of each other, and the loss of unifying core beliefs has been a long-running theme in American scholarship and public discourse, at least since David Riesman's *The Lonely Crowd* (1950).

In fact, some of the most influential nonfiction books of the last sixty-five years have played variants on this theme—notably, Christopher Lasch's *The Culture of Narcissism* (1979), Robert Bellah's *Habits of the Heart* (1985), and Robert D. Putnam's *Bowling Alone* (2000). Foundations, think tanks, scholars, and political leaders have devoted considerable effort to dissecting and trying to solve this set of issues. Lasch was invited to meet President Carter, and President Obama followed suit by hosting Putnam. The media and pollsters have probed these subjects at length.[2]

Few would argue with this narrative of the decline of Tocquevillean Man: Americans are much less likely to join civic, service, labor, and other types of groups aimed at improving the collective well-being. The armed forces find it hard to recruit sufficient numbers of people to serve their nation. Americans, who once generally saw their elected leaders and public institutions as beneficent and a symbolic embodiment of the country's democracy, are distrustful of, and angry toward, government. Mistrust and anger are the dominant feeling toward other institutions, such as big business and the media, as well as toward fellow Americans. Attendance at and involvement with religious congregations have cratered in large parts of the nation. National heroes are in short supply.

Ever since the Watergate scandal, every president has run against government. In the same year that Jimmy Carter was elected as the first of these presidents, during the nation's bicentennial, actor Peter Finch spoke for many Americans in the movie *Network* (1976) when he said, "I'm as mad as hell, and I'm not going to take it anymore!" During the 2016 campaign, Donald Trump was right when he said, "One of the key problems today is that politics is such a disgrace."[3]

However, the broad gender differences in the decline of de Tocqueville's America have received little attention, other than pollsters pointing to the gender gap in voting and pundits discovering the "angry white man." In fact, *civitas*—the idea of common purpose, responsibility, and community-mindedness—has sundered notably more among men than among women. Another early American concept, *humanitas*—connoting active participation in society and political life—also seems nearly as scarce among men as the waistcoats worn by Thomas Jefferson, one of the idea's great proponents.

Men in general are less likely to volunteer, participate in groups, engage in service, and vote and more likely to be mistrustful, angry, and self-isolating than women. Although many women act and think in similar ways, if anything, the great Tocquevillean American Man has been supplanted by the small but significant rise of the Tocquevillean Woman. To recast Putnam, it is men who bowl alone, while women read in book clubs and take Zumba classes together. Men as well as women work out at the gym, and some still read newspapers, but they do so alone. By contrast, women join and form groups, organize social movements, and take classes. As a health club spokesman said, "Women tend to like to work out together and feel like they are part of a community, while men . . . are more apt to go in, do their thing, and leave, often not engaging with others."[4]

If de Tocqueville's characterization of a thriving democracy (at the time, for white men) is not enough, let's turn to the father of our country. "Civic virtue"—what "binds the dutiful citizen to his country," as George Washington said in his farewell address—has withered. More and more men, once the standard-bearers of this responsibility (when women were excluded from public life), have abandoned this "duty." This too is a retreat for the gender that, until recent decades, was assigned sole custody of this virtue and duty.

This retreat is another part of the man out puzzle, fitting in with—not isolated from—the other manifestations of the sidelining of a sizable minority of American men. The behavioral, psychological, and ideational continuities are significant. This chapter examines men's declining membership and participation in service organizations, the military, and other forms of national service, their underrepresentation among volunteers, and—in comparison with women—their diminished religiosity and trust, and their antigovernment sentiments.

THE DECLINE OF FRATERNAL ORGANIZATIONS

The French enshrine *fraternité* as a core national value, but American men were once the joiners. They formed groups and met regularly to advance the needs of their community or a larger cause, to forge and sustain friendships, to support one another, and to do what we now call, with an impersonal utilitarianism, "networking."

Although Masonic lodges date to pre-Revolutionary America, in the decades just before and after the turn of the twentieth century, as a modern middle class was emerging, businessmen and other civic-spirited men created a host of all-male, nationwide service and fraternal organizations. They included the Knights of Columbus (1882), the Loyal Order of the Moose (1888), Rotary (1905), the Optimists (1911), the Kiwanis (1915), the Lions (1917), and the Jaycees (or Junior Chamber of Commerce, 1920). The Shriners and Elks were formed somewhat earlier, in the 1870s. So, too, were labor unions, with the Knights of Labor founded during Reconstruction and the more radical Industrial Workers of the World (or "Wobblies") established in 1905. Veterans organizations flourished after the establishment of the American Legion in 1919. College fraternity houses started to emerge in the 1890s (and sororities for the few female students of the time) as a way to bring young men together for sociability and to help each other in their academic and professional pursuits.

The funny names and rituals of these fraternal organizations, as well as their national conventions featuring dancing girls and Miss Americas, brought some mockery to these alleged Babbitts of the "booboisie" by Sinclair Lewis and H. L. Mencken in the 1920s and attacks from the National Organization for Women in the 1970s. Nonetheless, these service organizations thrived, enabling "professionals with diverse backgrounds [to] exchange ideas, form meaningful, lifelong friendships, and give back to their communities." Likewise, despite their post–*Animal House* (1978) image, fraternities professed their commitment to noble goals, such as "Friendship, Knowledge, Service, Morality, Excellence," in the case of Phi Gamma Delta.[5]

Meetings brought men together at "lodges" in small towns and big cities alike to eat, drink, talk, play bridge, take their wives out dancing, and plan charitable endeavors. In addition to projects to help their immediate communities, Rotary International has donated billions of dollars and sent members to provide medical care and literacy classes in poor countries and funded scholarships. The Lions have focused on vision care, the Elks have supported disabled children, and Kiwanis has funded various children's causes. "Service Above Self" has been Rotary's motto, "We Serve," for the Lions, and "Serving the Children of the World," for Kiwanis. The groups also helped knit communities together, sponsoring regular small-town fish fries and other events.

The YMCA arguably also had its heyday in the first decades of the twentieth century, as it became another men's organization. Unlike the largely middle-class service clubs, it geared its programs heavily toward working-class immigrants and rural migrants to big cities. With programs to promote character and provide vocational training, its numerous clubs both created fellowship and brought practical benefits to men. Today largely seen as a health club, its members generally come for a swim or a workout and take off.[6]

Taking a page from George Washington and de Tocqueville, the Rotarians' manual says the duty of members is "to be active as individuals in as many legally constituted groups and organizations as possible to promote, not only in words but through exemplary dedication, awareness of the dignity of all people and the respect of the consequent human rights of the individual."[7]

Unions, established to protect and advocate for working men, grew rapidly from the mid-1930s to the mid-1950s. More than one-third of America's wage and salary workers were members of unions in 1954, and about four-fifths of those members were men. Just as most towns and cities had Elks lodges and Rotary clubs, they also had union halls where men would gather. Unions not only had considerable bargaining power to improve workers' pay, benefits, and working conditions, they also provided a sense of collective identity to millions of working men.

During their heyday after World War II, all of these organizations brought millions of American men together. These men were the proverbial pillars of their communities, and the organizations counted almost every president from Woodrow Wilson to John F. Kennedy as members. Rotary proudly has boasted that it was invited to help draft the United Nations Charter and that President Eisenhower reputedly called the organization the greatest force for peace after the United Nations. Similarly, fraternities claim that 85 percent of Fortune 500 executives, 76 percent of U.S. senators, and a number of presidents since 1910 have been members.[8]

Then something changed during the 1970s and early 1980s, just as median wages began to stagnate for male workers, women entered the workforce in droves, divorce rates shot up, Tom Wolfe hailed the "Me Decade," attacks on unions increased during the Reagan administration, and the aftershocks of the cultural revolution of the 1960s and 1970s were spreading throughout society. Membership—at least among American men—started to plummet. The number of Elks fell by 50 percent between 1980 and 2012, from 1.6 million to 800,000. At its peak the downtown Kansas City Kiwanis chapter counted two hundred men as members; by 2016 there were fewer than twenty-five. An Elks lodge in Pendleton, Oregon, that had been in existence for 115 years shut down in 2017. The venerable Masons, which included so many of America's founders as members, saw membership collapse from four million in the mid-1960s to 1.1 million in 2016.[9]

As male membership has continued to fall, with few younger members, these service clubs have survived largely because of two changes—the court-ordered requirement that they admit women and the dramatic expansion of such organizations into scores of other countries. For example, only one-fourth of Rotary International's 1.2 million members in the mid-2010s were Americans, and women accounted for nearly 30 percent of their dwindling

U.S. membership. Between 2004 and 2014, the number of American male Rotarians declined by nearly one-fourth, to 240,000—fewer than in 1998. And the Shriners, which remains an all-male organization, in 2015 had one-fourth the membership it had in 1978.[10]

Frank, a middle-age white man, has been a longtime member of the Rotary Club, and before that the Jaycees, in the South Carolina town where he has lived. "We had an extremely vibrant club of young men," he recalled. "We had good fellowship, and the ladies had a separate club." In his district, including eighty-three clubs in the eastern part of the state, membership went down from 4,400 to 3,300 in just the five years before the end of 2016. He attributed much of the decline to "economic factors": the disappearance of textile factories, the decline of the tobacco industry, the North American Free Trade Agreement, underemployment, and the particularly difficult financial straits of the area's young adults.

Frank expressed mixed feeling about court rulings in the 1980s that forced these and other all-male clubs to admit women. On the one hand, he said, "I don't know what Rotary would do without women. They do more work than the guys do." On the other, he felt that "it changed the dynamics" at Jaycee meetings. "Guys act differently when their wives and other women are around."

In 2016 the percentage of union members who were men was less than one-third of what it was in 1954. Blame a changing economy, the business/Republican-led assault on organized labor, and an image problem stemming from perceptions of widespread corruption. Or blame broader trends in the withering of Tocquevillean America.[11]

Veterans of the wars in Iraq and Afghanistan have been less likely than older male vets to join the American Legion or Veterans of Foreign Wars. As both organizations have seen a falloff in membership and median ages approach 70, only about 15 percent of recent eligible vets had joined the VFW by 2014.[12]

Fraternities have continued to attract countless young men, but the raison d'être for many of them seems to have changed from knowledge, virtue, and humanitas to binge drinking, sexual assault, dangerous hazing rites, and a dark, quasi-criminality far beyond what John Belushi lampooned in *Animal House*. Counterculture descendants, political progressives, and most men with the genuine values that frats long ago proclaimed have abandoned Greek life in droves. However, one former fraternity member argues that frats still help combat loneliness and are less hostile to women.[13]

This flight from men's organizations extends to children and youth. Membership in the Boy Scouts, founded in 1910 with the same sort of idealistic motto as the fraternal organizations and fraternities—"leaving the world a better place"—fell from 6.2 million in 1968 to 2.4 million in 2014. The Mormon Church pulled its youth out of some programs, and Boy Scouts of America announced in late 2017 that girls could become Cub Scouts. Are there not enough males to keep these groups going? As is true of all of these male organizations, the sharp declines have occurred as the U.S. population has grown by nearly 50 percent since the 1970s.[14]

WHERE HAVE YOU GONE, GI JOE?

Just as fewer men join organizations for fellowship and to serve their communities, fewer men have been serving their country in recent decades. Some of the decline in military service can be attributed to disillusion with wars from Vietnam to Iraq, some to the end of the Cold War, and some to cuts in force levels.

Flag-waving crowds roar louder than ever when veterans are honored, polls show that the military is America's most respected institution, and pilots give a shout-out to active-duty servicemen (and women), eliciting passengers' applause. "Everyone appreciates soldiers, and America will thank someone in uniform for their service," said Andrea Zucker. "They love the military, but don't want to be in the military." Unlike in the mid- to late twentieth century, few Americans actually know someone on active duty; those in service to the nation are someone else, seen on TV, not in most people's dining rooms.[15]

Recruiters talk about the "disinterest," "not wanting to give back," and being "less propensed" to sign up. There's little sense of honor, integrity, duty, or pride; instead there's a lack of commitment and more of a sense of personal entitlement than a desire to work with others in service to the country, they say. They also ruefully say that most young men don't pass muster physically or psychologically to serve in the armed forces, although some are cautiously optimistic about the postmillennial generation.[16]

"There's a lack of a sense of community and a sense of it being 'our team,'" said Command Sergeant Major Gragg. Another recruiter spoke of the diminished "sense of ownership of the country" since World War II.[17]

Sergeant First Class Tifani Hightower, a center commander at the Army Recruiting Station in Brunswick, Georgia, echoed this observation: "Individuals don't really understand what it means to make a commitment to America . . . or anything."[18]

The armed forces include increasing numbers of women and are working to recruit more. While a victory over sexual discrimination, like the court decisions requiring service groups to admit women, which have kept Rotary and similar organizations alive, the army's ability to meet recruitment goals owes in part to the opening up of nearly all military occupations to women.[19]

PUBLIC SERVICE (DIS)CONTINUED

Men also are vanishing from other forms of national service. The Peace Corps, which drew heavily on idealistic young men after it was established in 1961, is now 62 percent female. Some staff privately say that men are more likely to join for adventure, whereas women are more drawn by development goals such as education, health, and the environment.[20]

AmeriCorps, which was created in 1993 as an expansion of the Kennedy-Johnson Volunteers in Service to America (VISTA) program and is part of the federal government's Corporation for National and Community Service (CNCS), includes an even smaller percentage of men among its 80,000 annual volunteers and approximately one million alumni. More than two out of three of the program's young adult alumni are women, and several studies indicate that more than 70 percent of twenty-first-century volunteers are female.[21]

DECLINING VOLUNTEERISM

Men are also underrepresented among volunteers for nonprofits, charities, churches, and other organizations, and their numbers have been trending downward. The annual CNCS survey of volunteering found that 21.8 percent of men volunteered in 2015, compared to 27.8 percent of women and 28.8 percent of men a decade earlier. The numbers for men include members of Rotary, Kiwanis, and other service groups. Among full-time workers there is the same gender gap, and volunteerism is lower for men who are not in the labor force and are unemployed than for those who are employed. One study found that part-time work boosts female volunteering but has no effect on men.[22]

Men accounted for only about 10 percent of the 5.5 million members of the national Parent Teacher Association in the early twenty-first century, although male participation has been inching up (even as overall membership has been declining). Young men are similarly underrepresented in newer national service organizations like Teach for America. In college, young women are not only more likely than men to volunteer but are also more likely to take courses that include community service.[23]

Women tend to be more responsive to solicitations to volunteer. YCorp, which tries to get young professionals to volunteer, reported that women accounted for 95 percent of the responses they got from a recruitment letter sent to equal numbers of men and women. When young people go out on city sidewalks trying to interest passersby in mentoring, women are more likely to stop and talk, while men are more likely to walk away, according to Tom Pollak, founder of the DC Tutoring and Mentoring Initiative.[24]

Is the lower propensity of men to volunteer yet one more example of at least a segment of the male population's flight from civic life? The fact that more working women volunteer than working men, who volunteer more than nonworking men, seems to suggest this. One nonprofit leader attributes this to irresponsible young "man-boys," but this fails to explain the difference at all ages. Another argues that women like to meet and socialize with like-minded women, whereas men don't see volunteering as an opportunity to connect with other men.[25]

THE MALE EMPTY-PEW SYNDROME

Go into a church or synagogue in much of America and you will see more women's faces than men's. To some extent this has been true for generations. Intriguingly, the reason may swing back to issues of masculinity. In an interesting piece by the Christian Broadcasting Network, "Why Men Hate Church," author David Murrow said, "The church has gained a reputation as a ladies' club in the minds of men. [Men don't] attend church for the same reason [they] don't wear pink." He added, "We live in a society with a female religion and a male religion: Christianity of various sorts for women and non-masculine men, and masculinity . . . for men."[26]

Although a religious man himself, Frank made a comment when discussing the admission of women to the Jaycees that bears out this idea. He described the feminization of the group as changing it "from being a guys club to being more like a Sunday school class."

The decline in church attendance and trust in organized religion has been going on for years as churches close, congregations consolidate, and pews get emptier. However, the gender gap is significant: 32 percent of men, compared to 40 percent of women, regularly attend services, and 47 percent of men say they pray every day, compared to 64 percent of women. Atheism, which has been on the rise in the twenty-first century, is more than twice as common among men than women. Whereas atheists tend to be college-educated and evangelism appears to draw conservative middle-class whites, church attendance has fallen most notably among less educated white men.[27]

COMMUNITY LITE

The decline of Tocquevillean Man is also exemplified by the much-bemoaned "decline of community life" and interpersonal trust. The mental pictograph for this idea often begins by conjuring up somewhat romanticized Norman Rockwell images of families gathered on the village green, kids playing on the street, and neighbors borrowing a cup of sugar. This did exist, but has community life "declined" or simply changed?

A similar working-class mystique surrounded the taverns and bars where men would head after the factory whistle blew. Small towns in the industrial Midwest like Horicon, often anchored by one giant plant, had main streets lined with these watering holes where men could find camaraderie and a couple of cold brews.

Today some neighborhoods have block parties, but they are often perfunctory affairs where no one really wants to eat the hot dogs or drink the cheap beer. They aren't the Friday night fish fries, the Rotary dances, or the bandstand concerts of yore. Although intense, overly organized sports leagues and competitions crowd the lives of upper-middle-class children and their parents, this lifestyle often feels more like drive-by fellowship than the easy, years-long associations based on scouting, Little League, or the playground. Just as contingent work has grown, so have such shallower contingent friendships.

The community associations where men were once "pillars" now look like the ruins of the Acropolis. As Horicon's mayor told me, no one shows up for town meetings that once drew men who believed it was part of their civic duty to participate.

Many older Americans spoke wistfully of the loss of community interaction and neighborliness. Small towns where everyone knew one another have become more anonymous. "There are no meeting places, no picnics like you used to have, and no bars where everyone knows your name," said Paul Pilconis, the Vietnam vet from Frackville. Suburban streets where kids played and mothers (and some fathers) talked have become ghostly as Google Calendar play dates take their place. Even some millennials, like Trevor from Missouri, spoke of how the smart phone generation seems unable to "foster the sense of community" of earlier generations.

Although women, too, especially those who are older, talk of the disappearance of this idyllic past, men appear to feel the greatest loss and insecurity. Trust in other people has fallen since 1972 among white people, men in particular.[28] Women still find ways to come together and form groups; for men, nothing has really taken the place of the Kiwanis, the union hall, the armed services, and community associations.

MALE ANGER, DISTRUST OF GOVERNMENT, AND THE HARD RIGHT

During and after the 2016 election campaign, there was endless talk about the emergence of "angry white men" as the swing voting bloc that enabled Donald Trump to win the presidency. As often happens with herd journalism, it was hard to find a media outlet that had not suddenly discovered these men. Even though polling indicated that well-to-do white college graduates gave 48–49 percent of their votes to Trump and that angry, good-ol'-boy white males accounted for only about one-fifth of the Trump vote, the "angry white men" theme was beaten to death, spun variously as "the triumph of" or "the last stand of."[29]

White working-class men in and out of the labor force are hardly the only Americans who have been angry at government or disgusted and disengaged from the political process. Black and immigrant men often feel that the power of the state is arrayed against them. Formerly incarcerated men are completely disconnected from the political process, a problem made worse by the disenfranchisement of more than six million former prisoners. Polling in the 2010s has shown that only about one in five Americans trust the federal government almost all or most of the time, compared to 77 percent when Lyndon Johnson was elected in 1964. At least since Ronald Reagan's proclamation that "government is the problem, not the solution," politicians and the public have expressed their wrath toward government as if it were a wartime enemy. More Americans had a favorable view of Vladimir Putin's Russia than of their own government before the 2016 election.[30]

Patriotism has become strangely divorced from allegiance to the government that represents the United States. Instead, many predominantly male Americans' allegiances are to "the flag," poorly understood and cherry-picked passages from the Constitution, and some amorphous notion of the United States as "Number 1." For reasons that lurk in the dark, racist corners of the

American psyche, military figures like Stonewall Jackson or Robert E. Lee seem more popular than true heroes like Eisenhower or George C. Marshall, not to mention the nothing-if-not-manly generals George S. Patton and Douglas MacArthur.

Twenty-first-century U.S. government certainly has many problems, but attacks on government have become a convenient distraction from many other fundamental problems, including ones that particularly beset marginal men. The internet—social media such as Facebook and Twitter in particular—has been a prime culprit in spreading conspiracy theories and "fake news" about the evils of government and politicians. It has also enabled faux engagement—expressing outrage and joining online crusades—that bespeak minimal commitment and involve little or no face-to-face solidarity or working together.[31]

Despite these society-wide shifts, a higher proportion of men than women distrusts and holds negative views of government. Men are half again as likely as women to see the feds as a "threat" to their privacy. White men account for about four out of five supporters of white supremacist and white nationalist hate groups, as well as of the "alt-right." Most American terrorists are white male loners. They are typically white male millennials who also hold misogynistic and homophobic views, according to George Hawley, author of *Making Sense of the Alt-Right*, although there are older, lone white guys too, like the perpetrator of the October 2017 Las Vegas massacre or the shooter at a Republican congressional baseball game in Virginia in June 2017. Simi Futtrell, a University of Maryland expert on domestic terrorism, found that those drawn to the radical right tend to have had "some kind of family disruption, whether that be divorce or parental abandonment, a parent being incarcerated, or substance abuse by one or both parents."[32]

The hard right turn among white men that has been noted in the Trump era had been building for some time. Figures like Pat Buchanan in 1992, Jesse Ventura in 1998, and Arnold Schwarzenegger in 2002 all built their bases around angry white guys, projecting a hypermasculinity that appealed especially to disaffected men. They are men who have felt ignored as the liberal lens has been focused on African Americans and other people of color, women, the LGBTQ community, and immigrants. Although undercurrents of antipathy toward government go back to Barry Goldwater and beyond, what is new in recent years is the implicit, and often explicit, link with masculinity. The men who rail against government today generally are not the von Hayek conservatives or Ayn Rand libertarians but rather those who have felt their masculinity threatened by their dwindling ability to be providers and the concurrent rise of feminism and women in the workplace and higher education. Government, in their view, is run by elites who ignore or look down on them and coddle immigrants, African Americans, Latinos, and women.

In many ways they are right that government, as well as business, has failed them. But what if the racist, misogynistic, nativist, and anti-elitist story that a lot of these men (and women) have learned is a smoke screen? The failure of government may be much less about it favoring the poor, people of color, women, and wealthy elites than about government and business having broken the promises of the post–World War II era. The structures by which government and business, working with organized labor, could guarantee white working men a fairly stable life and opportunity, and that started to provide opportunity for African Americans, have been largely dismantled, like an old movie set, beginning during the last two decades of the twentieth century. The biggest failures of government are rarely seen and feebly expressed by most Democrats unwilling to undertake a more systemic critique. Despite Reagan's humorous but disparaging remark about "I'm from the government and I'm here to help," the U.S. government has failed working men and women mostly by following the Reagan policy playbook. It has reduced protective regulations, shifted the risks for retirement (and other economic) security from business to individuals and families, scrimped on the safety net, failed to keep higher education affordable, emasculated unions, failed to provide child care and family leave to reduce family stress and enable both women and men to work, and passed trade deals that have left dislocated workers without retraining or support.

At the risk of diving too deeply into the psychoanalytic pool, the anger, hard-right beliefs, and attraction to strong, macho men may be a way of compensating for economic, political, and real and metaphorical impotence.

As many of these men turn right, it is superficially perplexing why "the party of individual responsibility, pulling yourself up by your bootstraps captures this crowd of white males who aren't terribly responsible in their private lives, fathering kids out of wedlock, while getting food stamps and disability," said Peter Fenn, a longtime Democratic Party strategist. "There's an attitudinal change that you blame your employer, blame the city, and blame the federal government for your situation."[33]

Men have been less likely to vote than women since 1980, and those who vote have increasingly leaned to the right. In the 2012 elections, men cast nearly ten million fewer ballots than women and single women have been more likely to vote than single men. Ten million fewer men than women were registered to vote in 2016, and the turnout gap in 2016 Democratic primaries was 16 percentage points. (However, the gender gap among African Americans was three times what it was among whites, in part a function of denying the vote to many black ex-offenders.) The overall gender voting gap between Trump and Hillary Clinton expanded to an unprecedented 24 percentage points. Disaggregating by race, Trump won the white male vote by 32 percentage points and outpolled 2012 Republican nominee Mitt Romney by 5 percentage points.[34]

Women also have become more likely to be activists, on both the right and left, playing leading roles in not only the #MeToo and Time's Up movements against sexual assault and harassment but also in the Tea Party, Occupy, and Black Lives Matter movements. Three-fifths of Obama's 2012 volunteers were women, and in the wake of the unfortunately named "Women's March" on January 21, 2017, and its 2018 successor, Democratic Party women were about 50 percent more likely than Democratic men to say they would be politically active.[35]

Even the men's rights groups who argue that there is skewed societal attention to women's problems acknowledge that women seem better at organizing. Getting men to join a "men's" group is like "herding chickens," said Harry Crouch, president of the National Coalition for Men.[36]

DISENGAGEMENT AND ISOLATION

For all the talk in recent years about declining civic engagement and "social capital," the multifaceted gender and class nature of the demise of what Washington called "civic duty" and Jefferson spoke of as "humanitas" has received little attention. Taking a cue from intersectionality, it is clear that women—especially millennial women—are leaving men in the dust when it comes to community group and church involvement, volunteerism, and political participation.

The demographics of male civic disengagement track other characteristics of men out. They are less likely to work. They feel their masculinity is threatened, in part by being sidelined from the "provider" role and the historical assumption that men are the leaders. They appear to be products and examples of family disintegration. They are especially prominent among millennial men, black men, and middle-age nonworking white men. Lack of group participation and free-floating anger go hand in hand with increasing interpersonal isolation and loneliness. Many men are isolated, and it is men who are having the most difficulty connecting with other men through either organized or informal groups.

While many good men are still active and engaged in public life and have group bonds with other men, the ranks of men on the sidelines in the civic sphere have been rising. This has taken its toll on communities, politics, our culture's values and norms, and men's psychological and social well-being.

CHAPTER 11

A Road to Recovery, or Men In?

With the gradual relaxation of discipline, morals first subsided, as it were, then sank lower and lower, and finally began the downward plunge which has brought us to our present time, when we can endure neither our vices nor their cure.

—Livy, c. 27 BC

Men are really going to have to change their act or have big problems.

—Harvard economist Richard Freeman

What can the United States do to bring several tens of millions of struggling, hurting, lost, angry, disengaged men from the sidelines to lead productive, fulfilling, happy lives? What can it do to prevent more men and boys growing into manhood from falling into the many-forked canyon of men out?

What happens if it doesn't try, can't succeed, or doesn't really understand the multifaceted nature of the problem? What if, as Livy suggested, the "cures" are too controversial or radical or rub too many people the wrong way so that we can't "endure . . . their cure"?

The first step is to recognize the issue of men out as a complex problem. This can't be swept under the rug or, more likely, pieces of it swept under different rugs. As Betty Friedan did, we need to bring this "problem that has no name" out of the shadows and into public discourse.[1]

The constellation of problems of men out can't be solved by focusing on just one or a few of the following issues: work and economics, masculinity, marriage, fatherhood, male-female relations, morality, civic life and politics, technology, criminal justice, health, mental health, or isolation. It can't be best addressed by restricting one's view to 2010s America; there are lessons to be learned from other countries and our own past. Nor can it be confronted only through a host of policy interventions or myriad cultural changes, although both are sorely needed.

Those with ideological axes to grind need to get beyond cocooning themselves with those who share their strong, and comfortable, predispositions. Many need to recognize that this is not overwhelmingly about economics, abetted by bad policies. Others need to accept that the increased number of men out is not primarily a moral or character problem, also abetted by what they view as bad policies. Feminists, and many women, need to see that there are also significant problems facing men worth discussing, even though women, on average, still have it worse than men, which has been true historically and remains so in the present. (Similarly, people in Zimbabwe, Bangladesh, and Haiti have it worse than most poor Americans; is that a reason not to care about the poor in America?) Some men's rights and pro-father types too easily slip into misogynistic venom. Some political demagogues are happy to exploit the anger of many of these men, but actually doing something about the underlying problems would destroy their reason for being. Progressive men's and gender-equity groups, who rightly denounce "toxic masculinity," sometimes seem loath to talk about or engage with those who emphasize the importance of marriage and family and, perhaps, some of the better aspects of traditional masculinity.

There are many earnest people calling for an end to, or a tempering of, hyperpartisanship, but, really, as the Beatles, Barack Obama, and James Madison said in different ways, we need to come together.

A multidisciplinary White House conference on men and boys (as others have suggested), a national commission, a series of town halls, more research, more media attention, and popular campaigns like Britain's Propamanda are good ways to begin, despite the often-deserved cynicism about hardworking, blue-ribbon commissions whose reports essentially end up in the circular file.

POLICY INTERVENTIONS

It's hard to know whether changing or adopting new policies or changing cultural values and norms is more difficult, although I'm inclined to think the latter—even as policymaking at the federal level has largely ground to a halt.

Nonetheless, many policies could make a difference for sidelined men. Ideally they should be bundled as much as possible. Despite the bad rap that it has gotten, Lyndon Johnson's Great Society used a bundling technique by proposing and enacting a wide range of antipoverty policies. There are also good arguments for testing different policies in states, the proverbial "laboratories of democracy," in the words of former Supreme Court justice Louis Brandeis.

Potential policy interventions largely fall into a handful of buckets, relating to the economy, work, and the safety net; families and fatherhood; reducing hate speech and sexual violence; public health; national service; and more controversial efforts that intrude on the realm of "culture," to teach character, civics, and a nontoxic masculinity.

Getting more men to work and have decent incomes to support themselves—and their children and families, if they have them—is a pretty uncontroversial idea supported by the left, right, and center. How to do so is where the disagreements emerge.

Increasing training and retraining, vocational education, and workforce development—all more or less synonymous—is one approach that enjoys bipartisan support, as well as backing by both business and workers. As noted, the United States spends about one-fifth as much per capita on training as other rich countries, such as Germany. The United States has had government-supported vocational-education programs since the Wilson administration, and private efforts like those of the YMCA date back even further, yet vocational education started to be looked down on during the last third of the twentieth century as socially prevailing norms all but dictated that going to college was the ticket to success. A college degree not only was prestigious but also became the necessary credential just to be considered for many a job. Based on very real data, the mantra of "the more you learn, the more you earn" was accepted by ever more parents and their children. Recognizing the continuing inequities in access to higher education, the idea of making at least two years of college universal was mooted by President Obama and others.[2]

As demand increased and government support, particularly for state universities, declined, colleges hiked up tuition. But this is where good old supply-and-demand curves went haywire as college costs soared beyond the median income, student debt grew to be more than the GDP of all but ten countries, and access to higher education by the 2010s became less equal than it was in the 1970s.

These trends, together with a growing mismatch between skills and available jobs, have led to a major rethink of whether a bachelor's degree should be the goal for all Americans. As we've seen, many college-educated young people are in jobs that hardly require undergraduate training in molecular biology, medieval history, or electrical engineering. And it's painfully easy to see that many youth are wasting their parents', the government's, or their own money going to college while some poorer, worthy students can't afford to get an education.

Community colleges, often partnering with business and with articulation agreements with high schools and four-year colleges, have stepped into the breach. States like Mississippi have a Workforce Enhancement Training Fund to help community colleges work with businesses to design curricula to teach basic and advanced career skills, some leading to industry-recognized credentials. The federal Trade Adjustment Assistance Community College and Career Training (TAACCCT) grant program has assisted more than seven hundred community colleges in developing industry-aligned curricula leading to stackable credentials. Federal funding is especially needed for community colleges in poorer, high-need areas, support that would be analogous to Title I funding for poorer K–12 schools.[3]

Career academies, "schools within schools" that provide skills training in about eight thousand high schools, are worth expanding. Teaching skills from hanging drywall to TV production, they have been shown to improve the job prospects, earnings, and even marriage rates for young men.[4]

Apprenticeships, which provide on-the-job training, a credential, and a path to full-time jobs, are available in scores of occupations—from able seaman to youth development practitioner—although fewer than 150,000 participated in 2012. This is one-eighteenth the number per capita in England, one-tenth the per capita number in France, and a fraction of the number that America usefully could have.[5]

The Job Corps, created under LBJ, has shown only mixed results. It provides free residential training in about one hundred career-technical occupations to about sixty thousand disadvantaged 16- to 24-year-olds each year.[6]

Training should not only be for in-demand occupations but should also include "soft skills" such as communication, teamwork, problem solving, creativity, and flexibility. Given that women are seen to be better at these "people skills," such training is especially important for many men. "Training" also should blur the lines between academic and vocational learning sufficiently so that we have well-rounded citizens.

However, for all the lip service paid to such training initiatives, the federal government has spent only about $90 million a year on apprenticeships, about $200 million a year on TAACCCT grants, and about $100 million for career academies, and funding for work-based training has fallen since the expiration of the Clinton-era School-to-Work Opportunities Act. These add up to an infinitesimally small fraction of the federal budget. President Trump's 2018 budget proposal called for 40 percent cuts in all federal job training programs, while French president Emmanuel Macron has called for 15 billion euros in new spending on training in a country with one-fifth the population of the United States.[7]

In addition to putting money where so many mouths are when it comes to training, youth development programs could be expanded for the millions of young people who are in neither school nor work. An Interagency Working Group on Youth Programs evaluates "positive youth development" programs in schools, but once again there is little public investment. Nonprofits like YouthBuild, which also receive support from the U.S. Department of Labor (DOL), need to be expanded to serve the large "not in education, employment or training" population.[8]

Training programs also need to be buttressed by strong job counseling and job placement services. The DOL's America's Job Network works with localities to operate 2,500 centers throughout the nation to help the unemployed, ex-offenders, older workers, veterans, the disabled, and others seeking work. While the centers do a yeoman's job, many who are not working—if they know about such centers at all—see them as grim government offices that they wouldn't be caught dead in. How do these men overcome problems of image, male pride, and lack of enthusiasm for work, especially in the absence of sufficient resources and strong partnerships with the private sector?

Public works programs like those created by FDR during the Great Depression could meet the needs both for jobs and for repairing and expanding the nation's infrastructure. Although this is seemingly a win-win proposition, most conservatives have been allergic to the idea of the government creating jobs and paying workers. Despite industry groups like the Business Roundtable calling for such investments, because of ideology or misplaced spending priorities, government infrastructure spending fell to its lowest percentage on record in early 2017.[9]

Since low wages and few employer-provided benefits make it hard for workers to keep their heads above water and may not make the jobs even worth it—given transportation and childcare costs and available public benefits—many on the left and the majority of Americans believe that raising the minimum wage would make work more attractive. More than two-fifths of working Americans—more women than men—are paid less than $15 an hour, and the federal minimum wage, at $7.25 an hour, is more than 25 percent lower than what it was in 1968, adjusting for inflation. It is also lower than in almost every other rich country. While many conservatives also can't stomach raising the wage floor, arguing that it eliminates jobs, most evidence from states and cities that have raised it suggests that a minimum wage of $12–$14 either has little effect on or actually increases employment. It should be raised and indexed to inflation.[10]

Wage insurance or subsidies are another way of increasing income and making work more attractive. For example, if a man lost a $70,000-a-year job and could only find one paying $35,000, which he might see as "below" him, the government could step in and provide a temporary subsidy to approach his former earnings. This would both salve male egos and get men back to work.[11]

Making it easier, rather than more difficult, for workers to join unions is another important way to raise wages, make work more appealing, and increase camaraderie. Unions were instrumental in winning good wages in the twentieth century, and unionized workers still are paid more and have better benefits, on average, than nonunionized workers. A Freelancers Union was created to try to represent gig economy workers,[12] and several men I spoke with established both a union and an advocacy group for the unemployed. Although organizing freelancers and the nonemployed may be like herding cats, both types of efforts are worth pursuing.

Providing all Americans with a universal basic income (UBI) or a guaranteed minimum income as a cushion against joblessness and poverty is increasingly discussed, as many fear that automation will eliminate millions of jobs. Technology leaders like Mark Zuckerberg, Bill Gates, and Elon Musk have been joined by the progressive Roosevelt Institute in calling for paying every American $1,000 a month. They argue that this would spur consumption-led economic growth, enable men and women to take the risks of starting a new business and looking for and changing jobs, and reduce inequality—while costing a fortune in new taxes. Most conservatives say that it could further deincentivize work, becoming the proverbial "hammock" for the lazy. However, Alaska's long-running payments to every state resident from oil-boom revenues have not harmed work rates. Bernie Sanders has supported the idea. So too has libertarian Charles Murray, although Murray wants to replace every social welfare program (including Social Security and Medicare) with a $13,000 annual payment for everyone to use as they see fit. Finland and Denmark are running small-scale experiments with guaranteed minimum incomes. President Nixon thought seriously about the idea, and thinkers going back to at least Thomas Paine have proposed it. It's politically unlikely to happen, its effects are unknown (although pilot programs could be tried), and it would be extremely costly.[13]

The earned income tax credit, which both enhances incomes for lower-wage workers and incentivizes work, is a policy that has long received bipartisan support. However, the EITC needs a number of fixes. Childless men, nonresident parents, and workers under 25 currently are largely ineligible for the tax credit; changing that could help many men. Similarly, many nonresident fathers, now ineligible for TANF benefits, should be eligible for these benefits if they spend significant time with their children. In addition, making EITC payments quarterly instead of annually would spread income throughout the year and reduce the temptation for the recipient to go on a spending spree when the yearly check arrives.[14]

Other tax credits, like the child tax credit (CTC), should be expanded and made refundable, like the EITC, actually putting money in people's pockets. If we want to support families, helping poorer parents to pay for their children's needs might make a small contribution to keeping families together. Without penalizing single mothers, perhaps an enhanced credit could be targeted to supporting greater father involvement.

Additional benefit reforms could also help struggling men and reduce some disincentives to working. Because SSDI limits the amount that a claimant can earn from work, there is little incentive to do much (at least on-the-books) work. Similarly, because one is either disabled or not, someone with a mild physical or psychological disability is treated the same as someone who is severely disabled. In the Netherlands, where disability claims had been so high that the problem was called the "Dutch disease," early twenty-first-century reforms have reduced disability cases by 60 percent since 2006 by making several changes: the burden was shifted from the state to the employer, leading employers to encourage workers with disabilities to get back to work, and distinctions were drawn between severely, permanently disabled workers and those who could at least work part-time. Those whose disabilities are not permanent or are less severe should be able to legally work and earn more. Even though nearly every American who goes on disability stays there—becoming a de facto welfare program for many—the Dutch, the British, and others have demonstrated the obvious: countless people get better and are able to work full-time again. And disability need not be an all-or-nothing condition with one-size-fits-all benefits. As a person's condition improves, benefits could be gradually scaled back. It could encourage people to not try to prove that they are disabled and instead get appropriate, affordable care, and incentivize them to work, thus saving taxpayer dollars.[15]

Unemployment insurance is less generous, covers fewer workers in the United States than comparable programs in other rich nations, and could be expanded. It is also mired in an old-economy mind-set. Much like disability, you're either unemployed or not. With the rise of the gig economy, independent contractors, irregular work hours, and more volatile incomes, UI should be extended to 1099 workers and be proratable for those who are underemployed. Employers of contract workers, like employers of full-time employees, should have to pay into the UI system and make other mandatory social payments, such as payroll taxes for Social Security and Medicare. America could follow the lead of French president Macron, who has advanced a legislative agenda that extends a measure of unemployment insurance to the self-employed and entrepreneurs.[16]

Conditional benefits—an idea that straddles policy and culture—have been championed by conservatives such as Lawrence Mead and liberals such as Olivia Golden, president of the Center for Law and Social Policy. Provide job training and cash assistance to struggling men if they can be responsible fathers, Isabel Sawhill at the Brookings Institution has suggested. Help men get jobs if they pay child support and see their kids.[17]

In Texas the state's child-support enforcement division teamed up with the state workforce commission, and later with federally supported responsible fatherhood programs to get nonworking noncustodial fathers to work, pay child support, and be more involved in their children's lives. "Each man had to have a participation contract—32 hours of employment activities, like TANF," a former Texas official said. In 2014, 4,100 mostly poor men with criminal records who were in arrears in child-support payments were ordered into the program: either participate or go to jail. After implementation, the program was evaluated. "They ran numbers multiple times and said they've never seen results this good," the ex-official said. "Seventy-five percent got jobs, and the average time from enrollment to employment was 7–8 weeks. Monthly child-support payments were $178, compared to $106 for those not in the program." The state spent about $7–$8 million per year, but child-support payments increased by $25 million, unemployment and food stamp claims went down, and the state also saved money by jailing fewer men. In addition, Texas issued orders that gave fathers more time with their children in conjunction with their child support orders, and included fathers in its Nurse-Family Partnership home visiting program, which had only mentored first-time mothers across the country during its thirty-year existence.[18]

"Everyone had the mind-set that these programs were for women," said Cynthia Osborne, director of the Center for Health and Social Policy at the LBJ School at the University of Texas. "We found that dads really valued these programs a lot. They were doing homework with their kids. They wanted their kids to be healthy and smart. When they heard their kids sing the numbers from one to ten, they thought their kids were smart." Mothers also stayed in the program seven months longer when the dads were involved, and relations between parents improved. Other states have started to copy the Texas program, and the federal government funded the National Child Support Noncustodial Parent Employment Demonstration Project in eight states, which concluded in September 2017.[19]

The criminal justice system cannot continue to chew up and discard so many men. Despite the horrible unemployment and recidivism rates, as well as the sad stories of so many formerly incarcerated men, "reentry" programs, with job training and placement, and wraparound services to address housing, health, and other critical issues, are too low a governmental priority.

Are there ways to go beyond "ban the box" to reduce discrimination against hiring men who have been imprisoned? Stronger laws that would enable those who feel they are the butt of discrimination to file complaints or lawsuits might deter some employers. An obvious fix going forward would be to simply stop imprisoning so many people in the first place. Aside from basic humanitarian reasons to not put people whose transgressions were minor in cages, crime rates have fallen significantly since the early 1990s, and prisons drain the public purse and crowd out funding for things like training and higher education. It is promising that the deincarceration movement has gained some bipartisan support and a number of states have been locking up fewer people in the 2010s. In addition, ex-offenders should not be disenfranchised for life. While this is a politically motivated problem, not giving people who have served their time the basic American right to vote only further alienates these men; rejection by the state, together with joblessness, breeds anger, which in turn breeds crime and other antisocial behavior.

America faces another culture-versus-policy conundrum with the uptick in older workers. Given the dearth of retirement savings, each year of additional work not only increases earnings and savings but also increases Social

Security benefits and investment earnings. It also helps keep the trillion-dollar-a-year Social Security program solvent a bit longer. Yet between the many 50-something men who aren't working, the reality of age discrimination against women and men, and many Americans spending one-third of their lives in retirement, what do we do? Social Security does provide the incentive for people to work longer, but whether by choice or out of need, most Americans claim benefits long before they max out. We not only need stronger "nudges"—as Richard Thaler, the winner of the 2017 Nobel Prize in economics, has demonstrated—we also need a labor market that is friendlier to "older" (over 55? over 60? over 45?) workers.[20]

Policy, for better and worse, is not just about economics.

Federal initiatives from the George W. Bush era, as well as a number of state initiatives, have sought to promote marriage. They have basically failed. One of the most promising, in Oklahoma, initiated by former Republican governor Frank Keating in 1999 and expanded with an influx of Bush-era funds, sought to reduce divorce rates by one-third. Despite money poured into "well-connected" government contractors, in the words of former Republican senator Tom Coburn, rates of divorce, single parenting, and cohabitation have increased.[21]

Family scholars differ on the value of such initiatives. Isabel Sawhill has said that we should focus on "responsible" parenting and give up on marriage promotion. Other leading scholars, such as Brad Wilcox and David Blankenhorn, believe it is in children's interest, America's interest, and men's and women's interests to keep up the good fight.

Although data show benefits of marriage, data are generally not a great way to get people to make probably the biggest emotional decision of a lifetime. Libertarians and liberals have a good point: Why should the state or some nonprofit with an agenda "teach" people to be married, especially when there's a whiff of sexism to promoting traditional marriage? Yet the Catholic Church at least has the right idea in providing marriage-preparation classes.

If marriage promotion or education makes one queasy, perhaps efforts to promote good parenting by couples, coparenting by yesterday's couples, and fatherhood by men are the best way to go. Premarital parenting instruction and mandated postdivorce coparenting classes are needed and could become much more thoughtful and intensive than the largely perfunctory affairs that they now are. The Children in Between program, based in Oregon, for example, tries to teach parents who don't live together how to respectfully communicate, share children, and not put their kids into loyalty conflicts, and Texas's Parent Education Responsibility workshops encourage both good parenting and workforce participation.[22]

"Responsible fatherhood" projects, like the one we visited in Baltimore, have been funded by the federal government since 2000, as well as by philan thropies such as the Annie E. Casey and the Ford Foundations. These have focused on counseling in parenting skills, peer support, coparenting, economic stability, and violence prevention, and they organize outings for fathers and their children. Most program leaders say that men want more efforts to connect missing fathers to their children, although they want activities that get them to their kids much more than classroom instruction or discussion sessions.[23] Curricula like Dads of Great Students, dad boot camps, and others that blend ways of being a good father with shedding toxic masculinity are helpful and have sprung up around the country. Yet teaching good fatherhood to men or parenting to couples is somewhere between teaching people to be kind and teaching them how to breathe. If baked into the culture, they should come naturally.

Sweden has had *pappas grupp*, or fathering groups, since the 1990s, to encourage men to be active parents from conception through childrearing. These discussion groups, facilitated by male psychologists, are a particularly successful model. However, they have been made possible by the country's pioneering parental leave policies. In 1974 Sweden became the world's first nation to replace maternity leave with parental leave. Couples get up to sixteen months of paid leave to be split between parents, with salary replacement between 80 and 90 percent; if fathers don't use at least 90 days, the couples lose them.[24]

The United States remains the only country among the thirty-five OECD nations that doesn't offer paid parental leave. Amounts of paid leave per newborn range from about half a year in France and Canada to a year in Germany. Japan—which is among thirty-one countries providing paternal leave—allows thirty weeks of paid leave for fathers alone.[25] Although 82 percent of Americans support paid maternity leave and 69 percent support paid paternity leave, along with advocates ranging from the center-right American Enterprise Institute to the liberal National Partnership for Women and Families, there has been little action at the federal level. A handful of states have enacted paid parental leave policies. Some, like California's, are funded solely by taxes on workers, whereas programs in New York and New Jersey are jointly funded by payroll taxes on employers and employees.[26] Paid family leave policies, which are known to benefit children and parents and ease the struggle for work-life balance, are long overdue in the United States.

Another policy reform that would help fathers and mothers and bring America in line with much of the rest of the world is subsidized or free pre-school and young child care. Despite government guidelines that child care should cost no more than 7 percent of a family's income, families in poverty spend 30–50 percent or more of their income—in many cases more than the cost of housing or public higher education. The annual cost of full-time care in Washington, D.C., was $22,000 in 2016, a bit under half the national median wage. The child and dependent care tax credit allows couples to claim up to $6,000 a year for two children, a pittance compared to cost. The Center for American Progress has proposed a tax credit of $14,000 a year per child for families with incomes up to 400 percent of the poverty level.[27]

Similarly, despite evidence that preschool is one of the best investments that a country can make in its citizens' long-term academic and emotional development and lifelong productivity, as well as providing a secure place for parents to have their 3- and 4-year-olds cared for, the United States ranks below about thirty other developed countries in early education. "I think we value our children less than other nations do," Arne Duncan, the former U.S. secretary of education, told the *Atlantic*. "I don't have an easier or softer or kinder way to say that." New York City and some states recently have instituted free, universal pre-K for children 3 and above, and many have introduced public preschool for 4-year-olds. In Oklahoma, three-fourths of 4-year-olds were in public preschools, but barely half of American 3- and 4-year-olds were in any preschool in 2015.[28]

By comparison, almost every other rich country has public universal early childhood education and care. France created its vaunted *écoles maternelles* in 1881, with antecedents founded in the eighteenth century in response to Jean-Jacques Rousseau's *Emile*. Virtually every French 3- to 5-year old is enrolled, as are many younger children. Free universal pre-K and child care would also not only help millions of working mothers trying to balance child care and work but would reduce the stress that many fathers feel because many employers still see it as more unseemly for men to take time off for child care. It might also prevent some young couples from splitting up. Although one cannot attribute causation, U.S. labor force participation rates were lower than in two dozen other rich countries with state-sponsored pre-K in 2016.[29]

Divorce law, as we have heard, is one of the things that most upsets many

fathers and other men and harms millions of children who have little or no contact with their fathers. Enact laws that go beyond vague joint-custody statutes
to establish the rebuttable presumption of joint physical custody, as a number
of states are considering. Adopt or go beyond the sort of child support reforms
that Texas has implemented that don't punish poor fathers. Require higher-
quality coparenting classes for couples who break up. Scrutinize assault allegations more carefully. Extend such family law reforms to unmarried parents.
All would considerably help children who need their fathers and the men who
miss their children and would reduce postbreakup animosity with ex-partners.
Some states have been making headway. Legislation in Utah increases noncustodial parents' time with their children from 80 to 145 days per year, bills have
been introduced in many states, and shared-parenting bills have passed the
Florida and Minnesota legislatures, only to have the Republican and Democratic governors, respectively, veto them. Opposition has come from plaintiff
lawyers for women and domestic violence-prevention advocates.[30]

Domestic violence is a serious problem, especially given some of the male
anger issues we have seen. However, rather than siloing the problem, a lot
could be gained by bringing together fatherhood and other masculinity initiatives with relationship and marriage programs. Colleges, divorce courts,
and society at large are caught between a rock and a hard place, as preventing
sexual and other physical assaults is critical, while it is also important to tease
out false allegations.

Although there are many other reasons for domestic violence, misogyny
is one that deserves a frontal attack. Much of what's needed is changing the
culture, which is hard to legislate. However, tougher policies on sexual ex-
ploitation and pornography, as well as assault and harassment—brought to
widespread public awareness by the #MeToo movement—are among the
things that government can enact and enforce. Given the greater recognition
of hate speech and its links to violence, the scourge of revenge porn, and of
broader issues like hacking and Russian meddling in U.S. elections, the still
Wild West of the internet is crying out for regulation and tougher enforcement. Even though Google and Facebook and some web-hosting services
have made greater efforts, in the wake of public and lawmakers' pressure, to
weed out vile content, either the Federal Communications Commission or
an internet-specific regulatory body should be given broader scope to deter
such activities on social media and websites, and law enforcement agencies
from the FBI to local police departments need the resources to go after the
individuals or groups engaging in this criminal online behavior.

Health is another arena where much can be done to help men and society at large. While there are federal Offices of Women's Health at the Centers for Disease Control and Prevention, the Food and Drug Administration, the National Institutes of Health, and the Health Resources and Services Administration, there is no Office of Men's Health. A congressional Men's Health Caucus was established in 2015 by Representative Donald Payne Jr. (D-N.J.) and Representative Markwayne Mullin (R-Okla.), but little has come of it during its first few years. Given men's lower average life expectancy, high substance abuse and addiction rates, widespread mental health and isolation problems that can lead to suicide and violence—a topic brought up with each new mass shooting incident—there is a crying need for at least one agency to increase and coordinate medical and psychological research, prevention, health maintenance, and treatment efforts. The correlations between poor health, nonwork, and disability-program use make this an economic issue as well as a public health issue. Once again, perhaps because men have become less likely to organize and advocate, the idea of focusing on men's health care has largely sat on the back burner.[31]

One of the most-needed drugs for men is a male birth control pill. Many men and women have called for it, as it would put more responsibility on men for contraception and would reduce the number of unintended pregnancies. Researchers around the world have explored hormonal and nonhormonal approaches to suppress sperm production, but one of the biggest impediments has been lack of funding for clinical trials. Another way to reduce the huge number of nonmarital pregnancies for couples who break up, with fathers going missing and children having every imaginable odd stacked against them, is to develop and promote long-acting reversible contraceptives (LARCs). Simply maintaining and strengthening publicly funded contraceptive services, which prevent more than two million pregnancies and seven hundred thousand abortions each year, is also essential, despite ideological opposition to government support.[32]

The other obvious health intervention is to limit the sale of prescription opioids. Thankfully, this has started to happen. The CDC and other medical groups have issued much more cautious guidelines on prescribing, pharmaceutical companies are being sued, and politicians in both major parties recognize that the opioid crisis must be addressed.[33]

Beyond these many worthwhile potential policies, there is a bigger-picture idea that Princeton economists Anne Case and Angus Deaton have hinted at. Although they point to declining incomes, jobs, and marriage, *The Economist* offered a radical but not so startling policy analysis of why white mortality in the United States has risen since 1999 while mortality has continued to decline by about 2 percent per year in Europe: America's "deaths of despair," including the rapidly growing number of men committing suicide and fatally overdosing on drugs and alcohol, may be a function of the nation's relatively poor safety net.

At least since Ronald Reagan, most Republicans and many Democrats have derided the European "welfare state" and its accompanying high taxes. If the only things certain in life are death and taxes, the United States seems to prefer death. Aside from the many other benefits of European welfare states—such as pre-K, family leave, and job training—they provide security through universal health care and strong income supports for anyone who has fallen on hard times. The United States does not provide such security.

"A more likely root cause for despair is the absence of a safety net for swathes of Americans, particularly in health care," *The Economist* asserts. "A lack of health insurance has obvious implications for mortality when illness strikes. But it causes the healthy anguish, too. . . . In other rich countries, people in dire straits need not worry about paying for health care. Broader social insurance is also lacking. The help available for workers who lose their jobs is paltry compared with their lifetime income losses." After also noting Americans' low saving rate, or personal safety net, the article says, "A perilous economic existence and a culture which almost indiscriminately holds people responsible for their circumstances are toxic for mental well-being."[34] American culture puts an especially heavy responsibility on men.

Radical policy changes that would make the United States look like Sweden, as well as many other reforms discussed above, do not appear to be in the offing, even if Bernie Sanders and some progressive Democrats support them. But policies such as these are needed. For a last time, we return to Moynihan: "The central conservative truth is that it is culture, not politics, that determines the success of a society. The central liberal truth is that politics can change a culture and save it from itself."[35]

CULTURAL CHANGE

So we arrive at culture.

Cultural change is at least as challenging as policy or economic change. How does one change many dimensions of a culture? You don't just run a massive public-awareness campaign (which some might call "propaganda") or even make dramatic, nationwide changes to school curricula.

There are no clear road maps, and the destination is much more difficult to define. The goals are hard to pin down, and the routes to them are generally not paved with policy interventions, although thoughtful "nudges" can help. Many would argue that culture changes organically or in reaction to significant social disruptions that are as different as the introduction of the automobile and the internet or World War I and mass prosperity. Unlike goals such as increasing the labor force participation rate by 5 or 10 percentage points, virtually ending opioid overdose deaths, or even eliminating roadblocks for millions of fathers to see their children, how does one even define what makes marriages successful, what male identities are sufficiently less harmful to women and men, what level of anger and distrust is tolerable, or what constitutes a good degree of engagement with other people?

There have been many big and smaller failures when it comes to intentional cultural change. Think of China's Cultural Revolution, Jacobin France, Prohibition, Nazi Germany, or George W. Bush's marriage-promotion initiatives.

Conversely, there have been some significant successes ranging from the acceptance of gay marriage and other rights to the reduction of teen pregnancy in the United States. The civil rights movement played a big part in reducing racism, but how much was a result of the legislation pushed by LBJ through the 89th Congress and how much of Motown Records, Richard Pryor, and movies and TV shows like *Guess Who's Coming to Dinner?* (1967) and *The Cosby Show?*

And then there are the cultural changes that are a function of unintended consequences. Think of college-educated hippies in the 1960s contributing to working-class cohabitation and nonmarital childbirths today or video games and social media like Facebook contributing to the decline of sociability.

Culture is an ocean wide and an ocean deep. It includes many tides and fish, swimming randomly and intentionally, and considerable debris.

When it comes to the overlapping set of issues characterizing men out in contemporary America, how do we change values and attitudes, norms and behavior?

Not easily.

But what is it that we want to change, and from what to what? Given the rise of cultural relativism, which can be seen as what Herbert Marcuse called "repressive tolerance" (an idea that has migrated from neo-Marxism to cultural conservatism), who has the right to say that it's better to live, think, and behave this way and not some other way? Evangelical Christians and upper-middle-class coastal liberals, meet Robespierre and Chairman Mao.

However, when there are identifiable problems—ones that are hurting people, the people around them, communities, and nations—"live and let live" is not the answer either.

Based on the preceding chapters, let's consider some broad ways to change the culture so that so many American men aren't on the sidelines:

1. Teach values like responsibility, hard work, respect for others, camaraderie or solidarity, empathy and kindness.

2. Ditch toxic masculinity. Replace it with genuine respect for women and all types of men, the idea that it's okay to express feelings and be vulnerable, and that being strong and seeking female companionship doesn't mean a default to rigidity and fighting or an endless sexorama. (And women and the media shouldn't generalize and trash men in toto any more than one should generically trash Jews, blacks, gays, Mexicans, Chinese, women, whites, or any other group.)

3. Recognize that certain jobs aren't "for women" any more than others are men's work; we would benefit in many ways if men were preschool teachers or personal-care providers.

4. Bestow greater dignity and status (as well as better pay) on all occupations in which men and women work hard and want to do their jobs well.

5. Restore faith in government; it's the only tangible, enduring entity we have that represents us as one people, as Americans (of course, contingent on government getting its act together and our democracy doing a much better job of living up to its democratic values).

6. Instill the values of service to others and to the nation, whether it's through the armed services, religious congregations, charities and other nonprofits, or universalizing AmeriCorps, the Peace Corps, or some form of required national service.

7. Understand that it's wrong to have children until you—men and women—are ready to take care of them and be engaged, supportive parents for life, and act accordingly. If you're not married or in an equally

committed relationship, birth control and—I'm sorry to say—early term abortion is better than sabotaging a child's life.

8. Enable and encourage men to form groups and friendships and provide more venues and opportunities for socializing and hanging out—with other men, with men and women, and with couples straight and gay.

9. Understand that whatever problems some poor people may have, it's not the poor who are to blame for your difficulties by taking government benefits (which we all do at one time or another); it's an unfair and rigged economic system that leaves too many Americans insecure and is baked in by bad policies, a political system that's too often for sale, and a culture in which this is second nature.

10. Get off the four-year college-is-for-all hobbyhorse (while acknowledging that too many who should be in college are shut out because of cost), and recognize that there are many types of honorable education and training that can lead to good jobs and lives.

11. It's fine to relax and enjoy oneself, which we have earned in a rich society, and some games and other play are healthy, but don't equate leisure with laziness or immersion in often addictive, antisocial, unproductive, and mind-numbing digital media and devices.

12. Don't blame all men out for their circumstances; most have not chosen to be where they are. (Moreover, telling people that they are bad usually doesn't make them good.)

13. Gender equality is not only about eliminating eons of discrimination and oppression of women. It is about treating fathers as equal parents, as long as they pull their weight, and women not expecting men simultaneously to be providers and hunks (i.e., sex objects) as well as sensitive, egalitarian, and never sexually aggressive. (Both women and men can provide for each other, be thoughtful toward each other, and still be sexy.)

14. Hate and violence almost never serve good ends. (If you really need to confront someone or some institution, we are a nation of laws; hate speech, misogyny, and other types of ranting on the internet are offensive and cowardly.)

15. Decency, manners, politesse, and kindness are not frills.

16. Elitism—the idea that we're better because we went to better schools, have higher-paying jobs, live in "better" neighborhoods, have art on the wall and tickets to the Galápagos—is prejudice. Wellesley may be a nicer place to live than Pittsfield, and parts of Brooklyn may be hipper than Staten Island, but living in either doesn't make you a better person.

There are other items that could be added to this list of cultural requisites, but let's start by considering these as basic premises for both a civilized nation and a society where men who are sidelined have a chance of making it into the mainstream and into better lives. Several of these items apply to all people, but many of them especially apply to men. Not everyone is going to agree with every item on this list, but let's try together to find a common core of values that will help make America a more decent, productive, inclusive, and happy nation.

How do we get there? As noted, policy changes and nudges can help.

Many conservatives and some liberals swear by the idea of conditional benefits: behave responsibly and productively, and the government will help you. The EITC is a long-standing example but far from the only type of policy initiative that could change behavior. The most successful implementation of a conditional benefits program was the expansion of Brazil's Bolsa Família under former president Luiz Inácio Lula da Silva: provide benefits to the needy on the condition that children go to school and get vaccinations and medical exams. A good American example is the Texas initiative that required men in arrears with child support to participate in a program to get training and a job in exchange for not sending them to jail, which worked wonders in increasing child support payments, improving men's incomes, increasing men's contact with their children, and reducing state welfare spending.

But much of the burden for changing values and behavior—that is, cultural change—must come from parents, schools, mentors, and that vague realm that social scientists and pundits call "civil society." Character education and civics education, dismissed mostly by the left in the post-counterculture era, deserve at least as much of a place in schools as some of the teach-to-the-test courses put in place under No Child Left Behind. Yes, schools and teachers already have a lot on their plates, but, just as many young women flourished in women's colleges, many young men might benefit from all-male life-skills classes or academies within schools, as long as they were not allowed to turn into breeding grounds for misogyny.

Excuses for substandard academic performance and for reckless, boorish, and proto-criminal behavior by boys and men (or anyone) cannot be allowed to stand. On the other hand, parents and teachers need to recognize that, in general, boys and girls develop differently and may learn differently; teachers' apparent proclivity to give poorer grades to boys than girls in gender-blind evaluations bespeaks a troubling reverse discrimination. As a *Time* magazine story aptly put it, "Boys are being judged unduly harshly and leniently."[36]

Public service announcements—which once did such a good job to get people not to litter, to wear seatbelts, and to stop smoking—could be resuscitated to convey many of these messages.

Parenting classes, which tend to be voluntary, haphazard, and for profit, should be required of newly married or expecting couples, with periodic refreshers at different stages in their children's life cycle. They should discuss values, be available at no charge, and be paid for by government. Some on the right and left may say that government has no business intruding on family life, but the job of good government is to protect and enhance the well-being of society at large. If behavior problems, crime, poor health practices, joblessness, irresponsible sex, and anger in boys and young men can be reduced— and replaced by good parental emotional and intellectual nurturing—the returns on investment could be enormous.

Once, the armed forces molded more than "a few good men." When the military reached deep into the heart of male America—beyond the class-based sliver that it does today—men learned respect and responsibility. We hardly need the size of the military that fought World War II or the Cold War, but there are strong moral and practical arguments for universally required national service, civilian or military. Not only does it bind citizens to their nation and meet essential national needs, but it also teaches lessons in character that are antithetical to the beer-internet-and-pajamas culture of men out. It also teaches skills and helps people become adults.

Everyday decency and manners aren't just artifacts of Emily Post or military requisites to say "Yes, sir." Rudeness, snobbishness, and brusqueness— more common among men—aren't cool; they're cruel. Many men out have reason to be angry with elites. But they are also culprits. Drivers going too slowly don't deserve the finger or driver's-seat aggression. Ex-partners, especially if they have children together, cannot act like the real or rhetorical guns are ready to blaze. Sincere thank-yous and apologies need to be more abundant. Those "random acts of kindness" bumper stickers may be trite, but they're not wrong.

Work is not just about a paycheck. When men say that a job is "below them," it may sound like laziness, but those in glass think tanks and executive suites shouldn't throw stones. These men got the idea that such jobs aren't valued from somewhere; remember the old Pogo comic strip quote about "We have met the enemy and he is us"? Other countries accord greater respect to unskilled workers. We once did to industrial workers, who weren't especially more skilled than retail salespersons or good waiters. Corporate responsibility is more than sourcing from organic farms; it also means not exploiting prison labor and treating workers as assets to invest in. Pope Leo XIII, in *Rerum novarum* (1891), not only spoke of living wages, unions, and social insurance but also emphasized that "working for gain is creditable, not shameful, to a man, since it enables him to earn an honorable livelihood; but to misuse men as though they were things in the pursuit of gain, or to value them solely for their physical powers—that is truly shameful and inhuman."[37]

My Brother's Keeper, President Obama's public-private alliance to help boys and young men of color, and many fatherhood and new-masculinity curricula are influencing the thinking of American men. Yet such initiatives are needed in every community and by virtually every young (or older) man.

The rapid cultural changes in desirable gender roles have given girls and women a goalpost but have left boys and men in quicksand. It's great to talk about gender equity, but that phrase is clearer and more aspirational for females while all too foggy for males. The paradox of oppression is that although freedom and justice are more difficult to attain, it is easier to understand what they mean than what it means to shed the role of the oppressor.

Boys and men need to be taught in many venues what it means to be egalitarian and responsible men if we are to attain a postpatriarchal world. Women are right that men need to change the diapers, do the laundry, and drive the kids to soccer games, as well as earn a living, just as women do. At the same time, men can't just be bludgeoned as eons-long oppressors. Women need to be careful about holding double standards for men and to provide better, concrete guidance to men about what they expect and is fair, rather than hurling high-minded abstractions like *égalité* at them, as if men could make the leap from the Declaration of the Rights of Man to the quotidian tasks of doing housework or reading *Goodnight Moon*.

Give men a break. But only so much of a break. When all the reasonable reasons and the spurious excuses have run their explanatory course, the fact of the matter is that many men have screwed up and need to get their acts together.

Similarly, there is much need for twenty-first-century versions of Rotary and Kiwanis clubs and other civic organizations that attract men. One can rightly object to these as sexist and uncool, but they did provide places for boys and men to bond over civic-spirited principles. Yes, Elks and Moose Lodges may be anything but hip, but do we not have the creativity to come up with new organizations that can accommodate both modern masculinity and community service?

Men may be less social creatures than women—who populate book clubs, churches, and fitness classes—but that is all the more reason to shore up and create new groups and settings for men to socialize in healthy, productive ways. Social networks are essential, but these need to be face-to-face networks with a purpose, not the pseudo-networks that are accessible with a smart phone or computer keystroke. And employers can do more to help foster friendliness and friendships in their work environments.

Finally, popular culture has a huge role to play. Nothing has had a greater influence on Americans'—and most people's—values and beliefs than the mass media that are often loosely called "Hollywood." Some movies and TV shows, some sports and popular music stars, have done much to model or instill a wide range of the values and behaviors that we've discussed. Participant Media and other thoughtful Hollywood producers, NBA players like LeBron James, Super Bowl champion Harry Sydney, and musicians like Bruce Springsteen, among many others, do portray or model a number of these values. Unfortunately, as we all know, too much of popular culture, including many video games, is garbage that idealizes bad behavior and values—particularly for boys and men. It shouldn't be so hard to tell stories of maleness that don't involve misogynists with Kalashnikovs or 40-year-old man-boys reliving their high school glory days.

Good movies, TV shows, novels, or games can't be dictated by a Politburo, but they don't need to play to, and reinforce, bad behavior and values. Some of the very best fiction and drama portray reprehensible actions, but they make us think about right and wrong. Popular culture doesn't need to play into the insidious cultural relativism in which all too much is permissible. The ways to change the mix are through increased supply, demand, public exhortation, or leadership by America's stars and "star-making machinery."

America's men out need to come back in—to a welcoming America, one that needs them. The men we've met in this book could easily be called "losers," or some gussied-up academic-sounding equivalent, but, despite mistakes they may have made, they need and deserve decent lives. From civic virtue to sociability, nonmisogynist masculinity to engaged, inclusive father-hood; from values like responsibility and drive to better public health and prisoner reentry; from workforce development and decent jobs to the kind of safety net that we've been told is impossible—we need it all. At least we need to start moving in that direction.

Notes

PREFACE

1. On the "end of men," see Hannah Rosin, *The End of Men: And the Rise of Women* (New York: Viking, 2012). On the "boy problem," see Leonard Sax, *Boys Adrift: The Five Factors Driving the Growing Epidemic of Unmotivated Boys and Underachieving Young Men* (New York: Basic Books, 2009); and Christina Hoff Sommers, *The War against Boys: How Misguided Policies Are Harming Our Young Men* (New York: Simon and Schuster, 2013). On the dwindling share of men in higher education, see Organization for Economic Cooperation and Development, "A Closer Look at Gender Gaps in Education and Beyond," *OECD Insights*, March 5, 2015; and Claudia Goldin, Lawrence Katz, and Ilyana Kuziemko, "The Homecoming of American College Women: The Reversal of the College Gender Gap," *Journal of Economic Perspectives* 20, no. 4 (2006): 113–56. One example of "snarky chick lit" is Maureen Dowd, *Are Men Necessary?* (New York: Penguin Group, 2005).

2. "Greater Appalachia" is J. D. Vance's term in *Hillbilly Elegy: A Memoir of a Family and Culture in Crisis* (New York: HarperCollins, 2016).

3. Ben Sasse, *The Vanishing American Adult: America's Coming-of-Age Crisis and How to Rebuild a Culture of Self-Reliance* (New York: St. Martin's Press, 2017).

4. The U.S. Census Bureau estimated that there were about 160 million males in the United States in 2017. About 43 million were between the ages of 0 and 19, and about 15 million were 70 or older. Whereas the traditional definition of the "prime working-age" population has been people between ages 25 and 54 and college attendance rates have increased, most men between their early 20s and late 50s work, and the one segment of the workforce that has been growing is people over age 60. Thus, if one defines the working-age population more realistically as those between 20 and 65, there were about 97 million working-age males. (If one uses the current Social

239

Security full retirement age, the number grows to about 98–99 million. Of course, there are many men younger than 20 and 65 and older who work, and many students between 20 and 25. Thus, for the purposes of this book, we will say that there are approximately 100 million working-age American men.

5. Kathryn Edin and Timothy J. Nelson, *Doing the Best I Can: Fatherhood in the Inner City* (University of California Press, 2013).

6. This estimate is discussed in chapter 1.

CHAPTER 1

1. Leonard Sax, *Boys Adrift: The Five Factors Driving the Growing Epidemic of Unmotivated Boys and Underachieving Young Men* (New York: Basic Books, 2009); and Christina Hoff Sommers, *The War against Boys: How Misguided Policies Are Harming Our Young Men* (New York: Simon and Schuster, 2013).

2. There were 115.7 million civilian, noninstitutionalized men 20 and older in February 2018; 80.2 million of these were employed. About 94 million men were between 20 and 64, more than 84 million were between 25 and 64, and another 13.5 million were between 65 and 74. Approximately 65.5 million 25 and older men were employed in 2017, 59 million of them in full-time jobs; virtually all of these were among the 97.5 million men between 25 and 74. These numbers and percentages are further complicated by 16- to 24-year-old men who are "not in school, not in employment" (or "disconnected youth"), men in prisons or jails, men working part-time or less than 35 hours per week who want to work full-time, and nonworking men 65 and older who want to work, as well as by men in the armed services and men 25 or older who are in school full-time. U.S. Department of Labor, Bureau of Labor Statistics (BLS), "Labor Force Statistics from the Current Population Survey," 2018; and BLS, "Employment Status of the Civilian Population by Sex and Age," March 2018. See the discussion in chapter 2.

3. The food stamp program is formally known as the Supplemental Nutrition Assistance Program, or SNAP, but the popular term "food stamps" is used throughout this book.

4. Robert D. Putnam's seminal work, *Bowling Alone: The Collapse and Revival of American Community* (New York: Simon and Schuster, 2000), described the descent of Americans from a Tocquevillean ideal of public-spirited joiners to an isolated/anomic world in which people are all but bereft of social engagement and "social capital."

5. Whereas the United Kingdom faces some similar issues as the United States, though less severe, organizations such as CALM (Campaign Against Living Miserably [www.thecalmzone.net]) have led public-awareness campaigns such as "Propamanda."

6. Simone de Beauvoir, *Le deuxième sexe* (Paris: Gallimard, 1949).

7. Federal Reserve Bank of St. Louis, "Civilian Labor Force Participation Rate: Men," February 2018.

8. Lawrence Mishel, Josh Bivens, Elise Gould, and Heidi Shierholz, Economic Policy Institute, *The State of Working America*, 12th ed. (Cornell University Press,

2012), 189; and U.S. Census Bureau, "Income, Poverty, and Health Insurance Coverage in the United States: 2016," Historical Income Tables: People, September 17, 2017.

9. Richard Fry, "New Census Data Show More Americans Are Tying the Knot, but Mostly It's the College-Educated," Pew Research Center, February 6, 2014.

10. Kids Count Data Center, "Children in Single-Parent Families," Annie E. Casey Foundation, n.d.

11. Jonathan Vespa, "The Changing Economics and Demographics of Young Adulthood: 1975–2016," U.S. Census Bureau, April 2017.

12. U.S. Department of Education, National Center for Education Statistics, Digest of Education Statistics.

13. Anne Case and Angus Deaton, "Rising Morbidity and Mortality in Midlife among White Non-Hispanic Americans in the 21st Century," *Proceedings of the National Academy of Sciences of the United States of America*, 112, no. 49 (September 17, 2015); and Laura Dwyer-Lindgren, Amelia Bertozzi-Villa, and Rebecca W. Stubbs, "Inequalities in Life Expectancy among US Counties, 1980 to 2014: Temporal Trends and Key Drivers," *JAMA Internal Medicine* 177, no. 7 (2017): 1003–11.

14. Harris Poll, "Less Than Half of Americans Trust Federal Government with Personal Info," July 16, 2013.

15. Danielle Paquette, "The Unexpected Voters behind the Widest Gender Gap in Recorded Election History," *Washington Post*, November 9, 2016.

16. "Service Clubs Push against Fading Influence to Find New Members," *Kansas City Star*, July 10, 2016; "Fading Tradition: Service Clubs Have Long Tradition, Uncertain Future," *Green Valley News*, September 2, 2015.

17. Citations will be provided when each of these issues is discussed in subsequent chapters. Richard Fry, "For First Time in Modern Era, Living with Parents Edges Out Other Living Arrangements for 18- to 34-Year-Olds," Pew Research Center, May 24, 2016; Sarah K. S. Shannon, Christopher Uggen, Jason Schnittker, Melissa Thompson, Sara Wakefield, and Michael Massoglia, "The Growth, Scope, and Spatial Distribution of People with Felony Records in the United States, 1948–2010," *Demography* (September 2017): 1–24.

18. Katy Steinmetz, "Beyond 'He' or 'She': The Changing Meaning of Gender and Sexuality," *Time*, March 16, 2017.

19. Stephanie Coontz, *The Way We Never Were: American Families and the Nostalgia Trap* (New York: Basic Books, 2016; first published 1992).

20. BLS, "Women's Earnings 83 Percent of Men's, but Vary by Occupation," January 15, 2016.

21. "Europe's Young Adults Living with Parents," *The Guardian*, March 24, 2014; Nick Squires, "Italy's 'Big Babies': Court Orders Father to Pay for Upkeep of 28-Year-Old Son," *The Telegraph*, April 27, 2016; "'Fasting Guys' Not Interested in Women—At All," *Japan Times*, January 24, 2013; and "Why Don't Japanese Men Like Having Sex?," *The Telegraph*, January 22, 2015.

22. Judith Warner, "Fact Sheet: The Women's Leadership Gap," Center for American Progress, March 7, 2014; Women and Hollywood, "Women and Holly-

wood: 2017 Statistics"; and Wendy Wang, Kim Parker, and Paul Taylor, "Breadwinner Moms," Pew Research Center, May 29, 2013.

23. "Forbes 400: Full List of America's Richest People," *Forbes*, September 29, 2014; Women Donors Network, "Who Leads Us," October 2014; National Women's Law Center, "Women Are 76 Percent of Workers in the 10 Largest Low-Wage Jobs," April 2014; and BLS, "Usual Weekly Earnings of Wage and Salary Workers Fourth Quarter 2017," January 17, 2018. These wage statistics are in current dollars.

24. Betty Hart and Todd R. Risley, "The Early Catastrophe: The 30 Million Word Gap by Age 3," *American Educator* 27, no. 1 (2003): 4–9.

25. Ivan Yip, quoted in "The Weaker Sex," *The Economist*, March 7, 2015.

26. Case and Deaton, "Rising Morbidity and Mortality in Midlife"; and T. G. Travison, A. B. Araujo, A. B. O'Donnell, V. Kupelian, and J. B. McKinlay, "A Population-Level Decline in Serum Testosterone Levels in American Men," *Journal of Clinical Endocrinology and Metabolism* 92, no. 1 (2007): 196–202.

27. U.S. Census Bureau, "Facts for Features: Fathers' Day 2017: June 18, 2017." A Pew study found that about 2 million fathers are at home with their minor children, although the census counts only one-tenth of those as staying at home to care for their children. Pew Research Center, "Six Facts about Fathers," June 16, 2016. This excludes the 2.6 million single-father-headed households.

28. H. C., "What Is the Manosphere?," *The Economist*, July 5, 2016.

29. Putnam, *Bowling Alone*.

30. Interview with Andrea Zucker, U.S. Army Marketing Research Group, January 13, 2017; and Eric Friedman and others, *New Methods for Assessing AmeriCorps Alumni Outcomes: Final Survey Technical Report* (prepared for the Corporation for National and Community Service, Office of Research and Evaluation) (Cambridge, Mass.: Abt Associates, 2016).

31. Stuart Lavietes, "Elliott Jacques, 86, Scientist Who Coined 'Midlife Crisis'" (obituary), *New York Times*, March 17, 2003; and Jonathan Rauch, "The Real Roots of Midlife Crisis," *The Atlantic*, December 2014.

32. "John Updike's *Rabbit Run*—Another American Story of Men Escaping Women," *The Guardian*, April 21, 2017.

33. Stephen M. Pollan and Mark Levine, *Fire Your Boss* (New York: HarperCollins, 2004); and William Sloane Coffin, "In Praise of Rest" (sermon, July 29, 1979), in *The Collected Sermons of the Rev. William Sloane Coffin: The Riverside Years*, vol. 1 (Louisville, Ky.: Westminster John Knox Press, 2008), 227.

34. Daniel Bell, *The Cultural Contradictions of Capitalism* (New York: Basic Books, 1976); and Christopher Lasch, *The Culture of Narcissism: American Life in an Age of Diminishing Expectations* (New York: W. W. Norton, 1979).

35. Daniel Patrick Moynihan, "Defining Deviancy Down," *American Scholar* 62, no. 1 (1993): 17–30.

36. Robert Paul Wolff, "Beyond Tolerance," in Robert Paul Wolff, Barrington Moore Jr., and Herbert Marcuse, *A Critique of Pure Tolerance* (Boston: Beacon Press, 1969).

37. Interview with Colonel Patrick R. Michaelis, U.S. Army 2nd Recruiting Brigade, February 2, 2017.

38. Daniel Patrick Moynihan, *Family and Nation: The Godkin Lectures, Harvard University* (San Diego: Harcourt Brace Jovanovich, 1986), 189.

CHAPTER 2

1. This expectation is especially well documented in Robert and Helen Lynd's ethnographic studies of Muncie, Indiana, in the 1920s and 1930s. See Robert S. Lynd and Helen Merrell Lynd, *Middletown: A Study in American Culture* (New York: Harcourt Brace, 1929), 25; and Robert S. Lynd and Helen Merrell Lynd, *Middletown in Transition* (New York: Harcourt Brace, 1937), 54.

2. Studs Terkel, *Working: People Talk about What They Do All Day and How They Feel about What They Do* (New York: Pantheon/Random House, 1974).

3. Union membership peaked in the ten to fifteen years after World War II at about 35 percent of all wage and salary workers, but disproportionate numbers of union members were men. Men accounted for 70 percent of the workforce and about 80 percent of union members. See Department of Labor, Bureau of Labor Statistics (BLS), "Union Members–2016," January 26, 2017; Gerald Mayer, "Union Membership Trends in the United States," Congressional Research Service, 2004; and "In Unity There's Strength," Center for Labor Education and Research, University of Hawaii–West Oahu: *Honolulu Record* Digitization Project, vol. 10, no. 18, November 28, 1957.

4. During the postwar era, but beginning in the nineteenth century, the ideal—and the reality for many—was that male wages would be high enough to support themselves, their wives, and their children. Although households always have had multiple earners, the family wage meant that one income was sufficient to support a family. Today criticized as patriarchal, it was also a de facto bargain between business and workers to pay relatively high and rising wages. As early as 1846, the *Ten Hour Advocate*, a labor publication, declared, "We hope the day is not distant when the husband will be able to provide for his wife and family, without sending the [wife] to endure the drudgery of the cotton mill." Quoted in Eric Arneson, *Encyclopedia of U.S. Labor and Working-Class History*, vol. 1 (New York: Routledge, 2007), 434. The influx of women into the workforce largely beginning in the last third of the twentieth century has been due at least as much to the demise of the family wage as to the movement to promote equal economic opportunity for women.

5. BLS, "Household Data," 2006; and BLS, "Alternative Measures of Labor Underutilization for States, Second Quarter of 2016 through First Quarter of 2017 Averages." U-3 is the officially reported unemployment rate.

6. BLS, "Labor Force Statistics from the Current Population Survey," April 6, 2018; Federal Reserve Bank of St. Louis, "Civilian Labor Force Participation Rate: Men"; U.S. Council of Economic Advisers, "The Long-Term Decline in Prime-Age Male Labor Force Participation," June 2016; BLS, "Civilian Labor Force by Age, Sex, Race and Ethnicity"; Steven F. Hipple, "Labor Force Participation: What Has Hap-

pened since the Peak?," PowerPoint presentation, BLS, December 8, 2016; Jennifer Schramm, "Labor Force Participation Rate for People Age 55+ Down Slightly in April," AARP, May 5, 2017; Alana Semeuls, "Maybe the Economy Isn't the Reason Why So Many Men Aren't Working," *The Atlantic*, March 22, 2017; and Jason Furman, remarks, "Men without Work," Harvard Kennedy School, April 26, 2017. Israel also has a lower male labor force participation rate, but the fact that many Orthodox Jewish men devote their time to study makes it a less apt comparison. Germany is the only major OECD country in which male workforce participation increased between 1990 and 2014.

7. Drew DeSilver, "Millions of Young People in U.S. and EU Are Neither Working Nor Learning," Pew Research Center, January 28, 2016; Martha Ross and Nicole P. Svajlenka, "Employment and Disconnection among Teens and Young Adults," Brookings Institution, May 24, 2016; James M. Quane, William Julius Wilson, and Jackelyn Hwang, "Black Men and the Struggle for Work," *Education Next* 15, no. 2 (2015); and U.S. Department of Justice, Bureau of Justice Statistics (BJS), "U.S. Correctional Population at Lowest Level since 2002," December 29, 2016.

8. BLS, "Labor Force Statistics from the Current Population Survey," March 9, 2018; BLS, "Employment Status of the Civilian Population by Sex and Age," March 9, 2018; Federal Reserve Bank of St. Louis, "Graph: Employment Rate: Aged 25–54: Males for the United States, 1955–2015"; Federal Reserve Bank of St. Louis, "Employment-Population Ratio—Men, Jan. 1948–Feb. 2018"; and email communication with Jacob Hacker, Yale University, June 28, 2017. It is important to distinguish between the *labor force participation rate*, which includes those actively seeking jobs and was 69 percent for all noninstitutionalized males 16 and older and 72 percent for males 20 and older in February 2018, and the *employment to population ratio*, which includes those who are not actively seeking jobs, which was 66.5 percent and 69 percent, respectively. If one includes men who are institutionalized, the percentage working becomes even smaller. Workers 55 and older are projected to make up one quarter of the workforce by 2022, according to the BLS. Because there is more black-market work in Europe than in the United States, the percentage of men working on the Continent is higher than official statistics show, according to Jason Furman, chair of President Obama's Council of Economic Advisers. Furman, remarks, "Men without Work."

9. BLS, "Labor Force Statistics from the Current Population Survey, 2016; BLS, "The Employment Situation: February 2018," March 9, 2018; BLS, "Employed and Unemployed Full- and Part-time Workers by Age, Sex, Race, and Hispanic or Latino Ethnicity," 2018. U.S. Census Bureau, "Income and Poverty in the United States: 2016," September 2017; and email communication with Jacob Hacker, June 28, 2017.

10. Estimates range upward from 7 percent of the workforce whose only income is from tax-reported contract work, to many more in gray- and black-market corners of the labor market. In 2018, the Labor Department estimated that 13.9 percent of workers were independent contractors, on-call day laborers, direct-hire temporary workers, agency temps, and contract workers for companies (BLS, "Contingent and Alternative Employment Arrangements—May 2017," June 7, 2018). See "Choice, Necessity, and the Gig Economy," McKinsey Global Institute, 2016; Annette Bernhardt and

Sarah Thomason, "What Do We Know about Gig Work in California? An Analysis of Independent Contracting," University of California, Berkeley, Labor Center, June 14, 2017; David Weil, *The Fissured Workplace: Why Work Became So Bad for So Many and What Can Be Done to Improve It* (Harvard University Press, 2014), 272; and Rudy Telles, "Digital Matching Firms: A New Definition in the 'Sharing Economy' Space," U.S. Department of Commerce, June 6, 2016.

11. Bernhardt and Thompson, "What Do We Know?"; Lauren Weber, "The Flip Side of the New U.S. Economy," *Wall Street Journal*, September 15, 2017; and interviews with Isabel Sawhill, December 5, 2016; Jacob Hacker, June 28, 2017; Sylvia Allegretto, July 6, 2017; David Autor, July 6, 2017; David Cooper, February 14, 2017; and Kathryn Edin, February 6, 2017.

12. U.S. Department of Labor, Women's Bureau, "Working Mothers Issue Brief," n.d.; Claudia Goldin and Joshua Mitchell, "The New Life Cycle of Women's Employment: Disappearing Humps, Sagging Middles, Expanding Tops," *Journal of Economic Perspectives* 31, no. 1 (2017): 161–82; and Elisabeth Jacobs, "Can Women's 'Sagging Middle' Help Explain the Fall in U.S. Labor Force Participation Rates?," Washington Center for Equitable Growth, February 17, 2017.

13. All are white except Tyrone, who is black.

14. David Card and John E. DiNardo, "Skill-Biased Technological Change and Rising Wage Inequality: Some Problems and Puzzles," *Journal of Labor Economics* 20, no. 4 (2002); and Eleanor Krause and Isabel Sawhill, "What We Know and Don't Know about Declining Labor Force Participation: A Review," Brookings Institution, May 2017.

15. Claudia Goldin and Lawrence Katz, "The Race between Education and Technology: The Evolution of U.S. Educational Wage Differentials, 1890 to 2005," NBER Working Paper 12984 (Cambridge, Mass.: National Bureau of Economic Research, 2007); Pew Research Center, "The Rising Cost of Not Going to College," February 11, 2014; Sandy Baum, "Higher Education Earnings Premium," Urban Institute, February 2014; and James Bessen, "Employers Aren't Just Whining—The 'Skills Gap' Is Real," *Harvard Business Review*, August 25, 2014.

16. Alan B. Krueger, "Where Have All the Workers Gone?," Federal Reserve Bank of Boston, October 4, 2016; Frank J. Lysy, "The Structural Factors behind the Steady Fall in Labor Force Participation Rates of Prime Age Workers," *An Economic Sense*, October 14, 2016; Alicia H. Munnell, "Why the Average Retirement Age Is Rising," *MarketWatch*, October 15, 2017; Lawrence Mead, *Expanding Work Programs for Poor Men* (Lanham, Md.: Rowman and Littlefield, 2011); BLS, "Table 1. Employment Status of the Civilian Noninstitutional Population by Disability Status and Selected Characteristics, 2016 Annual Averages"; BLS, "Table 1. Time Spent in Primary Activities and Percent of the Civilian Population Engaging in Each Activity, Averages per Day by Sex, 2016 Annual Averages"; BLS, "Summary Table 2. Number of Persons and Average Hours per Day by Detailed Activity Classification (Travel Reported Separately), 2015 Annual Averages: Not Employed"; and interview with Rose Woods, BLS, December 2, 2016.

17. A December 11, 2014, Kaiser Family Foundation/*New York Times*/CBS News "Non-Employed" poll found that 44 percent of prime-age nonworking men said there

were available jobs nearby but they were not willing to take them. Nicholas Eberstadt, *Men without Work: America's Invisible Crisis* (West Conshohocken, Penn.: Templeton Press, 2016), 111; Susan Chira, "Men Don't Want to Be Nurses; Their Wives Agree," *New York Times*, June 24, 2017; interview with David Autor, July 6, 2017; Men Care and Promundo, "State of America's Fathers 2016"; and Robert VerBruggen, "When Young Men Don't Work: Immigrants Replace Them in the Labor Force; Leisure Replaces Work in Their Lives," *American Conservative*, September 12, 2016.

18. Steven F. Hipple, "People Who Are Not in the Labor Force: Why Aren't They Working?," BLS, *Beyond the Numbers* 4, no. 15 (2015).

19. Richard Fry, "For First Time in Modern Era, Living with Parents Edges out Other Living Arrangements for 18- to 34-Year-Olds," Pew Research Center, May 24, 2016.

20. BLS, Unpublished Tabulations from the Current Population Survey, "Employment Status of the Civilian Noninstitutional Population by Marital Status, Sex, Age, Race, and Hispanic and Latino Ethnicity, Annual Average 2016"; David Autor and Melanie Wasserman, "Wayward Sons: The Emerging Gender Gaps in Labor Markets and Education," *Third Way*, March 2013; interview with Steven F. Hipple, BLS, December 8, 2016; Krause and Sawhill, "What We Know and Don't Know"; National Research Center on Hispanic Children and Families, "A Portrait of Latino Fathers: Strengths and Challenges," February 2017; and Mead, *Expanding Work Programs*, 15–16.

21. Gregor Aisch, Josh Katz, and David Leonhardt, "Where Men Aren't Working," *New York Times*, December 11, 2014.

22. BLS, "Table 1. Time Spent in Primary Activities"; Amanda Cox, "The Rise of Men Who Don't Work, and What They Do Instead," *New York Times*, December 11, 2014; BLS, "Summary Table 2. Number of Persons and Average Hours per Day"; interview with Rose Woods, December 2, 2016; Mark Aguiar and Eric Hurst, "The Increase in Leisure Inequality," prepared for the American Enterprise Institute, 2007; and Muriel Egerton, Kimberly Fisher, and Jonathan Gershuny, with contributions from John P. Robinson, Anne H. Gauthier, Nuno Torres, and Andreas Pollmann, "American Time Use 1965–2003: The Construction of a Historical Comparative File, and Consideration of Its Usefulness in the Construction of Extended National Accounts for the USA," ISER Working Paper 2005-28 (New York: Columbia University, Institute for Social and Economic Research, 2005); and Kaiser Family Foundation/ *New York Times*/CBS News, "Non-Employed Poll," December 31, 2014. Another survey found that 47 percent of prime-age nonworking men claimed to be disabled, with the number rising to 60 percent for those between the ages of 45 and 54.

23. Martha Nussbaum and Amartya Sen, *The Quality of Life* (Oxford University Press, 1993).

24. Binyamin Applebaum, "The Vanishing Male Worker: How America Fell Behind," *New York Times*, December 11, 2014; Jay Stewart, "Male Nonworkers: Who Are They and Who Supports Them?," *Demography* 43, no. 3 (2006); Derek Thompson, "The Missing Men," *The Atlantic*, June 27, 2016; Mona Chalabi, "How Many Women Earn More Than Their Husbands?," *FiveThirtyEight*, February 5, 2015;

Sarah Jane Glynn, "Breadwinning Mothers Are Increasingly the US Norm," Center for American Progress, December 19, 2016.

25. Applebaum, "The Vanishing Male Worker"; Krueger, "Where Have All the Workers Gone?"; Eberstadt, *Men without Work*, 114–19; Nicholas Eberstadt, "Our Miserable 21st Century," *Commentary*, February 15, 2017; BLS, "Employment Status of the Civilian Noninstitutional Population by Disability Status and Selected Characteristics, 2016 Annual Averages"; Federal Reserve Bank of St. Louis, "Working Age Population: Aged 25 to 54: Males in the United States"; and Ernie Tedeschi, "Will Employment Keep Growing? Disabled Workers Offer a Clue," *New York Times*, March 15, 2018.

26. Justin Gest, *The New Minority: White Working Class Politics in an Age of Immigration and Inequality* (Oxford University Press, 2016), 94–95; and Joan C. Williams, *White Working Class: Overcoming Class Cluelessness in America* (Boston: Harvard Business Review Press, 2017), 21.

27. Corporation for Enterprise Development, "2016 Asset and Opportunity Scorecard"; and Federal Reserve Bank of St. Louis, "Personal Saving Rate," December 2017.

28. Although the census does not break down data on assets by gender for those out of the labor force, or not working more generally, median net worth for households with no one working in the preceding year was a mere $10,040 in 2013, one-eighth the median for all U.S. households. Similarly, median net worth for Americans with a high school diploma or some college was about $37,000, compared to $148,000 for those with a college degree, and median net worth for single Americans, at about $42,000, was one-fourth that of the typical married couple. See U.S. Census Bureau, Wealth, Asset Ownership, and Debt of Households Detailed Tables: 2013, "Table 1: Median Value of Assets for Households, by Type of Asset Owned and Selected Characteristics: 2013."

29. Andrew Blevins, John Scott, Kevin Whitman, and Theron Guzoto, "Who's In, Who's Out: A Look at Access to Employer-Based Retirement Plans and Participation in the States," Pew Charitable Trusts, January 13, 2016; William J. Wiatrowski, "The Last Private Industry Pension Plans: A Visual Essay," BLS, *Monthly Labor Review*, December 2012; Barbara A. Butrica, Howard M. Iams, Karen E. Smith, and Eric J. Toder, "The Disappearing Defined Benefit Pension Plan and Its Potential Impact on the Retirement Income of Baby Boomers," *Social Security Bulletin* 69, no. 3 (2009); David A. Pratt, "Some Implications of the Changing Structure of Work for Worker Retirement Security, Pensions, and Healthcare," BLS symposium, December 10, 2015; and interview with C. Eugene Steuerle, Urban Institute, September 20, 2107.

30. BLS, "Labor Force Statistics from the Current Population Survey," January 19, 2018; Heidi Hartmann, Ariane Hegewisch, Barbara Gault, Gina Chirillo, and Jennifer Clark, "Five Ways to Win an Argument about the Gender Pay Gap," Institute for Women's Policy Research, 2017; Claudia Goldin, Sari Pekkala Kerr, Claudia Olivetti and Erring Barth, "The Expanding Gender Earnings Gap: Evidence from the LEHD-2000 Census," *American Economic Review* 107, no. 5 (May 2017); June Carbone and Naomi Cahn, *Marriage Markets: How Inequality Is Remaking the American Family* (Oxford University Press, 2014), 68; and Matthew Rouso, "Child-

less Women in Their Twenties Out-Earn Men. So?," *Forbes*, February 24, 2014. The gender pay gap, cited by the BLS at 83 cents to the dollar (and 79 cents by some advocates), is another contentious statistic, but no one disputes that even when everything else is held equal, men are paid more than women.

31. Elyse Shaw, Ariane Hegewisch, Emma Williams-Baron, and Barbara Gault, "Undervalued and Underpaid: Women in Low-Wage, Female Dominated Jobs," Institute for Women's Policy Research and Oxfam America, November 17, 2016; Miriam King, Steven Ruggles, J. Trent Alexander, and others, "Female and Male Income Percentile Calculator for the United States in 2016," DQYDJ.com, January 23, 2017; and Asset Funders Network, "Women and Wealth" (2015).

32. Demetrio Scopelliti, "Middle-Skill Jobs Decline as U.S. Labor Market Becomes More Polarized," BLS, *Monthly Labor Review*, October 2014; David Autor, "U.S. Labor Market Challenges over the Longer Term," MIT Working Paper, Department of Economics, October 5, 2010; interview with David Autor, July 6, 2017, and correspondence; and Megan W. Barker, "Manufacturing Employment Hard Hit during the 2007–2009 Recession," BLS, *Monthly Labor Review*, April 2011.

33. Autor and Wasserman, "Wayward Sons."

34. This trend can be seen at least since the turn of the century, as noted by Jacob S. Hacker, *The Great Risk Shift: The Assault on American Jobs, Families, Health Care, and Retirement and How You Can Fight Back* (Oxford University Press, 2006), 73.

35. Interview with Sylvia Allegretto, July 6, 2017.

36. Hipple, "People Who Are Not in the Labor Force"; Justin Worland, "2 in 5 Young Americans Don't Want a Job," *Time*, November 14, 2014; and "Age Comparisons among Workers," 2014 Retirement Confidence Survey Fact Sheet 4 (Washington, D.C.: Employee Benefits Research Institute, 2014).

37. Andrew J. Cherlin, *Labor's Love Lost: The Rise and Fall of the Working-Class Family in America* (New York: Russell Sage Foundation, 2014), 5, 17; and Charles Murray, *Coming Apart: The State of White America, 1960–2010* (New York: Crown, 2012), 182–83.

38. Claire Zillman, "The 10 Biggest Corporate Layoffs of the Past Two Decades," *Fortune*, September 20, 2015; and Henry S. Farber, "Job Loss in the Great Recession and Its Aftermath: U.S. Evidence from the Displaced Workers Survey," Discussion Paper 9069, Princeton University, May 2015.

39. Nelson D. Schwartz, "Economy Needs Workers, but Drug Tests Take a Toll," *New York Times*, July 24, 2017; and interviews with Colonel Patrick Michaelis, February 2, 2017, and Master Sergeant Jeffrey Klimek, March 2, 2017.

40. David J. Deming, "The Growing Importance of Social Skills in the Labor Market," NBER Working Paper 21473 (Cambridge, Mass.: National Bureau of Economic Research, August 2015); Korn Ferry, "New Research Shows Women Are Better at Using Soft Skills Crucial for Effective Leadership and Superior Business Performance," March 2016; and Sarah Kruger, "Are Soft Skills a Competitive Advantage for Women?," Accenture, January 2017.

41. Tyler Cowen, *Create Your Own Economy: The Path to Prosperity in a Disordered World* (New York: Dutton, 2009); Aspen Institute, "Income Volatility: A

Primer," May 2016; and Jared Bernstein, *All Together Now: Common Sense for a Fair Economy* (San Francisco: Berrett-Koehler, 2006), 3–4.

42. Kimberly Palmer, "Ten Things You Should Know about Age Discrimination," AARP, n.d.; David Neumark, Ian Burn, and Patrick Button, "Is It Harder for Older Workers to Find Jobs? New and Improved Evidence from a Field Experiment," NBER Working Paper 21669 (Cambridge, Mass.: National Bureau of Economic Research, October 2015); Gary Koenig, Lori Trawinski, and Sara Rix, "The Long Road Back: Struggling to Find Work after Unemployment," AARP Public Policy Institute, March 2015; and National Opinion Research Center, General Social Survey, "Quality of Working Life," 2016.

43. Kathryn J. Edin and H. Luke Shaefer, *$2 a Day: Living on Almost Nothing in America* (New York: Houghton Mifflin Harcourt, 2016), xvii; National Alliance to End Homelessness and Homelessness Research Institute, "The State of Homelessness in America 2016"; and Tom Matlack, "Why Are Men More Likely to Be Homeless?," Good Men Project, January 28, 2012.

44. Lawrence Mishel, Elise Gould, and Josh Bivens, "Wage Stagnation in Nine Charts," Economic Policy Institute, January 6, 2015; U.S. Census Bureau, "Historical Census of Housing Tables"; and Andrew L. Yarrow, *Measuring America: How Economic Growth Came to Define American Greatness in the Late Twentieth Century* (University of Massachusetts Press, 2010), 197.

45. "1950s Cars," *Fifties Web*.

46. Nelson Lichtenstein, *The Most Dangerous Man in Detroit: Walter Reuther and the Fate of American Labor* (New York: Basic Books, 1995).

47. Michael Harrington, *The Other America: Poverty in the United States* (New York: Macmillan, 1962). Harrington's revelations about "our fifty million poor" were first published in *Commentary* in July 1959.

48. There are many different baseline years that one could choose to chart changes in the U.S. economy. The years 1979, just before the Reagan administration, or 2000, at the end of the Clinton-era boom, are frequently used, but 1973 is a particularly good benchmark because that was when real median wages—the inflation-adjusted earnings of a worker at the statistical middle of the earnings distribution—peaked in U.S. history.

49. U.S. Census Bureau, Historical Income Tables, "Table P-5. Regions—People by Median Income and Sex"; "Income and Poverty in the United States: 2016"; Mead, *Expanding Work Programs*, 60; Lawrence H. Summers, "Economic Forum: Policy Responses to Crises," remarks at the Fourteenth Jacques Polak International Monetary Fund Annual Research Conference, Washington, D.C., November 8, 2013; and Alvin H. Hansen, "Capital Goods and the Restoration of Purchasing Power," *Proceedings of the Academy of Political Science* 16, no. 1 (April 1934). Adjusting wages for inflation is based on the Consumer Price Index, although many factors make this difficult to apply throughout the United States and over time, because there can be regional variations in costs such as housing, and the goods that different people buy in the 2010s compared to the 1970s differ in many ways. See BLS, "Consumer Price Index Research Series Using Current Methods (CPI-U-RS)," 2016.

50. Department of Labor, "1965 Handbook on Women Workers: Women's Bureau Bulletin, no. 290" (1965); Federal Reserve Bank of St. Louis, "Civilian Labor Force Participation Rate: Women"; Ravi Balakrishnan, Mai Dao, Juan Solé, and Jeremy Zook, "Lost Workers," *Finance and Development* 52, no. 3 (September 2015); "All the Working Ladies: Women Alone Are Driving a Recovery in Workforce Participation," *The Economist*, August 19, 2017.

51. Chad Stone, Danilo Trisi, Arloc Sherman and Roderick Taylor, "A Guide to Statistics on Historical Trends in Income Inequality" (Washington D.C.: Center on Budget and Policy Priorities, November 7, 2016).

52. President Barack Obama, cited in *Washington Post*, December 4, 2013; David Autor, "The Polarization of Job Opportunities in the U.S. Labor Market: Implications for Employment and Earnings," Center for American Progress and the Hamilton Project, April 2010; and Weil, *The Fissured Workplace*, 284, 281.

53. BLS, "Estimating the U.S. Labor Share," *Monthly Labor Review*, February 2017.

54. Lawrence Katz and Alan Krueger, "Documenting Decline in U.S. Economic Mobility," *Science* 356, no. 6336 (2017); Robert B. Reich, "The Secession of the Successful," *New York Times Magazine*, January 20, 1991; Richard Reeves, *Dream Hoarders: How the American Upper Middle Class Is Leaving Everyone Else in the Dust, Why That Is a Problem, and What to Do about It* (Brookings Institution Press, 2017), 52; and Raj Chetty, David Grusky, Maximilian Hell, Nathaniel Hendren, Robert Manduca, and Jimmy Narang, "The Fading American Dream: Trends in Absolute Income Mobility since 1940," NBER Working Paper 22910 (Cambridge, Mass.: National Bureau of Economic Research, December 2016).

55. Emmanuel Saez, "The Evolution of Top Incomes in the United States (Updated with 2015 Preliminary Estimates)," University of California, Berkeley, June 30, 2016; Federal Reserve Bank of Atlanta, "Divergence: Wealth and Income Inequality in the United States," *EconSouth* 16, no. 3 (September to December 2014); Mishel and others, "Wage Stagnation in Nine Charts"; Weil, *Fissured Workplace*, 281; Stone, Trisi, and others, "Guide to Statistics on Historical Trends in Income Inequality"; Steven Clifford, *Excess at the Top: The CEO Pay Machine* (New York: Blue Rider, 2017); Lawrence Mishel and Jessica Schieder, "CEOs Make 276 Times More Than Typical Workers," Economic Policy Institute, August 3, 2016; Reeves, *Dream Hoarders*; Williams, *White Working Class*, 10; and "Everything Is Awesome! Now Is the Time to Sell Your Stock," *Wall Street Journal*, July 7, 2017.

56. Hacker, *Great Risk Shift*, 67; and Peter Gosselin, *High Wire: The Precarious Financial Lives of American Families* (New York: Basic Books, 2008), 23 and 11ff.

57. Benjamin Landy, "Graph: How the Financial Sector Consumed America's Economic Growth," Century Foundation, February 25, 2013; and Steve Denning, "Wall Street Costs the Economy 2% of GDP Each Year," *Forbes*, May 31, 2015.

58. "Bravo's 'The Real Housewives of Orange County' to Premiere March 21," *Reality TV World*, January 6, 2006.

59. Cork Gaines, "The 25 Highest-Paid NFL Players," *Business Insider*, February

3, 2017; and "The World's Highest Paid Musicians of 2016," *Forbes*, November 30, 2016.

60. Brink Lindsey and Steven M. Teles, *The Captured Economy: How the Powerful Enrich Themselves, Slow Down Growth, and Increase Inequality* (Oxford University Press, 2017); and Benjamin I. Page, Larry M. Bartels, and Jason Seawright, "Democracy and the Policy Preferences of Wealthy Americans," *Perspectives on Politics* 11, no. 1 (2013); Demos, "Stacked Deck: How the Dominance of Politics by the Affluent and Business Undermines Economic Mobility in America," 2013; and Thomas Piketty, *Capital in the 21st Century* (Harvard University Press, 2014), 20, 35.

61. "Since 1980s, the Kindest of Tax Cuts for the Rich," *New York Times*, January 18, 2012; and Congressional Budget Office, "The Budget and Economic Outlook: 2018 to 2028," April 9, 2018.

62. National Right to Work Committee; AFL-CIO, "Right to Work"; Jake Rosenfeld, Patrick Denice, and Jennifer Laird, "Union Decline Lowers Wages of Nonunion Workers," EPI, August 30, 2016; interview with David Autor, July 6, 2017; and Kate Rogers, "Adjusted for Inflation, the Federal Minimum Wage Is Worth Less Than 50 Years Ago," CNBC, July 21, 2016.

63. Murray, *Coming Apart*, 173, 181–83, 170–71; Scott Winship, "How to Fix Disability Insurance," *National Affairs* (Spring 2015): 3–25; and U.S. Council of Economic Advisers, "Long-Term Decline." As suggested earlier, the percentage claiming disability benefits is smaller than the percentage "qualifying" for such benefits.

64. Quoted in Alexis Pozen, "Health Insurance," *Washington Post*, July 2, 2017.

65. Eberstadt, *Men without Work*, 5, 127; and Nicholas Eberstadt, *A Nation of Takers: America's Entitlement Epidemic* (West Conshohocken, Penn.: Templeton Press, 2012).

66. Jose A. DelReal, "Carson Says Living in Poverty a 'State of Mind,'" *Washington Post*, May 25, 2017.

67. Kaiser Family Foundation/*New York Times*/CBS News Non-Employed Poll, December 11, 2014; interview with David Lapp, December 14, 2016; Krause and Sawhill, "What We Know and Don't Know"; and interview with Amanda White, John Deere factory, Horicon, Wisc., March 28, 2017.

68. Sara E. Rix, "America's Aging Labor Force," AARP Public Policy Institute, September 2014.

69. World Bank, "GDP per Person Employed (Constant 2011 PPP $)"; Federal Reserve Bank of St. Louis, "Compensation of Employees: Wages and Salary Accruals/Gross Domestic Product."

70. Email communication with Jacob Hacker, June 28, 2017; Congressional Budget Office, "The Budget and Economic Outlook: 2017 to 2027," January 2017, "Table 2-3. Key Inputs in CBO's Projections of Potential GDP"; Stephanie Aaronson, Tomaz Cajner, Bruce Fallick, Felix Galbis-Reig, Christopher Smith, and William Wascher, "Labor Force Participation: Recent Developments and Future Prospects,"

Brookings Papers on Economic Activity, Fall 2014; and Jim Puzzanghera, "The U.S. Labor Force's Guy Problem: Lots of Men Don't Have a Job and Aren't Looking for One," *Los Angeles Times*, November 21, 2016.

71. Congressional Budget Office, "The Budget and Economic Outlook: 2018 to 2028," April 19, 2018.

FRACKVILLE, PENNSYLVANIA

1. Pennsylvania Department of Corrections, "SCI Frackville" and "SCI Mahanoy."

2. Steve Esack, "Frackville State Prison to Remain Open, SCI Pittsburgh to Close," *Morning Call*, January 26, 2017.

3. "Warehouse Product Selector Full Time, Wegmans Food Markets," Pottsville, Penn., February 27, 2018; and "Wegmans Food Markets Product Selector Salaries in United States," Glassdoor.com.

4. Kehillat Israel Society, "Jewish Community Records of Shenandoah, Pa.," December 19, 2007; interviews with Loraine Stanton, March 9, 2017, and April 17, 2018; and Akiva Males, "The Story of Mahanoy City: The Disappearance of a Jewish Community in a Small American Town," *Jewish Action*, June 14, 2012.

5. David Wenner, "Pa. Overdoses Surge by 37 Percent: Updated Death Toll for Each County," *PennLive*, July 27, 2017.

6. Amy Marchiano, "Suicide Rate Rising in Schuylkill County," *Standard Speaker*, October 18, 2016.

7. Julianne Hing, "Luis Ramirez's Attackers Get Nine Years in Prison for Deadly Beating," *Colorlines*, February 24, 2011; and Bob Kalinowski, "Ex-Shenandoah Chief Nestor Sentenced to 13 Months in Prison; Moyer Gets 3 Months," *Republican Herald*, June 2, 2011.

CHAPTER 3

1. Department of Justice, Federal Bureau of Investigation, *2015 Crime in the United States*, "Table 42. Arrests by Sex, 2014"; Department of Justice, Bureau of Justice Statistics, "Criminal Victimization 2015," October 2016; and Mark Follman, Gavin Aronsen, and Deanna Pan, "U.S. Mass Shootings, 1982–2017: Data from *Mother Jones*' Investigation," *Mother Jones*, June 14, 2017.

2. Terry A. Kupers, "Toxic Masculinity as a Barrier to Mental Health Treatment in Prison," *Journal of Clinical Psychology* 61 (2005): 713–24; R. W. Connell, *Masculinities* (University of California Press, 1995); Campaign against Living Miserably, "Propamanda"; and interview with Sergeant First Class Robert W. Dodge, Chattanooga East Army Recruiting Center, January 31, 2017.

3. Megan K. Maas, Cindy L. Shearer, Meghan M. Gillen, and Eva S. Lefkowitz, "Sex Rules: Emerging Adults' Perceptions of Gender's Impact on Sexuality," *Sex Culture* 19, no. 4 (2015); and Brian Heilman, Gary Barker, and Alexander Harrison, "The Man Box: A Study on Being a Young Man in the U.S., U.K., and Mexico," Promundo, rev. March 29, 2017.

4. Markham Heid, "The Truth about Erectile Dysfunction," *Men's Health*, October 28, 2014; Nancy Jo Sales, "Tinder and the Dawn of the 'Dating Apocalypse,'"

Vanity Fair, August 6, 2015; and Nicola Davis, "Sperm Counts among Western Men Have Halved in Last 40 Years—Study," *The Guardian*, July 25, 2017.

5. Thomas Foster, ed., *New Men: Manliness in Early America* (New York University Press, 2011), 1.

6. Joan C. Williams, *White Working Class: Overcoming Class Cluelessness in America* (Boston: Harvard Business Review Press, 2017), 92.

7. "Dwayne Johnson: Man of the Century," *Muscle and Fitness*, December 2015; and Natalie Robehmed, "The World's Highest-Paid Actors 2016: The Rock Leads with Knockout $64.5 Million Year," *Forbes*, August 25, 2016.

8. Peter Moore, "The Decline of the Manly Man," *YouGov*, May 23, 2016; and Heilman, Barker, and Harrison, "The Man Box."

9. Interview with Tyvon Hewitt, Latin American Youth Center, July 14, 2017.

10. Simone de Beauvoir, *Le deuxième sexe* (Paris: Gallimard,1949); and Betty Friedan, *The Feminine Mystique* (New York: W. W. Norton, 1963).

11. Ronald Brownstein, "Poll: American Men Embracing Gender Equality," *The Atlantic*, April 30, 2015; and Victoria Shannon, "Equal Rights for Women? Survey Says: Yes, but . . . ," *New York Times*, July 1, 2010.

12. Diane M. Negra, "Alan Alda," Museum of TV and Broadcasting; and Logan Hill, "Dark Horse," *New York Magazine*, February 14, 2005.

13. Mark Simpson, "The Metrosexual Is Dead. Long Live the 'Spornosexual,'" *The Telegraph*, June 10, 2014; and Kevin Roose, "Are You a Yummy?," *New York Magazine*, March 25, 2014.

14. If it needs repeating, this is not to say that sexism has vanished from Wall Street, Washington, Hollywood, or anywhere else, or that women are more likely to be less successful economically and politically.

15. Francisco J. Sánchez, Stefanie T. Greenberg, William Ming Liu, and Eric Vilain, "Reported Effects of Masculine Ideals on Gay Men," *Psychology of Men and Masculinity* 10, no. 1 (2009); interview with Naomi Goldberg, Movement Advancement Project, January 25, 2017; and Tara Bahrampour, "Nearly Half of Homeless Youth Are LGBTQ, First-Ever City Census Finds," *Washington Post*, January 13, 2016,

16. Straightacting.com, "The Butch Board IV.1." This board is no longer active

17. Ritch C. Savin-Williams and Kenneth M. Cohen, "Mostly Straight, Most of the Time," *Good Men Project*, January 24, 2018.

18. Gail Sheehy, *Understanding Men's Passages* (New York: Random House, 1998), chapter 1; and "Friedanisms," *New York Times*, November 29, 1970.

19. "Robertson Letter Attacks Feminists," *New York Times*, August 26, 1992.

20. Andrew Tobin, "Women Don't Really Go for 'Nice' Guys, Study Indicates," *Times of Israel*, August 17, 2014; Eric W. Dolan, "Wives with Masculine Husbands Are More Satisfied at Peak Fertility, Study Finds," *PsyPost*, May 8, 2017; Amanda Prestigiacomo, "Study: Women Love Them Some Toxic Masculinity," *Daily Wire*, May 17, 2017; and Kevin Voight, "Who Pays? NerdWallet Study Finds Gender Roles Remain Strong among Couples," *NerdWallet*, September 17, 2014. This survey found that 77 percent of heterosexual couples believe that men should pay for at least the first date.

21. Michael S. Kimmel, *Manhood in America: A Cultural History* (New York: Free Press, 1996), 21, 122, 151, 177, 247, 261–62, 278; and Arthur M. Schlesinger Jr., *The Politics of Hope and The Bitter Heritage: American Liberalism in the 1960s*, (Princeton University Press, 2007, first published 1963), 292.

22. Lionel Tiger, *The Decline of Males: The First Look at an Unexpected New World for Men and Women* (New York: Golden Books, 1999), 21, 56, 179, 77, 3; Guy Garcia, *The Decline of Men* (New York: HarperCollins, 2008); and Hanna Rosin, *The End of Men: And the Rise of Women* (New York: Riverhead Books, 2012).

23. U.S. Department of Education, National Center for Education Statistics, *Digest of Education Statistics*, "Table 105.20. Enrollment in Elementary, Secondary, and Degree-Granting Postsecondary Institutions, by Level and Control of Institution, Enrollment Level, and Attendance Status and Sex of Student: Selected Years, Fall 1990 through Fall 2025"; Matt Rocheleau, "On Campus, Women Outnumber Men More Than Ever," *Boston Globe*, March 28, 2016; Mark Hugo Lopez and Ana Gonzalez-Barerra, "Women's College Enrollment Gains Leave Men Behind," Pew Research Center, March 6, 2014; U.S. Department of Commerce, "Latest Census Data on Educational Attainment Shows Women Lead Men in College Completion," March 30, 2016; June Carbone and Naomi Cain, *Marriage Markets: How Inequality Is Remaking the American Family* (Oxford University Press, 2014), 67; and Richard V. Reeves, "Sex, Race, Education and the Marriage Gap," *Newsweek*, April 15, 2015.

24. Tom Loveless, "Girls, Boys, and Reading," part 1 of 2015 Brown Center Report on American Education, Brookings Institution, March 24, 2015; Erika Christakis, "Do Teachers Really Discriminate against Boys?," *Time*, February 6, 2013; David Autor, David Figlio, Krzysztof Karbownik, Jeffrey Roth, and Melanie Wasserman, "Family Disadvantage and the Gender Gap in Behavioral and Educational Outcomes," Institute for Policy Research, Northwestern University, Working Paper Series, October 21, 2015; and J. D. Vance, *Hillbilly Elegy: Memoir of a Family and Culture in Crisis* (New York: HarperCollins, 2017), 245.

25. Loveless, "Girls, Boys, and Reading"; "The Weaker Sex," *The Economist*, March 7, 2015; Jesse Singal, "That Men's Book Clubs Article Mostly Just Made Me Sad," *New York Magazine*, May 5, 2016; Richard Hofstadter, *Anti-Intellectualism in American Life* (New York: Alfred A. Knopf, 1963); and Kenneth Olmstead, Amy Mitchell, and Tom Rosenstiel, "Navigating News Online," Pew Research Center, May 9, 2011.

26. "Women Make up Majority of U.S. Law Students for the First Time," *New York Times*, December 16, 2016; Valentina Zarya, "Why Women in Their Early 20s Are Out-Earning Men," *Fortune*, April 12, 2016; "Workplace Salaries: At Last, Women on Top," *Time*, September 1, 2010; and Carbone and Cahn, *Marriage Markets*, 68. Like the "gender wage gap" statistic often cited by those on the left, this stat, largely put forth by conservatives, is misleading because both compare earnings of all workers without taking into account occupational differences. Carbone and Cahn report that under-30 women in New York City have median incomes that are 117 percent those of under-30 men, although this is skewed by notably higher incomes among African American and Latina women relative to men. Young women in places like Manhattan

and Washington, D.C., more broadly may be earning more because there are more college-educated women than men in these cities. However, when men and women reach their early to mid-30s, a time when these better-educated women are having children, men are paid more than women overall and within occupations. The issue of declining male public engagement is addressed in chapter 10.

27. "'Materialism Decides Your Machismo': Bono on Male Gender Norms," *Daily Mail*, November 1, 2016.

28. Eileen Patten and Kim Parker, "A Gender Reversal on Career Aspirations," Pew Research Center, April 19, 2012; and "Men Adrift," *The Economist*, May 30, 2015.

29. Eloise Salholz, "The Marriage Crunch," *Newsweek*, June 2, 1986; and "See the Ratio of Single Men to Women Where You Live," *Time* Labs, August 24, 2015.

30. Lauren Martin, "Real Men vs. New York Men: 13 Reasons New York Women Can't Find Love," *Elite Daily*, October 22, 2014; "8 Signs That Your Boyfriend Is Actually Trash," *Gurl*, May 15, 2017; and StraightWhiteBoysTexting.org.

31. Lisa Jones, "The Top 20 Traits Women Want in a Man," *Men's Health*, March 31, 2015; Deborah Tannen, *You Just Don't Understand: Men and Women in Conversation* (New York: HarperCollins, 1990); and Andrew P. Smiler, presentation at the American Psychological Association, Washington, D.C., August 5, 2017.

32. Olga Khazan, "Why College Students Need a Class in Dating," *The Atlantic*, July 2, 2014; and Justin Garcia, Chris Reiber, Sean G. Massey, and Ann M. Merriwether, "Sexual Hookup Culture: A Review," *Review of General Psychology* 16, no. 2 (2012): 161–76.

33. e-Harmony, "Why Successful Women Can't Find a Great Man," n.d.

34. Wendy Wang and Kim Parker, "Record Share of Americans Have Never Married," Pew Research Center, September 24, 2014; Wendy Wang and Kim Parker, "Never-Married Young Adults on the Marriage Market," Pew Research Center, September 24, 2014; Wendy Wang, "The Best and Worst Cities for Women Looking to Marry," Pew Research Center, October 2, 2014; and Susan Patton, "Letter to the Editor: Advice for the Young Women of Princeton: The Daughters I Never Had," *The Princetonian*, March 28, 2013.

35. Linsey Davis and Hana Karar, "Single, Black, and Female—and Plenty of Company," ABC News, December 22, 2009; Carbone and Cahn, *Marriage Markets*, 71; and Robin M. Boylorn, "Black, Single, and Waiting," *Slate*, May 21, 2017.

36. Maureen Dowd, *Are Men Necessary? When Sexes Collide* (New York: Berkley Publishing Group, 2006).

37. Match.com, "Online Dating by the Numbers," July 16, 2017; and James Tozer, "What the Numbers Say: Online Dating," *The Economist 1843*, June/July 2017.

38. Ad for Tinder app on iTunes store; Lea Rose Emery, "Here's How Many Women vs. Men Use Tinder," *Bustle*, April 12, 2016; Eve Livingston, "It May Be Shallow and Salacious, but Don't Blame Tinder for Online Misogyny," *The Guardian*, April 8, 2016; and Abigail Beall, "Why Tinder Is Making Women Miserable: Men Swipe Right for an Ego Boost with No Intention of Speaking to Matches," *Daily Mail*, July 27, 2016.

39. Shani Silver, "Tinder Is a Modern Day Whorehouse. I Said It," *Bullshitist*, February 14, 2017; and Sales, "Tinder and the Dawn."

40. NPR, "Hookup Culture: The Unspoken Rules of Sex on College Campuses," February 14, 2017; and Lisa Wade, *American Hookup: The New Culture of Sex on Campus* (New York: W. W. Norton, 2017).

41. Garcia and others, "Sexual Hook-Up Culture"; Isabel Sawhill, *Generation Unbound: Drifting into Sex and Parenthood without Marriage* (Brookings Institution Press, 2014), 23–24.

42. Rosin, *The End of Men*, 21–22, 45; Sawhill, *Generation Unbound*, 24.

43. Garcia and others, "Sexual Hook-Up Culture"; Sales, "Tinder and the Dawn"; and Amber Lapp, "Transforming Hookup Culture: A Review of *American Hookup* by Lisa Wade," *Family Studies*, February 15, 2017.

44. In a letter to *Time* magazine published in its September 16, 2000, issue, Steinem credited Australian feminist Irina Dunn with coining the phrase. "The Phrase Finder"; Cathy Young, "Feminists Treat Men Badly. It's Bad for Feminism," *Washington Post*, June 30, 2016; and Lauren Oyler, "Men Are Creepy, New Study Confirms," *Broadly*, April 11, 2016.

45. Kathleen Geier, "The New Misogyny," *Washington Monthly*, March 11, 2012; Southern Poverty Law Center, "Misogyny: The Sites," *The Intelligence Report*, Spring 2012; and Gina Bellafante, "Misogyny Is Back; Did It Ever Go Away?," *New York Times*, October 14, 2016.

46. "Three Cheers for 'Misogyny,'" *The Economist*, August 21, 2015; and Peter Beinart, "Fear of a Female President," *The Atlantic*, October 2016.

47. Camile Sardina, "This Is What Happens When Men Act Like 'Pick-Up Artists' on Dating Apps," *Teen Vogue*, March 12, 2016; Ronald Weitzer and Charis E. Kubrin, "Misogyny in Rap Music: A Content Analysis of Prevalence and Meanings," *Men and Masculinities* 12, no. 1 (2009); Catherine Taibi, "'Keep Calm and Rape' T-Shirt Maker Shutters after Harsh Backlash," *Huffington Post*, June 25, 2013; and Alice H. Wu, "Gender Stereotyping in Academia: Evidence from an Economics Job Market Rumors Forum," August 2017.

48. Josephine B. Yurcaba, "Misogyny Is Killing Women in the U.S., but Society Is Blaming It on Mental Illness," *Bustle*, July 26, 2015; and "Elliot Rodger's California Shooting Spree: Further Proof That Misogyny Kills," *The Guardian*, May 24, 2014; and "Incel," *Vox*, April 25, 2018.

49. "Statistics about Sexual Violence," National Sexual Violence Resource Center, 2015; "Scope of the Problem: Statistics," Rape, Abuse & Incest National Network (RAINN); interview with Chuck Derry, Gender Violence Institute, March 24, 2017; David A. Fahrenthold, "Statistics Show Drop in U.S. Rape Cases," *Washington Post*, June 19, 2006; Kevin Drum, "Rape Is Way Down over the Past Two Decades—but So Is All Violent Crime," *Mother Jones*, December 18, 2014; "US: Soaring Rates of Rape and Violence against Women," Human Rights Watch, December 18, 2008; and Joseph Shapiro, "Campus Rape Reports Are Up, and Assaults Aren't the Only Reason," NPR, April 30, 2014.

50. "Sexual Violence," Centers for Disease Control and Prevention, 2012.

51. T. Rees Shapiro, "College Men Use Anti-Bias Law to Fight Sex-Assault Findings," *Washington Post*, May 2, 2017; interview with Harry Crouch, president, National Coalition for Men, December 14, 2016; Sheila Coronel, Steve Coll, and Derek Kravitz, "'A Rape on Campus': What Went Wrong," *Rolling Stone*, April 5, 2015; Sydney Ember, "Rolling Stone to Pay $1.65 Million to Fraternity over Discredited Rape Story," *New York Times*, June 13, 2017; *Community of the Wrongly Accused*; Emma Brown, "DeVos: Obama-Era Sexual Assault Policy Unfair," *Washington Post*, July 14, 2017; and Erica L. Green and Sheryl Gay Stolberg, "Campus Rape Policies Get a New Look as the Accused Get DeVos's Ear," *New York Times*, July 12, 2017.

52. Joseph H. Pleck, *The Myth of Masculinity* (Boston: MIT Press, 1981); and Robert Bly, *Iron John: A Book about Men* (New York: Addison-Wesley, 1990), 146, 55.

53. Interview with David Blankenhorn, January 4, 2017; interview with Joe Cordell, December 15 and 19, 2016; Institute for American Values, "Fatherless America," June 1, 1993; David Blankenhorn, *Fatherless America: Confronting Our Most Urgent Social Problem* (New York: Basic Books, 1995); David Blankenhorn, Wade Horn, and Mitch Pearlstein, eds., *The Fatherhood Movement: A Call to Action* (Lanham, Md.: Lexington Books, 1999); Michael A. Fletcher, "The Million Man March: Its Effect May Be Debatable. Its Significance Is Not," *Washington Post*, October 9, 2015; and Promise Keepers, "About."

54. Warren Farrell, *The Liberated Man* (1974) and *The Myth of Male Power* (2001); MGTOW, "The Manosphere"; interview with Warren Farrell, January 10, 2017; and Marilyn Webb, "The Joys and Sorrows of Joint Custody," *New York Magazine*, November 5, 1984, 38–45.

55. "Obama Speaks on Importance of Fatherhood," *USA Today*, February 17, 2013; and National Fatherhood Initiative. This issue is discussed in greater detail in chapter 7.

56. Interview with Harry Crouch, December 14, 2016; National Coalition for Men, "Issues"; and interview with J. Steven Svoboda, attorney for Rights of the Child, December 28, 2016.

57. Rebecca Cohen, "Welcome to the Manosphere: A Brief Guide to the Controversial Men's Rights Movement," *Mother Jones*, January/February 2015; and H. C., "What Is the Manosphere?," *The Economist*, July 5, 2016,

58. Stephen Marche, "Swallowing the Red Pill: A Journey to the Heart of Modern Misogyny," *The Guardian*, April 14, 2016; "The Red Pill"; and *The Red Pill: A Feminist's Journey into the Men's Rights Movement*.

59. Men Going Their Own Way (MGTOW.com, www.facebook.com/MenGoing TheirOwnWay/).

60. Interview with Rob Okun, MenEngage and *Voice Male*, March 23, 2017; and Society for the Psychological Study of Men and Masculinity.

61. Michael S. Kimmel and Michael A. Mess ed., *Men's Lives*, 7th ed. (Boston: Pearson, 2007); Promundo, "Manhood 2.0: Breaking Up with Stereotypes and Encouraging Relationships Based on Consent, Respect, and Equality in the United

States," August 23, 2016; interview with Gary Barker, president and CEO, Promundo-US, March 2, 2017; Hewitt interview, July 14, 2017; and Society for the Psychological Study of Men and Masculinity.

62. Interview with Julie Vogtman, director of income support policy and senior counsel for the Family Economic Security Program, National Women's Law Center, February 7, 2017.

CHAPTER 4

1. U.S. Census Bureau, "Historical Marriage Tables: Table MS-2. Estimated Median Age at First Marriage, 1890 to Today," November 2017.

2. Richard Fry, "For First Time in Modern Era, Living with Parents Edges Out Other Living Arrangements for 18-to-34-Year-Olds," Pew Research Center, May 24, 2016; and Matthew Rousu, "Childless Women in Their Twenties Out-Earn Men. So?," *Forbes*, February 24, 2014.

3. Jonathan Vespa, "The Changing Economics and Demographics of Young Adulthood: 1975–2016," U.S. Census Bureau, April 2017; U.S. Department of Education, National Center for Education Statistics (NCES), *The Condition of Education 2017*, "Annual Earnings of Young Adults," 2017; Fry, "For First Time in Modern Era"; Richard Fry, "A Rising Share of Young Adults Live in Their Parents' Home," Pew Research Center, August 1, 2013; Pew Research Center, "Applicability of Generational Traits," Marketing Charts, September 2015; Roberto Stefan Foa and Yascha Mounk, "The Danger of Deconsolidation: The Democratic Disconnect," *Journal of Democracy* 27, no. 3 (July 2016); Pew Research Center, "Atheists," Religious Landscape Study 2017; Peter Beinart, "Breaking Faith," *The Atlantic*, April 2017; "New Low of 52% Extremely Proud to Be Americans," Gallup, July 1, 2016; Gina Kolata and Sarah Cohen, "Drug Overdoses Propel Rise in Mortality Rates of Young Whites," *New York Times*, January 16, 2016; and Anne Case and Angus Deaton, "Mortality and Morbidity in the 21st Century," Brookings Institution, March 23, 2017.

4. Brad Tuttle, "6 Insulting Terms for Adults Who Live with Their Parents," *Time*, April 23, 2014; and Kay Hymowitz, *Manning Up: How the Rise of Women Has Turned Men into Boys* (New York: Basic Books, 2011), 1–2.

5. "Hotel Mama: Bad Economy Has Young Europeans at Home," *Spiegel Online*, January 15, 2013; and Tomoyuki Hoshino, *Me: A Novel* (New York: Akashic Books, 2017).

6. In this chapter and book, all references to age groups, such as 18- to 34-year-olds, will be to people who were those ages around 2015. Similarly, all references to millennials will be to those born between about 1981 and 1996, whereas references to 18- to 34-year-olds will be identified by specific years in the mid-2010s when data were collected.

7. Richard Fry, "Millennials Projected to Overtake Baby Boomers as America's Largest Generation," Pew Research Center, March 1, 2018; U.S. Census Bureau, "Millennials Outnumber Baby Boomers and Are Far More Diverse, Census Bureau Reports," June 25, 2015; Eileen Patten and Richard Fry, "How Millennials Today Compare with Their Grandparents 50 Years Ago," Pew Research Center, March

19, 2015; Alex Williams, "Move over Millennials, Here Comes Generation Z," *New York Times*, September 18, 2015; Sparks and Honey, "Meet Generation Z: Forget Everything You Learned about Millennials," 2014; and Jean M. Twenge, *iGen: Why Today's Super-Connected Kids Are Growing Up Less Rebellious, More Tolerant, Less Happy—and Completely Unprepared for Adulthood* (New York: Atria, 2017), 6.

8. Only 24 percent of male and female 25- to 34-year-olds had achieved the first four milestones in 2016, compared to 45 percent in 1975; see U.S. Census Bureau, "Changing Economics."

9. Jeffrey Jensen Arnett, *Emerging Adulthood: The Winding Road from the Late Teens through the Twenties* (Oxford University Press, 2004); and Erik Erikson, *Childhood and Society* (New York: W. W. Norton, 1950) and *Identity and the Life Cycle* (New York: W. W. Norton, 1959).

10. Interview with Jean Twenge, December 19, 2016.

11. "Adulting," Urban Dictionary.

12. Gary Cross, *Men to Boys: The Making of Modern Immaturity* (Columbia University Press, 2008).

13. 1 Corinthians 13:11.

14. Andrew L. Yarrow, "Alpha Moms and Helicopter Parents," *San Francisco Chronicle*, June 11, 2006; Wendy Mogel, *Blessings of a B-Minus: Using Jewish Teachings to Raise Resilient Teenagers* (New York: Simon and Schuster, 2010); and Anna Almendrala, "5 Signs You Were Raised by Helicopter Parents, and What to Do about It," *Huffington Post*, September 30, 2015.

15. "Millennials Are Selfish and Entitled, and Helicopter Parents Are to Blame," *Time*, August 21, 2014; and "Blame Parents for Millennials' Laughable Fragility," *National Review*, May 14, 2016.

16. Greg Lukianoff and Jonathan Haidt, "The Coddling of the American Mind," *The Atlantic*, September 2015; "I Just Got My BA. Why Do I Feel So Blue?" *Washington Post*, August 8, 2017; and "Microaggressions: Power, Privilege, and Everyday Life," n.d.

17. Interview with Sergeant First Class Tifani Hightower, February 10, 2017.

18. National Center for Health Statistics, "Attention-Deficit Hyperactivity Disorder," *Health, United States, 2016, With Chartbook on Long-term Trends in Health* (Hyattsville, Md., 2017); and American Psychiatric Association, *Diagnostic and Statistical Manual-5* (New York: American Psychiatric Association, 2013), 461ff. The *Diagnostic and Statistical Manual* (DSM), the bible for therapists and health insurance companies, has updated what conditions are considered psychological disorders four times, most recently in 2013, with the *DSM-5*. Reflecting the culturally and historically specific nature of many mental health diagnoses, earlier editions of the *DSM* did not include these diagnostic categories. Girls are more likely to be diagnosed with depression.

19. David Autor and Melanie Wasserman, "Wayward Sons: The Emerging Gender Gaps in Labor Markets and Education," Third Way, March 2013.

20. A higher percentage of women than men had low incomes in 2016, although the percentage with incomes of less than $30,000 declined significantly for women

since 1975, in contrast to the significant increase among men. U.S. Census Bureau, "Changing Economics"; U.S. Census Bureau, "New Census Bureau Statistics Show How Young Adults Today Compare with Previous Generations in Neighborhoods Nationwide," December 4, 2014; Jim Tankersley, "American Dream Collapsing for Young Adults, Study Says, as Odds Plunge That Children Will Earn More Than Their Parents," *Washington Post*, December 8, 2016; Equality of Opportunity Project, December 2016; and "Changes in U.S. Family Finances from 2010 to 2013: Evidence from the Survey of Consumer Finances," *Federal Reserve Bulletin* 1000, no. 4, September 2014; Wendy Wang and Kim Parker, "Record Share of Americans Have Never Married," Pew Research Center, September 24, 2014; Economic Policy Institute, "Wage Stagnation in Nine Charts," January 6, 2015; and Patten and Fry, "How Millennials Today Compare."

21. Andrew Sum, Ishwar Khatiwada, Joseph McLaughlin, Sheila Palma, "No Country for Young Men," in *Young Disadvantaged Men: Fathers, Families, Poverty, and Policy*, ed. Timothy M. Smeeding, Irwin Garfinkel, and Ronald B. Mincy, special issue, *Annals of the American Academy of Political and Social Science* 635 (May 2011): 24–55.

22. NCES, Digest of Education Statistics, "Table 318.10, Degrees Conferred by Postsecondary Institutions, by Level of Degree and Sex of Student: Selected Years, 1869–70 through 2025–26"; Fry, "For First Time in Modern Era"; Ana Swanson, "Study Finds Young Men Are Playing Video Games Instead of Getting Jobs," *Chicago Tribune*, September 23, 2016; and Ana Swanson, "Why Amazing Video Games Could Be Causing a Big Problem for America," *Washington Post*, September 23, 2016.

23. Drew DeSilver, "Millions of Young People in the US and EU Are Neither Working Nor Learning," Pew Research Center, January 28, 2016; Martha Ross and Nicole P. Svajlenka, "Employment and Disconnection among Teens and Young Adults," Brookings Institution, May 24, 2016; and James M. Quane, William Julius Wilson, and Jackelyn Hwang, "Black Men and the Struggle for Work: Social and Economic Barriers Persist," *Education Next* 15, no. 2 (2015).

24. U.S. Census Bureau, "Changing Economics"; and Buck Wargo, "Why So Many Millennials Are Financially Supporting Their Parents," *Huffington Post*, August 24, 2015.

25. Minda Zetlin, "63 Percent of Millennials Have More Than $100,000 in Student Debt. They'll Be Paying for Decades," *Inc.*, January 11, 2017; "A Look at the Shocking Student Loan Debt Statistics for 2017," *Student Loan Hero*, May 17, 2017; U.S. Census Bureau, "Changing Economics"; and Federal Reserve Bank of St. Louis, "Why Are More Young Adults Still Living at Home?," October 26, 2015.

26. U.S. Census Bureau, "Changing Economics"; Fry, "For First Time in Modern Era"; Fry, "Rising Share"; Jim Puzzanghera, "The U.S. Labor Force's Guy Problem: Lots of Men Don't Have a Job and Aren't Looking for One," *Los Angeles Times*, November 21, 2016; Swanson, "Study Finds Young Men Are Playing Video Games"; Paula Lavigne, "Roommates: It's a Guy Thing," *Dallas Morning News*, January 9, 2004; and Belinda Luscombe and Chris Wilson, "This State Has the Most Millennials Living with Their Parents," *Time*, September 15, 2016.

27. U.S. Census Bureau, "Changing Economics"; Fry, "Rising Share"; Bureau of Labor Statistics, "America's Young Adults at 29: Labor Market Activity, Education, and Partner Status: Results from a Longitudinal Survey," April 8, 2016; U.S. Census Bureau, "How Young Adults Today Compare"; Dan Kadlec, "How to Avoid Paying for Your Kids Forever," *Money*, September 10, 2014; and Child Care Aware of America, "Checking In: A Snapshot of the Child Care Landscape: 2017 Report."

28. Wargo, "Why So Many Millennials Are Financially Supporting Their Parents."

29. Samuel D. James, "America's Lost Boys," *First Things*, August 2, 2016.

30. Eastern and southern European countries have even higher rates of young adults living with parents than the United States.

31. Swanson, "Why Amazing Video Games"; James, "America's Lost Boys"; and Quentin Fottrell, "Women Leave Nest, Men Stay with Parents," *Market Watch*, August 5, 2013.

32. Justin Worland, "2 in 5 Young Americans Don't Want a Job," *Time*, November 14, 2014.

33. Binyamin Appelbaum, "The Vanishing Male Worker: How America Fell Behind," *New York Times*, December 11, 2014; and interview with Jean M. Twenge, December 19, 2016.

34. Jerry Nelson, "Helicopter Parents Share the Blame for Millennials' Alcoholism," *Medium*, July 21, 2016; and Lydia Saad, "In U.S., 38 Percent Have Tried Marijuana, Little Changed since '80s," Gallup, August 2, 2013.

35. Heather Krause, "Guess Who Cares for Young Adults When They Move Back Home," *FiveThirtyEight*, May 5, 2014; Casey Dowd, "The Price You Pay When Adult Children Move Back Home," *Fox Business News*, August 20, 2015; Kadlec, "How to Avoid Paying"; and Mary W. Quigley, "How to Handle Return of Boomerang Kids," AARP, May 13, 2016.

36. Interview with Irene Caniano, December 28, 2106.

37. Fry, "For First Time in Modern Era"; and Mark Mather, "In U.S., a Sharp Increase in Young Men Living at Home," Population Reference Bureau, September 2011.

38. Frederick Marx, "The Sensitive but Angry Man," Good Men Project, April 7, 2012; and interview with Frederick Marx, March 13, 2017.

39. Ernst & Young, "EY Studies Race, Gender and Exclusion: The Top Takeaways," October 6, 2017.

40. American Psychological Association, "2015 Stress in America."

41. Rahiel Tesfamariam, "Breaking Hip-Hop's Silence: Kid Cudi Speaks on Mental Health," *Washington Post*, January 17, 2013.

42. American Foundation for Prevention of Suicide, "Suicide Statistics," 2016.

43. Raven Molloy, Christopher Smith, and Abigail Wozniak, "Reconciling the Decline in Job Changing with Trends in Employment Tenure," and Henry Farber, "Labor Unions and the Decline in Long Term Employment Relationships in the United States," American Economic Association conference, Philadelphia, January 6, 2018; MetLife, "Work Redefined: A New Age of Benefits," 2017; "The 2016 Deloitte Millennial Survey," Deloitte, 2016; American Management Association, "Survey

Finds Employees Less Loyal Than Five Years Ago," January 6, 2015; and Knowl-edge@Wharton, "Declining Employee Loyalty: A Casualty of the New Workplace," May 9, 2012.

44. "2016 Deloitte Millennial Survey"; Brandon Rigoni and Amy Adkins, Gallup, "What Millennials Want from a New Job," *Harvard Business Review,* May 11, 2016; and Eileen Patten and Kim Parker, "A Gender Reversal on Career Aspirations," Pew Research Center, April 19, 2012.

45. Sean Bisceglia, "Outside Opinion: Millennials Frustrate HR Execs," *Chicago Tribune,* September 5, 2014.

46. Interview with Colonel Patrick R. Michaelis, February 2, 2017.

47. Interview with Master Sergeant Jeffrey A. Klimek, March 2, 2017.

48. Janet Al-Saad, "What Employers Really Think of Millennials," *The Street,* June 18, 2014.

49. Pew Research Center, "Applicability of Generational Traits."

50. U.S. Census Bureau, "Changing Economics"; Beth Brophy, "Millennials Slower Than Boomers to Reach Milestones," AARP, April 21, 2017; Fry, "For First Time in Modern Era"; Gillian B. White, "The Institution of Marriage: Still Going Strong," *The Atlantic,* June 16, 2015; U.S. Census Bureau, "Historical Marriage Status Tables," November 2017; Wendy Wang, "The Link between a College Education and a Lasting Marriage," Pew Research Center, December 4, 2015; and Wang and Parker, "Record Share of Americans."

51. Zetlin, "63 Percent of Millennials"; and interview with Ron Haskins, November 16, 2016.

52. Robert Lerman and W. Bradford Wilcox, "For Richer, For Poorer: How Family Structures Economic Success in America," American Enterprise Institute and Institute for Family Studies, 2014; Robert Rector, "Marriage: America's Greatest Weapon against Child Poverty," Heritage Foundation, September 16, 2010; Andrew L. Yarrow, "Falling Marriage Rates Reveal Economic Fault Lines," *New York Times,* February 6, 2015; and Pew Research Center, "Applicability of Generational Traits."

53. Interview with June Carbone and Naomi Cahn, April 5, 2017.

54. U.S. Census Bureau, "Changing Economics"; Ariel Kuperberg, "Does Premarital Cohabitation Raise Your Risk of Divorce?," Council on Contemporary Families, March 20, 2014; and June Carbone and Naomi Cahn, "Nonmarriage," *Maryland Law Review* 76 (2016): 55.

55. June Carbone and Naomi Cain, *Marriage Markets: How Inequality Is Remaking the American Family* (Oxford University Press, 2014), 73.

56. W. Bradford Wilcox and Wendy Wang, "The Millennial Success Sequence: Marriage, Kids, and the 'Success Sequence' among Young Adults," American Enterprise Institute and Institute for Family Studies, June 14, 2017; and Patten and Fry, "How Millennials Today Compare."

57. Robert Putnam, *Our Kids: The American Dream in Crisis* (New York: Simon and Schuster, 2015), 67; and Isabel Sawhill, *Generation Unbound: Drifting into Sex and Marriage without Parenthood* (Brookings Institution Press, 2014), 19–20, 71–72.

58. Interview with Isabel Sawhill, December 5, 2016.

59. Interview with Theresa Apple, April 28, 2017.

60. Twenge, *iGen*, 20, 290.

CHAPTER 5

1. This chapter's opening epigraph is from "Tim Berners-Lee on the Future of the Web: 'The System Is Failing,'" *The Guardian*, November 15, 2017. Caitlin Dewey, "A Surprising Map of Where Men Outnumber Women Online—and Where They Don't," *Washington Post*, May 20, 2014; and Jim Puzzanghera, "The U.S. Labor Force's Guy Problem: Lots of Men Don't Have a Job and Aren't Looking for One," *Los Angeles Times*, November 21, 2016.

2. Entertainment Software Association, "2015 Sales, Demographic, and Usage Data: Essential Facts about the Computer and Video Game Industry."

3. Nielsen, "The Digital Age: Young Adults Gravitate toward Digital Devices," October 10, 2016; "Limiting Screen Time Improves Sleep, Academics, and Behavior, ISU Study Finds," Iowa State University News Service, March 31, 2014; Nielsen, "2016 Social Media Report"; Jean M. Twenge, "Have Smartphones Destroyed a Generation?," *The Atlantic*, September 2017; interview with Jean M. Twenge, December 19, 2016; Nielsen, "The Men, the Myths, the Legends: Why Millennial 'Dudes' Might Be More Receptive to Marketing Than We Thought," December 20, 2014; Nielsen, "Facts of Life: As They Move through Life Stages, Millennials' Media Habits Are Different and Distinct," March 24, 2016; and Erik Hurst, "Video Killed the Radio Star," *Chicago Booth Review*, September 1, 2016.

4. Maeve Duggan, "Gaming and Gamers," Pew Research Center, December 15, 2015.

5. "What Is the True Definition of a Toxic Player?," League of Legends discussion, Reddit, 2015.

6. Interview with Command Sergeant Major Michael Gragg, January 7, 2017.

7. Interview with Kimberly Young, December 13, 2016; and George Will, "How to Restore American Self-Reliance," *Washington Post*, May 28, 2017.

8. On-Line Gamers Anonymous, "OLGA Reflections: Our Best Lives Now," November 11, 2013.

9. Duggan, "Gaming and Gamers"; and Entertainment Software Association, "2016 Sales, Demographic, and Usage Data."

10. Mark Aguiar, Mark Bils, Kerwin Charles, and Erik Hurst, "Leisure Luxuries and the Labor Supply of Young Men," September 15, 2016; Samuel D. James, "America's Lost Boys," *First Things*, August 2, 2016; Derek Thompson, "What Are Young, Nonworking Men Doing?," *The Atlantic*, July 25, 2016; Ana Swanson, "Study Finds Young Men Are Playing Video Games Instead of Getting Jobs," *Chicago Tribune*, September 23, 2016; Puzzanghera, "U.S. Labor Force's Guy Problem"; and Ana Swanson, "Why Amazing Video Games Could Be Causing a Big Problem for America," *Washington Post*, September 23, 2016.

11. Michael Castleman, "Dueling Statistics: How Much of the Internet Is Porn?," *Psychology Today*, November 3, 2016; "Porn Sites Get More Visitors Each Month

Than Netflix, Amazon, and Twitter Combined," *Huffington Post*, May 4, 2013; and Covenant Eyes, "Pornography Statistics: 2015 Report."

12. Jason S. Carroll, Dean M. Busby, Brian J. Willoughby, and Cameron Brown, "The Porn Gap: Gender Differences in Men's and Women's Pornography Patterns in Couple Relationships," *Journal of Couple & Relationship Therapy* 16, no. 2 (2017).

13. Jonathan Merritt, "Pornography: A Christian Crisis or Overblown Issue?," Religion News Service, January 20, 2016.

14. Kirstein Weir, "Is Pornography Addictive?," *APA Monitor on Psychology* 45, no. 4 (2014); Mike Wendling, "Is 'Porn Addiction' a Real Thing?," BBC, February 29, 2016; Kevin B. Skinner, "Is Pornography (Sexual) Addiction Real?," *Psychology Today*, November 3, 2014; Gina Bellafonte, "Misogyny Is Back: Did It Ever Go Away?," *New York Times*, October 14, 2016; William Struthers, *Wired for Intimacy: How Pornography Hijacks the Male Brain* (Downer's Grove, Ill.: Intervarsity Press, 2009); Camila Domonoske, "Utah Declares Porn a Public Health Hazard," NPR, April 20, 2016; and NoFap, "Get a New Grip on Life."

15. "The New Scarlet Letter," *Time*, July 10–17, 2017; Soraya Chemaly, "There's No Comparing Male and Female Harassment Online," *Time*, September 9, 2014; Charlotte Alter, "'It's Like Having an Incurable Disease': Inside the Fight against Revenge Porn," *Time*, June 13, 2017; Hayley Tsukayama, "Facebook to Crack Down on 'Revenge Porn' Images," *Washington Post*, April 6, 2017; Sarah Horner, "Anoka Man Charged under New 'Revenge Porn' Law for Posting Nudes of Ex, Charges Say," *Twin Cities Pioneer Press*, February 28, 2017; Jake Russell, "Details Emerge on Superintendent's Firing," *Morris Herald-News*, June 6, 2012; Erica Goode, "Victims Push Laws to End Online Revenge Posts," *New York Times*, September 23, 2013; and "Rob Kardashian and Blac Chyna Reality Show Not on E! Schedule, Network Says," *Variety*, July 8, 2017.

16. National Network to End Domestic Violence, "Safety Net Project," n.d.; and interview with Chuck Derry, April 5, 2017.

17. United Nations, "Global Report on Trafficking in Persons 2012," December 2012; and Chemaly, "There's No Comparing."

18. Interview with Kimberly Young, December 13, 2016.

19. Ian Kerner, "Too Much Internet Porn: The SADD Effect," *Ask Men*, December 16, 2010.

20. Dennis Thompson, "Study Sees Link between Porn and Sexual Dysfunction," *Web MD*, May 12, 2017; B. Y. Park, G. Wilson, J. Berger, M. Christman, B. Reina, F. Bishop, W. P. Klam, and A. P. Doan, "Is Internet Pornography Causing Sexual Dysfunctions? A Review with Clinical Reports," *Behavioral Sciences* 6, no. 3 (2016); Philip G. Zimbardo and Nikita Duncan, "'The Demise of Guys': How Video Games and Porn Are Ruining a Generation," CNN, May 24, 2012; Kerner, "Too Much Internet Porn"; Michael Castleman, "The Real Problem with Porn: It's Bad for Sex," *Psychology Today*, August 1, 2012; Jill Hamilton, "Has Porn Ruined Our Sex Lives Forever?," *Dame*, February 26, 2014; and Maia Szalavitz, "Does Men's 'Bond' with Porn Ruin Them for Real-Life Sex?," *Time*, February 9, 2011. Older research suggests little change in the early 2000s; see B. W. Schouten, A. M. Bohnen, F .P. Groeneveld,

G. R. Dohle, and Thomas S. Bosch, "Erectile Dysfunction in the Community: Trends over Time in Incidence, Prevalence, GP Consultation, and Medication Use— The Krimpen Study: Trends in ED," *Journal of Sexual Medicine* 7 (2010): 2547–53.

21. Castleman, "Dueling Statistics."

22. Liftoff, "Mobile Dating 2015: User Acquisition Trends and Benchmarks," February 12, 2016.

23. David Kushner, "Scammer and Spammers: Inside Online Dating's Sex Bot Con Job," *Rolling Stone*, February 1, 2016.

24. Ryan Buxton, "AARP's Dating Expert Reveals the Differences between Older Men and Women Who Date Online," *Huffington Post*, January 9, 2015.

25. James, "America's Lost Boys."

26. Camile Sardina, "This Is What Happens When Men Act Like 'Pick-Up Artists,'" *Teen Vogue*, March 12, 2016.

27. Amanda Hess, "Why Women Aren't Welcome on the Internet," *Pacific Standard*, January 6, 2014; Caitlin Dewey, "The Only Guide to Gamergate You Will Need to Read," *Washington Post*, October 14, 2014; and "How the World Was Trolled," *The Economist*, November 4, 2017.

28. Jamie Bartlett, "Misogyny on Twitter," Demos, May 10, 2014; and Dean Schabner and Matt Negrin, "Rush Limbaugh Apologizes for Calling Sandra Fluke a 'Slut,'" ABC News, March 3, 2012.

29. Leora Tanenbaum, "The Truth about Slut-Shaming," *Huffington Post*, June 15, 2015; and Bartlett, "Misogyny on Twitter."

30. Chris Cillizza, "Kellyanne Conway Offers Alternative Fact to Explain Why Trump Isn't Lying," CNN Politics, July 24, 2017; and *Daniel Patrick Moynihan: A Portrait in Letters of an American Visionary*, ed. Steven R. Weisman (New York: Public Affairs, 2010).

31. "About Andrew Anglin," Southern Poverty Law Center, n.d.

32. Ibid.; Angela Nagle, "Brotherhood of Losers," *The Atlantic*, December 2017; and Ron Nixon and Eileen Sullivan, "U.S. Rescinded Grant to Combat Extremism of Right-Wing Groups," *New York Times*, August 16, 2017.

33. Ian Sherr, "How to Scrub Hate Off Facebook, Twitter, and the Internet," CNET, November 27, 2017; Maeve Duggan, "Men, Women Experience and View Online Harassment Differently," Pew Research Center, July 14, 2017; and CNN/ORC International Poll, September 13, 2015.

34. Ed Leefeldt, "Hacker's Paradise: Secrets of the Dark Web," CBS News, May 17, 2017; Gabriel Weimann, "Terrorist Migration to the Dark Web," *Perspectives on Terrorism* 10, no. 3 (2016); and Max Berger, "How to Understand the Roots of White Male Terrorism," *The Nation*, November 30, 2015; Erin Calabrese and Elisha Fieldstadt, "Charleston Church Shooter Dylann Roof Was Loner Caught in 'Internet Evil': Family," *NBC News*, June 20, 2105; and N. R. Kleinfield, Ray Rivera, and Serge F. Kovaleski, "Newtown Killer's Obsessions, in Chilling Detail," *New York Times*, March 28, 2013.

35. Veronica Jarski, "How Women and Men Use Social Media and Mobile," *Marketing Profs*, June 10, 2014.

36. Catey Hill, "Millennials Engage with Their Smartphones More Than They Do Actual Humans," *MarketWatch*, June 21, 2016; and Jean M. Twenge, *iGen: Why Today's Super-Connected Kids Are Growing Up Less Rebellious, More Tolerant, Less Happy—and Completely Unprepared for Adulthood—and What That Means for the Rest of Us* (New York: Simon and Schuster, 2017), 2, 4–5.

37. Yolanda (Linda) Reid Chassiakos, Jenny Radesky, Dimitri Christakis, Megan A. Moreno, and Corinn Cross, "Children and Adolescents and Digital Media," American Academy of Pediatrics, October 2016; and Ravin Jesuthasan and Anne-Marie Jentsch, "How Does Digital Media Really Affect Us?," World Economic Forum, January 28, 2016.

38. New York Behavioral Health, "The Impact of Social Media Use on Social Skills," n.d.; and Andrew L. Yarrow, "In Public, We're All Preoccupied with Ourselves," *San Francisco Chronicle*, April 13, 2016.

39. Sean Bisceglia, "Outside Opinion: Millennials Frustrate HR Execs," *Chicago Tribune*, September 5, 2014; and On-Line Gamers Anonymous, "OLGA Reflections."

40. Twenge, "Has the Smartphone Destroyed a Generation?," and *iGen*, 5.

41. Maura Keller, "Social Media and Interpersonal Communication, *Social Work Today* 13, no. 3 (2013).

42. Aaron Smith, "U.S. Smartphone Use in 2015," Pew Research Center, April 1, 2015.

CHAPTER 6

1. Interview with Steven F. Hipple, U.S. Department of Labor, Bureau of Labor Statistics (BLS), December 8, 2016.

2. Public Health Service, U.S. Department of Health, Education, and Welfare (HEW), "100 Years of Marriage and Divorce Statistics, 1867–1967," 1973.

3. Robert S. Lynd and Helen Merrell Lynd, *Middletown: A Study in American Culture* (New York: Harcourt Brace, 1929), 110, 116.

4. U.S. Census Bureau, "America's Families and Living Arrangements: 2016: Adults (A table series)"; U.S. Census Bureau, "Families and Living Arrangements"; HEW, "100 Years of Marriage and Divorce Statistics"; and Wendy Wang and Kim Parker, "Record Share of Americans Have Never Married," Pew Research Center, September 24, 2014.

5. *Obergefell v. Hodges*, quoted in "Supreme Court Orders States to Recognize Same-Sex Marriage," *Time*, June 26, 2015.

6. Brigid Schulte, "Survey: Majority of Men Want Flexible Work," *Washington Post*, October 21, 2014; U.S. Census Bureau, "Facts for Features: Father's Day: June 18, 2017"; Gretchen Livingston, "Growing Number of Dads Home with the Kids," Pew Research Center, June 5, 2014; Kim Parker and Gretchen Livingston, "Six Facts about American Fathers," Pew Research Center, June 16, 2016.

7. Livingston, "Growing Number"; Parker and Livingston, "Six Facts"; U.S. Census Bureau, "Fathers' Day 2017: June 18, 2017"; Steven F. Hipple, "People Who Are Not in the Labor Force: Why Aren't They Working?," *Beyond the Numbers* 4, no. 15, BLS, December 2015; and interview with Rose Woods, BLS, December 2, 2016.

8. Interview with Katharine Gallagher Robbins, January 12, 2017; and Schulte, "Survey: Majority of Men."

9. Isabel Sawhill, *Generation Unbound: Drifting into Sex and Marriage without Parenthood* (Brookings Institution Press, 2014), 48; Robert D. Putnam, *Our Kids: The American Dream in Crisis* (New York: Simon and Schuster, 2015), 73–74; Mona Chalabi, "How Many Women Earn More Than Their Husbands?," *FiveThirtyEight*, February 5, 2015; and Amanda MacMillan, "Women Thrive as the Primary Breadwinner While Men Suffer, Study Finds," *Fox News*, August 25, 2016.

10. U.S. Census Bureau, "Unmarried and Single Americans Week: Sept. 17–23, 2017," *Facts for Features*, August 14, 2017.

11. Centers for Disease Control and Prevention (CDC), National Vital Statistics System, Vital Statistics Rapid Release, Report no. 002, "Births: Provisional Data for 2016," June 2017; interview with David Autor, MIT, July 6, 2017; Sawhill, *Generation Unbound*, 58; and Thomas Edsall, "The Increasing Significance of the Decline of Men," *New York Times*, March 16, 2017.

12. Sawhill, *Generation Unbound*, 145.

13. Larry M. Bartels, Ron Haskins, and Isabel V. Sawhill, "The Decline of the American Family: Can Anything Be Done to Stop the Damage?," *Annals of the American Academy of Political and Social Science* 667, no. 1 (2016): 8–34; Wang and Parker, "Record Share"; Child Trends, "Births to Unmarried Women," 2014; Andrew L. Yarrow, "Falling Marriage Rates Reveal Economic Fault Lines," *New York Times*, February 6, 2015; Derek Thompson, "How America's Marriage Crisis Makes Income Inequality So Much Worse," *The Atlantic*, October 1, 2013; and Sean McElwee and Marshall I. Steinbaum, "No, the Decline in Marriage Did Not Increase Inequality," *New Republic*, January 16, 2015.

14. Richard V. Reeves, "The Dangerous Separation of the American Upper Middle Class," Brookings Institution, September 3, 2015; Yarrow, "Falling Marriage Rates"; interview with Ron Haskins, November 16, 2016; Sawhill, *Generation Unbound*, 5; and William Emmons and Lowell Ricketts, "The Link between Family Structure and Wealth Is Weaker Than You Might Think," Federal Reserve Bank of St. Louis, *On the Economy*, May 9, 2017.

15. U.S. Census Bureau, "New Census Bureau Statistics Show How Young Adults Today Compare with Previous Generations in Neighborhoods Nationwide," December 4, 2014; U.S. Census Bureau, "America's Families and Living Arrangements: 2016: Adults (A table series)"; and Barry Schwartz, *The Paradox of Choice: Why More Is Less* (New York: HarperCollins, 2004).

16. Brigid Schulte, "Till Death Do Us Part? No Way: Gray Divorce on the Rise," *Washington Post*, October 8, 2014; Gretchen Livingston, "Four-in-Ten Couples Are Saying 'I Do,' Again," Pew Research Center, November 14, 2014; and Marcia Carlson and Katherine Magnuson, "Low-Income Fathers' Influence on Children," in *Young Disadvantaged Men: Fathers, Families, Poverty, and Policy*, ed. Timothy M. Smeeding, Irwin Garfinkel, and Ronald B. Mincy, special issue, *Annals of the American Academy of Political and Social Science* 635 (May 2011): 108.

17. U.S. Census Bureau, "America's Families and Living Arrangements: 2016"; Renee Stepler, "Number of U.S. Adults Cohabiting with a Partner Continues to Rise, Especially among Those 50 and Older," Pew Research Center, April 6, 2017; William E. Gibson, "Far More 50+ Couples Shacking Up," AARP, May 8, 2017; Charles Q. Strohm, Judith A. Seltzer, Susan D. Cochran, and Vickie M. Mays, "'Living Apart Together' Relationships in the United States," *Demographic Research*, August 13, 2009; and University of Missouri Health, "Older Adults Embracing 'Living Apart Together,'" *Science Daily*, February 9, 2017.

18. U.S. Census Bureau, "The Changing Economics and Demographics of Young Adulthood: 1975–2016," April 2017.

19. June Carbone and Naomi Cahn, "Nonmarriage," George Washington University Law School Public Law Research Paper 2017-8, GWU Legal Studies Research Paper 2017-8, Minnesota Legal Studies Research Paper 17-08, March 4, 2017.

20. CDC, "Trends in Attitudes about Marriage, Childbearing, and Sexual Behavior: United States, 2002, 2006–2010, and 2011–2013," National Health Statistics Reports 92, March 17, 2016; W. Bradford Wilcox and Laurie DeRose, "Ties That Bind: Childrearing in the Age of Cohabitation," Institute for Family Studies, February 16, 2017; Putnam, *Our Kids*, 67; Stephen J. Blumberg, Anjel Vahratian, and Joseph H. Blumberg, "Marriage, Cohabitation, and Men's Use of Preventive Health Care Services," CDC, June 2014; June Carbone and Naomi Cahn, *Marriage Markets: How Inequality Is Remaking the American Family* (Oxford University Press, 2014), 79; Isabel Sawhill, "Beyond Marriage," *New York Times*, September 13, 2014; BLS, "America's Young Adults at 29: Labor Market Activity, Education and Partner Status: Results from a Longitudinal Survey," April 8, 2016; Frank F. Furstenberg Jr., "How Do Low-Income Men and Fathers Matter for Children and Family Life?," in Smeeding, Garfinkel, and Mincy, eds., *Young Disadvantaged Men*, 133; and History Cooperative, "The History of Divorce Law in the United States," n.d.

21. Interview with David Lapp, December 14, 2016; interview with Isabel Sawhill, December 5, 2016; interview with Naomi Cahn and June Carbone, April 6, 2017; Naomi Cahn and June Carbone, "New Research on Unmarried Mothers and Family Formation," Institute for Family Studies, April 6, 2017; Sawhill, *"Beyond Marriage"*; Jennifer S. Barber, Yasamin Kusunoki, and Heather Gatny, "Relationships Dynamics and Social Life Study," University of Michigan Population Studies Center; Kathryn Edin and Timothy J. Nelson, *Doing the Best I Can: Fatherhood in the Inner City* (University of California Press, 2013), 43.

22. Interviews with Brad Wilcox, December 7 and 9, 2016.

23. Sawhill, *Generation Unbound*, 62, 8, 104.

24. Interview with Isabel Sawhill, December 5, 2016.

25. Barbara Dafoe Whitehead, "Dan Quayle Was Right," *The Atlantic*, April 1993.

26. Interview with Lawrence Mead, November 14, 2016.

27. Nicola Twilley, "How T.G.I. Friday's Helped Invent the Singles Bar," *New Yorker*, July 2, 2015.

28. Christopher Lasch, *The Culture of Narcissism: American Life in an Age of Diminishing Expectations* (New York: W. W. Norton, 1979), 9.

29. Interview with Brad Wilcox, December 7, 2016.

30. Brad Wilcox, "Be a Man. Get Married," YouTube, May 2016.

31. Sara S. McLanahan, Irwin Garfinkel, and others, "Fragile Families and Child Wellbeing Study," Princeton University, 1998–2018 (ongoing); Nancy E. Reichman, Julien O. Teitler, Irwin Garfinkel, and Sara S. McLanahan, "Fragile Families: Sample and Design," *Children and Youth Services Review* 23, nos. 4/5 (2001); and Sarah W. Whitton, Galena K. Rhoades, Scott M. Stanley, and Howard J. Markman, "Effects of Parental Divorce on Marital Commitment and Confidence," *Journal of Family Psychology* 22, no. 5 (2008).

32. McLanahan, Garfinkel, and others, "Fragile Families"; U.S. Census Bureau, "Families and Living Arrangements"; Edin and Nelson, *Doing the Best I Can*, 17–18, 30–31; Mitch Pearlstein, *Broken Bonds: Why Family Fragmentation Matters* (Lanham, Md.: Rowman and Littlefield, 2014); Smeeding, Garfinkel, and Mincy, eds., introduction to *Young Disadvantaged Men*, 12; MenCare and Promundo, "State of the World's Fathers 2016," MenCare, 2016; Simon R. Crouch, Elizabeth Waters, Ruth McNair, Jennifer Power, and Elise Davis, "Parent-Reported Measures of Child Health and Wellbeing in Same-Sex Parent Families: A Cross-Sectional Survey," *BMC Public Health* 14 (June 2014); Guttmacher Institute, "Declines in Teen Pregnancy Risk Entirely Driven by Improved Contraceptive Use," August 30, 2016; Gretchen Livingston and Kim Parker, "A Tale of Two Fathers: Living Arrangements and Father Involvement," Pew Research Center, June 15, 2011; and interview with Kathryn Edin, February 6, 2017. Fewer than 20 percent of unmarried parents are not romantically involved at the time of the child's birth, the Fragile Families study found.

33. U.S. Census Bureau, "Multiple Partner Fertility Brief," March 2017. One in six women have had children with more than one man.

34. Interview with Ron Haskins, November 21, 2016.

35. Mary Meghan Ryan, ed., "Table 1-45: Employment Status of the Population, by Sex and Marital Status," March 1995–March 2016, *Handbook of U.S. Labor Statistics 2017* (Lanham, Md.: Bernan Press), 121; and Eleanor Krause and Isabel Sawhill, "What We Know and Don't Know about Declining Male Labor Force Participation: A Review," Brookings Institution, May 2017.

36. Krause and Sawhill, "What We Know."

37. Charles Murray, *Coming Apart: The State of White America, 1960–2010* (New York: Crown Forum, 2012), 182; interview with Melissa Boteach, Center for American Progress, January 12, 2017; Pearlstein, *Broken Bonds*, 5; and Shawn Fremstad and Melissa Boteach, "Valuing All Our Families," Center for American Progress, January 2015.

38. Interview with David Blankenhorn, January 4, 2017.

39. Matthew J. Breiding, Sharon G. Smith, Kathleen C. Basile, and others, "Prevalence and Characteristics of Sexual Violence, Stalking, and Intimate Partner Violence Victimization—National Intimate Partner and Sexual Violence Survey, United States, 2011," CDC, *Morbidity and Mortality Weekly Report, Surveillance Summaries* 63, no. 8 (2014), "Table 6. Lifetime and 12-Month Prevalence of Intimate Partner Violence Victimization, by Sex of Victim and Time Period"; interview with Chuck

Derry, Gender Violence Institute, April 5, 2017; and interview with Tom Grazio, The Tree House, August 7, 2017.

40. Robert N. Bellah, Richard Madsen, William M. Sullivan, and Steven M. Tipton, *Habits of the Heart: Individualism and Commitment in American Life* (University of California Press, 1985), 111; Murray A. Strauss, "Thirty Years of Denying the Evidence on Gender Symmetry in Partner Violence: Implications for Prevention and Treatment," *Partner Abuse* 1, no. 3 (2010); Christin L. Munsch, "Her Support, His Support: Money, Masculinity, and Marital Infidelity," *American Sociological Review* 80, no. 3 (2015); Caroletta Shuler, "Male Victims of Intimate Partner Violence in the United States: An Examination of the Review of Literature through the Critical Theoretical Perspective," *International Journal of Criminal Justice Sciences* 5, no. 1 (2010); Alison Bonaguro, "The #1 Reason Women Cheat," *Men's Health*, September 28, 2015; "Women More Likely Than Men to Initiate Divorces, but Not Non-Marital Breakups," *Science Daily*, August 22, 2015; and Lynd and Lynd, *Middletown*, 126.

41. BLS, "America's Young Adults at 29"; and National Center for Health Statistics, "Marriage, Cohabitation, and Men's Use of Preventive Health Care Services," NCHS Data Brief 154, June 2014.

42. It is noteworthy that even as interclass marriage has become less common, the number of interracial marriages has gone up. See Richard D. Kahlenberg, "Harvard's Class Gap," *Harvard Magazine*, May–June 2017.

43. BLS, "America's Young Adults at 29"; and Stephanie Coontz, "Marriage Suits Educated Women," *New York Times*, February 11, 2012.

44. Interview with Mark Kiselica, August 18, 2017.

45. See Guy Standing, *The Precariat: The New Dangerous Class* (London: Bloomsbury, 2011).

46. Interview with Joseph Cordell, December 15, 2016.

47. Interviews with Brad Wilcox, December 7 and 9, 2016.

48. Margaret Mead, Statement before the Subcommittee on Children and Youth, Committee on Labor and Public Welfare, U.S. Senate, in *Congressional Record* 119 (September 28, 1973), 31962.

CHAPTER 7

1. Jo Jones and William D. Mosher, "Fathers' Involvement with Their Children, 2006–2010," National Health Statistics Report 71, December 20, 2013; Gretchen Livingston, "Fewer Than Half of U.S. Kids Today Live in a 'Traditional' Family," Pew Research Center, December 22, 2014; Annie E. Casey Foundation, *2017 Kids Count Data Book*; and Lindsay M. Monte, "Multiple Partner Fertility Brief," U.S. Census Bureau, March 2017.

2. U.S. Census Bureau, "America's Families and Living Arrangements: 2017"; Monte, "Fertility Research Brief"; U.S. Census Bureau, "Facts for Features: Father's Day: June 18, 2017," June 8, 2017; Timothy Grall, "Custodial Mothers and Fathers and Their Child Support: 2013," U.S. Census Bureau, January 2016; interview with Lindsay Monte, U.S. Census Bureau, December 5, 2017; ChildStats.gov, "Family Structure and Children's Living Arrangements"; National Center for Fathering, "The

Extent of Fatherlessness"; Gretchen Livingston, "The Rise of Single Fathers," Pew Research Center, July 2, 2013; Annie E. Casey Foundation, *2017 Kids Count Data Book*; Karen Benjamin Guzzo and Krista K. Payne, "Living Arrangements of Fathers and Their Children," National Center for Family and Marriage Research, Bowling Green University, 2013; National Research Center on Hispanic Children and Families, "A Portrait of Latino Fathers: Strengths and Challenges," February 2017; and Linda Searing, "When Divorced Parents Share Custody, It's Better for Their Kids' Health," *Washington Post*, May 11, 2015.

Although the U.S. Census Bureau's Survey of Income and Program Participation collects fertility data for women and men, its Current Population Survey collects data on married, single, and custodial fathers (and mothers) living with minor children, and the Census and National Center for Health Statistics collect data on co-residential parents, there are a number of reasons why precise numbers of all fathers with biological or adoptive minor children and fathers not living with their children are impossible to determine. These include issues of defining "single parent" and "custody," fathers' reporting of fertility and involvement, cohabitation with partners with children from other unions, reporting on "co-residential" parents (whether step-children and other children are counted), and children who live with grandparents or no parents. More precise statistics on the numbers of nonresidential fathers who see their children frequently, once a week, or never are also impossible to ascertain, given the large numbers of unmarried fathers and the consequent widespread lack of formal custody agreements and the problems of self-reporting. Custody arrangements, especially for poor and working-class fathers but also middle-class and more well-to-do fathers, do not exactly mirror behavioral realities.

3. David Autor and Melanie Wasserman, "Wayward Sons: The Emerging Gender Gap in Labor Markets and Education," Third Way and NEXT, 2013.

4. History.com staff, "Father's Day," History.com, 2009.

5. Andrew J. Cherlin, *Marriage, Divorce, Remarriage* (Harvard University Press, 1981).

6. Elaine Tyler May, *Homeward Bound: American Families in the Cold War* (New York: Basic Books, 1988); Lawrence R. Samuel, *Fatherhood: A Cultural History* (Lanham, MD: Rowman and Littlefield, 2016), 20; Kyle A. Cuordileone, *Manhood and American Political Culture in the Cold War* (New York: Routledge, 2005), 154; David Blankenhorn, Wade Horn, and Mitch Pearlstein, eds., *The Fatherhood Movement: A Call to Action* (Lanham, MD: Lexington Books, 1999), 105ff; and Guy Garcia, *The Decline of Men* (New York: HarperCollins, 2008), 7.

7. Ross D. Parke and Armin A. Brott, *Throwaway Dads: The Myths and Barriers That Keep Men from Being the Fathers They Want to Be* (Boston: Houghton Mifflin, 1999), 87.

8. Kyle D. Pruett, *The Nurturing Father* (New York: Warner Books, 1987); Ross D. Parke, *Fatherhood* (Harvard University Press, 1996); Doyin Richards, "Five Ways Being a Good Dad Is Damn Sexy," *Huffington Post*, November 2, 2014; Emily Bobrow, "The Man Trap," *The Economist 1843*, June/July 2017; interviews with Dan Singley, MenExcel, June 28, 2017; Rob Okun, MenEngage Alliance, April 5,

2017; Gary Barker, Promundo, February 22, 2017; Katherine Gallagher Robbins and Melissa Boteach, January 12, 2017; and Sonia Molloy, September 5, 2017; and Debra G. Kilman and Rhiana Kohl, *Fatherhood U.S.A.* (New York: Garland Publishing, 1984), xix.

9. Daniel Patrick Moynihan, *The Negro Family: The Case for National Action*, U.S. Department of Labor, 1965; and Robert I. Lerman and Theodora J. Ooms, eds., *Young Unwed Fathers: Changing Roles and Emerging Policies* (Temple University Press, 1993).

10. Ronald Reagan, State of the Union Address, February 4, 1986; Barack Obama, speech, Chicago, June 15, 2008; Kathryn Edin and Timothy J. Nelson, *Doing the Best I Can: Fatherhood in the Inner City* (University of California Press, 2013); Mitch Pearlstein, *Broken Bonds: What Family Fragmentation Means for America* (Lanham, Md.: Rowman and Littlefield, 2014), xxix; and Vicki Turetsky, "Legislation in Brief: Responsible Fatherhood and Healthy Family Act of 2007," Center for Law and Social Policy, July 9, 2008. Senator Obama, together with Senator Evan Bayh (D-Ind.), introduced the Responsible Fatherhood and Healthy Family Act of 2007.

11. Edin and Nelson, *Doing the Best I Can*.

12. Fatherhood Project, "Research Review: The Fatherhood Project at MGH," Massachusetts General Hospital Partners HealthCare System, 2014, 4–5.

13. Emily Alpert Reyes, "Survey Finds Dads Defy Stereotypes about Black Fatherhood," *Los Angeles Times*, December 20, 2013.

14. Interview with Sonia Molloy, September 5, 2017.

15. Fatherhood Project, "Research Review," 8; S. Katherine Nelson, Kostadin Kushlev, Tammy English, Elizabeth W. Dunn, and Sonja Lyubomirsky, "In Defense of Parenthood: Children Are Associated with More Joy Than Misery," *Psychological Science*, November 30, 2012; MenCare and Promundo, "State of the World's Fathers 2016" (Washington, D.C.: Promundo, 2016); Sharon Jayson, "Are Parents Happier? Dads May Be, but Not Moms, Singles," *USA Today*, January 15, 2013; and I. Alger and D. Cox, "The Evolution of Altruistic Preferences: Mothers versus Fathers," *Review of Economics and the Household* 11, no. 3 (2013).

16. Fatherhood Project, "Research Review," 3.

17. Laura Tach and Kathryn Edin, "The Relationship Contexts of Young Disadvantaged Men," in *Young Disadvantaged Men: Fathers, Families, Poverty, and Policy*, ed. Timothy M. Smeeding, Irwin Garfinkel, and Ronald B. Mincy, special issue, *Annals of the American Academy of Political and Social Science* 635 (May 2011): 79; Edin and Nelson, *Doing the Best I Can*, 40; interview with Vernon Wallace, Baltimore Responsible Fatherhood Project, February 6, 2017; interview with Donald Gordon, Center for Divorce Education, June 29, 2017.

18. Edin and Nelson, *Doing the Best I Can*, 167, 215; and Reyes, "Survey Finds Dads Defy Stereotypes."

19. Edin and Nelson, *Doing the Best I Can*, 58–62, 168.

20. Interview with David Blankenhorn, January 4, 2017.

21. National Women's Law Center, "National Snapshot: Poverty among Women and Families, 2015," 2015; Institute for Women's Policy Research, "Undervalued and

Underpaid in America: Women in Low-Wage, Female-Dominated Jobs," November 2016; Alana Semeuls, "How Poor Single Moms Survive," *The Atlantic*, December 1, 2015; and Alana Semeuls, "The End of Welfare as We Know It," *The Atlantic*, April 1, 2016.

22. U.S. Census Bureau, "The Majority of Children Live with Two Parents, Census Bureau Reports," November 17, 2016; U.S. Census Bureau, "Mother's Day: May 8, 2016"; J. D. Vance, *Hillbilly Elegy: A Memoir of a Family and Culture in Crisis* (New York: HarperCollins, 2016), 20–21; Robert Rector, "How Welfare Undermines Marriage and What to Do about It," Heritage Foundation, November 17, 2014; and U.S. Census Bureau, "Father's Day: June 18, 2017."

23. William J. Bennett, *The Broken Hearth: Reversing the Moral Collapse of the American Family* (New York: Broadway Books, 2001), 93.

24. Edin and Nelson, *Doing the Best I Can*, 1; "Text of Obama's Fatherhood Speech," *Politico*, June 15, 2008; and Julie Basman, "Obama Sharply Assails Absent Black Fathers," *New York Times*, June 16, 2008.

25. Hossein Berenji, "Six Reasons Some Divorced Dads Check Out of Their Children's Lives," Good Men Project, May 25, 2016.

26. Cynthia Miller and Virginia Knox, "The Challenge of Helping Low-Income Fathers Support Their Children: Final Lessons from Parents' Fair Share," MDRC, November 2001, v–vi.

27. "The Fragile Families and Child Wellbeing Study, Princeton and Columbia Universities"; interview with Kathryn Edin, February 6, 2017; and David Blankenhorn, "Are We Still Married? Family Structure and Family Policy in the Emerging Age of the Unformed Family," Institute for American Values, n.d.

28. David Blankenhorn, "Fatherless America," Institute for American Values, June 1, 1993.

29. "Responsible Fatherhood," Office of Family Assistance, Administration for Children and Families, U.S. Department of Health and Human Services, November 10, 2016.

30. Ronald B. Mincy, Monique Jethwani, and Serena Klempin, *Failing Our Fathers: Confronting the Crisis of Economically Vulnerable Nonresident Fathers* (Oxford University Press, 2015).

31. Mary Meghan Ryan, ed., "Table 3: Employment Status of the Civilian Noninstitutionalized Population by Sex, Age, Presence and Age of Youngest Child, Marital Status, Race, and Hispanic Origin," *Handbook of U.S. Labor Statistics, 2017*; interview with David Blankenhorn, January 4, 2007; interview with Ron Haskins, November 21, 2016; Rich Morin, "The Disappearing Male Worker," Pew Research Center, September 13, 2013; and Frank F. Furstenberg Jr., "How Do Low-Income Men and Fathers Matter for Children and Family Life?," in Smeeding, Garfinkel, and Mincy, eds., *Young Disadvantaged Men*, 134.

32. Edin and Nelson, *Doing the Best I Can*, 90; and interview with David Lapp, December 9, 2016.

33. Smeeding, Garfinkel, and Mincy, eds., *Young Disadvantaged Men*, 6–7, 12, 77–84; and Edin and Nelson, *Doing the Best I Can*, 30–32, 42, 53–54, 77–98.

34. Wendy D. Manning, Susan L. Brown, and J. Bart Stykes, "Family Complexity among Children in the United States," *Annals of the American Academy of Political and Social Science* 654 (July 1, 2014); Smeeding, Garfinkel, and Mincy, eds., introduction to *Young Disadvantaged Men*, 12; Tach and Edin, "Relationship Contexts," 82–88; Pearlstein, *Broken Bonds*, 4; Edin and Nelson, *Doing the Best I Can*, 190–91; Lawrence M. Berger and Callie Langton, "Young Disadvantaged Men as Fathers," in Smeeding, Garfinkel, and Mincy, eds., *Young Disadvantaged Men*; and interview with Tom Grazio, The Tree House, August 7, 2017.

35. Blankenhorn, Horn, and Pearlstein, *Fatherhood Movement*, 118.

36. Interviews with Joseph Cordell, December 12, 2016, and Harry Crouch, National Coalition for Men, December 14, 2016.

·37. Joseph E. Cordell, "Shared Parenting Movement Gaining Momentum in 2015," *Huffington Post*, June 17, 2015.

38. J. Herbie DiFonzo, Kristin Pezzuti, Nicole Guliano, and Diana Rivkin, "Joint Custody Laws and Policies in the Fifty States: A Summary Memorandum," Massachusetts Legal Services, February 7, 2013.

39. Kim Parker and Gretchen Livingston, "Six Facts about American Fathers," Pew Research Center, June 15, 2017; Parke and Brott, *Throwaway Dads*, 17ff, 29, 55, 79, 95–96; and Office of Child Support Enforcement, "Effect of Male Employment on Child Support Payments," April 22, 2014.

40. Interviews with Joseph Cordell, December 15 and 19, 2016.

41. Interview with Donald Gordon, June 29, 2017.

42. Interview with Ron Haskins, November 21, 2016.

43. Interview with Joseph Cordell, December 15, 2016

44. Interview with J. Steven Svoboda, December 28, 2016; interview with Joseph Cordell, December 15, 2016; interview with Kathryn Edin, February 6, 2017; Timothy Grall, "Custodial Mothers and Fathers and Their Child Support: 2011," U.S. Census Bureau, October 2013; Timothy Grall, "Custodial Mothers and Fathers and Their Child Support: 2013," January 2016, U.S. Census Bureau; and National Responsible Fatherhood Clearinghouse, "Dad Stats," n.d.

45. Family Research Council website, n.d.; Cordell, "Shared Parenting Movement"; interview with Warren Farrell, January 12, 2017; and Fatherhood Project, "Research Review," 4.

46. Interview with Joseph Cordell, December 15, 2016.

47. Blankenhorn, Horn, and Pearlstein, *Fatherhood Movement*, 115.

48. Interview with Warren Farrell, January 9, 2017.

49. "Women's Rights Groups to Rally in Tally against Alimony Bill," *Florida Politics*, April 8, 2016; Interview with Warren Farrell, January 9, 2017; and National Organization for Women, "California Family Courts Helping Pedophiles, Batterers Get Child Custody," March 9, 2011.

50. Darlena Cunha, "The Divorce Gap," *The Atlantic*, April 28, 2016; Prentice Reid, "Opposing Shared Parenting: The Feminist Track Record," *A Voice for Men*, March 15, 2015; and interview with Sonia Molloy, September 5, 2017.

51. Henry Gornbein, "Why Equal Child Custody Should Not Be Presumed," *Huffington Post*, August 29, 2012; and Cathy Young, "The Feminist Leader Who Became a Men's-Rights Activist," *The Atlantic*, June 13, 2014.

52. Interview with Donald Gordon, June 29, 2017; interview with Warren Farrell, January 12, 2017; interview with Joseph Cordell, December 15, 2016; and Grall, "Custodial Mothers and Fathers and Their Child Support: 2013."

53. Office of Child Support Enforcement, Administration of Children and Families, U.S. Department of Health and Human Services, "2015 OCSE Annual Report."

54. Jennifer Ludden, "From Deadbeat to Dead Broke: The 'Why' behind Unpaid Child Support," NPR, November 19, 2015.

55. Grall, "Custodial Mothers and Fathers and Their Child Support: 2013"; Furstenberg, "How Do Low-Income Men and Fathers Matter?," 150; and interview with Kathryn Edin, February 6, 2017; Marcia Carlson and Katherine Magnuson, "Low-Income Fathers' Influence on Children," in Smeeding, Garfinkel, and Mincy, eds., *Young Disadvantaged Men*, 105; Isabel Sawhill, *Generation Unbound: Drifting into Sex and Marriage without Parenthood* (Brookings Institution Press, 2014), 68, 90–91, 62; and Ludden, "From Deadbeat to Dead Broke."

56. Furstenberg, "How Do Low-Income Men and Fathers Matter?," 147.

57. Interview with Cynthia Osborne, University of Texas, September 27, 2017; and Michael Alison Chandler, "D.C. Tries to Get Child Support on Track," *Washington Post*, September 10, 2017.

58. Interview with Olivia Golden, president, Center for Law and Social Policy, March 13, 2017; Marcia Cancian, Daniel R. Meyer, and Eunhee Han, "Child Support: Responsible Fatherhood and the Quid Pro Quo," in Smeeding, Garfinkel, and Mincy, eds., *Young Disadvantaged Men*, 151–57; Office of Child Support Enforcement, "Effect of Male Employment"; Nino Rodriguez, "Noncustodial Parents, and Child Support and EITC Policy: Are We Moving Families toward Economic Security?," Center for Family Policy and Practice, December 2013; Elaine Sorenson, "Initial Results from the New York Noncustodial Parent EITC," Brief 16, *Urban Institute*, August 2010; Virginia Knox, Philip A. Cowan, Carolyn Pape Cowan, and Elena Bildner, "Policies That Strengthen Fatherhood and Family Relationships: What Do We Know and What Do We Need to Know?," in Smeeding, Garfinkel, and Mincy, eds., *Young Disadvantaged Men*, 150; and Marah A. Curtis, Sarah Garlington, and Lisa S. Schottenfeld, "Alcohol, Drug, and Criminal History Restrictions in Public Housing," *Cityscape: A Journal of Policy Development and Research* 15, no. 3 (2013), U.S. Department of Housing and Urban Development.

59. Interview with Cynthia Osborne, September 27, 2017.

60. Jones and Mosher, "Fathers' Involvement with Their Children"; Gretchen Livingston, "Less Than Half of U.S. Kids Today Live in a 'Traditional' Family," Pew Research Center, December 22, 2014; and U.S. Census Bureau, "Table C3. Living Arrangements"; Liz Hamel, Jamie Firth, and Mollyann Brodie, "Kaiser Family Foundation/*New York Times*/CBS News Non-Employed Poll," December 11, 2014; and Derek Thompson, "The Missing Men," *The Atlantic*, June 27, 2016.

61. Interview with Gail Melson, March 9, 2017; Ariel Kalil and Kathleen Ziol-Guest, "Parental Employment Circumstances and Children's Academic Progress," *Social Science Research* 37, no. 2 (2008); and Gail F. Melson, "Parents Lose Jobs and Children Suffer," *Psychology Today*, January 22, 2014.

62. Sawhill, *Generation Unbound*, 8.

63. Sara McLanahan and Isabel Sawhill, "Marriage and Child Wellbeing Revisited," *The Future of Children* 25, no. 2 (2015); 2–9; Fatherhood Project, "Research Review," 23–24, 32; Jones and Mosher, "Fathers' Involvement with Their Children"; Richard A. Warshak, "After Divorce, Shared Parenting Is Best for Children's Health and Development," *Stat*, May 26, 2017; National Responsible Fatherhood Clearinghouse, "Dad Stats"; Valarie King and Juliana M. Sobolewski, "Nonresident Fathers' Contributions to Adolescent Well-Being," *Journal of Marriage and the Family* 68, no. 3 (2006): 537–57; Marcia J. Carlson and Kimberly J. Turner, "Fathers' Involvement and Fathers' Well-Being over Children's First Five Years" (Madison, WI: Institute for Research on Poverty, 2010); Robert Bly, *Iron John: A Book about Men* (New York: Addison-Wesley, 1990), 31; Parke, *Fatherhood*; Kyle D. Pruett, *Fatherneed: Why Father Care Is as Essential as Mother Care for Your Child* (New York: Free Press, 2000); and Christine Winquist Nord, DeeAnn Brimhall, and Jerry West, *Fathers' Involvement in Their Children's Schools*; *National Household Education Survey* (U.S. Department of Education, National Center for Education Statistics, 1997).

64. Autor and Wasserman, "Wayward Sons"; interview with Brad Wilcox, December 7, 2016; Putnam, *Our Kids*, 109–114; and Carlson and Magnuson, "Low-Income Fathers' Influence," 100.

65. Sara McLanahan and Christine Percheski, "Family Structure and the Reproduction of Inequalities," *Annual Review of Sociology* 34 (2008): 257–76; U.S. Census Bureau, America's Families and Living Arrangements: 2016, "Table C8. Poverty Status, Food Stamp Receipt, and Public Assistance for Children under 18 Years by Selected Characteristics: 2016"; Sara McLanahan, Laura Tach, and Daniel Schneider, "The Causal Effects of Father Absence," *Annual Review of Sociology* 39 (July 2013); U.S. Department of Health and Human Services, ASEP Issue Brief, "Information on Poverty and Income Statistics," September 16, 2014; Robert I. Lerman, "Impacts of Marital Status and Parental Presence on the Material Hardship of Families with Children," Urban Institute, July 1, 2002; Ray Williams, "The Male Identity Crisis and the Decline of Fatherhood," *Psychology Today*, June 8, 2014; National Fatherhood Initiative, "The Father Absence Crisis," February 16, 2017; and Nicholas Kristof, "When Liberals Blew It," *New York Times*, March 11, 2015.

66. Sid Kirchheimer, "Absent Parent Doubles Suicide Risk," *WebMD*, January 23, 2003; "Child Abuse," *Psychology Today*; Sawhill, *Generation Unbound*, 58; Esma Fuller-Thompson and A. D. Dalton, "Suicidal Ideation among Individuals Whose Parents Have Divorced: Findings from a Representative Canadian Community Survey," *Psychiatric Research* 187, nos. 1–2 (2011); Williams, "Male Identity Crisis"; interview with Lawrence Mead, New York University, November 14, 2016; interview with Mark Kiselica, August 18, 2017; Bly, *Iron John*, 55; and National Responsible Fatherhood Clearinghouse, "Dad Stats."

67. James J. Heckman, "Promoting Social Mobility," *Boston Review*, September 1, 2012; Autor and Wasserman, "Wayward Sons"; Paul R. Amato, "The Impact of Family Formation Change on the Cognitive, Social, and Emotional Well-Being of the Next Generation," *Future of Children* 15, no. 2 (2005): 75–96; Marianne Bertrand and Jessica Pan, "The Trouble with Boys: Social Influences and the Gender Gap in Disruptive Behavior," NBER Working Paper 17541, (Cambridge, Mass.: National Bureau of Economic Research, October 2011); and Williams, "Male Identity Crisis."

68. Andrea N. Allen and Celia C. Lo, "Drugs, Guns, and Disadvantaged Youths: Co-occurring Behavior and the Code of the Street," *Journal of Urban Health* 58, no. 6 (2012); and Sharonne D. Herbert, Elizabeth A. Harvey, Claudia I. Lugo-Candelas, and Rosanna P. Breaux, "Early Fathering as a Predictor of Later Psychosocial Functioning among Preschool Children with Behavior Problems," *Journal of Abnormal Child Psychology* 4, no. 5 (2013): 691–703.

69. Interviews with Brad Wilcox, December 7 and 9, 2016; Raj Chetty, Nathaniel Hendren, Frina Lin, Jeremy Majerovitz, and Benjamin Scuderi, "Childhood Environment and Gender Gaps in Adulthood," NBER Working Paper 21936 (Cambridge, Mass.: National Bureau of Economic Research, January 2016); and Delia L. Lang, Traci Rieckmann, Ralph J. DiClemente, Richard A. Crosby, Larry K. Brown, and Geri R. Donenberg, "Multi-Level Factors Associated with Pregnancy among Urban Adolescent Women Seeking Psychological Services," *Journal of Urban Health* 90, no. 2 (2013).

70. Chetty and others, "Childhood Environment and Gender Gaps."

71. Andrew L. Yarrow, "Fathers' Unemployment Taking Huge Toll on Children," *San Francisco Chronicle*, April 27, 2017.

72. National Fatherhood Initiative, "The One Hundred Billion Dollar Man: The Annual Public Costs of Father Absence."

CHAPTER 8

1. Anne Case and Angus Deaton, "Rising Morbidity and Mortality in Midlife among White Non-Hispanic Americans in the 21st Century," *Proceedings of the National Academy of Sciences* 112, no. 49 (2015); Anne Case and Angus Deaton, "Mortality and Morbidity in the 21st Century," *Brookings Papers on Economic Activity*, March 23–24, 2017; Joseph E. Stiglitz, "When Inequality Kills," *Project Syndicate*, December 7, 2015; Krueger, "Where Have All the Workers Gone?," Federal Reserve Bank of Boston, October 4, 2016; and Andrew L. Yarrow, "Are Americans Popping Too Many Pain Pills?," *San Francisco Chronicle*, May 5, 2016.

2. Kenneth D. Kochanek, Sherry L. Murphy, Jiaquan Xu, and Elizabeth Arias, "Mortality in the United States 2016," NCHS Data Brief 293, December 2017; Jiaquan Xu, Sherry L. Murphy, Kenneth D. Kochanek, and Elizabeth Arias, "Mortality in the United States 2015," NCHS Data Brief 267, December 2016; Brian W. Ward, Tainya C. Clarke, Colleen N. Nugent, and Jeannine S. Schiller, "Early Release of Selected Estimates Based on Data from the 2015 National Health Interview Survey," NCHS, May 2016; and interview with J. Steven Svoboda, December 28, 2016.

3. Christopher R. Tamborini, "The Never-Married in Old Age: Projections and Concerns for the Near Future," *Social Security Bulletin* 67, no. 2 (2007).

4. National Center for Health Statistics (NCHS), "Health, United States 2015," May 2016; Virginia M. Freid, Amy B. Bernstein, and Mary Ann Bush, "Multiple Chronic Conditions among Adults Aged 45 and Over: Trends over the Past 10 Years," NCHS Data Brief 100, July 2012; Lena H. Sun, "Rural Americans More Susceptible to Top Causes of Death," *Washington Post*, January 13, 2017; and Joel Achenbach and Dan Keating, "A New Divide in American Death," *Washington Post*, April 10, 2016.

5. Emily Bobrow, "The Man Trap," *The Economist 1843*, June/July 2017; Stephen J. Blumberg, Anjel Vahratian, and Joseph H. Blumberg, "Marriage, Cohabitation, and Men's Use of Preventive Care Services," NCHS, June 2014; and Christin Munsch, "Relative Income, Psychological Well-Being, and Health: Is Breadwinning Hazardous or Protective?," paper presented at the 111th Annual Meeting of the American Sociological Association, August 19, 2016.

6. NCHS, "Health, United States, 2015"; Roger B. Fillingim, Christopher D. King, Margarete C. Ribeiro-Dasilva, Bridgett Rahim-Williams, and Joseph L. Riley III, "Sex, Gender, and Pain: A Review of Recent Clinical and Experimental Findings," *Journal of Pain* 10, no. 5 (2009); National Institutes of Health (NIH), National Center for Complementary and Integrative Health, "What Complementary and Integrative Approaches Do Americans Use? Key Findings from the 2012 National Health Interview Survey," n.d.; Institute of Medicine of the National Academies, *Relieving Pain in America: A Blueprint for Transforming Prevention, Care, Education, and Research* (Washington, D.C.: National Academies Press, 2011), 77.

7. Krueger, "Where Have All the Workers Gone?"; Justin R. Pierce and Peter K. Schott, "Trade Liberalization and Mortality: Evidence from U.S. Counties," November 2016; and Harriet Ryan, Lisa Girion, and Scott Glover, "More Than 1 Million OxyContin Pills Ended Up in the Hands of Criminals and Addicts: What the Drugmaker Knew," *Los Angeles Times*, July 10, 2016.

8. "The Opioid Menace," *AARP Bulletin*, June 2017; Lenny Bernstein, "Study Links Greater Opioid Use, Mental Disorders," *Washington Post*, June 26, 2017; Grace Medley, Rachel N. Lipari, Jonaki Bose, and others, "Sexual Orientation and Estimates of Adult Substance Use and Mental Health: Results from the 2015 National Survey on Drug Use and Health," U.S. Department of Health and Human Services, Substance Abuse and Mental Health Service Administration (SAMHSA), October 2016; and Case and Deaton, "Mortality and Morbidity."

9. NCHS, "Data Brief 294. Drug Overdose Deaths in the United States, 1999–2016," December 2017; "America's Opioid Epidemic Is Driven by Supply," *The Economist*, January 29, 2018; Josh Katz, "Drug Deaths in America Are Rising Faster Than Ever," *New York Times*, June 5, 2017; Lenny Bernstein, "Deaths from Drug Overdoses Soared in the First Nine Months of 2016," *Washington Post*, August 8, 2017; and American Society of Addiction Medicine, "Opioid Addiction: 2016 Facts and Figures." A number of states and localities are suing pharmaceutical companies for their alleged complicity.

10. National Institute on Drug Abuse, "Substance Use in Women and Men," January 2016; SAMHSA, "Prescription Drug Use and Misuse in the United States: Results from the 2015 National Survey on Drug Use and Health"; Medley and others,

"Sexual Orientation and Estimates"; Centers for Disease Control and Prevention (CDC), "Today's Heroin Epidemic," 2015; Mark S. Woodford, *Men, Addiction, and Intimacy* (New York: Routledge, 2012), 2; John Rosengren, "America's Addiction to Pain Pills," Special Report: The Opioid Epidemic, *AARP Bulletin*, June 2017; and "Pain, Anxiety Meds Are a Deadly Mix," *AARP Bulletin*, February 19, 2018.

11. Nelson D. Schwartz, "Economy Needs Workers, but Drug Tests Take a Toll," *New York Times*, July 24, 2017; interview with Andrea Zucker, U.S. Army Marketing Research Group, January 13, 2017; and interview with Master Sergeant Jeffrey A. Klimek, Army Virtual Recruiting, March 2, 2017.

12. SAMHSA, "Prescription Drug Use and Misuse"; CDC," Excessive Alcohol Use and Risks to Men's Health," 2016; National Institute on Alcohol Abuse and Alcoholism (NIAAA), "Alcohol Facts and Statistics," February 2017; NCHS, "Health, United States, 2015"; Matt Gonzales, "Binge Drinking and Alcoholism Increasing among Older Adults," DrugRehab.com, December 20, 2016; Robert Jimison, "Americans over 60 Are Drinking More, Study Finds," CNN, April 3, 2017; Karla Pequenino, "Women Now Drink Nearly as Much Alcohol as Men, Study Finds," CNN, October 25, 2016.

13. NIAAA, "Alcohol Facts and Statistics"; Schwartz, "*Economy Needs Workers*"; Krueger, "Where Have All the Workers Gone?"; Case and Deaton, "Mortality and Morbidity"; and Dan Munro, "Inside the $35 Billion Addiction Treatment Industry," *Forbes*, April 27, 2015.

14. Interview with Andrew Smiler, August 18, 2017.

15. Vivek Murthy, "Work and the Loneliness Epidemic," *Harvard Business Review*, September 2017; Bobby Baker, "The Biggest Threat Facing Middle-Age Men Isn't Smoking or Obesity. It's Loneliness," *Boston Globe*, March 9, 2017.

16. Ward and others, "Early Release of Selected Estimates"; SAMHSA, "Prescription Drug Use and Misuse"; National Institute for Mental Health (NIMH), "Serious Mental Illness (SMI) among U.S. Adults," 2015; and interview with Pierre Azzam, September 12, 2017. According to official CDC statistics, 4.3 percent of 18- to 44-year-old women report mental distress in any given month, compared to 3.1 percent of their male peers.

17. Interview with Daniel Singley, June 28, 2017.

18. Brian Heilman, Gary Barker, and Alexander Harrison, "The Man Box: A Study on Being a Young Man in the US, UK, and Mexico," Promundo, March 2017.

19. National Opinion Research Center, General Social Survey; and Pierce and Schott, "Trade Liberalization and Mortality."

20. NIMH, "Men and Depression," n.d.; Matthew A. Davis, Lewei A. Lin, Haiyin Liu, and Brian D. Sites, "Prescription Opioid Use among Adults with Mental Health Disorders in the United States," *Journal of the American Board of Family Medicine* 30, no. 4 (2017): 407–17; and Kira Asatryan, "Surprising Differences between Lonely Women and Lonely Men," *World of Psychology*, November 26, 2015.

21. Robin Simon and Anne Barrett, "Non-Marital Romantic Relationships and Mental Health in Early Adulthood: Does the Association Differ for Women and Men?," *Journal of Health and Social Behavior* 51 (June 2010): 168–82; "The Emo-

tional Health of Our Sons," Proposal to Create a White House Council on Boys and Men Steering Committee, n.d.; and BLS, American Time Use Survey, "Average Hours per Day Spent in Selected Activities by Employment Status and Sex," June 17, 2017.

22. Markham Heid, "Erectile Dysfunction Increasing in Men Under 40," *Prevention*, August 21, 2013.

23. Sally C. Curtin, Margaret Warner, and Holly Hedegaard, "Suicide Rates for Females and Males by Race and Ethnicity: United States, 1999 and 2014," NCHS, April 2016; NCHS, "Deaths: Leading Causes for 2015," *National Vital Statistics Reports* 66, no. 5, November 27, 2017; NCHS, "Health, United States, 2015"; Augustine J. Kposowa, "Unemployment and Suicide: A Cohort Analysis of Social Factors Predicting Suicide in the U.S. National Longitudinal Mortality Study," *Psychological Medicine* 31, no. 1 (2001): 127–38; Augustine J. Kposowa, "Marital Status and Suicide in the National Longitudinal Mortality Study," *Journal of Epidemiology and Community Health* 54, no. 4 (2000); White House Council on Boys and Men Steering Committee, "Emotional Health of Our Sons"; Medley and others, "Prescription Drug Use and Misuse"; and Alaska Bureau of Vital Statistics, "Alaska Suicide Facts and Statistics."

24. Medley and others, "Prescription Drug Use and Misuse"; and Pierce and Schott, "Trade Liberalization and Mortality."

25. National Alliance to End Homelessness, "Homelessness in America"; and Tom Matlack, "Why Are Men More Likely to Be Homeless?," Good Men Project, January 28, 2012.

26. David Autor and Mark Duggan, "The Growth in the Social Security Disability Rolls: A Fiscal Crisis Unfolding," NBER Working Paper 12436 (Cambridge, Mass.: National Bureau of Economic Research, August 2006).

27. Derek Thompson, "The Missing Men," *The Atlantic*, June 27, 2016; Social Security Administration, "Monthly Statistical Snapshot," February 2018; Social Security Administration, "FY 2018 President's Budget: Key Tables"; Department of Veterans Affairs, "Department of Veterans Affairs Statistics at a Glance," June 30, 2017; Nicholas Eberstadt, *Men without Work: America's Invisible Crisis* (West Conshohocken, Penn.: Templeton Press, 2016), 116–17; Center on Budget and Policy Priorities, "Chart Book: Social Security Disability Insurance," August 1, 2017; Stephanie Aaronson, Tomaz Cajner, Bruce Fallick, Felix Galbis-Reig, Christopher L. Smith, and William Wascher, "Labor Force Participation: Recent Developments and Future Prospects," Finance and Economics Discussion Series, Divisions of Research and Statistics and Monetary Affairs, Federal Reserve Board, Washington, D.C., 2014; and BLS, "Persons with a Disability: Labor Force Characteristics—2015," news release, June 21, 2016. The SSDI numbers include 1.7 million spouses and children of disabled workers. The total number of disabled workers on SSDI has gone down slightly between 2014 and 2018, from about 9.0 million to 8.8 million. Eighteen percent of Americans with a disability were employed in 2016, including about one-third of workers on SSDI who work part time.

28. Krueger, "Where Have All the Workers Gone?"; and BLS, "Persons with a Disability: Labor Force Characteristics Summary—2016," June 21, 2017.

29. U.S. Census Bureau, "America's Families and Living Arrangements: 2016: Unmarried Couples" (UC Table Series); A. C. Patterson and G. Veenstra, "Loneliness and Risk of Mortality: A Longitudinal Investigation in Alameda County, California," *Social Science Medicine* 71, no. 1 (2010); Murthy, "Work and the Loneliness Epidemic"; AARP, "Loneliness among Older Adults," September 2010; Baker, "Biggest Threat"; David Lester, *Suicide in Men* (Springfield, Ill.: Charles C. Thomas Publisher, 2014); Richard S. Schwartz and Jacqueline Olds, *The Lonely American: Drifting Apart in the 21st Century* (Boston: Beacon Press, 2009); and John T. Cacioppo, *Loneliness: Human Nature and the Need for Social Connection* (New York: W. W. Norton, 2008).

30. Rhonda Kruse Norton, "Yesterday's Love Stories: The Gray Divorce Phenomenon," Institute for Family Studies, March 21, 2017.

31. David Figura, "Middle-Aged Men Need Good Friends, Too," Good Men Project, July 20, 2011.

32. Interview with Pierre Azzam, September 12, 2017.

33. "I Am 42 Years Old and Have No Friends," *Quora*; and "How Relationships and Online Dating Differ for Introverted Loner Men versus Women," AdultSocialSkills.com.

34. The Red Pill, "Men without Friends," podcast; and Daniel Duane, "Do Men Suck at Friendship?," *Men's Journal*, April 22, 2014.

HORICON, WISCONSIN

1. U.S. Census Bureau, American Fact Finder, "Horicon City, Wisconsin."

2. Olivia Barrow, "Horicon Manufacturer Lays Off 39 Employees in Plant Shutdown," *Milwaukee Business Journal*, July 5, 2016.

3. Public School Review, "Horicon High School"; and Education Data Partnership, "Horicon Elementary."

4. Wisconsin Department of Public Instruction, "Wisconsin School District Performance Report: Horicon," 2015–16; and Dan Larson, "Horicon, Husty Join Forces—Have High Hopes Merger Will Bear Fruit," *Beaver Dam Daily Citizen*, August 18, 2016.

5. "Blue Zones Project Kicks Off in Dodge County Next Week," *Beaver Dam Daily Citizen*, April 11, 2017.

6. "Year at a Glance: Overview," Church Trends, February 22, 2018.

7. "Danny Boys Irish Pub," Yelp.

CHAPTER 9

1. "Formerly incarcerated" is arguably a less demeaning term than "ex-felons," "ex-prisoners," or "ex-convicts," and will be used in most instances.

2. Lauren C. Porter, Shawn D. Bushway, Hui-Shien Tsao, and Herbert Smith, "How the U.S. Prison Boom Has Changed the Age Distribution of the Prison Population," *Criminology* 54, no. 1 (2016): 30–35.

3. Interview with Ronald Day, December 13, 2016.

4. Matthew Friedman, "Just Facts: As Many Men Have Criminal Records as College Diplomas," Brennan Center for Justice, November 17, 2015; Prison Policy Initia-

tive, "United States Incarceration Rates by Sex"; Gary Fields and John R. Emshwiller, "As Arrest Records Rise, Americans Find Consequences Can Last a Lifetime," *Wall Street Journal*, August 18, 2014; Sarah Shannon, Christopher Uggen, Jason Schnittker, Michael Massoglia, Melissa Thompson, and Sara Wakefield, "The Growth, Scope, and Spatial Distribution of People with Felony Records in the United States, 1948–2010," April 19, 2017 draft, *Demography* 54 (2017): 1795–1818; Robert D. Putnam, *Our Kids: The American Dream in Crisis* (New York: Simon and Schuster, 2015), 77; Gregg Bernstein, "A Forgiveness Certificate for Ex-Offenders," *Baltimore Sun*, April 1, 2016; Putnam, *Our Kids*; Steven Raphael, "Incarceration and Prisoner Reentry in the United States," in *Young Disadvantaged Men: Fathers, Families, Poverty, and Policy*, ed. Timothy M. Smeeding, Irwin Garfinkel, and Ronald B. Mincy, special issue, *Annals of the American Academy of Political and Social Science* 635 (May 2011): 194; U.S. Department of Justice, Bureau of Justice Statistics (BJS), "U.S. Correctional Population at Lowest Level since 2002," December 29, 2016; BJS, "In 2016, State and Federal Prison Populations Declined for Third Consecutive Year," January 18, 2018; BJS, "Jail Incarceration Rate Was Down from Midyear 2012 to Midyear 2016," February 22, 2018; BJS, "Probation and Parole in the United States 2015," December 2016; "World Prison Brief," Institute for Criminal Policy Research, 2017; and Jennifer L. Truman and Rachel E. Morgan, "Criminal Victimization, 2015," BJS, October 2016.

5. Although there are incarcerated and formerly incarcerated women, since 90 percent of this population are male and men are the focus of this book, men are the focus of this chapter.

6. BLS, "Occupational Outlook Handbook."

7. Peter Wagner and Bernadette Rabuy, "Mass Incarceration: The Whole Pie 2017," Prison Policy Initiative, March 14, 2017; Carimah Townes, "The True Cost of Mass Incarceration Exceeds $1 Trillion," *Think Progress*, Center for American Progress, September 12, 2016; "Prison Labour Is a Billion-Dollar Industry, with Uncertain Returns for Inmates," *The Economist*, March 16, 2017; "How Prison Labor Is the New Slavery and Most of Us Unknowingly Support It," *Return to Now*, June 13, 2016.

8. Devah Pager, *Marked: Race, Crime, and Finding Work in an Era of Mass Incarceration* (University of Chicago Press, 2007), 3; Justice Center, Council of State Governments, "NRRC Facts and Trends," n.d.; Porter and others, "How the U.S. Prison Boom Has Changed"; Smeeding, Garfinkel, and Mincy, eds., introduction to *Young Disadvantaged Men*, 39–40; and Christy Visher, Nancy LaVigne, and Jeremy Travis, "Returning Home: Understanding the Challenges of Prisoner Maryland Pilot Study: Findings from Baltimore," Urban Institute, 2004.

9. BJS, "Prisoners in 2016," January 2018.

10. National Resource Center on Children and Families of the Incarcerated, "Children and Families of the Incarcerated Fact Sheet 2014"; Smeeding, Garfinkel, and Mincy, eds., introduction, *Young Disadvantaged Men*, 11; Lawrence Berger and Callie Langton, "Young Disadvantaged Men as Fathers," in Smeeding, Garfinkel, and Mincy, eds., *Young Disadvantaged Men*, 81–82; Sentencing Project, "Incarcerated Parents and Their Children: Trends 1991–2007," February 2009; and Annie E.

Casey Foundation, "A Shared Sentence: The Devastating Toll of Parental Incarceration on Kids, Families and Communities," April 2016.

11. "Multi-Site Family Study on Incarceration, Parenting, and Partnering: Parenting and Partnership When Fathers Return from Prison: Findings from Qualitative Analysis," U.S. Department of Health and Human Services, July 2016; and Andrew Sum, Ishwar Khatiwada, Joseph McLaughlin, Sheila Palma, "No Country for Young Men," in Smeeding, Garfinkel, and Mincy, eds., *Young Disadvantaged Men*, 67.

12. Interview with Philip Hall, January 8, 2017.

13. U.S. Department of Justice, National Institute of Justice (NIJ), "Offender Re-Entry," 2015.

14. Nicole Flatow, "The Prison Doors Open and You're Released. You Have No Money or Transportation. Now What?" Center for American Progress, June 21, 2015.

15. Interview with Ronald Day, December 13, 2016.

16. Christopher Uggen, Ryan Larson, and Sarah Shannon, "Six Million Lost Voters: State-Level Estimates of Felony Disenfranchisement, 2016," Sentencing Project, October 6, 2016; and interview with Sonia Molloy, September 5, 2017.

17. NIJ, "Research on Reentry and Employment," n.d.; Tanzina Vega, "Out of Prison and Out of Work," CNN Money, October 30, 2015; and Appelbaum, "The Vanishing Male Worker: How America Fell Behind," *New York Times*, December 11, 2014.

18. Pager, *Marked*, 5; and Bruce Western and Becky Pettit, "Incarceration and Social Inequality," *Daedalus*, Summer 2010, American Academy of Arts and Sciences.

19. Devah Pager and Bruce Western, "Investigating Prisoner Reentry: The Impact of Conviction Status on the Employment Prospects of Young Men," prepared for the U.S. Department of Justice, October 2009.

20. Beth Avery and Phil Hernandez, "Ban the Box: U.S. Cities, Counties and States Adopt Fair Hiring Policies," National Employment Law Project, August 1, 2017; Gary Fields and John R. Emshwiller, "As Arrest Records Rise, Americans Find Consequences Can Last a Lifetime," *Wall Street Journal*, August 18, 2014; Heather Long, "From the Jailhouse to a Job," *Washington Post*, January 28, 2018.

21. Raphael, "Incarceration and Prisoner Reentry," 209; NIJ, "Research on Reentry and Employment"; and Pager and Western, "Investigating Prisoner Reentry."

22. Fields and Emshwiller, "As Arrest Records Rise."

23. Raphael, "Incarceration and Prisoner Reentry," 208; and "How Prison Labor Is the New Slavery," *Return to Now*, June 13, 2016.

24. Raphael, "Incarceration and Prisoner Reentry," 208.

25. Matthew R. Durose, Alexia D. Cooper, and Howard N. Snyder, "Recidivism of Prisoners Released in 30 States in 2005: Patterns from 2005 to 2010," BJS, April 2014; NIJ, "Recidivism," n.d.; Jeremy Travis, Amy L. Solomon, and Michelle Waul, "From Prison to Home: The Dimensions and Consequences of Prisoner Reentry," Urban Institute, June 2001, 31; and Center for Family and Policy Research, University of Missouri, "Programs for the Re-entry of Incarcerated Individuals & the Children of Incarcerated Parents in Missouri," November 2016.

26. Ingrid A. Binswanger, Marc F. Stern, Richard A. Deyo, Patrick J. Heagerty, Allen Cheadle, Joann G. Elmore, and Thomas D. Koepsell, "Release from Prison—A High Risk of Death for Former Inmates," *New England Journal of Medicine* 356 (2007): 157–65; Travis, Solomon, and Waul, "From Prison to Home"; and Jay Hancock, "Out of Jail, Uninsured, Ex-Inmates Face Health Care Challenges," *Baltimore Sun*, September 13, 2017.

27. Annie E. Casey Foundation, "Shared Sentence"; and Bruce Western and Natalie Smith, "Formerly Incarcerated Parents and Their Children," Harvard University, February 2017.

28. Devah Pager, "Young Disadvantaged Men: Reactions from the Perspective of Race," in Smeeding, Garfinkel, and Mincy, eds., *Young Disadvantaged Men*, 127; and "I'm Back," October 26, 2016.

29. Shannon and others, "Growth, Scope, and Spatial Distribution," 1795–1818.

CHAPTER 10

1. Alexis de Tocqueville, *Democracy in America*, ed. Richard D. Heffner (New York: New American Library, 1956), 198.

2. Christopher Lasch, *The Culture of Narcissism: American Life in an Age of Diminishing* Expectations (New York: W. W. Norton, 1979); Robert N. Bellah, Richard Madsen, William M. Sullivan, and Steven M. Tipton, *Habits of the Heart: Individualism and Commitment in American Life* (University of California Press, 1985); and Robert D. Putnam, *Bowling Alone: The Collapse and Revival of American Community* (New York: Simon and Schuster, 2000).

3. Donald Trump, Twitter, August 10, 2016.

4. Ted Balcolm, "Why So Few Men Join Book Groups," *Booklist Reader*, July 8, 2011; Pamela Burger, "Women's Groups and the Rise of the Book Club," *JSTOR Daily*, August 12, 2015; and "Why Are There More Women in Group Exercise?," International Health, Racquet & Sportsclub Association, September 10, 2014.

5. Rotary, "Our History"; Rotary International, *1970 Proceedings: Sixty-First Annual Convention of Rotary International* (Evanston, IL: Rotary International, 1970); and *The Rotarian* 137, no. 2 (1980).

6. YMCA, "History"; *Thomas Winter, Making Men, Making Class: The YMCA and Workingmen, 1877–1920* (University of Chicago Press, 2002).

7. Rotary District 7530, "Rotary's Core Beliefs"; and Maria Konnikova, "18 U.S. Presidents Were in College Fraternities," *The Atlantic*, February 21, 2014.

8. Joyce Steward, "The Chartering of the United Nations and Rotary's Continuing Relationship—from San Francisco to New York City," RotaryFirst100.org, January 21, 2003; and Konnikova, "18 U.S. Presidents."

9. Ruth Serven, "Service Clubs Push against Fading Influence to Find New Members," *Kansas City Star*, July 10, 2016; "Fading Tradition: Service Clubs Have Long Tradition, Uncertain Future," *Green Valley News*, September 2, 2015; Stuart Taylor Jr., "High Court Rules That Rotary Clubs Must Admit Women," *New York Times*; Antonio Sierra, "Pendleton Elks Close Lodge," *East Oregonian*, April 11, 2017; and Masonic Service Association of North America, "Masonic Membership Statistics, 2015–16."

10. Statistics provided by Rotary International; "Rotary," *Look*, July 6, 1948; "Fading Tradition"; Shriners International, "Shriners' Myth Sheet," 2012.

11. Gerald Mayer, "Union Membership Trends in the United States," Congressional Research Service, 2004; "In Unity There's Strength: 18 1/2 Million U. S. Workers Now in Unions; 3 1/2 Million Are Women," Center for Labor Education & Research, University of Hawaii–West Oahu: Honolulu Record Digitization Project, *Honolulu Record* 10, no. 18, Thursday, November 28, 1957; and U.S. Department of Labor, Bureau of Labor Statistics (BLS), Union Members Summary, January 26, 2017.

12. Jacqueline Klimas, "Younger Veterans Bypass VFW, American Legion for Service, Fitness Groups," *Washington Times*, October 19, 2014.

13. Caitlin Flanagan, "The Dark Power of Fraternities," *The Atlantic*, March 2014; Rob Fox, "Abolish Fraternities," *Bloomberg View*, January 7, 2014; and Peter Jacobs, "I Joined a Fraternity and It Was One of the Best Decisions I Ever Made," *Business Insider*, January 8, 2014.

14. "The History of Scouting"; and Reuters, "Boy Scout Membership Falls Again in 2014," January 17, 2015; "Boy Scouts to Lose 185,000 Mormon Members, as Church Starts Its Own Program," *Dallas Morning News*, May 11, 2017; and Eli Rosenberg and Ellie Silverman, "Boy Scouts, in Historic Move, Will Accept Girls," *Washington Post*, October 12, 2017.

15. Interview with Andrea Zucker, January 13, 2017.

16. Interviews with Sergeant First Class Robert W. Dodge, January 31, 2017; Colonel Patrick R. Michaelis, February 2, 2017; Sergeant First Class Robert W. Dodge, February 10, 2017; Command Sergeant Major Michael L. Gragg, February 10, 2017; Brian Sutton, U.S. Army Recruiting Command, December 20, 2016; Master Sergeant Jeffrey A. Klimek, March 2, 2017; Colonel Patrick R. Michaelis; and Andrea Zucker.

17. Interview with Michael Gragg, February 10, 2017; and interview with Sergeant First Class Robert W. Dodge, February 10, 2017.

18. Interview with Sergeant First Class Tifani Hightower, February 2, 2017.

19. U.S. Army, "Women in the Army"; U.S. Marine Corps, "U.S. Marine Corps Jobs for Women"; and "Army Looks to Recruit More Women, Adapt Physical Testing," Military.com, February 13, 2016.

20. Peace Corps, "Fast Facts."

21. Abt Associates Inc. for Corporation for National and Community Service (CNCS), "2016 Alumni AmeriCorps Alumni Outcomes Final Survey Technical Support," August 2016; and CNCS, Office of Research and Policy Development, "AmeriCorps: Changing Lives, Changing America," Washington, D.C., 2007; and Abt Associates Inc., "Serving Country and Community: A Study of Service in AmeriCorps," 2001.

22. CNCS, "Volunteering and Civic Life in America"; BLS, "Volunteering in the U.S., 2015," February 25, 2016; Dan Kopf, "Why Don't Men Volunteer as Much as Women?," Priceonomics; and Hiromi Taniguchi, "Men's and Women's Volunteering: Gender Differences in the Effects of Employment and Family Characteristics," *Nonprofit and Voluntary Sector Quarterly* 35, no. 1 (2006).

23. Lisa Belkin, "Dads in the PTA," *New York Times*, January 6, 2009; Kei Kawashima-Ginsberg and Nancy Thomas, "Civic Engagement and Political Leadership among Women—a Call for Solutions," Center for Information and Research on Civic Learning and Engagement (CIRCLE), Tufts University, May 2013; Teach for America, "69% of Teach for America Members Are Women"; Krista Jenkins, "Gender and Civic Engagement: Secondary Analysis of Survey Data," CIRCLE, June 2005; and Ray Franke, Sylvia Ruiz, Jessica Sharkness, Linda DeAngelo, and John Pryor, "Findings from the 2009 Administration of the College Senior Survey (CSS): National Aggregates," Cooperative Institutional Research Program at the Higher Education Research Institute at UCLA, 2010.

24. Kopf, "Why Don't Men Volunteer?"; and interview with Tom Pollak, November 18, 2016.

25. Ibid

26. David Murrow, "Why Men Hate Church," Christian Broadcasting Network, 2005.

27. "The Gender Gap in Religion around the World," Pew Research Center, March 22, 2016; Gallup, "Confidence in Institutions," 2017; "10 Facts about Atheists," Pew Research Center, June 1, 2016; National Opinion Research Center, General Social Survey, "How Often Respondent Attends Religious Services"; Will M. Gervais and Maxine B. Najle, "How Many Atheists Are There?," *PsyArXiv*, March 3, 2017; and Peter Beinart, "Breaking Faith," *The Atlantic*, April 2017.

28. "Poll: Americans Don't Trust One Another," *USA Today*, November 30, 2013.

29. Wayne Allyn Root, "Why 2016 Is the Year of the Angry White Male," Fox News, August 24, 2016; Chris Weigant, "Angry White Men Triumphant," *Huffington Post*, November 9, 2016; Sally Cohn, "The Old White Man's Last Hurrah," *Time*, February 29, 2016; Deroy Murdock, "Beyond 'Angry White Men,'" *National Review*, December 30, 2016; and Hadley Freeman, "I've Heard Enough of the White Male Rage Narrative," *The Guardian*, November 10, 2016.

30. "Beyond Distrust: How Americans View Their Government," Pew Research Center, November 23, 2015; interview with Ronald Day, December 13, 2016; and Art Swift, "Americans See Russia Less Negatively, as Less of a Threat," Gallup News, February 18, 2016.

31. SafeHome, "Hate on Social Media," n.d.

32. "Demographics and American Values," Pew Research Center, June 4, 2012; and Harris Interactive, "Less Than Half of Americans Trust Federal Government with Personal Info," Harris Poll, PR Newswire, July 16, 2013; Caroline Kitchener, "The Women behind the 'Alt-Right,'" *The Atlantic*, August 18, 2017; "Why They Join," Southern Poverty Law Center, February 25, 2014; and George Hawley, *Making Sense of the Alt-Right* (New York: Columbia University Press, 2017).

33. Interviews with Peter Fenn, December 13 and 16, 2017.

34. Center for American Women and Politics, Rutgers University, "Gender Differences in Voter Turnout," 2016; "The Unexpected Voters behind the Widest Gender Gap in Recorded Election History," *Washington Post*, November 9, 2017; Barbara

Norrander, "Women Vote at Higher Rates Than Men," *Washington Post*, June 27, 2016; and interviews with Peter Fenn, December 13 and 16, 2016.

35. Lauren Leader-Chivée and Courtney Emerson, "Vote vs. Voice: Women in American Democracy," *The Hill*, February 6, 2015; and Scott Clement, Sandhya Somashekhar, and Michael Alison Chandler, "United by Post-Inauguration Marches, Democratic Women Plan to Step Up Activism," *Washington Post*, February 1, 2017. The marches, not solely about "women's issues," could have more fruitfully and inclusively dropped the "women's" moniker.

36. Interview with Harry Crouch, National Coalition for Men, December 14, 2016.

CHAPTER 11

1. The Richard Freeman epigraph is from Thomas B. Edsall, "The Increasing Significance of the Decline of Men," *New York Times*, March 16, 2017.

Betty Friedan, *The Feminine Mystique* (New York: W. W. Norton, 1963), 16.

2. The White House, "Fact Sheet—White House Unveils America's College Promise Proposal: Tuition-Free Community College for Responsible Students," January 9, 2015.

3. Northern Mississippi Industrial Development Association, "Workforce Training"; Andrew L. Yarrow, "Capacity Building in Community Colleges for Student Career Success," Aspen Institute, October 1, 2016; and Richard Reeves, *Dream Hoarders: How the American Upper Middle Class Is Leaving Everyone Else in the Dust, Why That Is a Problem, and What to Do about It* (Brookings Institution Press, 2017), 134–36.

4. David Autor and Melanie Wasserman, "Wayward Sons: The Emerging Gender Gaps in Labor Markets and Education," Third Way, March 2013.

5. U.S. Department of Labor, Employment and Training Administration, "Available Occupations"; and Sarah Ayres Steinberg and Ethan Gurwitz, "The Underuse of Apprenticeships in America," Center for American Progress, July 22, 2014.

6. Peter Z. Schochet, John Burghardt, and Sheena McConnell, "National Job Corps Study and Longer-Term Follow-Up Study: Impact and Benefit-Cost Findings Using Survey and Summary Earnings Records Data Final Report," Mathematica Policy Research Inc., August 2006.

7. James J. Kemple, "Career Academies: Long-Term Impacts on Work, Education, and Transitions to Adulthood," MDRC, June 2008; Ovetta Wiggins, "Obama to Announce Federal Grants to Help Prepare Students for Careers," *Washington Post*, April 7, 2014; U.S. Department of Labor, "FY 2017 Congressional Budget Justification Employment and Training Administration: Job Corps"; Office of Management and Budget, "America First: A Budget Blueprint to Make America Great Again," May 23, 2017, 31; Wiggins, "Obama to Announce Federal Grants"; Patrick Gillespie, "Trump Budget Proposes 40% Cut to Job Training Programs," CNN Money, May 24, 2017; and Peter S. Goodman, "Europe Is Back. And Rejecting Trumpism," *New York Times*, January 24, 2018.

8. Youth.gov, "Positive Youth Development," n.d.; and YouthBuild, "About YouthBuild," n.d.

9. Business Roundtable, "Road to Growth: The Case for Investing in America's Transportation Infrastructure," September 2015; and Federal Reserve Bank of St. Louis, "Total Public Spending on Infrastructure," April 2017.

10. Claire Zillman, "Who Makes Less Than $15 per Hour?," *Fortune*, April 13, 2015; David Cooper, "Testimony before Maryland Committee in Support of SB543," March 8, 2015; Michael Reich, Sylvia Allegretto, and Anna Godoey, "Seattle's Minimum-Wage Experience, 2015–2016," Center on Wage and Employment Dynamics, Institute for Research on Labor and Employment, University of California, Berkeley, June 2017; and Congressional Budget Office, "The Effects of a Minimum-Wage Increase on Employment and Family Income," February 18, 2014.

11. Jason Furman, remarks, Harvard Kennedy School, April 26, 2017; and Lawrence Mead, *Expanding Work Programs for Poor Men* (Lanham, Md.: Rowman and Littlefield, 2011), 25.

12. Freelancers Union.

13. Michalis Nikiforos, Marshall Steinbaum, and Gennaro Zezza, "Modeling the Macroeconomic Effects of a Universal Basic Income," Roosevelt Institute, August 2017; David Z. Morris, "Universal Basic Income Could Grow the U.S. Economy by an Extra 12.5%," *Fortune*, September 3, 2017; and Charles Murray, "A Guaranteed Income for Every American," *Wall Street Journal*, June 3, 2016.

14. Interview with Ron Haskins, August 22, 2017; Marcia Cancian, Daniel R. Meyer, and Eunhee Han, "Child Support: Responsible Fatherhood and the Quid Pro Quo," in *Young Disadvantaged Men: Fathers, Families, Poverty, and Policy*, ed. Timothy M. Smeeding, Irwin Garfinkel, and Ronald B. Mincy, special issue, *Annals of the American Academy of Political and Social Science* 635 (May 2011): 143; and Elaine Maag, "A Plan to Radically Expand the Earned Income Tax Credit," *Forbes*, September 15, 2017.

15. Marcel Einerhand and Erik Swart, "Reform of the Dutch Sickness and Disability Arrangements," European Union, February 2010; David Autor and Mark Duggan, "The Rise in the Disability Rolls and the Decline in Employment," MIT, 2003; Social Security Administration, "How Many SSDI Beneficiaries Leave the Rolls for Work? More Than You Might Think," Disability Research Policy Brief 10-01, April 2010; Shawn Fremstad and Rebecca Vallas, "The Facts on Social Security Disability Insurance and Supplemental Security Income for Workers with Disabilities," Center for American Progress, May 30, 2013; and David Autor, "The Unsustainable Rise of the Disability Tolls in the United States: Cause, Consequences, and Policy Options," NBER Working Paper 17697 (Cambridge, Mass.: National Bureau of Economic Research, December 2011).

16. Interview with Anna Polivka, U.S. Department of Labor, Bureau of Labor Statistics (BLS), June 8, 2017; Jacob S. Hacker, *The Great Risk Shift: The Assault on American Jobs, Families, Health Care, and Retirement and How You Can Fight Back* (Oxford University Press, 2006), 79–80; David Weil, *The Fissured Workplace: Why Work Became So Bad for So Many and What Can Be Done to Improve It* (Harvard University Press, 2014), 9–10; and "French Business Applauds Macron's Labour Reforms," *Financial Times*, September 1, 2017.

17. Interviews with Olivia Golden, Center for Law and Social Policy, March 13, 2017; Lawrence Mead, November 14, 2016; and Isabel Sawhill, December 5, 2016; and World Bank, "Bolsa Família: Brazil's Quiet Revolution," November 4, 2013.

18. Cynthia Osborne, Andrea Michelson, and Kaeley Bobbitt, "Fatherhood EFFECT Evaluation Final Report: A Comprehensive Plan for Supporting Texas Fathers and Families," Child and Family Research Partnership, University of Texas at Austin, Lyndon B. Johnson School of Public Affairs, August 2017; and "Dads Need Help Too," Nurse-Family Partnership.

19. Interview with Cynthia Osborne, September 27, 2017; and Carmen Solomon-Fears and Jessica Tollestrup, "Fatherhood Initiatives: Connecting Fathers to Their Children," Congressional Research Service, December 28, 2016.

20. Alicia H. Munnell and Steven Sass, *Working Longer: The Solution to the Retirement Income Challenge* (Brookings Institution Press, 2008), 8, 36, 41; and Richard H. Thaler and Cass R. Sunstein, *Nudge: Improving Decisions about Health, Wealth, and Happiness* (Yale University Press, 2008).

21. "Oklahoma Marriage Program Has Spent $70 Million in Mostly Welfare Dollars," *Tulsa World*, December 2, 2013.

22. Interview with Ron Haskins, August 22, 2017; interview with Isabel Sawhill, December 6, 2016; "Oklahoma Watch· Effectiveness of Oklahoma Marriage Initiative Is Questioned by Some," *The Oklahoman*, December 1, 2013; interview with Donald Gordon, June 29, 2017; and interview with Cynthia Osborne, September 27, 2017.

23. U.S. Department of Health and Human Services, Administration on Children and Families, Office of Family Assistance, "About Healthy Marriage and Responsible Fatherhood"; Solomon-Fears and Tollestrup, "Fatherhood Initiatives"; interview with Vernon Wallace, February 6, 2017; and Center for Men's Excellence.

24. BBC, "Where New Dads Are Encouraged to Take Months off Work," January 6, 2016; and "Sweden's Pioneering Fathers' Groups," *Voice Male*, Spring 2017.

25. Gretchen Livingston, "Among 41 Nations, U.S. Is the Outlier When It Comes to Paid Parental Leave," Pew Research Center, September 26, 2016.

26. Steven Findlay, "Paid Parental Leave May Be the Idea That Transcends Politics," *USA Today*, July 22, 2017, and National Partnership for Women and Families, "State Paid Family Leave Insurance Laws," July 2017.

27. Child Care Aware, "Parents and the High Cost of Child Care: 2016"; and Danielle Paquette, "The $90 Billion Question: Do We Need Government-Supplied Daycare?," *Washington Post*, April 6, 2016.

28. Child Care Aware, "Parents and the High Cost"; Paquette, "$90 Billion Question"; and National Center for Education Statistics, Digest of Education Statistics 2016, "Table 202.10. Enrollment of 3-, 4-, and 5-Year-Old Children in Preprimary Programs, by Age of Child, Level of Program, Control of Program, and Attendance Status: Selected Years, 1970 through 2015," 2017.

29. Lillian Mongeau, "Why Does America Invest So Little in Its Children?," *The Atlantic*, July 12, 2016; Ministère de l'éducation nationale (France), "Les niveaux et les établissements d'enseignement: L'école maternelle," 2017; and OECD, "Labour Force Participation Rate, 15–64 Year-Olds, % in Same Age Group, 2016."

30. Joseph Cordell, "Shared-Parenting Movement Gaining Momentum in 2015," *Huffington Post*, June 17, 2016; Jonathan Ellis, "Shared Parenting Could Be New Divorce Outcome," *USA Today*, January 27, 2014; interview with Cynthia Osborne, September 27, 2017; and Solomon-Fears and Tollestrup, "Fatherhood Initiatives."

31. Editors of *Men's Health*, "The Most Important Thing You Can Do for Your Health Today: A Federal Office of Men's Health Is Needed to Address the Health Risks of Men—and You Can Help Make It Happen," *Men's Health*, November 17, 2015; and Men's Health Caucus of the American Public Health Association, "Bi-Partisan Congressional Men's Health Caucus Established," April 2, 2015.

32. Emily Mullin, "Why We Still Don't Have Birth Control Drugs for Men," *MIT Technology Review*, November 11, 2016; Isabel Sawhill, *Generation Unbound: Drifting into Sex and Parenthood without Marriage* (Brookings Institution Press, 2014), 9, 102; interview with Naomi Cahn and June Carbone, April 6, 2017; Council for a White House Conference on Boys and Men, "Proposal for a White House Council on Boys and Men"; and interview with Warren Farrell, January 9, 2017.

33. Centers for Disease Control and Prevention, "CDC Guideline for Prescribing Opioids for Chronic Pain—United States, 2016," March 18, 2016; and Scott Higham and Lenny Bernstein, "Drugmakers and Distributors Face Barrage of Lawsuits over Opioid Epidemic," *Washington Post*, July 4, 2017.

34. "Economic Shocks Are More Likely to Be Lethal in America," *The Economist*, March 25, 2017.

35. Daniel Patrick Moynihan, *Family and Nation: The Godkin Lectures, Harvard University* (San Diego: Harcourt Brace Jovanovich, 1986), 189.

36. Camille Terrier, "Boys Lag Behind: How Teachers' Gender Biases Affect Student Achievement," School Effectiveness and Inequality Initiative, MIT and NBER, Working Paper 2016.07, November 2016; Christopher Cornwell, David B. Mustard, and Jessica Van Parys, "Noncognitive Skills and the Gender Disparities in Test Scores and Teacher Assessments: Evidence from Primary School," *Journal of Human Resources* 48 (January 2013): 236–64; and Erika Christakis, "Do Teachers Really Discriminate against Boys?," *Time*, February 6, 2013.

37. *Rerum Novarum*: Encyclical of Pope Leo XII on Capital and Labor Rights and Duties of Capital and Labor, 1891, paragraph 20.

Index

employment-to-population ratio and, 28; fantasy of starting a successful business and, 33–34, 99; as fathers, 162–64; government benefits and, 31, 35; health issues of, 171; how they spend their time, 33–34, 110, 124, 125; income sources of, 34–37, 42–43; job search by, 33, 34, 43, 98, 140, 169; lack of education as factor, 30, 32; lower paying jobs, men forced to take, 52; as "men out" key characteristic, 25–26, 106; "middle skill" jobs, effect of disappearance of, 30–31, 37–38; moral crisis created by, 51; new class created by, 30–32; parents supporting, 35; part-time jobs and, 28; pension and retirement-savings plans and, 36–37; post-1973 transformation and, 45–54; reasons for, 37–43, 50; refusal to take jobs "beneath them," 31, 52; savings of, 36; skill-biased technological change and, 30; statistics on, 26–28; traditionally unacceptable status of nonworking male, 24; women supporting, 34–37, 73. *See also* "Men out" examples; Millennial men; Unemployed men
NOW (National Organization for Women), 82, 159, 203
Nursing profession, 32

Obama, Barack: Council of Economic Advisers for, 50; on criminal records and hiring, 195; on fatherhood, 82, 144, 153; on fragmentation of the family, 149–50; growing up without a father, effect on, 149; My Brother's Keeper program and, 235; online racism targeted at, 119; Putnam and, 201; on rising economic inequality, 14, 46; on stereotyping Rust Belt workers, 16; on universal college education, 217
Obamacare. *See* Affordable Care Act
Objectification of opposite sex, 118
Occupy Wall Street, 47, 213

OECD countries, 27, 29, 86, 225. *See also specific countries*
Oklahoma proposal to reduce divorce rates, 224
Okun, Rob, 83
Older male workers (age 60 and above), 31, 38, 53, 223–24
One percenters, 14, 47, 48
The Onion Router (browser), 120
Online abuse, 79
Online anger, 118–21
Online dating and hookups, 75–77, 110, 115, 131, 134, 142
On-Line Gamers Anonymous, 113, 123
Online porn and sexting, 26, 63, 79, 110, 114–18
Ooms, Theodora, 149
Open-mindedness, 13
Opioid addiction: economic costs of, 173; effects of, 172–73; examples of, 102–03; in Frackville, 58; Naloxone (treatment drug), 39; Narcan (treatment drug), 58; overdoses and death due to, 86, 99, 101–02, 172, 184; pain and health issues requiring opioid treatment, 172; proposals to address, 228
Optimists clubs, 202
Osborne, Cynthia, 161, 223
Out-of-wedlock births, 57–58, 86, 132, 145, 153
Overwatch (video game), 112
Ozzie and Harriet (TV show), 44

Pager, Devah, 195
Paid parental leave, proposal for, 225–26
Paine, Thomas, 221
Palazzolo, Piera, 104
Parent Education Responsibility workshops, 222–23, 225, 233
Parenting: classes for, 234; cultural change regarding trends, 231–32; expectations for children, 90–93; gay and lesbian parents, 135; grandparents